Healing Developmental Trauma

A Systems Approach to Counseling Individuals, Couples, & Families

Janae B. Weinhold, PhD
Barry K. Weinhold, PhD

LOVE PUBLISHING COMPANY®
Denver • London • Singapore

DEDICATION

We dedicate this book to our children,
Margie, Mark, Greg, and Chad, and
our grandchildren, Aaron, Brandon, Sophia, and Ena
and all the other young people who inspire us to
create a better world. We also dedicate this book to
those who feel responsible for the
"seventh generation yet unborn."

Published by Love Publishing Company
P.O. Box 22353
Denver, Colorado 80222
www.lovepublishing.com

Fifth Edition

Library of Congress Control Number: 2009939848

Printed in the United States of America
ISBN 978-0-89108-349-8

Contents

PART FIVE

Developmental Process Consultation 385

Figures

Tables

Preface

At end of the first decade of the 21st century, many people are stuck in their lives and repeating self-defeating and self-destructive patterns of behavior. They seem depressed and unhappy and often use a variety of addictive activities and substances, including prescription drugs, to temporarily lift themselves out of their suffering. Some use manipulative, aggressive, and violent behaviors to try to get their needs met. Others lie, cheat, steal, and refuse to accept limits on their behavior, saying they are entitled to pursue their grandiose schemes without anyone ever questioning their logic or sustainability. They use denial, projection, and rationalizations to avoid taking responsibility for their actions.

Most of those who are considered wealthy are greedy and quest after material resources far beyond what they actually need or can ever use. Their compulsion to dominate and overconsume still does not make them happy. Some use the people in their close relationships as objects to be consumed and then discarded. Others lack the capacity for true intimacy and resign themselves to lives of quiet desperation after failing in numerous attempts to create a loving, close relationship with another person.

To support their flagrantly addictive, overconsumptive, and unsustainable lifestyles, many citizens of Planet Earth are rapidly squandering our precious nonrenewable resources. The human race has now reached a critical stage in its history where it has the potential to destroy both our planet and us as a species. Nevertheless, in the face of an extinction of our own making, we have the power to change the way we live our lives. People living with the unrecognized and unhealed chronic effects of shock, trauma, or stress, unfortunately, do not believe that they have the ability to change their lives. Their only hope is to be sufficiently hypervigilant to avoid re-experiencing the dreaded feelings hidden somewhere in their memory of their early experiences of developmental shock, trauma, and stress.

The hidden effects of these chronic states of shock, trauma, and stress control our lives and keep us stuck in a cultural trance that makes us not only vulnerable to the cynical manipulation of advertisers and propagandists, but to the collective reenactment of our shocks, traumas, and stresses through domestic violence, child abuse, wars, and other destructive acts. Many organizations such as schools, churches, corporations, and governments have failed to help their members create a sense of community that provides feelings of safety and security and places where people can sustain the basic trust that is necessary for promoting the common good. In our primarily dominator-based system, chronic states of unrecognized and unhealed shock, trauma, and stress keep us looking outside of ourselves for the deep emotional connections that we needed as children and never received. And so we are rocked to sleep with the sweet lullaby of overconsumption, addictions, distractions, and dependency.

Why do people persist in using self-destructive behaviors? Do they really want to break free of them? How can we help those who really want out of this evolutionary trap? This book offers our perspective on these and related questions.

It is possible to free ourselves both individually and collectively from entrapment in chronic states of unrecognized and unhealed shock, trauma, and stress to release the "pause button" on the evolution of human consciousness. What we each need in order to advance in our evolution is the ability to direct our lives from a solid internal foundation. Without this inner guidance system, we are subject to the whims of those who serve only themselves and wish to dominate us and keep us stuck in fear.

Our understanding of developmental trauma grew out of our clinical practice, where we had many adult clients with symptoms of unrecognized and unhealed shock, trauma, and stress who could not recall any instances of shock, trauma, or stress in their history. This led us to look deeper for the source of their symptoms. We also began looking at our own relationship issues and traced them back to our early childhood experiences of shock, trauma, and stress.

From this personal and clinical experience, we began to understand the long-lasting effects of subtle energetic disconnects in the relationships between infants and young children and their adult caregivers and how these disconnects disrupt the completion of essential developmental processes related to bonding and separation.

We believe that human development is continuous and that completing certain early developmental processes at optimal times builds the foundation for human evolution. When essential developmental processes are not completed at the optimal time, they are carried into the next stage of development, making successive stages more difficult to complete.

Because of the innate drive of human evolution for completion, any incomplete developmental processes continue to press for completion when opportunities present themselves, particularly in our adult relationships. The events that disrupted our early developmental lives reappear as traumatic reenactments in intimate relationship conflicts as adults. Once we recognized this phenomenon, we understood why subtle relational disconnects during the first 3 years of our own lives were emerging as unrecognized and unhealed developmental shock, trauma, and stress. We saw this not only in our own relationship but those of our clients. At this point, we began creating tools that worked for us and with our clients. Between 1987 and 2000, our university courses in conflict resolution strategies and DPW, our clinical work with clients in our private practices, and our personal work and therapy served as the laboratory for our heuristic research on developmental trauma.

In psychology, heuristic research involves a subjective search through which one discovers the nature and meaning of an experience, which leads to the creation of methods and procedures for further investigation and analysis. Heuristic methodologies help explain how and why people make decisions, come to judgments, and solve their problems. Our heuristic research helped us discover everything we could about developmental trauma from a personal, conceptual, theoretical, clinical, and systemic perspective. Simultaneously, we were problem-solving and testing a variety of clinical interventions, processes, and practices for helping ourselves and others heal the effects of developmental trauma.

We have conducted numerous national and international trainings for professionals, teaching them our approach for healing developmental trauma. Our approach is breaking new ground not only in the fields of developmental psychotherapy and traumatology, but also in many other fields where professionals are encountering people who are reenacting their unrecognized and unhealed developmental shocks, traumas, and stresses. We also train professionals who do not practice psychotherapy but are in an excellent position to intervene in people's lives during spiritual emergencies,when their developmental traumas are reactivated. These "first responders" need to recognize that what they are seeing is a developmental issue and respond appropriately.

As we were writing this book, we encountered new research about shock and how it is often confused with trauma. We have incorporated this new research into this book in order to help clear up confusion in the helping professions about the differences between shock and trauma and the treatment each requires. We also recognized that if these differences are not clearly articulated, improper clinical interventions can harm clients.

The purpose of this book is to present our developmental model for advancing human evolution through the use of the following core concepts:

1. *Developmental Systems Theory,* which identifies the essential developmental processes or building blocks that must be completed in four stages of evolution (codependent, counterdependent, independent, and interdependent) in six increasingly more complex human systems (individual, couple, family, organization, culture/nation–state, and the human race).
2. *Developmental Shock, Trauma, and Stress* and their role in blocking the successful completion of these processes and stalling human evolution.
3. *Developmental Process Work,* a treatment modality for healing the seven components of unrecognized and unhealed developmental shock, trauma, and stress.
4. *LOVEvolution,* a blueprint for optimal growth and development of human systems.

If you are a therapist or other helping professional, it is important to first identify and heal your own developmental shocks, traumas, and stresses before attempting to help others. This will help you open your heart and become more present so that you are more emotionally available and supportive in your work with others. This is the surest way we know to develop empathy and compassion for the wounds of others, which are essential components of the healing process.

It is our sincere hope that reading this book helps you identify and heal any previously unrecognized and unhealed developmental shocks, traumas, and stresses that might be preventing you from using all your God-given talents and resources or interfering with your capacity to build sustainable, loving relationships. We can testify that it requires spiritual courage to look at yourself and your life in the ways that we describe in this book. If you are using this book as a self-help tool, we urge you to consult occasionally with a professional therapist who can offer you support and help guide your efforts. We recommend that if you are working with a therapist, you share what you are learning by reading this book and get his or her cooperation and support.

What we have learned as we have walked down our paths of self-discovery is that the self-reflective work required to evolve is absolutely worth doing. Our own lives have become incredibly richer and more fulfilling as a result of healing our own developmental shocks, traumas, and stresses. Naturally, there were times when we wanted to give up or turn away from the task because the challenge seemed overwhelming. In these moments we surrendered and asked for help. By surrendering, we always seemed to find the way through our challenges. We hope that the work we have done and the tools that we developed will be useful for your journey and make it easier for you and those with whom you work professionally.

Please read this book with an open mind and an open heart. At times, you may feel upset or touched to tears by memories that surface as you read this material. We hope that you take the parts of the book that work for you and use them to change your life and the lives of others. We wish you well on your journey toward wholeness.

Acknowledgments

We thank the many students, clients, and workshop participants who helped co-create our developmental paradigm over the past 25 years. We would like to particularly acknowledge the graduate students in our DPW and conflict resolution classes at the University of Colorado at Colorado Springs who helped us conduct action research on DST and its application, DPW.

We also acknowledge the many pioneers in the fields of counseling and family systems therapy, developmental psychology, traumatology, psychobiology, cell biology, and the quantum sciences, whose research and practice provide the foundation on which we build our paradigm.

We also acknowledge the long-term support of Stan Love and Carrie Watterson, our friends and colleagues at Love Publishing. They have been instrumental in helping our work reach a larger audience. Carrie has particularly been supportive in the conception, gestation, and delivery of this book, and we really appreciate her dedicated efforts both as an administrator and editor in its publication.

About the Authors

Janae B. Weinhold, PhD, is a former adjunct professor at the University of Colorado at Colorado Springs, where she taught in the School of Education's Counseling and Human Services MA program. She is a licensed professional counselor and the author or coauthor of 10 books and more than 100 professional articles. A specialist in children's mental health, she regularly consults and trains early childhood educators and childcare professionals. Since 1990, she has actively been involved in humanitarian projects with ROZRADA, CICRCL's sister NGO in Kiev, Ukraine. Since 1994, she has provided ongoing training in practical psychology to Ukrainian psychologists and has been instrumental in getting the Weinholds' books on codependency and counterdependency translated into Russian. Janae currently serves as a codirector of the Carolina Institute for Conflict Resolution & Creative Leadership (CICRCL) near Asheville, North Carolina.

Barry K. Weinhold, PhD, is Professor Emeritus at the University of Colorado at Colorado Springs, where he founded the School of Education's Counseling and Human Services MA program and taught for 30 years, serving many years as the chair of the program. He is the author or coauthor of 40 books and more than 100 professional articles. He is also a licensed psychologist; a consultant to schools, agencies, and community organizations; and director of a violence prevention program known as The Kindness Campaign. The Kindness Campaign has been implemented in 13 communities and more than 600 schools in the U.S. and Canada. He currently codirects CICRCL.

For updated information on *Healing Developmental Trauma* and all the other training, counseling, and consulting activities of the Weinholds, please visit them at their websites, where they welcome questions that arise from reading this book. Here you can also find additional information and resources and interact with them on their forums.

Their flagship website: www.weinholds.org
Their website for this book: www.weinholds.org/devtrauma
Their website for their conflict resolution book: www.weinholds.org/rcr
Their website for parenting support: www.weinholds.org/parenting
Their Developmental Process Work website: www.weinholds.org/dpw
Their Developmental Systems Theory website: www.weinholds.org/dst
Their You Can Heal Yourself website: www.weinholds.org/youcanheal
Their Kindness Campaign website: www.weinholds.org/kindness
Their website on LOVEvolution: www.weinholds.org/lovevolution
Their website on 2012: www.weinholds.org/2012

You can also email them at cicrcl@weinholds.org

A lifetime without love is of no account
Love is the water of life
Drink it down with heart and soul.

Rumi

Introduction

This book presents an expanded paradigm for understanding the pervasive influence of unrecognized and unhealed shock, trauma, and stress on humanity's evolution, along with a comprehensive approach for healing them. We examine the chronic impact of shock, trauma, and stress that occurs during the first 3 years of life on the development of all human systems, particularly those of individuals, couples, and families. A wealth of information and research findings is readily available that concentrates on the science behind and technologies for treating the effects of acute trauma. In this book, we look in a different direction. We focus specifically on the subtle relational aspects of early shock, trauma, and stress both as causative and curative factors. We use the terms *developmental shock, trauma,* and *stress* to identify this specific focus.

Developmental Shock, Trauma, and Stress: A New Paradigm

In this book, we synthesize a wide range of scientific research and information into a paradigm that not only presents a new perspective on humanity's problems but also offers a practical and hopeful approach for addressing them. During our review of the literature for this book, we discovered that much of the information emerging from the hard sciences about shock, trauma, and stress contains contradictory terminologies and highly technical and clinical language. We have simplified this information and translated it into more readable language and a more accessible conceptual framework.

Because our approach is a synthesis of new information and research from many fields, this book may feel a little compacted as you read it. We suggest taking time to digest and assimilate it. We would like to begin by summarizing some of the new contributions that this book makes to the fields of traumatology, developmental psychology, and complementary medicine. We will discuss each of these contributions more fully later in the book.

Synthesizes New Research from the Fields of Attachment Theory, Biology, Psychology, Traumatology, Brain Development, Energy Medicine, and the German New Medicine

Our concept of developmental shock, trauma, and stress builds on the study of many other researchers and practitioners whose work has focused primarily on acute causes of shock, trauma, and stress. Only recently have a few researchers recognized the effects of subtle disruptions in the social interactions between the mother and child and the emotional dysregulation during early childhood as causes of later experiences involving shock, trauma, and stress. These findings indicate that early childhood shock, trauma, and stress are caused by small daily disruptions in the social interactions between mother and child; that they have profound long-term effects on human development; and that they interfere with the ability to form functional, sustainable adult relationships. We also include new research that correlates developmental shock, trauma, and stress with degenerative conditions.

Differentiates among Shock, Trauma, and Stress

These three terms currently are used almost interchangeably in the field of traumatology. Even posttraumatic stress incorporates two of these terms. Our research revealed that these states have unique characteristics and involve different parts of the brain, different parts of the autonomic nervous system, and differences in time orientation. Most importantly, they require very different kinds of treatment interventions. We differentiate and simplify some of the commonly used concepts, terminologies, and intervention approaches that have made the study of traumatology both confusing and difficult. Because shock, trauma, and stress disrupt human development, we describe them as *developmental shock*, *developmental trauma,* and *developmental stress.*

Expands the Traditional Definitions of Shock, Trauma, and Stress

Much of the focus in the field of early childhood traumatology has been on the long-term effects of acute childhood events involving sexual or physical abuse or severe physical or emotional neglect. What we discovered in our personal experience and clinical research is that "ordinary" day-to-day relational experiences during early childhood can cause lasting effects of developmental shock, trauma, and stress. These ordinary relational events are just as damaging to human development as acute events but are not typically recognized by adults as shocking, traumatic, or stressful.

We believe that many professionals ignore the potential harm caused by these "normal" early childhood relational incidents that involve developmental shock, trauma, and stress. This blindness can cause professionals to misdiagnose people's symptoms and to use inappropriate clinical interventions. We believe that the chronic effects of unrecognized and unhealed developmental shock, trauma, and stress are far more extensive and widespread than previously thought and hope that this book will spur more research into this area of traumatology.

Our research revealed that the long-term social, relational, and behavioral problems of those who experienced developmental shock, trauma, and stress during the first 3 years of life are virtually identical: difficulties in regulating emotions; problems sustaining reciprocal, intimate relationships; and the tendency to perpetuate intergenerational histories involving abuse, neglect, addiction, and fractured relationships. What we also find significant about unrecognized and unhealed developmental shock, trauma, and stress is that they are typically overlooked as sources of posttraumatic stress disorder (PTSD).

The long-term effects of unrecognized and unhealed developmental shock, trauma, and stress can cripple people's capacity for relational intimacy as adults. It can impair their ability to effectively parent and care for their children and cause degenerative conditions later in life. From our expanded definition of shock, trauma, and stress, much of the *Diagnostic and Statistical Manual* (*DSM-IV*, 1994) of the American Psychiatric Association (APA, 1994) can be viewed as a handbook describing the impact of developmental shock, trauma, and stress on the human mindbody.

We believe the primary sources of developmental shock, trauma, and stress during early infancy involve experiences of too frequent or too lengthy relational separations from their primary caregivers. These separations overwhelm an infant's nervous system and cause repeated experiences of emotional dysregulation and dissociation. We found these kinds of events far more difficult to recognize and treat than acute events involving physical abandonment, abuse, and neglect. Dissociated memories of early subtle relational shocks typically lie dormant for many years until sensory cues trigger them into reenacting the events in their intimate adult relationships. These dormant memories can also trigger reenactment events in adults with their children while parenting, with their supervisors and colleagues at work, or in interpersonal conflicts with friends when they feel threatened in some way.

Identifies the Symptoms of Developmental Shock, Trauma, and Stress

This book can help you identify the behavioral, biological, and relational symptoms of unrecognized and unhealed developmental shock, trauma, and stress in yourself and your clients, and it can also help you understand how they impact your life and the lives of your clients. It will also help you see how the effects of unrecognized and unhealed developmental shock, trauma, and stress can ripple out into other parts of the world through phenomena such as *traumatic reenactment* and the *repetition compulsion*. These phenomena involve unconscious replays or the restaging of past experiences of developmental shock, trauma, and stress in present time. This book also describes how unresolved intractable conflict involving dormant memories related to experiences of shock, trauma, and stress during the first 3 years of life is the most common cause of mindbody breakdowns that weaken the immune system and contribute to degenerative conditions.

Identifies New Intervention Tools

This book not only differentiates among development shock, trauma, and stress and expands their definitions, but it also describes new and proven interventions for healing them. As the field of traumatology grew, new knowledge about the nature and impact of trauma became a catalyst for creating many new intervention modalities for treating trauma. Many trauma intervention models, in our opinion, fail to differentiate among shock, trauma, and stress but focus on "trauma reduction" through the use of "power therapies." These intervention models tend to ignore or minimize the social and relational components of shock, trauma, and stress. In Chapters 9 through 13, we present a comprehensive list of intervention tools we recommend for healing the effects of developmental shock, trauma, and stress in individuals, couples, and families.

Presents a Hopeful, Practical, and Systemic Framework

This book uncovers many of the hidden causes of present-time relational conflicts and social issues in individuals, couples, and families. In our systemic approach, we avoid finding fault or blaming others for triggering our emotional responses during conflicts. We believe that emotional reactions that emerge during a triggering episode are evidence of unrecognized and unhealed shock, trauma, and stress that is stored in our nervous systems. Our approach offers comfort and reassurance; coping strategies; and practical, proven interventions for helping people heal the effects of developmental shock, trauma, and stress. Our clinical modality, Developmental Process Work (DPW), uses an array of mindbody tools for identifying and treating common behavioral problems caused by developmental shock, trauma, and stress.

Heightens Sensitivity to the Social, Emotional, and Relational Needs of Children

We emphasize the inherently sensitive and empathic nature of prenates, infants, and small children and their critical need for emotional attunement with their adult caregivers, particularly their mothers. Through our personal experience and heuristic research, we have identified the essential developmental processes that prenates, infants, and young children must complete in order to build a solid foundation for a fully functioning adult self. This book specifically identifies the kinds of social, emotional, and relational experiences involving developmental shock, trauma, and stress that are common between conception and 36 months of age. These early experiences interfere with the completion of the essential developmental processes. They limit children's capacities for connection and reciprocity in subsequent relationships and lay the foundations for adult relational conflicts, for impaired mental health, and for degenerative conditions.

Defining Developmental Shock, Trauma, and Stress

An amazing amount of information is now available for both professionals and laypersons on the topics of trauma or stress. In comparison, there is very little information on the topic of shock. Part of our challenge in writing this book has been reviewing a wide range of literature in the field of traumatology, identifying common concepts that are expressed using different technical languages, and then placing our work within this context. In this section, we summarize the most current synthesis of our paradigm.

Developmental shock, developmental trauma, and developmental stress are breakthrough concepts in the fields of mental health, pre- and perinatal psychology, developmental psychology, traumatology, and complementary medicine. They emphasize the invisible but pervasive impact of overwhelming emotional experiences between conception and the age of 3 in disrupting evolution in all human systems.

Before looking at the more clinical and scientific aspects of developmental shock, trauma, and stress, we would like to paint a word picture to help you understand what these terms look like in real time. The inspiration for this word picture comes from a 1986 NOVA film, "Life's First Feelings," illustrating the results of a research investigation into the important biological and social functions emotions serve in the early development of a child's personality (NOVA, 2000).

Early in the film, chief investigator Dr. Edward Tronick describes an interactive dance of communication that he observes between an infant about the age of 5 months and his mother. In this dance, the infant is sitting in a carrying seat and the mother is standing in front of him. She is instructed to interact with her child for several minutes while being videotaped. Sometimes she puts her face too close to her son, and he fusses, looks stressed, withdraws, and looks at his hands.

Then she backs away and again comes in close several times. Sometimes she makes sounds, wipes the drool off his chin, or waves her hands close to his face. When the boy becomes overly stimulated and gets a little upset, he withdraws and soothes himself by breaking eye contact and looking at his hands. Then he looks back at his mother and smiles really big in an effort to reengage with her.

This part of Tronick's experiment is an excellent illustration of the infant–mother dance of communication. The next part of the experiment, however, contains something that would not be done today because we now understand that it causes experiences of shock, trauma, and stress in infant research subjects.

Tronick does a short "cold mother" experiment in which he asks the mother to keep a blank face and not respond to her child's attempts to engage with her. It is obvious after the previous playful exchanges with his mother that the infant does not anticipate her withdrawal. At first he looks surprised, and then he smiles really big at her in an attempt to draw her in. When she stays stony-faced, he looks off to one side and again peers at his hands. Then he looks back at his disengaged mother's face and smiles and tries to reengage with her.

When he sees that she is still not responding to him, this causes a series of things to happen very fast—so quickly that they are almost invisible. First the pupils in the boy's eyes dilate, then his eyes bulge, and his face becomes blank. Then he has what looks like a severe hiccup, and finally he vomits a little bit.

Tronick does not comment about the look of terror on the infant's face, the change in his eyes, or his hiccup. He does remark about the child's "loss of bodily fluids" and then shifts the focus. An announcer in the background asks the question, "If this response occurs in the laboratory, what happens when infants are emotionally deprived over long periods of time?"

This short video segment illustrates four important points. The first point is the difference between developmental shock, trauma, and stress. This process begins in the first part of the experiment when the invasive mother overstimulates her child. He shows signs of developmental stress and then flees his mother's overstimulating behavior by looking at his hands and self-soothing, at which point he then attempts to reengage with his mother.

He first shows signs of disorientation during the cold mother experiment when he is unable to reengage her in their dance. Then he quickly drops into a state of developmental shock that is visible in the dilation of his pupils, his bulging eyes, his blank facial expression, his hiccupping, and finally his vomiting. The experiment becomes a shattering experience for this small boy, who dissociates and becomes immobile.

The second point the video illustrates is the immense power of the interactive dance between the child and mother and what happens to the child when the mother disengages from it. The third point it illustrates is how few resources this child has to cope with his mother's disengagement and how rapidly this causes him to move from stress into trauma, where he attempts to reregulate himself by looking at his hands, and then into shock when his mother does not respond to his efforts to engage.

The fourth point that this video segment demonstrates is the sequences of state-shifting from developmental stress, into developmental trauma, and then into developmental shock; from higher-order brain functions to more primitive defensive responses contained in the limbic system and reptilian brain; and from newer parts of the autonomic nervous system to the older. These are the primary components of what we call the *trauma continuum*, which we describe briefly in the next section.

By definition, developmental shock, trauma, and stress are inflicted on infants and children unconsciously and most often without malicious intent by adult caregivers who are unaware of children's social and emotional needs. Infants and children require energetic attunement; skin-to-skin, eye-to-eye, and right brain–to–right brain contact; kind and comforting words; and protection and safety during gestation, birth, and the first 3 years of life. Most adults, including many mental health professionals, have not been educated about these needs, and many lacked these personal experiences of emotional attunement when they were children. Adults also do not correlate these developmental deficits with the day-to-day struggles they experience in their lives. Consequently, they are unaware when they are shocking, traumatizing, or stressing their own children and are not able to recognize the symptoms of developmental shock, trauma, or stress in themselves, their children, or others.

In this book you will learn how custodial adults—parents, grandparents, childcare providers, healthcare providers, teachers, ministers, therapists, and institutions, including churches, schools, corporations, and governments—unconsciously create and perpetuate systems that inflict developmental trauma on themselves and each other. Adults and the systems they create generally do not understand or adequately provide for the developmental needs of young children. How they relate to the needs of young children may also involve a need to unconsciously defend against encountering memories of their own unhealed developmental shock, trauma, or stress. The bottom line is that adults who do not recognize or heal their own developmental issues are the primary transmitters of developmental shock, trauma, and stress throughout our culture.

Early shock, trauma, or stress inflicted by trusted caregivers is quantitatively and qualitatively more destructive than any other kind of stressor and has the most potential for causing subsequent psychopathology. Experiences of developmental shock, trauma, or stress can happen even in families where the parents are "good enough," meaning that they can function at a sufficiently high enough level to meet their children's physical needs. However, they lack the skills and understanding to effectively and quickly restore emotional resonance with their children when it is disrupted. We believe that the effects of parents' own unrecognized and unhealed developmental shocks, traumas, or stresses also interfere with their ability to stay attuned to their child in ordinary day-to-day interactions.

The Trauma Continuum

Our study of developmental trauma coincided with our research in conflict resolution, which we summarized in our book, *Conflict Resolution: The Partnership Way* (2009). In this book we show how unresolved interpersonal conflicts in adult relationships are often caused by invisible and unhealed developmental shocks, traumas, or stresses that happened during early childhood. We also showed how the adrenal stress response (ASR) activates freeze, flight, and fight reactions during a conflict, and how each of these responses involves different parts of the brain and the central nervous system.

In order to help us better understand all of this complex information, we placed the ASRs of freeze, flight, and fight on a continuum. Then we described each of these responses and how different parts of the brain, the central nervous system, and behaviors are activated.

Table I.1 presents an overview of our trauma continuum. It begins with common behavioral symptoms and then identifies the parts of the brain that are active, the parts of the autonomic nervous system that are involved, the internal orientation to time, and intervention approaches for each. Chapter 5 provides a more detailed version of this table.

TABLE 1.1

The Trauma Continuum

Classification	Developmental Shock	Developmental Trauma	Developmental Stress
Behavioral symptoms	Collapsed, withdrawn	Overwhelmed, hypervigilant	Anxious, engaged
Brain part active	Brain stem, reptilian brain, ectoderm tissue	Limbic brain	Neocortex
Autonomic nervous system part involved	Parasympathetic nervous system	Sympathetic nervous system	Social engagement system (SES)
Time orientation	Dissociated No time	Socially disengaged Regressed Caught between present time and past	Socially engaged In present time
Intervention	Attuning with clients, empowering them, and helping them re-embody	Attuning with clients and calming them so that they can experience life in present time	Attuning with clients to keep them socially and emotionally engaged in present time

As we better understood the dance between mothers and children and sometimes between fathers or other adult caregivers and children, we reached the following conclusion:

> Every intense emotional experience can be classified as shock, trauma, or stress and can be easily distinguished by observing a person's appearance, behaviors, and social interactions.

In our model, it is irrelevant whether emotionally overwhelming events are acute or chronic, whether they happen through observing or directly experiencing an event, as are the exact circumstances of an event. What is relevant are how people look, what they feel, how they behave, how they communicate during these experiences, and how they perceive these experiences. These behavioral characteristics indicate which part of the brain is activated, which part of the autonomic nervous system is impacted, and the person's orientation to time. Only after evaluating these behavioral, biological, and temporal cues is it possible to determine a person's state of awareness and the appropriate treatment intervention.

Differentiating among these criteria and using them to determine the most appropriate intervention appears to be something not known or used in the field of traumatology. We discuss the implications of our trauma continuum throughout the remainder of the book.

Because *all* experiences of shock, trauma, or stress interfere with human development, we classify them as developmental shock, trauma, or stress. Because all humans have experienced developmental shock, trauma, or stress that has not been recognized or healed, by definition we are all developmentally delayed—individually, systemically, and as a species. Some of us are delayed more and some less, depending on the amount of developmental shock, trauma, or stress that we have experienced, how it was or was not addressed at the time it happened, and what we have done to heal it.

As early as the late 1880s, science divided the autonomic part of the central nervous system into two branches: the sympathetic, which is linked with fight-and-flight responses, and the parasympathetic, which is linked to freeze responses (Dykema, 2006). This paradigm has been almost religiously adhered to for more than 100 years.

Stephen Porges' new research (1995, 2001, 2003), which he synthesized from the fields of neurobiology, psychology, endocrinology, neuro-anatomy, and psychiatry, revealed some of the limitations of this early paradigm. His new information about the evolution of the human brain and the autonomic nervous system revealed the presence of a third more evolved and sophisticated part of the nervous system that he calls the social engagement system (SES). It is linked to cranial nerves that control facial expression, body language, and verbal communication.

Its primary function is to help people become and remain socially and emotionally engaged with other people.

According to Porges, each part of the autonomic nervous system is connected to a different part of the brain, each of which has developed in tandem during the course of human evolution. The parasympathetic nervous system, which is the oldest, links to the brain stem and the cerebellum or reptilian brain and helps to slow things down, restore calm, and refocus attention (1995, p. 310). The sympathetic nervous system developed next. It is linked to the limbic or mid-brain and is activated during fight-or-flight reactions that we call trauma. The SES is the newest part of the autonomic nervous system. It links to the new brain or neocortex and controls facial expressions, body language, and spoken language, all of which support social and emotional interactions.

Porges' model of the autonomic nervous system, which he calls polyvagal theory, helped us identify the shock/trauma/stress continuum. In addition, his theory also helped us understand why developmental shock, trauma, or stress each requires very different interventions. We saw that any intervention had to be based on which parts of the brain and autonomic nervous system has stored the information during past emotionally dysregulating events. With this information, the pieces of the puzzle fell into place, and our paradigm became both more precise and more encompassing.

Using Porges' polyvagal model, we were able to associate freeze responses with developmental shock; fight and flight responses with developmental trauma; and developmental stress responses with his SES. Differentiating shock, trauma, and stress also helped us understand the effects of developmental shock, trauma, and stress during the prenatal period.

Developmental Shock

Developmental shock reactions register in the brain stem and cerebellum (Hamer, 2000), which control the large muscles, manage autonomic body functions, and are responsible for instinctive survival behaviors. During shock, the brain stem and cerebellum actually suppress the production of adrenaline; deactivate the parasympathetic nervous system; and cause dissociation, lowered vitality, increased depression, and a defeated look. This accounts for people's frozen appearance, glassy eyes, immobile body, and dissociative responses when they are experiencing present-time shock or re-experiencing memories of early developmental shock.

Developmental shocks and the internal conflicts associated with them are stored in the mindbody and reactivated by later events that activate the memory of the early shock or subsequent shock events. Unless the effects of this early developmental shock are recognized and healed, the person is likely to develop a degenerative conditions later in life. Evidence suggests that the cumulative effects of chronic developmental shock, trauma, and stress may become part of a "the straw that breaks the camel's back" syndrome and can activate the onset of degenerative conditions (Brodie, 2001).

"Shock recapitulates globally," according to pre- and perinatal psychologist William Emerson (cited in Mines, 2003, p. 27). A developmental shock experience is like dropping a rock in a large pond. The initial impact creates a large splash in the water that eventually disappears, but ripples continue to radiate out from the point of impact to the edge of the pond or lake. In humans, developmental shocks leave what is known in the field of energy psychology (Feinstein, Eden, Craig, & Bowden, 2005) as *energetic imprints*, the energetic residue of an experience that is stored in the body's energy system or fluids (Thayer & Nathanson, 1997, p. 276). Energetic imprints are a way of storing early experiences, some of which may be traumatic or shocking, and about which we may have no conscious awareness (Mines, 2003, p. 27).

Our theory states that when a subsequent shock registers in the brain, the ripples from the new shock energetically resonate with the imprinted memory of an unhealed developmental shock from the past. This *shock wave resonance* creates a synergistic interaction that both connects the present and past events and also amplifies them. Because the earliest shock experiences impact the parts of the old brain and the embryonic tissue layers, very few people correlate these very early experiences of developmental shock with subsequent events involving shock. We believe that recognizing the correlation between early developmental shock and later shock wave resonance is critical for understanding the emergence of degenerative conditions later in life.

To treat developmental shock, the parasympathetic nervous system needs relational support that empowers and helps the individual to awaken authentic responsiveness and self-protective mechanisms. We discuss interventions for healing developmental shock, trauma, and stress in more detail in Chapters 9 through 13.

Developmental Trauma

Developmental trauma, the middle category in our continuum, can occur at any time during infancy, but it most often occurs between the ages of 6–8 and 36 months. This is when children have more resources for coping with emotionally upsetting experiences. At this age, they have more developed limbic brains and sympathetic nervous systems, are able to protect themselves by physically disengaging or fleeing from upsetting events, and have some sense of personal power and control. Toddlers are also able to use limbic-based fight-or-flight defenses to defend against or modulate the effects of traumatizing experiences. The older the child in this stage of development, the more of these defenses he or she will have in place.

Developmental trauma is caused by seemingly ordinary, normal, or subtle daily events that most adults do not recognize or perceive as traumatic to a child.

Many parents believe these things "happen to everyone," or they simply lack an awareness of the effects that their "good enough" parenting has on their developing child. These "ordinary" events hardwire the brain and nervous system of the child for a life structured around avoidance of anything that might trigger a memory of a developmental shock or trauma with the underlying conflict and anxiety that accompany it. If their efforts fail, they will react with a posttraumatic response that causes them to fight or flee or with a post-shock reaction that causes them to freeze during a present-time reenactment.

Porges said that if the flight or fight responses fail to reregulate escalated feeling states that are associated with an earlier event, people will regress into a freeze or shock reaction. We saw that progression in the example with the mother and the 5-month-old child in Tronick's experiment. Porges' theory states that our physiological responses are hierarchically organized and behaviorally follow the same sequence in which the systems evolved. During a conflict situation, the initial autonomic nervous system reaction is through the SES's fight response. If that fails to provide the social support or protection, the next response is the less sophisticated sympathetic nervous system's flight response. If it fails to provide the needed safety, then the next response is the least sophisticated parasympathetic nervous system's freeze response.

Flight reactions triggered by either the memory of a past developmental trauma or a present traumatic event involve the more sophisticated protective mechanisms of the limbic brain. It activates the sympathetic nervous system and cause the medulla to secrete adrenal hormones. These hormones increase heart rate, increase metabolic rate, constrict blood vessels, dilate the bronchioles, increase blood glucose, inhibit gastrointestinal activity, dilate the pupils of the eyes, and prepare the person to encounter danger.

Sympathetic nervous system responses are designed to support active, aggressive, and extremely physical protective behaviors. They stimulate repeated bursts of adrenaline with only the slightest exposure to triggering stimuli, causing hyperactivity; hypervigilance; driving, relentless behavior that nothing seems to stop; and an inability to rest at appropriate times. They can also stimulate a deep, obsessive need for action and a resistance to rest, almost like a raging fire that cannot be controlled. This eventually leads to adrenal fatigue and exhaustion, causing cellular breakdown and degenerative physical conditions. To treat developmental trauma, it is necessary to calm and quiet the sympathetic nervous system. We discuss recommended interventions for healing developmental trauma in more detail in Chapters 9 through 13.

As indicated, developmental trauma commonly occurs during the process of psychological and emotional separation between the ages of 6–8 months and 36 months. This period of development is critical for the creation of a sense of Self and the completion of the *psychological birth* by about 36 months. This concept is explained more fully in Chapter 4. Common traumas during the emotional separation process involve issues such as too many, too few, or too restrictive limits; harsh discipline involving physical punishment, shaming, and humiliation; and reversals in which children are not allowed to separate but are instead used to take care of their parents' social and emotional needs.

The task of primary caregivers is to provide consistent nurturing and protection for helpless and dependent infants and very young children and to help them learn how to regulate themselves biologically and emotionally when they become shocked, traumatized, or stressed. When a trusted caregiver is the cause of the developmental stress, this has significant short- and long-term consequences on children's developing minds and bodies (Schore, 2003a, p. 182).

The authors of the new *DSM-V* edition, to be published in 2012, are now considering the inclusion of developmental trauma as a new diagnostic category. Preliminary reports indicate they will be using the term developmental trauma to identify the symptoms of acute early childhood trauma (DeAngelis, 2007). Our definition of developmental trauma recognizes the chronic effects of subtle emotional disconnects that draw no caregiver attention to children's symptoms of shock, trauma, or stress. We believe these effects are far more widespread than is currently understood by the therapeutic community.

Once we began to understand the more subtle nuances of developmental shock, trauma, and stress, we saw how pervasive they are. We saw well-meaning but unaware parents and other caregiving adults everywhere inflicting them on openhearted, receptive infants and young children who have no defenses to protect themselves. We can honestly say that this process of recognition was at times shocking and traumatizing, and gave us fodder for continued work on our own developmental histories and issues.

Currently, we might describe our state of awareness more as stressful, because our levels of empathy have deepened so much that we experience the kind of suffering the 14th Dalai Lama mentioned when he accepted the Nobel Peace Prize in 1989 that drives his vision of "building a better world through human understanding and love, and that in doing so we may reduce the pain and suffering of all sentient beings." Ultimately, we recognized the immense need to provide accurate information and training to parents to help them respond effectively to the social and emotional needs of infants for touch, for emotional attunement, and for their consistent physical presence.

Developmental Stress

During developmental stress, which falls on the mild end of our continuum, the neocortex is still active and the SES of the autonomic nervous system helps the person who is experiencing developmental stress to maintain communication, stay emotionally and socially engaged, to use fight response mechanisms, and to experience life in present time. While the individual may exhibit some anxious or overly active behaviors, the body is able to produce bursts of adrenaline to cope with a short-term crisis and then return to balance when the perceived danger is past.

SES reactions involve the use of facial muscles to both help people quiet themselves inside and to draw others to them for emotional support. Facial muscles control smiling, eyebrow and eyelid lifting, winking, hearing, voice intonation, head nodding, and eye contact—all of these nonverbal cues that indicate whether a person is open and receptive to social interaction. These are also common behaviors between mothers and their infants and between newly found lovers and are considered part of the language of love.

When a person's level of developmental stress moves from a short-term experience to one that is longer lasting, it becomes difficult to keep the SES active. This is because the SES is part of the autonomic nervous system, and the urge to flee or fight starts taking over at a biological level. Disrupting this process requires the person to notice his or her internal reactions and biological states and take conscious control of them. In other words, the challenge is to make unconscious and involuntary actions more conscious and voluntary. We discuss how to do this in more detail in Chapters 9 through 13.

The Four Stages of Human Development

We have divided all human development into four distinct stages: codependent, counterdependent, independent, and interdependent. In each stage, we have identified the essential developmental processes that the individual must complete in order to evolve to the next stage. Any that are not completed on schedule during any stage are carried forward into the next stage, which then makes it even more difficult to complete the essential developmental processes of the subsequent stage.

Through our research, we have expanded this four-stage model to include the essential developmental processes that need to be completed in each stage of development at all levels of human systems: couples, families, organizations, cultures, nation-states, and the history of the whole human race. We will discuss this expanded model, which we call developmental systems theory (DST), in more detail in Chapters 1 and 2.

Our Binary Model of Human Evolution

During our study of developmental shock, trauma, and stress, we found concepts and terms from both quantum physics and biology very useful in describing the subtleties of the human experience, particularly at energetic and cellular levels. They are also compatible with language used in the field of energy psychology.

Terms such as energy, harmonics, attunement, resonance, and synchrony helped us to better understand and describe the nuances of social interactions. When we gave presentations about bonding and trauma, we discovered that people immediately understood these concepts when we introduced them with terms such as "on the same page," "bad vibes," and "out of synch."

Quantum physics provides language to describe moments in which things are vibrating at the same frequency. This frequency is known as the system's *resonance frequency*. An example of a system experiencing resonance frequency is when members of an orchestra are tuning their musical instruments to one tone or frequency before they play music together. In humans, the process of attunement is biological, psychological, and energetic. This attunement is sometimes known as *limbic resonance,* as it involves a complex and rapid exchange of information, largely nonverbal, between two people about their emotional states and their emotional adaptations to one another. Limbic resonance is part of the mechanism of love (Lewis, Amini, & Lannon, 2000, p. 76).

Physicists also theorize that the cosmos is held together through a similar phenomenon known as *orbital resonance*. This self-regulating process allows all the galaxies, black holes, quasars, and masers to attune with each other in ways that form a stable, cohesive cosmic system. Smaller systems, whether planetary or human, construct and stabilize themselves through this same principle. When a system, such as a piano, emits more than one tone, it creates a *harmonic,* making it possible for other instruments to simultaneously attune to multiple tones. This is the principle behind any orchestral composition. It is also the main principle behind our concept of *LOVEvolution*, which we describe in more detail in Chapter 3.

At the point when we recognized that we were mapping two very different evolutionary tracks of development—LOVEvolution and a devolutionary track involving developmental shock, trauma, and stress—we began describing them in our books on codependency and counterdependency (Weinhold & Weinhold, 2008a & 2008b). By the time we published the first edition of *Conflict Resolution: The Partnership Way* (2000b), we saw developmental trauma as the primary cause of devolution. In this book, we now recognize that the primary causes of devolution are developmental shock, developmental trauma, and developmental stress.

In this book, we use quantum language to describe our binary, or two-track, model of human evolution. When two people empathically engage with each other, for example, they create a field of energy in which their hearts, right brains, and sensory systems are attuned in a shared relational field. In this field, they are each able to regulate intense emotions and to sustain feelings of pleasure and interconnectedness that support their mutual growth and evolution. This is the track of LOVEvolution. When this field of supportive and pleasurable energy gets disrupted or breaks down, people become emotionally dysregulated, socially disengage from each other, and energetically closed down. They shift into the devolutionary track of developmental shock and developmental trauma.

We believe intense or lengthy breaks in this relational field of interconnectedness begin first as developmental stress. If the break is repaired in a timely manner through comforting responses that calm and help reregulate the emotions, then the disruption is just a psychological "owie." If the disruption is not quickly repaired, then it turns into a break that overwhelms the autonomic nervous system and the brain. The experience can shift quickly from developmental stress into a developmental trauma state. If an intervention does not relieve the symptoms of overwhelm, then the person falls into a developmental shock state.

While emotional dysregulation is consciously experienced as an emotional event, it also produces an invisible biochemical event that involves a trackable sequence of quantifiable biochemical reactions in the body. The experience of dysregulation begins at the cellular level and then travels through the neural circuitry to the brain and nervous system. From there it goes to the endocrine system, which produces hormones that mobilize the person into protective, survival-oriented behaviors.

By this definition, many people are walking around in a chronic state of shock, trauma, or stress and do not know it. They may be chronically dissociated, or hypervigilant and subconsciously watching for some sign of danger from which they must protect themselves. These unconscious reactions related to early shocks, traumas, or stresses control a large percentage of human behavior.

You, for example, may have no conscious memory of a past experience involving shock, trauma, or stress and therefore do not understand why you are getting an inner biological signal telling you there is something dangerous about a current situation or person. You recognize from experience, however, that certain situations and people stir uncomfortable feelings. The way people typically avoid these feelings is by compulsively using some addictive substance or activity to numb or distract themselves. By definition, all addictions are attempts to avoid feelings.

Developmental Shock, Trauma, and Stress as Primary Causes of Human Suffering

This book identifies the intergenerational and systemic reenactment of developmental shock, trauma, and stress as the primary causes of all human suffering and the arrested or delayed evolution in all human systems. According to our metatheory, DST, developmental shock, trauma, and stress are transmitted intergenerationally via *fractal* patterns of relational dynamics. The geometric concept of fractals was made famous by the mathematician Benoît Mandelbrot (1980) and his recognition of regular and repeating patterns in nature. For example, the structure of a tree and its branches is very similar to the structure of the airways and blood vessels in human lungs. Even before Mandelbrot appeared on the scene, biologists referred to the architecture of the human lung as the "human bronchial tree." (Horsfield, Dart, Olson, Filley & Cumming, 1971)

We apply Bruce Lipton's concept of fractal evolution (2005, pp. 17–98) to the transmission of precise patterns of relationship dynamics that are repeated throughout microsystems (individuals, couples, and families) and macrosystems (groups, organizations, nation–states) that ultimately obstruct the evolution of the human race. Two common relationship fractals that are repeated throughout all human systems are the dominator/dominated or master/slave pattern and the victim/victimizer patterns. For example, a person who was dominated and traumatized as a child may end up dominating and traumatizing his or her own spouse or children or employees at work. All of these behavior patterns are rooted in humanity's very earliest experiences within the nuclear family and then reenacted throughout all human systems and structures.

DST affirms the basic premise of family systems theory, which states that you must look at the whole system for the cause of a problem, be it the whole individual as a system or a larger microsystem like a family. DST then expands this theory to include all human macrosystems and shows how developmental shock, trauma, and stress can block or even completely stall the evolution of human civilization.

The fractal patterns of relational shock, trauma, and stress are transmitted from one system to another through a mechanism that Freud identified as the *repetition compulsion* (Freud, 1921). The repetition compulsion is part of a human's natural learning style, which is to repeat something that is unhealed or misunderstood until it becomes consciously understood and healed. Once you understand the cause-and-effect correlation between these early traumatic events and current relational conflicts, it is possible to heal the effects of the underlying developmental shocks, traumas, and stresses. Without an understanding of the effects of these unrecognized and unhealed shocks, traumas, and stresses, it is difficult to see the fractal patterns of behavior that affect the evolution of larger human systems. With this understanding, it is not only possible to recognize the effects of patterns produced by the reenactment of shock, trauma, and stress, it is also possible to change them. This is what ultimately advances evolution in all human systems.

Unfortunately, it seems that many people do not understand this reenactment or recapitulation process and continue to accept its accompanying chaos, isolation, pain, and suffering as part of the human condition. They do not know there is a way out of this suffering. When the two of us began our relationship, we chose not to live in this paradigm. We really believed that once we understood the causes of our suffering and discovered how to change them, then we (and humanity) could have a quite different destiny—one of harmony, community, affiliation, functional parenting, and spiritual evolution that goes far beyond struggle and suffering. We believe that we can consciously change our reactions to unhealed developmental shocks, traumas, and stresses and prevent them from interfering with our ability to create and sustain happy, healthy relationships.

Developmental Shock, Trauma, and Stress as Causes of Degenerative Conditions

The Chinese have known for thousands of years that emotional stress is an underlying cause of degenerative conditions such as heart conditions, diabetes, and cancer (Zhang, 2007). Candace Pert (1997) and Louise Hay (1984) more recently presented this same premise in contemporary literature. Recent holistic research has revealed a very precise link between these health conditions and prior experiences of acute or chronic shock, trauma and stress. For example, German oncologist and researcher, Dr. Ryke Hamer (2000), and an American oncologist and researcher, Dr. W. Douglas Brodie (1997), discovered independently how unhealed developmental shock, trauma, or stress suppresses the immune system.

Hamer discovered that in almost every case, the onset of cancer was preceded by some inescapable shock or unresolved emotional conflict (trauma) within the previous 1 to 2 years of the diagnosis. Both Hamer and Brodie independently found that episodes of acute shock or trauma not only damaged the immune system but also damaged the emotional center in the brain that emits condition-fighting proteins. These doctors began utilizing psychotherapy to treat cancer and achieved remarkable results. We discuss Hamer's and Brodie's work in more detail in Chapter 8.

Our research on the role of unrecognized and unhealed developmental shock, trauma, and stress in illness and degenerative conditions actually extends the work of Hamer and Brodie by looking at the systemic impact of unrecognized and unhealed developmental shock, trauma, and stress over the lifespan. It also expands and extends their work by looking at the impact of unrecognized and unhealed developmental shock, trauma, and stress at a species level. We believe that shocking, traumatic, or stressful experiences during conception, gestation, and birth have the most profound impact on human development. The energetic, biological, and psychological environment in which a fertilized egg gradually transforms into a complete human being determines much of its future. Experiences after birth and up through the first 3 years reinforce these prenatal experiences of developmental shock, laying down the foundation for a person's propensities toward certain kinds of degenerative health conditions.

Developmental Process Work: Tools for Healing Developmental Shock, Trauma, and Stress in Individuals, Couples, and Families

DPW is our comprehensive interventions model for healing developmental shock, trauma, and stress in individuals, couples, and families. DPW emphasizes the importance of clearing imprints of shock, trauma, and stress from the central nervous system, resolving intractable conflicts, rebuilding fractured relationship dynamics, restoring the experience of deep emotional resonance and connection, and helping people learn how to regulate their emotional states. This focus provides the necessary foundation for building sustainable, loving adult relationships. DPW also provides practical tools for identifying and tracking the shock, trauma, and stress aspects of an emotionally dysregulating event. Most importantly, it offers the possibility of changing the quality of a person's life.

After first using DPW tools with ourselves and then with our clients, we found they were also effective as an interventions model for helping individuals, couples, and families heal developmental trauma. In early 1990, we began introducing these tools to counselors-in-training in our graduate classes in conflict resolution and other counselor training classes at the University of Colorado at Colorado Springs.

DPW is a relational rather than a power or informational approach to therapy that relies on the effectiveness of the therapeutic relationship to provide communication tools, understanding, and processes for healing the effects of developmental shock, trauma, and stress and for creating heartfelt, resonant connections in the therapist–client relationship. We believe that it is necessary to heal your own developmental shock, trauma, or stress if you wish to fully attune emotionally with your children, partners, siblings, parents, friends, clients, students, and coworkers. Whether you are a helping professional or not, this means being personally able to open your heart and fully extend genuine empathy and compassion to others in ways that facilitate the healing of developmental shock, trauma, and stress.

DPW interventions also modulate the impact of shock on the parasympathetic nervous system and help people re-embody after experiences of dissociation. DPW heals the impact of developmental trauma on the sympathetic nervous system and helps people recover from regressive episodes that mix memories of past experiences with present-time events. It treats seven different components of developmental shock, trauma, or stress:

1. Sensory system distortions (visual memory, auditory memory, proprioceptive memory, kinesthetic memory)
2. Body memories
3. Distorted cognition and beliefs
4. Dysregulated emotions
5. The split within the self
6. Distorted relational dynamics between self and other
7. Intractable conflicts in intimate relationships

We believe that our unique synthesis of practical tools, anchored in a systemic, evolutionary framework, can help all human systems move forward in their evolution.

PART ONE

Developmental Systems Theory

God must become an
activity in our consciousness.

Joel S. Goldsmith

CHAPTER ONE

What Is Developmental Systems Theory?

Developmental Systems Theory (DST) is a binary metatheory for understanding human evolution. Track one of this theory, LOVEvolution, provides an optimal model of development for advancing the evolution of six levels of human systems. Track two of this theory, developmental trauma, looks at how early experiences of shock, trauma, and stress prevent this optimal development and interfere with the evolution of these human systems.

DST as a metatheory identifies the essential developmental processes that must be completed in order for each human system to evolve. It describes evolution as a continuous process that moves through four developmental stages, each building on the previous one. DST is our version of a unified developmental systems theory that includes the study of all human systems, what they require in order to evolve, and the human experiences that interfere with their evolution.

In this chapter, we share how our personal search for intimacy as a couple led to the creation of the microsystems component of DST. We also look at the scientific principles of general systems theory and then present an overview of both the micro and macro components of DST. In Chapter 2, we describe our heuristic research, how we created the microsystems component of DST, and the theoretical foundations of DST.

A Personal Context for Developmental Systems Theory

We have been conducting personal research on DST in what we came to call "our laboratory" since we were married in 1984. We had no idea that patterns of unrecognized and unhealed developmental shock, trauma, and stress transmitted to us from our family-of-origin systems would impact our efforts to experience intimacy. When they appeared, we looked for ways to identify the barriers to intimacy and then create tools for healing them. We closed the exits that we had used to avoid looking at ourselves in our previous relationships—addictions, distractions, defenses, excuses—and began working in earnest.

The fact that we were both mental health practitioners also gave us extra motivation to work on ourselves and our relationship. We realized that doing this work was equally essential for creating healthy and ethical relationships with our clients. So we had deep personal and professional reasons for charting our particular course.

First, we learned to recognize that the overreactions we had during our conflicts were being triggered by unrecognized and unhealed shock, trauma, and stress from the past. We began to recognize that our intergenerational patterns of unhealed shock, trauma, and stress were anchored in our early childhood development. We gradually saw how our patterns were complementary and that this was one of the reasons we were attracted to each other. Eventually we understood that a central purpose of our relationship was to help each other heal the lingering effects of our early experiences of shock, trauma, and stress and to change our perceptions of them.

We both had been in therapy prior to our relationship and were under the illusion that we had already healed the effects of our early shock, trauma, and stress. We soon realized, however, that the depth of intimacy we were experiencing in our relationship was triggering older and deeper levels of unhealed early developmental shock, trauma, and stress and causing increasingly more frequent periods of disharmony and feelings of emotional separation.

We noticed during conflicts that our exaggerated emotional reactions were much greater than the situation called for. Emotional escalation was the first signal that we were being triggered by unrecognized and unhealed shock, trauma, and stress and that we were dissociating or regressing. We had worked in therapy on our more obvious experiences of shock, trauma, and stress, such as Janae's abandonment by her mother at 13 years when her mother committed suicide. Barry had done extensive reparenting therapy to help him heal the effects of early bonding breaks with his mother.

We finally recognized that the closeness and intimacy of our relationship, greater than we ever had in previous relationships, was making it safe enough for deeper levels of previously unrecognized and unhealed shock, trauma, and stress to surface. We then began experimenting with ways to help each other heal the lingering effects of these experiences. It soon became clear to us that this was a challenging process and that some of the ways we were using to heal these wounds were not very effective.

What made it seem even more difficult was that our intergenerational patterns of shock, trauma, and stress seemed to mesh perfectly. When Barry did something that reminded Janae of her mother's abandonment, she would feel deep feelings of fear and sadness from her abandonment trauma. This would cause her to project her mother's face on Barry, lash out at him, and push him away like she did her mother. This would trigger Barry's memories of being verbally attacked by his mother and his feelings of abandonment after her attacks. So we were often two scared, angry, and regressed little children attempting to resolve a current conflict that was anchored in our past experiences involving the unhealed effects of shock, trauma, and stress.

When we got triggered during a relationship conflict, we quickly found ourselves feeling emotionally mis-attuned and disconnected from each other. The trigger cues and signals often gave us clues that helped us identify the developmental sources of our conflict. From this we surmised that we must have had numerous bonding breaks with our mothers during our early infancy. We also recognized that when we were regressed or dissociated we had intense emotions that made it very difficult for us to function as adults. In these situations we sometimes resorted to using old defenses such as blaming each other, fleeing physically or emotionally, or even just freezing and not knowing what to say or do, to keep us from regressing or dissociating.

Recognizing these time-distorting experiences slowly helped us connect present-time conflicts with unhealed developmental shocks, traumas, and stresses that we experienced as infants. We realized that we both had mothers who were unable to consistently attune with us emotionally. As we understood more about our mothers' childhood histories, we recognized that they were struggling with their own unrecognized and unhealed developmental shock, trauma, and stress, which made it difficult for them to be present with us.

As we looked at our mothers and their own mother–child experiences, we understood in a very personal way how these subtle patterns of developmental shock, trauma, and stress are transmitted intergenerationally. As we created tools that helped us reregulate our feelings during our periodic traumatic reenactments, we began to use them with clients who had similar issues in their relationships.

In our clinical work we began to focus more intensely on helping individuals recognize their first signs of posttraumatic stress. We helped them to connect the dots between problems they were having in their current life situations with experiences involving shock, trauma, and stress during their first 3 years of life. Then we used our tools to help them complete these developmental processes in present time and to help heal the lingering effects of shock, trauma, and stress from their relationships, bodies, and nervous systems. Finally, we served as comforting figures that were able to empathize with them and witness their emotional struggles. We discovered that people in the helping professions—therapists, social workers, and teachers—are most effective when they shared about their own process of becoming whole and individuated persons at appropriate times in their work with others.

We also worked with many couples who came to us in the midst of breakdown and we taught them how to use our tools to heal their developmental shock, trauma, and stress. We discovered that our systems framework could help them quickly identify their core couple issues. We also taught them how to work cooperatively to help each other heal the developmental shock, trauma, and stress that they had brought into their relationships.

Then we began to see the same symptoms of early shock, trauma, and stress in our clinical work with families. We worked with intact families, blended families, and single-parent families who were all facing serious problems. In each case, the family system was threatened by the lack of sustained emotional resonance and inability of members to regulate their emotions. Many had serious conflicts involving children who needed more emotional support from the parents in order to complete the essential developmental processes of both their codependent and counterdependent stages. We saw how difficult it was for parents to support their children when they were not securely bonded with each other and their children.

Here it was clear how the parents' unhealed developmental shock, trauma, and stress were impacting both the couple structure and the whole family system. It was also here that we learned how to work systemically to heal developmental shock, trauma, and stress. Our first focus was on helping individuals learn how to regulate themselves during escalated emotional states, then teaching couples how to help each other do this, and finally working with the whole family to teach them these skills. The ripple effect of change we saw moving among these three systems always amazed us, particularly how quickly the children adapted once the adults became more whole and functional.

One of our most effective intervention strategies involved the use of home visits in which we helped couples integrate their work into their families. This particular practice gave us a lot of experience in honing the DST microsystem component strategies and skills. It also triggered deeper family-of-origin issues for us to address in our own relationship.

The feedback from our clients and the countertransference issues they generated for us to work on helped us refine our tools, which we then tested in our own relationship. Once we refined them and researched them more thoroughly, we began teaching these tools to counselors in training through our graduate classes at the University of Colorado at Colorado Springs. They gave us feedback on their effectiveness in their therapy work with themselves and with their clients. Finally, we began writing books to share our philosophy and approach more widely. We can say that we are still in the midst of a living laboratory and drawing on all our life experiences as resources for learning and evolving. Our websites contain our writings about the latest learning and evolving we have done since the book was published.

A Scientific Context for Developmental Systems Theory

General systems theory originated in the early 1940s as mathematicians, physicists, and engineers searched for functional and structural rules that could describe all physical (nonhuman) systems. Norbert Weiner (1954) first applied these principles as he developed the Norden bombsight during World War II. He coined the term *cybernetics* to describe this emerging field of study.

Books by Buckley (1968) and von Bertalanffy (1968) made early attempts to apply systems concepts to human systems. Ten years later, James Miller (1978) wrote a book applying the concepts of general systems theory to human systems. Lerner and Ford's work on DST and the work of Miller and others are responsible for generating widespread agreement today that general systems theory, as a model of self-organization, can be used to describe how complex human systems change and evolve. It also demonstrates how complex human systems can create new forms and still retain continuity.

Based on what we were learning in our personal laboratory, we started our heuristic research on how to facilitate evolution in all human systems by focusing first on understanding individual development. Then over a period of about 15 years, we gradually applied the principles of individual development to larger, more complex human systems: couples, families, groups/organizations, cultures/nation–states, and the human race. By the time that we published our book on conflict resolution in 2000, we understood how all of these systems evolved through the same four stages of development: codependent, counterdependent, independent, and interdependent.

This part of our research also involved understanding the role of fractal patterns related to shock, trauma, stress, incomplete developmental processes, and unmet developmental needs. We saw that these patterns repeat concisely through each system and operate as templates for all biological, psychological, and material development in that system.

Finally, we consolidated our research into our systemic metatheory of DST and based it on principles of fractal evolution in which a reiterated pattern of "structures" nests within one another. More specifically, the pattern of the whole is reflected in the parts of the whole (Lipton, 2005, pp. 197–198). When we applied fractal principles to the history of the human race, we could see that the evolutionary fractal pattern of the whole human race is also reflected in the cells of the individual human.

This holographic perspective emphasizes the interconnectedness of all life. In a hologram any small part of a larger image contains the pattern of the whole, When you look at a nation–state as a human system and then focus on one citizen of that nation–state, it is possible to understand how that person behaves. Likewise, looking at one citizen of a nation–state will help you understand how the larger system behaves. Behaviorally, energetically, and structurally, they serve as mirrors for each other.

Lipton's work helped us understand the functional structure and behavior of a cell, which made it easier to understand and map the organization and behavior of the individual as a system. Once we understood the functional structure of the individual human system, it helped us understand and map the organizational and behavioral level of larger and more complex human systems such as couples, families, groups/organizations, cultures/nation–states, and humans as a species. A fractal framework for evolution shows how each larger system contains the same patterns of organization and behavior that are found in the subsystems contained within it.

While we may be among the first to map human evolution using principles from fractal geometry, others have recognized the value of a comprehensive and integrative theory of development. In 1992, Ford and Lerner presented the need for this approach in their groundbreaking book, *Developmental Systems Theory: An Integrative Approach.* While Ford and Lerner's integrative approach to a theory of development contains many useful concepts that we were able to incorporate into our work, it still embraced many neo-Darwinian beliefs about the characteristics of biological systems that did not fit a fractal model of evolution. Neo-Darwinian proponents view evolution in the following way:

- All developmental processes support evolution by continually creating new structures.
- Each new structure transcends the structures from which it came and has its own unique systemic characteristics, information, functions, and laws.
- Conversely, each new structure is ultimately reducible to any lower or higher levels of structure even with its unique systemic characteristics. It still has much in common with its lower or higher structures.
- The major developmental processes through which life evolves can only be accounted for by incorporating many more layers of structure and process than allowed by the usual concepts of genes and environment.

Based on the new research we found, we came to believe that these early models are outdated and should be replaced with Lipton's model of fractal evolution. His model offers an alternative theory to neo-Darwinism, basing the primacy of development on the individual cell receptors' perception of its environment rather than on nature or genetics.

Lipton's biological premise, which draws from unified field theory, asserts that receptors on the membranes of individual cells read the field surrounding them. The cells' perception of the field determines how they respond. When the cells perceive danger, their receptors close and direct the organism into a protective mode. When the cells perceive safety, the receptors open, and they direct the organism into a growth mode.

Lipton's model provides no middle ground: cells and organisms can only be in one mode at a time. Cells are either in a growth mode and able to give and receive information, sustenance, and unconditional love, or they are in a protection mode and unable to receive supportive information and energy. We find Lipton's model of fractal evolution along with principles from quantum sciences, particularly quantum biology and neuroscience, very supportive of the framework we began developing for DST in the early 1990s.

Lipton's pioneering work in the field of epigenetics (2005, pp. 67–73) also provided us with a scientific foundation for our clinical model, Developmental Process Work (DPW). Epigenetics, a revolutionary field in biology, establishes that DNA is mutable, rather than fixed as "destiny" in a Darwinian sense, and can be modified without changing the basic blueprint. The DNA blueprint cannot only be damaged through nutrition, stress, and emotional states, but it can also by healed through modalities designed to treat the damage. We examine this process at more length in Chapter 9.

Schore (2003a) presented a similar rationale by applying three interacting principles of dynamic systems theory to the study of normal and abnormal human development. His first key concept was *state changes*. This concept involves looking for the underlying complex psychobiological states that evoke change in humans. In individuals, the brain and nervous system determine and regulate these state changes. Advances in brain imaging technology have made it easier to identify the internal states that cause changes in the brain and nervous system and ultimately cause a system to shift. For example, the study of infant bonding now examines the developing brain and nervous system as a child evolves into a self-organizing being.

Schore's second key concept was the *psychobiological state* that marks the common boundary between the psychological and biological sciences and helps reunite mind and body. His third key concept of *self-organization* is essential for identifying the impact of early childhood experiences on brain development, particularly the development of the right hemisphere. Perry (1996) and others recognized the developing brain as use-dependent: The quality of the bonding interactions between infants and their mothers determines which parts of the brain fully develop and which do not.

Schore's review of recent brain research suggested that "the self-organization of the brain occurs in the context of another self, another brain" (1996, p. 58). He contended that an infant's early bonding experiences with his or her mother involve the energetic attunement of his or her right brain with the right brain of the mother. If the mother has a functional right brain and is able to attune to her child's right brain through mutual gazing, kind words, soft singing, and gentle touch, then the infant's cell receptors open and allow the brain and nervous system to grow and develop.

Schore focused much of his attention on the experience-dependent maturation of the frontolimbic system in the human brain. This part of the brain directs traffic and regulates psychobiological states and organismic energy flow and balance (2003a, p. 92). He contended that less than optimal gene–environment interactions (developmental shocks, traumas, or stresses) during the crucial bonding and separation developmental processes produce a frontolimbic brain organization that is vulnerable to a later spectrum of psychopathologies (1994).

The work of both Lipton and Schore utilized the language from quantum mechanics, particularly quantum biology, that recognizes the psychobiological transfer of energy that is generated during shared emotional states between living systems, both at micro- and macroscopic levels. Schore's description of the mother–child relationship is sprinkled with quantum language such as attunement, energetic resonance, and synchronization. In Chapter 3 we look at some of the research showing that the beating human heart generates some 2.5 watts of electrical activity with each heartbeat that creates a pulsing electromagnetic field of energy around the body.

We know that the developing brain demands massive amounts of energy and matter to fuel its growth, making a young child's brain operate at a much faster metabolic rate than an adult brain. This is why it can shift more rapidly into self-organization. We also know that self-organization increases the rate of energy/matter transfer, so the more open a complex system is to receiving energy, the faster and easier the energy/matter flows in that system (Goerner, 1995, pp. 17–38). This concept supports Lipton's notion that when the cell perceives that it is safe to open and receive new energy/matter, it relays this information on to the frontolimbic brain, which increases the rate of self-organization.

Based on his review of the new research on neurobiology and neurochemistry, Schore listed a number of important systems principles that are useful in the study of self-organizing developmental systems (for a more detailed analysis, please consult Schore, 2003a, pp. 92–95). The following are principles that describe how humans get their needs met and evolve:

- They are open to interact with their particular environment. For human infants, it is important to monitor their interactions with the social environment, particularly their primary caregivers.
- Infants' ongoing development requires an open system in which both matter and energy can be openly exchanged with the environment. This is the same principle

that Lipton observed at a cellular level. If the receptors on the lining of the cell wall perceive the environment as safe, they open and receive both matter and energy that support growth.

- At certain key moments in the development of a system, a flow of new energy/matter from the environment allows the components of infants' self-organizing systems to become increasingly more interconnected. We describe these as *essential developmental processes*. An example of this is the secure bonding that occurs over time as the result of an infant's consistently repeated experiences of connecting, disconnecting, and reconnecting with the mother and other adult caregivers. Completing the essential developmental process of bonding allows children to build basic trust and move on to the separation stage of development.
- Self-organization occurs when the developing infant uses incoming energy/matter to move from a state of equilibrium into a state of disequilibrium and then reorganizes into a higher state of equilibrium.
- As the patterns of energy/matter transfer among the components of a self-organizing infant become increasingly interconnected and well ordered, the infant is better able to maintain stability in relation to the input he or she is receiving from the environment.
- Given a current state of self-organization, an infant is able to tolerate a range of states without becoming too unstable.
- As an infant passes through a succession of states, he or she must eventually return to the state previously entered. The path a system takes to return to its previous state is called its trajectory.
- If an infant is forced out of a stationary state by new inputs from the environment, the infant will tend to return to his or her original state, but in a new way.
- The time it takes for an infant to return to a stationary state determines his or her stability. The people who created aerobics, for example, use this principle to define *fitness*. The quicker your pulse and heart rate return to normal after the stress of an aerobic exercise, the more physically fit you are considered. The same principle can be applied to psychological fitness.
- Self-organization proceeds systematically and hierarchically, with each level of self-organization building upon the one that preceded it. However, systems never develop in a straight line—they are always nonlinear.
- All human systems, including infants, function hierarchically. One can track the path of their development to see where environmental input (developmental shocks, traumas, stresses, or exceptional developmental support) may have caused the system to modify its trajectory.
- The different organizational levels of both human individuals and larger and more complex human systems unfold through a hierarchical process of development and maturation. This unfoldment is characterized by an alternation between rapid and slower rates of development that finally plateaus and sets the limits on the stages of development. Thus, a plateau in development marks the

end of one stage of development before an acceleration of development marks the beginning of the next stage.

- Developmental change is the result of a series of alternating states of stability and instability. These changes are marked by transitions that irreversibly alter the trajectory of the system and help it reach new and higher levels of self-organization.
- Complex systems are sensitive to bifurcation points where the system can choose to divide. At these sensitive points, small differences in inputs can become amplified and are able to activate large system effects over many cycles of change. In chaos theory these inputs are called *strange attractors*. When these inputs are integrated into the system, they have the potential to produce system-altering changes.
- Strange attractors can be introduced deliberately to either stabilize a system or to rapidly change the path of a system trajectory to a desired state. They also cause systems to become more flexible in their performance and more open to adapting to changes in their environment. Those who perform this function in organizations are known as *change agents,* or in our terminology, *developmental process consultants (DPCs).*
- Information is a special kind of energy that is required to establish biological order. Emotion (e-motion or energy in motion) acts as a strange attractor to direct the system's attention to relevant information coming in from its environment. It helps the system monitor and interpret environmental events according to their significance to the system.
- Interpersonal strange attractors also determine the stability of a system. They help maintain the system's equilibrium and effectively regulate any disequilibrium caused by emotions.

We know someone who went through the kind of life-altering experience Schore described. His name is Fleet Maull, and we met him in Boulder, Colorado, through his Peacemaker Institute when we still lived in Colorado Springs. Maull was an adventuresome young man who got caught trafficking in drugs in 1989 and was sentenced to 14 years in a federal maximum-security penitentiary. During this time, he had to face the consequences of his action in circumstances more demeaning and violent than he ever imagined. This experience turned out to be a transition point for him—he could succumb to the horror his life had become or he could make a decision to live in spite of his bleak future.

He chose to face his fate head-on by diving into Tibetan Buddhist meditation practices, teaching literacy classes to other prisoners during the day, and providing hospice care for dying inmates during the night. During his time behind bars, he completed a strenuous Tibetan initiatory practice that entailed performing 100,000 prostrations in his tiny cell, took vows to become a novice monk, and managed to navigate the unspoken and often life-threatening maze of social codes that govern prison life.

Since his early release for good behavior in 1999, Maull has become a leading prison activist and the founder of two national organizations, the Prison Dharma Network and the National Prison Hospice Association, which promote contemplative spirituality and compassionate end-of-life care in our prisons and jails. He is also an adjunct faculty member at Naropa University in Boulder, Colorado, where he directs the activist training components of the master's degree program in Engaged Buddhism; teaches courses in engaged spirituality, contemplative social action, and peacemaking; and directs the Institute for Transformative Justice.

Maull also works as a management consultant and executive coach, training business and nonprofit leaders in the arts of genuine relationship and authentic leadership. He is a shining example of not only what can happen when a person is willing to open and receive new information and support during a critical bifurcation point in his life, but how this choice can change his or her trajectory or life path.

We can use Maull's story of transformation to understand the use of systems principles in the study of infant development. Let's use the example of the communication that occurs in the mother–infant system during the bonding process. Any interactions between the two that trigger highly emotional states eventually cause a period of disequilibrium between them. This experience forces their relationship to go through a reorganization.

If the mother responds to her child's unregulated emotions by quickly offering soothing or comforting behavior, then the infant calms down, the resonance between them is restored, and the mother–child system reorganizes. If the mother fails to respond to her infant's cry for help in a calming manner that helps reregulate his or her emotions, the infant will disengage from the mother.

If a mother repeatedly fails to respond to her infant's unregulated emotions, the infant will develop self-soothing substitute mechanisms such as sucking a thumb or pacifier or cuddling with a blanket. This not only creates a chaotic internal system structure for the child who struggles with repeated experiences of disequilibrium, it also lays the foundation for oral addictions later in life.

Infants may also protect themselves from feeling their overwhelming need for an unavailable mother by dissociating, particularly if their relational attunement breaks down repeatedly very early in life. These infants learn that engaging with the mother is painful and even shocking, traumatic, or stressful, forcing them to build defenses against experiencing the feelings associated with the breakdowns and disequilibrium.

A good place to begin studying the evolution of human systems is with the principle of *openness to change*. We have developed inventories that assess this. If we use the mother–child system described above, we would look at the openness of both the mother and the infant. Unless infants have experienced serious neurological damage at birth or prenatally, it is safe to assume that they are open to change.

The mother, however, may or may not be open enough to operate effectively in the mother–child system. In addition, we would want to know how open the father is and how supportive a role he plays in the family system. We might also want to know how open the extended family system is to this mother–child system and the couple system. We also might look at what kind of support is available in the neighborhood and community for the mother–child dyad, the couple, and the extended family.

Table 1.1 lists some of the systemic risk factors to consider when assessing the openness of the mother–infant system, as well as systemic compensating factors that might neutralize or reduce the effects of the risk factors in the dyadic system. As you can see in the table, both positive and negative factors present in the various systems provide input into the mother–infant system. In assessing the openness of any level of human system, it is important to consider the external influences that are also impacting it. Otherwise it will be difficult to effectively control the research.

Developmental Systems Theory: The Essential Developmental Processes for Advancing Human Evolution

Any theory must be clearly stated in order for researchers to validate its premises. Any scientific study of human development should meet the following criteria:

1. Description—This includes an accurate portrayal of the essential developmental processes to be completed to support human evolution.
2. Explanation—The reasons that these processes are essential for development must be clear.
3. Prediction—The essential processes must be sufficiently articulated in order to predict what will happen when they are successfully completed or not.
4. Modification—We can use this knowledge to prevent developmental problems from occurring and to promote good development.

Bowlby (1969) suggested a different set of criteria for evaluating a scientific theory: "The merits of a scientific theory are to be judged in terms of the range of phenomena it embraces, the internal consistency of its structure, the precision of the predictions it can make and the practicality of testing them" (p. 173).

In order to evaluate the efficacy of DST as an emerging theory, we clearly spell out its central elements. DST was designed to meet Bowlby's criteria and the first set of four criteria listed. As an emerging theory, however, we offer it as a set of heuristic hypotheses that can be tested and evaluated by experimental, clinical, and other heuristic researchers. DST, as presented in this book, can be evaluated

TABLE 1.1

Systemic Assessment of Developmental Shock, Trauma, or Stress: Compensatory and Risk Factors

	Parental History Systems Level	Couple/Family Systems Level	Extended Family, Neighborhood, Community Systems Level	State/Federal Systems Level
COMPENSATORY FACTORS	• High IQ • Awareness of and therapy to heal past developmental shocks, traumas, or stresses • History of a positive relationship with parents; good modeling • High self-esteem • Special talents • Physical attractiveness • Good social engagement skills	• Good prenatal care • Healthy mother • Healthy siblings • Supportive spouse • Economic security/ stable employment/ savings in the bank • Healthy role models in family • Timely therapeutic interventions in the couple or family system when problems arise	• Good family support; close-knit families • Supportive neighbors and friends • Few stressful events in neighborhood • Strong, supportive religious affiliation • Positive school experiences and peer relations • Positive adult role models in neighborhood and community	• Cultures that promotes a sense of shared responsibility in caring for the community children • Cultures opposed to violence • Economic prosperity • Good family leave/flex-time policies • Affordable health insurance for families/children
RISK FACTORS	• History of developmental shocks, traumas, stresses, abuse, etc., or lack of awareness of its effects • No H.S. education • Low self-esteem • Low IQ • Poor social engagement skills • Poor peer relations as a child • Poor relations with parents • Evidence of alcohol/drug abuse	• Poor or no prenatal care • Marital discord • Children with behavior problems • Premature or unhealthy children • Frequent moves by family • Drug/alcohol abuse • Single parent • Teen parent • Family income below poverty level • High stress in the family	• High unemployment and poor job prospects • Isolation; lack of extended family support • Poor supportive services for children and families • Economic and social breakdown in neighborhood or community • High stress in the neighborhood and community	• Cultural acceptance of corporal punishment • View of children as possessions • Economic recession or depression • Lack of acceptance of the rule of law to keep order • Lack of trust in government policies

Source: Adapted from "The Intergenerational Transmission of Abuse," by J. Kaufman and E. Zigler, in *Child Maltreatment: Theory and Research on the Causes and Consequences of Child Abuse and Neglect,* D. Cicchetti and V. Carlson (Eds.), 1990, New York: Cambridge University Press.

against these criteria. This chapter describes one of the central elements of the theory: the essential developmental processes for each level of human systems—the individual, the couple, the family, the group/organization, the culture/nation–state, and the human race.

Figure 1.1 and Tables 1.2 and 1.3 describe the six levels of human systems and the essential developmental processes that must be completed in each stage to ensure healthy psychosocial development. Our goal is to describe the theory in such a way that the reader can see how the next stage builds on the successful completion of the developmental processes in the previous stage. When some essential developmental processes are not completed in the previous stage, it makes it more difficult for the system to complete the essential developmental processes of the next stage.

We think the most important system to understand is the individual, because individual development contains the fractal pattern for the evolution of all other human systems. It is also the simplest and most personal system to study.

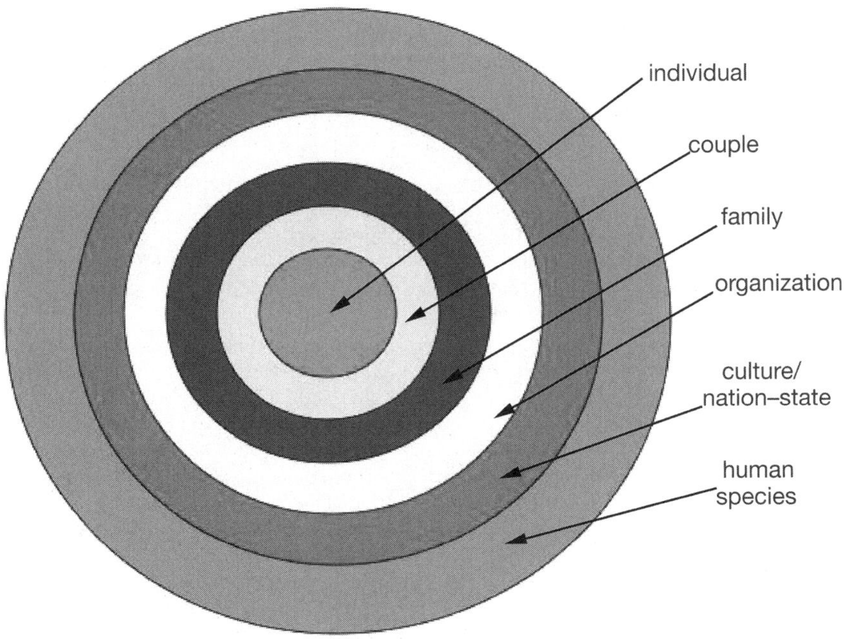

FIGURE 1.1

The Systemic Evolution of All Human Systems

TABLE 1.2

The Developmental Evolution of Human Microsystems

Stage of Development / Primary Task	Essential Developmental Processes of an Individual	Essential Developmental Processes of a Couple	Essential Developmental Processes of a Family
Codependent Stage (Bonding)	• Mother receives good prenatal care and support • Experience a nonviolent birth with immediate interventions to heal any shocks or birth trauma • Experience secure bonding/attachment with mother and or other adult caregivers • Build primal trust with both parents through a consistent resonant connection • Learn emotional resiliency skills • Create a secure internal model of self/other • Build healthy emotional communication and social engagement skills with both parents and others • Achieve secure bonding experiences with siblings and extended family • Promote effective communication and social engagement skills with parents and others	• Create secure and consistent bonding experiences with each other • Establish deep primal trust in each other • Develop ways to quickly repair any disruptions to couple resonance • Establish good communication and social engagement skills with each other • Establish an identity as a couple • Create secure bonding experiences in the family between parents and children • Establish primal trust among family members • Establish healthy emotional communication and social engagement skills among family members • Establish an identity as a family	• Create secure bonding experiences in the family between parents and children • Establish primal trust of family members with one another • Establish healthy emotional communication and social engagement skills among family members • Initiate a healthy family vision and induct family members into it • Establish a healthy identity as a family
Counterdependent Stage (Separation)	• Achieve complete psychological separation from both parents • Learn to explore one's environment in safe ways	• Become functionally separate individuals in the relationship • Identify and accept individual differences in thoughts, feelings, and behaviors in each other	• Parents and children learn to assert their individual needs and have them supported by other family members

(continued)

TABLE 1.2 *(continued)*

Stage of Development / Primary Task	Essential Developmental Processes of an Individual	Essential Developmental Processes of a Couple	Essential Developmental Processes of a Family
Counterdependent (continued)	• Learn to trust and regulate one's own thoughts, feelings, behaviors in socially appropriate ways • Internalize appropriate physical and social limits • Develop healthy narcissism • Resolve internal conflicts between oneness and separateness • Bond with self • Continue to build secure internal working model of reality • Successfully complete the psychological birth process	• Resolve internal conflicts between needs of self and other • Develop effective partnership ways to resolve conflicts of wants and needs, and conflicts of values and beliefs	• Use fair, equitable, and nonshaming methods of limit setting and discipline • Parents are able to set effective limits for themselves and their children • Resolve conflicts effectively between needs of parents and needs of children
Independent Stage (Mastery)	• Master basic self-care • Master the process of becoming a functionally autonomous individual separate from parents • Develop object constancy • Develop trust in core values and beliefs • Achieve secure bonding experiences with nature • Learn effective social engagement skills • Develop secure internal working model of self/other • Achieve secure bonding with peers	• Listen empathically and nondefensively to each other • Communicate feelings directly and responsibly • Take responsibility for the influence of past shocks, traumas, or stresses on behavior • Master financial, psychological, and professional self-sufficiency within the relationship • Move beyond an idealized, romanticized approach to love and intimacy • Develop core values and beliefs as a couple • Achieve object constancy as a couple • Bond with nature as a couple	• Support development of individual initiative in family members • Develop individual and couple autonomy within the family structure • Set limits on children, selves, extrafamily involvement to preserve couple relationship/ couple autonomy within the family structure • Develop core values and beliefs as a family • Achieve object constancy as a family • Bond with nature as a family

(continued)

TABLE 1.2 *(continued)*

Stage of Development / Primary Task	Essential Developmental Processes of an Individual	Essential Developmental Processes of a Couple	Essential Developmental Processes of a Family
Interdependent Stage (Cooperation)	• Learn how to cooperate with others • Learn how to negotiate with others to get needs met • Learn to accept responsibility for personal behaviors and life experiences • Experience secure bonding with peers and other adults • Develop a social conscience • Achieve a secure bonding experience with the main culture • Develop a secure bonding experience with the planet • Live out of an authentic adult self • Achieve secure bonding with own children • Understand the influence of incomplete developmental processes on own life and how to heal own developmental shocks, traumas, or stresses successfully	• Create a well-differentiated and clearly defined sense of self • Support partner's development • Learn to cooperate with each other in getting important needs met in the relationship • Experience the deepest human connection possible with each other • Develop equality in the relationship • Cooperate to help each other heal developmental shocks, traumas, or stresses • Cooperate to develop each person's fullest human potential	• Build consensus in decision-making skills among family members • Teach family members to cooperate with each other so all get important needs met. • Create rituals that sustain the spiritual dimension of the family • Create divisions of labor based on individual interests and abilities • Help family members cooperate to help each other to heal their developmental shocks, traumas, or stresses • Teach family members how to cooperate to develop each member's fullest potential as human being

We believe that individual evolution is now stalled at the counterdependent stage because most of humanity has not yet successfully completed enough of the essential developmental processes in the codependent and counterdependent stages. This also affects all the other human systems in the same way. We believe that the effects of unrecognized and unhealed developmental shock, trauma, and stress are the primary obstacles to the evolution of the whole human race.

Incomplete developmental processes in individual development create fractal relational patterns that block the evolution of couples, families, groups/organizations, cultures/nation–states, and the human race. Individuals unconsciously carry

TABLE 1.3

The Developmental Evolution of Human Macrosystems

Stage of Development / Primary Task	Essential Developmental Processes of an Organization	Essential Developmental Processes of Cultures and Nation–States	Essential Developmental Processes of the Human Race
Codependent Stage (Bonding)	• Create bonding experiences for employees • Build trust between employers and employees • Create an organizational identity • Provide for basic needs of employees and managers • Foster healthy emotional communication and social engagement skills with employees and employers • Build organizational esprit de corps	• Create bonding experiences that unify all subcultures around common values and practices • Build trust between leaders and citizens • Create healthy national identity • Establish healthy emotional communication and social engagement skills for all citizens • Provide opportunities for all citizens to get their basic needs met • Understand the true history of the nation • Build national esprit de corps	• Establish secure bonding with the world of nature • Create a respect for the supernatural and spiritual elements of human life • Establish a unique identify as a species • Promote the development of right-brain functions within the individual • Understand the true history of the human race
Counterdependent Stage (Separation)	• Support employees to assert their needs and have them taken seriously by employers • Identify and promote unique contributions of each employee to the organization • Use fair, equitable, and nonshaming methods of limit setting with employees • Establishing rules and policies in equitable ways • Resolving internal conflicts between the needs of employees and the needs of employers in partnership ways	• Encourage all citizens to assert their needs and insist they are taken seriously by leaders • Guarantee freedom of expression and protect minority and cultural rights • Identify and promote unique contributions of every citizen to the nation • Establish fair, equitable, and nondiscriminating laws and national policies • Use rule of law to provide equal justice for all citizens	• Explore ways to become functionally separate from nature • Establish and respect diversity in the species • Develop left-brain functions within the individual • Create separate nation–states • Create religions based on beliefs in the supernatural and separate from Nature • Resolve conflicts between nations and religions in partnership ways

(continued)

TABLE 1.3 *(continued)*

Stage of Development / Primary Task	Essential Developmental Processes of an Organization	Essential Developmental Processes of Cultures and Nation–States	Essential Developmental Processes of the Human Race
Counterdependent *(continued)*	• Understand the influence of incomplete developmental processes on work performance and provide ways to heal developmental shocks, traumas, or stresses that show up at work	• Identify unique strengths of cultures and nations • Develop effective ways to resolve conflicts of needs between cultural groups and between nations • Understand how incomplete developmental processes influence national health and provide ways to heal developmental shocks, traumas, or stresses of all citizens	• Understand how incomplete developmental processes influence human development and provide ways to heal developmental shocks, traumas, or stresses of all humans
Independent Stage (Mastery)	• Create an organizational culture with mutually determined values and beliefs • Support individual autonomy within the organizational structure • Give employees responsibility for self-regulation of emotion and self-care • Support employees' achievement of true pride in their work • Provide specialized training and development for each employee to enhance individual contributions to the organization	• Create a national culture that honors and protects diversity of all cultures • Create economic/social safety net for those in need • Insure that voting rights of all citizens are guaranteed • Teach citizens how to take responsibility for self-regulation of emotion and self-care • Help citizens develop true cultural and national pride	• Reunite with the world of nature as partners • Develop whole-brain thinking functions including both/and thinking • Create & support individual cultures • Celebrate diversity among all cultures • Resolve conflicts of needs between cultures in partnership ways • Provide for the basic needs of all citizens • Utilize systemic thinking in making major decisions
Interdependent Stage (Cooperation)	• Create organizations run cooperatively by employees and employers	• Citizens and their representatives cooperate to create three interdependent and balancing branches of	• Establish a planetary partnership culture based on cooperation and respect for differences

(continued)

TABLE 1.3 *(continued)*

Stage of Development / Primary Task	Essential Developmental Processes of an Organization	Essential Developmental Processes of Cultures and Nation–States	Essential Developmental Processes of the Human Race
Interdependent Stage *(continued)*	• Utilize cooperative team-building activities • Promote cooperation building among teams • Create rituals that build and sustain employee morale • Create divisions of labor based on individual interests and abilities • Foster cooperation that helps each employee develop his or her fullest potential as a human being	government with equal power to govern • Leaders cooperate to build consensus policies to handle relations between cultural groups and between nations • Leaders cooperate to create meaningful national rituals that build and sustain citizen morale • Create equal opportunities for all citizens to develop their fullest potential	• Develop the global brain and utilize global thinking in major decision-making bodies • Develop trans-systemic thinking

their incomplete developmental processes with them into their couple relationships and try to complete them there. When that does not work, they may switch partners. If that fails, they may decide to have children. This creates families that simply replay unrecognized and unhealed developmental shocks, traumas, and stresses and pass them on to their children. When the family is not able to heal these shocks, traumas, and stresses, the members carry them into schools, the workplace and the community. These fractal relationship patterns then continue to permeate higher and higher levels of systems and are acted out in larger and larger arenas where they have more widespread effects. This process is illustrated in Figure 1.1.

The Essential Developmental Processes for Advancing the Evolution of Individuals

We identified the essential developmental processes required for optimal development of an individual through our own heuristic research in developmental psychology and that of other developmental psychologists. We believe that these processes create the fractal relational template that drives evolution in all human systems, including the human race. Without these critical developmental descriptors, it would be very difficult to determine the actual impact of shocking, traumatic, and stressful early childhood events on human evolution.

Because most people lack information about what constitutes optimal human development, the effects of shocking, traumatic, and stressful early childhood events have become accepted as part of the "human condition." This attitude helps hide the true impact of unrecognized and unhealed developmental shock, trauma, and stress on optimal human development. We believe that it is time to create a collective vision of what is humanly possible: *the possible human*. Only then can we identify and remedy what interferes with achieving this ideal.

Recent advances in related fields of developmental psychology—developmental and quantum biology, neurobiology, and neurochemistry—now clearly reveal the devastating lifelong impact of shock or trauma on early childhood development. Schore (2003a) wrote, "Current developmental conceptions that integrate the psychological and biological realms are bringing us closer to a complex biopsychosocial model that can serve as a source of not only the next level of questions for science, but also for pragmatic application." He added, "These deeper investigations of infant mental health, of the primary forces that impact the development of human nature, can do more than alter the intergenerational transmission of psychopathology. They can also significantly increase the numbers of individuals who possess an intuitive sense of emotional security, and thereby improve the quality of life of the infant child, and adult members of our societies" (p. xvii).

Our contribution to the field of infant and early childhood mental health is identifying subclinical symptoms of developmental shock, trauma, and stress that prevent the completion of essential developmental processes and showing how they block the evolution of all human systems, including the human race. Our research helped us correlate these effects with developmental issues to show how they manifest as fractal patterns in larger human systems and obstruct evolution.

In addition to identifying the building blocks for creating a possible human, those who care for our children need blueprints and tools to help children experience optimal development. This will make it possible to not only raise the standards of parenting and childcare but to advance the evolution of the human race.

In our next book we will discuss in more detail the essential developmental processes that affect macro systems and the evolution of groups/organizations, cultures/nation–states, and the human race. In this chapter we present a brief overview of the essential developmental processes for each human system and suggest ways to successfully complete them.

According to our theory, individuals move through four stages of development: codependent, counterdependent, independent and interdependent. In each stage, we have identified the essential developmental processes that an individual must complete successfully to provide the proper foundation for moving on to the next stage of development.

The Codependent Stage

The essential developmental processes for the codependent stage of individual evolution focus on bonding and building a solid social, emotional, and relational foundation to help individuals give and receive unconditional love. This involves emotional and psychological preparation on the part of both parents prior to conceiving a child. Ideally, both parents would have healed their developmental issues and created a secure economic, social, and psychological vessel in which to raise a child.

Because this has not been part of the context for conceiving children, it is urgently necessary to educate prospective parents about how to avoid inflicting early shock, trauma, or stress on the developing infant, particularly during the first trimester of prenatal development. We must also teach parents and adult caregivers how to help infants repair the effects of early shock trauma, and stress. We recognize the importance of couples conceiving children with as much love and consciousness as possible. The consciousness of couples before, during, and after conception enhances the potential for their children's optimal development (Lipton, 2005, pp. 141–142).

After conception, the mother should avoid drugs and alcohol and begin regular prenatal care. The mother also needs the support of her partner and an extended family to keep her as free as possible from stress. Both the mother and father need to spend time communicating in loving ways with the incoming child. The birth should be completed with the assistance of a doula or support person for the mother as well as using the latest gentle, natural, and nonviolent birthing procedures available. Even with these procedures in place, it is crucial to have processes in place to help the child heal any birth shock, trauma, or stress as quickly as possible. This might include time floating in water, gentle infant massage, and maximum skin-to-skin contact with the mother and father.

Infants need immediate and prolonged skin-to-skin contact with both parents during the first 36 hours following the birth. They also need continuous and consistent contact with their mother in the weeks and months after the birth. Any prolonged physical separations between the two should be avoided, even in the case of an illness of the mother or child or a premature birth. Building secure bonding between the mother and child is the most important developmental process of this stage and requires the focused and consistent attention of the mother with support from the father, friends, and extended family.

Any emotional disruptions in the bonding and attunement process between the child and the parents and other adult caregivers should be repaired as quickly as possible to restore the resonance between them. If at all possible, the mother should provide full-time care for the infant during the first year, and particularly for the first 2 months. The codependent stage ends between 6 and 8 months when children begin to crawl or walk and can venture away from their mothers in order to safely explore their immediate world. See Chapter 3 for a much more extensive description of the essential developmental processes of this stage.

The Counterdependent Stage

While the previous stage was all about bonding, this stage is all about separation. The essential developmental processes of this stage support the child building a self that is psychologically and emotionally separate from the parents. The separation process involves a gradual moving away from the closeness with the mother, while still requiring her presence if and when the child becomes frightened or needs comfort. The mother of bonding during the first stage of development must gradually shift into being the mother of separation. Now she must set limits, cope with the child's frustration, and gradually help modulate the child's ego.

The key parent–child interactions involve setting limits and using emotionally supportive methods to enforce the social and physical limits needed to protect the child. Parents should use nonshaming methods that respect the needs of the child, while also responding empathically to the child's frustration when encountering natural limits to his or her exploration. Healthy limit setting during this stage of development also helps to effectively modulate the child's developing ego without damaging it. This process will slowly bring into balance behaviors of grandiosity, entitlement, euphoria, and omnipotence that are typical of this stage of development.

Many developmental traumas that occur during this stage are created by parents who do not know how to help their child handle frustration and too often use punitive and shaming responses to their child's cries for help. For example, parents should not send their children to another room for a time out when they misbehave or have temper tantrums. Instead, they should hold them and provide empathic listening responses to help them calm down so that they can reregulate their feelings. While this is a key intervention at any stage of development, it is particularly useful during this stage.

The separation process goes through several subphases, including a splitting phase in which children see their mother and father as all good or all bad, depending on whether or not they are available when needed. The resolution of this phase involves parents knowing how to respond empathically to children's feelings and helping to reregulate them when necessary. The final resolution involves the child being able to see him- or herself and the parents as separate people and everyone as "okay." The successful completion of the essential developmental processes of the separation stage fosters the *psychological birthing* of the individual.

During this stage, children learn to experience themselves as emotionally and psychologically separate from their primary caregivers and develop the cognitive ability for *both/and thinking.* We see completed individuation as the most important developmental marker in the evolution of the individual. It means that a person must be securely bonded and attached in order to complete the developmental tasks related to the 1st year of life. If they successfully navigate the process of becoming a separate, fully functioning human being by around age 3, they are able to experience what is known as the *psychological birth.*

When children are able to trust their own internal feelings and impulses, they can operate from their *internal power*. This means the child has developed the foundation to become a self-directed rather than other-directed person. This process should ideally be completed between ages 2 to 3. Chapter 4 contains a much more extensive description of how children develop this self-directedness and *object constancy*—the ability to maintain good feelings about themselves when they encounter criticism that challenges their narcissistic urges.

Challenging children's narcissistic urges can cause them to split their perception of themselves into good and bad parts. They learn to hide their unacceptable parts not just from others, but from themselves. This internal good/bad split manifests externally as the two-against-one game in which the child allies with one parent against the other by sharing secrets or taking sides. Here, the child not only tests the strength of the bond between the parents or caregivers but also the adults' psychological maturity.

The Independent Stage

During this stage, children learn to master their immediate environment. This includes learning to dress, toilet train, and feed themselves, as well as engaging in creative play designed to master coordination and motor skills. The role of the parents is to support their efforts by making the home environment "child friendly" and giving positive feedback to the toddler's efforts toward mastery.

Although the building blocks for self-mastery began in the previous stage, object constancy becomes firmly established in this stage. This means that children are able to maintain an internal image of themself as "okay." They are able to maintain a sense of equanimity even when something challenges their narcissistic urges, when they feel criticized, or when something does not go as they want. This is a major achievement in mastering self-regulation and self-determination. Object constancy also helps them become more resilient, which supports them in the successful completion of the next stage of development.

Another important skill during this stage is mastering parallel play with other children. This involves learning social engagement skills outside the family and is an important building block for going to school. This stage should be completed by age 5 or 6.

The Interdependent Stage

This stage spans about 25 years or so and should be completed by age 29. When we first began using these stages and ages, our children were still in their late teens and early 20s. We could see how they still needed our support in mastering the world of adulthood. All of them returned to live with either us or their other parent during this period while they were attempting to establish themselves professionally and relationally. Initially, we thought this stage ended at age 18, but observing our children and others helped us see that individuals may not be ready to be truly interdependent until around the age of 30.

This stage builds on the successful completion of the developmental processes in the three previous stages. Much physical growth takes place during this stage and requires an equivalent amount of emotional growth to support it. The most important developmental processes are learning how to cooperate with others and learning to negotiate effectively in order to meet important needs and wants. If the essential developmental processes of the previous three stages have been completed successfully, this stage will unfold more smoothly.

Generally, it is incomplete developmental processes from the three previous stages that delay interdependence. If so, these processes will continue to press for completion. For example, between the ages of 12 and 16, teenagers cycle back through the first 4 years of their development. If incomplete developmental processes or developmental shocks or traumas from either the codependent or counterdependent stages remain, they will show up during this period. They can become clingy between 12 and 13 and rebellious between 13 and 14, as they test any limits and attempt to complete their separation process.

If they have few or no unhealed developmental traumas or incomplete developmental processes to delay them, they will not replay the "terrible twos" as teen rebellion between ages 14 and 16. They will have minimal narcissistic defenses and can accept responsibility for their behavior and feelings. They will not operate out of victim consciousness, use the two-against-one game known as the drama triangle, which we describe in more detail in Chapter 7, to get their needs met, or blame others for their problems. Instead of playing on the drama triangle as a victim, persecutor or rescuer, they will recognize the presence of unhealed developmental shocks, traumas, or stresses in their peers and will be able to help them with these issues.

Unfortunately, there are not many people who have completed this stage of individual evolution. We can point to great leaders of movements like Dr. Martin Luther King, Jr. or Mahatma Gandhi and spiritual leaders like Jesus, Buddha, Mother Theresa, or Rumi as possible examples of fully individuated humans. What we really need is a critical mass of individuated people who can energetically support those who are moving toward true interdependence.

The Essential Developmental Processes for Advancing the Evolution of Couples

Couples follow the same four-stage sequence of development as individuals. Chapter 12 explores in greater detail how many of the stages and essential developmental processes are similar in principle but different in the expression or practice.

The Codependent Stage

The decision to create a long-term relationship usually begins while couples are engaged in the bonding process. Couples, like individuals, go through a bonding stage and the hugging, tender words, intimacy, and resonance that appears looks much like the bonding between a mother and infant. The partners are also creating a bond of trust and establishing a friendship with each other—doing things together and finding common interests and values.

Like the early bonding period of infancy, a couple needs large blocks of time together and lots of skin-to-skin contact. They need to minimize outside distractions that keep them either preoccupied with other things or separated physically. This process begins during the "honeymoon" stage but continues in order to sustain their intimacy and closeness.

To build this bond of trust and friendship, they find ways to show respect for each other and to validate each other's needs, thoughts, beliefs, values, and feelings. They also validate each other's spiritual essence with expressions of unconditional love and acceptance. Ideally, partners also need to help each other to recognize any unhealed developmental shocks, traumas, and stresses from their childhood that they are bringing with them into the relationship. They will need to create ways within the relationship that support the healing of the effects of these unrecognized developmental shocks, traumas, and stresses. During the bonding stage, it is helpful to expand the definition of intimacy to include the appearance of any conflicts that arise and to commit to resolving them in ways that heal the developmental shocks, traumas, or stresses that might be imbedded in them.

The Counterdependent Stage

The counterdependent stage begins when partners recognize that there are substantive differences between them. These differences may initially have seemed small and insignificant but eventually indicate a growing sense of difference and uniqueness. The safety established through bonding during the codependent stage allows partners to discuss both their differences and the effects of previously unrecognized and unhealed developmental shocks, traumas, and stresses that may be surfacing in the relationship.

It is important for a couple to recognize that the emergence of unhealed developmental shocks, traumas, or stresses from the past is actually an indication of the strength of their relationship. If they recognize this and agree to help each other heal the effects of these shocks, traumas, or stresses, the couple can use them as opportunities for becoming even closer.

Many couples need some coaching or therapy during this stage because they often lack the skills necessary for helping each other recognize and heal the effects of these developmental shocks, traumas, or stresses. We found that many couples can learn these skills quickly and then require only periodic support when they need new skills.

As partners learn how to maintain their personal identity in a close relationship, they may need encouragement from their partner to explore interests outside the relationship. As with the exploratory behavior of toddlers, the relationship serves as a safe place to which they can return for sharing, validation, and support. Both people must identify their own unique and separate goals, values, and beliefs that they wish to retain while in the relationship. Conflicts of values and beliefs should be resolved in ways that show respect and acceptance of any differences.

Partners also need to learn to differentiate between nurturing touch and sexual touch as they learn how to respect each other's boundaries and needs. They also must learn to negotiate directly with one another to get their needs and wants honored and met. Developing boundaries in a close relationship means learning to distinguish between what is "mine" and what is "not mine." This can involve personal possessions as well as "my needs" and "your needs."

The Independent Stage

If the essential developmental processes are completed in the previous two stages, providing bonding and psychological separateness as a solid foundation for the couple relationship, then this stage will involve each person learning to master self-sufficiency within the relationship. It also means achieving some equality in the relationship so that both persons feel their contributions to the success of the relationship are valued and appreciated. Roles may still be defined in the relationship, but they are negotiated freely so that neither person feels burdened by his or her role. Mastering this, of course, often involves some trial-and-error experiments.

It is also important to recognize and respond to each other as autonomous individuals. This means honoring and acknowledging the growth and gains in autonomy each person is making in the relationship. It also means mastering the ability to negotiate for any additional autonomy either person needs. This is a process of mastering self-responsibility, rather than waiting for the partner to guess what these needs are and being willing to ask directly to get these needs met. This keeps partners from acting out the drama triangle and taking turns playing victim, persecutor, or rescuer roles.

The Interdependent Stage

In this stage of a relationship, partners learn to negotiate and cooperate with each other to get their needs and wants met. Again, it takes the successful completion of the essential developmental processes of the previous three stages to fully complete this stage. Couples in this stage learn how to experience the deepest human connection possible between two people. They have no secrets, yet mystery remains because they both know how multifaceted they each are and how the essence of the other can become fully visible in any given moment.

Not only are they committed to sustaining the spiritual connections they have built together, they desire to cooperate fully to support each other's spiritual evolution. This may involve using the synergy of the relationship to support causes and projects that help others develop their full potential.

This stage also typically involves a recapitulation of the previous three stages. The vacillation between wanting to be very close and codependent and wanting to be totally separate and counterdependent may continue. From the outside, this stage can appear to be codependent, counterdependent or independent. Internally, the flow between oneness and separateness is valued and consciously negotiated. The critical difference between a codependent and an interdependent relationship is that in an interdependent relationship this flow is acknowledged and intimacy levels are consciously negotiated.

Even though this stage represents what couples typically say they want in their relationship, it is still very rare. We hope for more couples who are willing to master the challenges, particularly those who can model the individuation process and inspire other couples to do the necessary hard work. We believe that interdependent relationships offer people the best opportunity for evolving further and faster. Couple relationships, based on a deep, abiding love and commitment to each other, provide an ideal container for the evolution of both partners' souls.

The Essential Developmental Processes for Advancing the Evolution of Families

Families follow the same four-stage sequence of development as individuals and couples. Chapter 13 explores in greater detail how many of the stages and essential developmental processes are similar in principle but different in the expression or practice.

The Codependent Stage

From a systems perspective, families officially begin when a child arrives and changes the couple dyad into a triad. The first stage of family development involves the bonding process between the mother and the child. It is important for the couple to have planned for the child's birth so that it does not cause any unnecessary turmoil in the family. Both parents must be involved in the bonding process in order to create a secure, consistent family environment in which a child can bond.

Both parents need time to attune to an infant's unique rhythms. This will likely disrupt the couple's normal routine for a while, as sleeping and feeding cycles of the infant will require major adjustments for both parents. A new child is a 24/7 project and many parents are surprised by the intensity that the constant focus involves.

It is important for each parent to recognize and acknowledge the other's willingness to accept the new parenting roles that a child requires of them. Many new parents do not fully realize the responsibility they have taken on until the reality of it forces them to look to each other and to members of the extended family for support and comfort.

It is important for both parents to recognize and acknowledge the essence of the newborn child and to surround the infant with an atmosphere of unconditional love. Parents need to provide the infant with nurturing touch and gentle talking and singing to help solidify the bonding. If there are other children in the family, they too need to be part of this welcoming process. As much as possible, the family needs to use this occasion as a way of extending the bonding process to reinforce the sense of being a secure, bonded family, a securely bonded couple, and securely bonded individuals.

Families must learn to create their own identity so that any challenge to it is met nondefensively. The more solid the object constancy of each individual in the family, the more a family can maintain its center in responding to outside challenges, such as parental illnesses, a loss of job, living by different values such as religion or home schooling, the need to move to a new location due to a job transfer, or the need to take in and care for an aging parent or relative.

Counterdependent Stage

The opportunities and challenges during this stage are numerous for an evolving family, particularly the need for family members to continue their efforts to become separate individuals. Children go to school and get involved in activities, and parents change jobs, go back to school, or find new hobbies or interests.

It is important to recognize the unique talents and interests of each family member. It is also necessary to reestablish boundaries that allow parents to have some separate time without the children. Parents may need a night out away from their children or need time at home when they can interact without being interrupted by the demands of parenting. Respite care provided by a babysitter or a relative is important for recharging parents so that they can carry out their roles in the family.

Families also need effective tools for resolving conflicts that emerge. Sometimes conflicts arise about how to parent children. Parents need cooperative methods for resolving conflicts involving wants and needs and those involving values and beliefs, particularly those related to parenting. If parents come from families that used very different approaches to parenting, this stage is likely to be more complicated and conflictual.

Independent Stage

If the essential developmental processes of the first two stages have been completed successfully, this stage proceeds more easily. The major tasks and processes of this stage involve providing children with independence training in mastering money, time, peer relationships, school, and extracurricular activities. Parents also have to learn how to implement consequence-based discipline methods that help their children develop self-mastery, particularly in cause-and-effect thinking.

Boundaries must respect the autonomy of the couple and the individuals within the family structure. Children and other family members must also be supported to develop interests outside the family structure. This may involve parents providing "taxi services" to take children to music lessons or after-school activities.

Again, it is important for parents to find ways to get their needs met within the family and to have their needs respected and honored. Families with strong object constancy can work together to cope with stresses and conflicts that emerge without seriously disturbing the family's emotional resonance.

Family activities help members establish a bond with nature. Family vacations and activities that involve hiking, camping, fishing, skiing, picnicking, and gardening can help foster this bonding.

The Interdependent Stage

This stage can be really fun for families who have successfully completed the essential developmental processes of the three previous stages. Family meetings help foster skills in consensus building and decision making. Here family members can also learn to cooperate so that everyone feels heard and included in making major family decisions, such as where they vacation. This also applies to the day-to-day decisions that need to be made, such as food preferences, recreational activities, and meal times.

It is also important to equalize the power between the adults and children so that no one resorts to drama and power plays in order to get needs met. Parents need to retain the final say on how to spend family resources since they are generating them. If children are contributing to the family resources in some area, they need to have some input on how those resources are used. All agreements must be written and posted where all family members can see them. If necessary, items can be renegotiated between the family members who are directly involved in them.

The family also should provide high levels of physical, mental, emotional, and spiritual resources to help all family members develop their fullest potential. This may involve some sacrifice on the part of parents in order to provide financial support for children's activities or further education. It could also include regular and unique rituals that help family members sustain their spiritual values.

The Essential Developmental Processes for Advancing the Evolution of Organizations

Organizations follow the same four-stage sequence of development as individuals, couples, and families. Chapter 14 explores in greater detail how many of the essential developmental processes are similar in principle but different in expression or practice.

The Codependent Stage

The developmental crucible grows larger and more complex at the group/organizational level of evolution, which involves schools, businesses, nonprofits, and churches. In this stage, the major objective is to help members of the organization bond with each other.

Schools use extramural competitive sports, special colors, and school songs to help create a common culture. They build trust by using fair discipline and grading practices. This is even more important in schools, because students usually do not choose to be members. They are required to be there, while employees and church members are there by choice.

Businesses and nonprofit organizations can use logos, mottos, or slogans to help unite employees. They build trust with fair wages, employment benefits, and equitable policies regarding job promotion. The needs of organizational members must be respected and taken seriously.

Churches use community-building activities and regular rituals and orders of service with specific creeds or prayers to unite parishioners. In addition to the governing groups, churches also need small groups of parishioners to meet and discuss common interests and values.

Organizations must establish a wide bandwidth of direct interpersonal communication in order to promote effective social engagement skills among members. This may involve many face-to-face meetings or extramural or intramural activities.

School assemblies, employee meetings, and church socials help build an organizational esprit de corps. Organizations must invest in these kinds of events in order to sustain this feeling, or members may lose their sense of purpose.

Counterdependent Stage

Organizations need regular methods for recognizing the unique talents, individual achievements, and contributions of members through honor assemblies, employee-of-the-week programs, or member recognition in the weekly church bulletin. Different curricular offerings, differential workloads, flexible time schedules, and different roles and responsibilities for members help demonstrate a respect for individual differences.

Organizations operating in this stage provide methods that encourage students, employees, and members to give input about their needs and ideas, and the leaders of the organization take this input seriously. Organizations need to develop fair, nonshaming methods of limit setting and consequences for their members, such as restorative justice, which focuses on restoring or preserving the relationship between those involved in disputes.

In general, it is best to have a minimum number of rules and regulations and to encourage self-governance. The organization needs to focus on giving positive feedback to its members using the "twice as many yes's as no's" guideline.

Effective organizations also establish structures and guidelines for resolving conflicts between members and teach conflict resolution skills to all members. Organizational leaders recognize the influence of incomplete developmental processes or developmental shocks, traumas, or stresses on the behavior of its members. It is helpful to have people who are trained to identify these issues and have skills in healing the impact of unhealed shock, trauma, and stress on organizations when they emerge in member interactions.

Organizational decisions should be made as close as possible to the level of implementation. Top-down decisions are often perceived as domination and imposition if those involved in the implementation are not consulted during the decision-making process. The most effective leaders perceive themselves as "servants" of their organization and model their behavior and communication in ways that support esprit de corps.

The Independent Stage

During this stage, members of the organization are encouraged to help bring the organizational culture into alignment with their personal values and beliefs. The organizational culture supports, encourages, and rewards individual achievements and regards personal and professional integrity as a vital part of the organization.

After members learn effective communication and conflict resolution skills, they take personal responsibility for regulating their own emotions, for resolving their own conflicts, and for getting their needs met. They ask for what they want directly with those from whom they want it and avoid playing on the drama triangle.

All members receive positive feedback and recognition for their individual efforts to improve the organization, which encourages self-development, autonomy, and strength. In addition, members receive special training that enhances their personal development in ways that also contribute to the overall welfare of the organization.

The Interdependent Stage

An organization that has completed the essential developmental processes from the previous three stages is functioning at a high level and is poised to become a model organization. These kinds of organizations practically run themselves. Members cooperate to a high degree, which makes the work of the organization a joyfully successful experience for all involved.

Teams of members collaborate to carry out the organization's essential functions. When teams need to collaborate on a project or work toward a goal, they coordinate their work cooperatively. They create regular rituals to help build and sustain group morale and encourage people to go beyond what is expected of them (discretionary *effort*) so that they can not only achieve more of their own goals, but also the organization's goals. Everyone in the organization recognizes that helping each other develop their fullest potential as human beings is an outcome of their collaboration. Cooperation rather than competition rules the day-to-day operations of this kind of organization. At this stage, individual development and organizational develop become mutually supportive and are recognized as such.

The Essential Developmental Processes for Advancing the Evolution of Cultures and Nation–States

Nation–states are amalgamations of cultures that contain numerous subsystems (states, cultures, groups/organizations, families, couples, individuals), with each of them containing incomplete developmental processes, unhealed developmental shocks, traumas, stresses, and unmet developmental needs. The evolutionary stage of a nation–state correlates with the average stage of evolution of its subsystems. It is difficult for a larger system to evolve if a significant number of its cultural subsystems are stalled in their development. A priority for the leaders of a nation–state is developing public policies and national practices that ensure that the essential developmental processes of each subsystem are completed and that any debris of unhealed developmental shock, trauma, or stress does not block the evolutionary trajectory of the nation–state.

The Codependent Stage

It is possible to facilitate cultural and national bonding and esprit de corps through songs, dances, and patriotic holidays that truly honor the historic traditions of the nation–state and inspire subcultures to work together for their common good. Bonding within a culture and nation–state happens in many ways. It begins by learning its true history—a process that can be difficult, as its history is often slanted either intentionally or unintentionally in favor of certain values, beliefs, or ideas that are congruent with industrialization and globalization. In the case of the United States, the truest representation of this country's history is Howard Zinn's book, *The People's History of the United States* (2001). In indigenous cultures the true history is often carefully preserved through oral traditions and passed between generations by the wise ones and elders of the culture. Those who study the oral traditions of indigenous people often find huge discrepancies between them and the written history that shows up in textbooks.

Secure bonding between subcultures is essential to nation building. If a subculture feels discriminated against or not included in the national fabric, this group will resist and even sabotage efforts to build an effective nation–state. Subcultural diversity can contribute to the vitality of a nation and help create bonds of trust between the groups. An important part of building trust is a real commitment to protecting the rights of all citizens regardless of their cultural, ethnic, or racial background. Healthy governments are particularly concerned with creating effective safely nets to protect the welfare of their poor, disadvantaged, and disabled citizens.

Effective mechanisms should be built into nation–states that safeguard the public trust in the institutions of government. The elected representatives of the people must be honest and ethical in their lawmaking. They must be seen as trustworthy stewards of the people and make decisions that reflect the collective will of the people. Elections need to be fair and honest and preserve the rights of citizens to participate in the electoral process. Healthy governments also provide equal education for all citizens regardless of race or ethnic background. In addition, the laws of the land should have built-in protections for the rights of minorities. Discrimination of any kind undermines the secure bonding between the government and its citizens, so laws must limit this behavior. The health and welfare of all citizens must be a real priority. All citizens must have free or low-cost health insurance and equal access to quality medical services.

The Counterdependent Stage

In this stage, citizens need the legal right to ask directly to get their wants and needs met and to have national leaders take their requests seriously. Freedom of speech and expression must be guaranteed and supported equally among all the members without favoring cultural subgroups. A free press allows the presentation and discussion of divergent ideas.

Rule-of-law principles and practices provide equal justice for all citizens and guarantee an independent justice system that is not overly influenced by political and ideological issues. The nation must make an effort to recognize the unique contributions that all individuals and subcultures contribute to the nation's strength. The government also needs to provide fair and equitable ways to resolve internal conflicts between subcultures, as well as external conflicts between itself and other nations. The use of any kind of force is considered a last resort never to be used to intimidate or dominate.

National leaders recognize the potential influence of collective incomplete developmental processes, and developmental shocks, traumas, and stresses associated with them, on the health and welfare of the nation. They should develop processes to collectively address these issues and help those coping with the effects of unrecognized and unhealed shock, trauma, or stress to receive the help they need to heal them. The government should also prevent wounded individuals from acting out their unrecognized and unhealed shock, trauma, or stress in ways that undermine the national goals. Effective procedures should be in place to remove leaders who persist in reenacting their personal developmental issues on the national stage in ways that harm the nation.

The Independent Stage

In this stage of development, nation–states create a national culture that honors and protects the rights of all cultural groups. The leaders create national policies and laws that support diversity and the rights of all subcultures. For example, countries with democratic structures protect voting rights to ensure a one person–one vote principle. They also create public financing of their elections to prevent wealthy individuals or special interest groups from controlling the government.

During this stage, governments also create a strong economic and social safety net that allows people to maintain their dignity. For example, laws should set the minimum wage at the living wage level so citizens can afford to pay for their basic needs.

Citizens need to be allowed to get involved in a national goal-setting process by becoming elected representatives who truly represent the wishes of the people they serve. The number of people they represent needs to be somewhat equalized so they each serve about the same number of citizens.

In this stage, citizens learn how to heal their developmental issues and to parent their children effectively. National family leave policies allow parents to take time from work with pay to stay home and provide the care that we know newborn infants need. Educational institutions train citizens to take responsibility for their lives and to regulate their own emotions and lifestyles.

The Interdependent Stage

To reach this level of development, nation–states must have achieved a level of consciousness in which citizens and governing representatives understand the operation of complex human systems and work together to implement effective, systemic management principles and practices. Without this level of consciousness, it is very difficult for a nation–state to achieve and sustain the interdependent stage of evolution.

Essential for the fullest expression of this human system, leaders and citizens create three independent branches of government with equal power to provide checks and balances on each other. Nation–state leaders focus on creating cooperative rather than competitive economic and social policies. There is no state religion, and religious expression is protected.

The leaders create policies that promote peaceful interdependence among cultural groups and with other nations. They promote fair trade agreements among all nations that protect both the rights of workers and the environment. They cooperate to create meaningful national rituals that build and sustain morale of all citizens. People are motivated and mobilized to work together to achieve important national goals through special days that honor cultural diversities. National projects, such as a domestic peace corps, encourage young people to volunteer for national service.

When they reach this stage of development, nation–states should operate as stewards of the environment. National laws and policies are used to protect the environment and to preserve the quality of life inherent with stewardship.

A national commitment to equal opportunities helps citizens develop their fullest potential. Public financing of higher education, trade schools, and continuing education ensure access to post–high school learning.

The Essential Developmental Processes for Advancing the Evolution of the Human Race

As we looked at the evolutionary history of the human race, we saw that the same developmental dynamics from microsystems are present in the history of the human race. It stands to reason that the developmental history of the human race would follow the same developmental patterns found in its subsystems.

We divide the history of the human race into prerecorded history (prior to 2500 B.C.E.) and recorded or written history since that time. With the advent of carbon dating and the translation of ancient texts and other archeological evidence, it is now possible to look even further back into our history and understand more about our developmental roots. This prehistoric evidence tells the story of a matrifocal era of human history that emphasized feminine values.

Riane Eisler (1987), who built on the work of archeologist Maria Gimbutas (1982), described how the ancient Minoan culture on Crete flourished without war for more than 1,500 years (3000–1500 B.C.E.). The Minoan family and social practices emphasized cooperation rather than competition as a major way of social engagement. Archeological evidence also shows that from 7000 to 3500 B.C.E. small settlements in parts of Asia Minor practiced equal gender relations and peaceful relations with their neighboring settlements.

Using this larger perspective on the history of the human race, we see parallels between the evolution of the human race and the evolution of the individual and all other human systems. For example, the matrifocal period of human evolution parallels the codependent stage of individual evolution and the patrifocal period parallels the counterdependent stage of individual evolution. Contemporary history brings us up to the edge of the independent stage of individual evolution.

We have no idea how long it will take for the human race to evolve fully into the independent and interdependent stages, but we do know that we must recognize that it is stuck in the counterdependent stage of its evolution and explore ways to facilitate its further evolution. We believe understanding the relationship between the evolution of the human race and the evolution of the individual can produce forward movement in all other human systems, including the human race. In order to do this, we must first understand the need for civilizations that are based on matrifocal values, beliefs, and practices. This will help build a more secure foundation for human evolution and anchor life-giving, humanitarian values into our culture. A matrifocal culture will also help couples and families integrate these values and practices in their relationships.

The Codependent Stage

From archeological data, it appears that prehistoric humans instinctually valued and supported secure bonding practices between mothers and infants. These practices were supported by their understanding of their symbiotic relationship with nature, which also helped them bond with the natural world. In this partnership crucible, early people regarded nature as the mother who provided them with food. Gimbutas (1982) also found evidence that property and lineage passed through women and family life and was centered on the activities of the women, while the men had the role of finding food for the family.

The critical factor during the matrifocal period of human history, however, was its emphasis on feminine values such as inclusion, life giving, nurturing, and equality. These values promoted peaceful interdependence among the people and suggest that during this stage the right hemisphere of the brain might have been more developed and the left hemisphere less developed.

Their religions were centered on the supernatural world, and people worshipped deities based on their perceptions of the great power that the supernatural world held over them. Their codependence was based on their dependence on Mother Earth and their feelings of powerlessness over the forces of nature to provide food and water for them, and so they performed religious rituals to please Mother Nature so she would provide sustenance for them. Later religions during this period shifted to goddess worship. Evidence suggests that these matrifocal values eventually changed, and that women began to dominate the men, followed by a gradual shift to more patrifocal or masculine values of exclusion, life taking, and the domination of women by men.

The Counterdependent Stage

Some historians mark the shift from the codependent to the counterdependent stage of the evolution of the human race with the beginning of agriculture. When humans pierced Mother Earth with sticks, spades, shovels, and plows, they argue, it marked an attempt to dominate and control the Earth and a shift away from a codependent attitude toward Mother Earth as the "eternal provider." Agriculture altered the natural relationship humans had with the Earth and marked the beginning of a period in which humans also began dominating each other.

The desire to become self-sufficient food producers represents a collective effort to separate psychologically. Wandering and gathering humans had been dependent on wild animals and wild fruits and berries and often had to travel great distances to find food. With the advent of agriculture and the domestication of animals, however, they could settle in favorable locations with rich soil and grow their own food.

The other critical events that may have helped shift humanity's value base from feminine to masculine were the widespread invasions of patrist marauders from Saharasia. Between 4300 and 2300 B.C.E. several waves of these invaders seem to have gradually fragmented the nomadic tribes and trampled the matrist values found in the peaceful cultures of Old Europe. The widespread destruction inflicted by the patrists on the matrifocal values of Old Europe gave these people their first exposure to war, separation, shock, and trauma. It happened so many times that humans' psyches and nervous systems began changing.

Rather than developing on the LOVEvolution track, they began evolving on the developmental trauma track of human evolution. This fractured the long-held matrist values and many cycles of uninterrupted symbiosis with Mother Earth. The repeated exposure to the violence of the Saharasian marauders gradually shifted the matrifocal culture into one dominated by patrist values and collective experiences of shock, trauma, and stress.

Over the course of human history, various divisions of the human race emerged based on skin color. With the advent of agriculture and permanent locations, feudal empires and nation–states began rising. The patrist values were institutionalized into religions that significantly reduced the role of women. These organized religions also separated people from the pagan, Earth-based religions of the previous stage and severely punished those who tried to practice them. This campaign of repression culminated in the Catholic Church's Inquisition, in which maybe millions of people were put to death as witches or heretics (Sjoo & Mor, 1987, p. 192).

Certainly the Industrial Revolution and Western civilization's addiction to a petroleum-based lifestyle has become part of the domination of Nature and the rape of the Earth of her natural resources. At a species level, we are currently stuck in a split between the matrifocal and patrifocal value systems. During the codependent stage of evolution, the patrist values were seen as bad and the matrist values seen as good, then the two were reversed during the counterdependent stage of evolution.

The Independent Stage

The markers for movement into the independent stage of evolution include all the efforts to equalize gender relations and create a set of values that does not make the opposite "bad." This is the challenge of the independent stage of evolution. This stage requires us to create ways to honor equally both genders and both sets of values for their contributions to the evolution of humanity.

This also means reuniting with the Earth and Nature as partners to co-create a way of living on the Earth that honors and protects the Earth from destruction. It also means moving out of a petroleum-based economy into an economy based on sustainable agriculture and energy practices. This task is now being forced on humanity because of the destructive impact of our dependence on fossil fuels on the Earth and its atmosphere.

At the same time we must find ways to peacefully resolve the conflicts between and among religions, cultures, and nation–states to avoid destroying the planet and us with it. The use of nuclear weapons represents the ultimate threat of using patrifocal values to govern our lives. As a species, we must stop splitting atoms and instead focus on healing the split between the polarities and incongruities in our psyches. We need to create a new value system that supports living in harmony as a full partner with the Earth.

In order to make this leap in consciousness, humans need whole brains that can think systemically. This allows us to view the Earth and life on it as a set of interlocking systems that can be changed. While consciousness is moving in this direction, we now must evolve more quickly. It requires a massive effort to get enough people up to speed to make the shift into interdependence in time.

The Interdependent Stage

If we survive the current crisis in our evolution and heal the split in our individual and collective psyches, we can create a world based on a new set of values. At this time (2010) the odds are less than 50–50 that we will make it to the next stage of evolution.

Attempts at healing this split, such as the creation of the United Nations and the European Union, have failed to provide the right structures to support this kind of a shift in consciousness. While the UN has made modest gains in eradicating some diseases, it is not working because there is no true cooperation beyond national interests. Nations belong to it out of a need to find a way to protect their national interests, and the deliberations of this group focus on making sure that none of its decisions adversely affect the national interests of one side or the other. The EU is facing some of the same hurdles as it attempts to homogenize the varied cultures and nation–states of Europe without recognizing the contributions of the diversity that they provide.

International trade agreement groups have become tools for wealthy corporations to use as mechanisms for greed and domination. Nation–states are competing with each other over the real scarcity of petroleum reserves and other shrinking resources such as crop production and potable water. It is time to scrap these flawed and biased trade agreements and work cooperatively to preserve the world's shrinking resources so that they can be shared equitably.

Nation–states can cooperate in the creation of a global plan to share resources to end poverty, hunger, and starvation and bring the base level of human existence up to a higher level. An enlightened media drives the awareness of the seriousness of the problem. Lester Brown outlined a practical plan in his fine book, *Plan B 3.0* (2008), for completely moving humanity to a new level. In 2003 Franz Joseph Radermacher and several colleagues and organizations proposed a Global Marshall Plan in Tikkun Magazine (Quilligan, 2007) that moves the world's leaders from using "Strategies of Domination" to using "Strategies of Generosity." These efforts overcome inaction based on ignorance and depression and inspire us with hope and a sense of global purpose.

When enough people wake up to the urgency of the environmental crisis and the possibility that the human race may not survive unless we take drastic collective action immediately, it will hopefully produce the cooperation that is necessary to turn the tide. Information on the problem and the practical solutions to it are not lacking. What is lacking is merely the collective will and the consciousness to make it happen. Everyone appears to be in a collective trance and deep state of dissociation and denial because of unhealed developmental shock, trauma, and stress.

It is our hope that the information in this book will help people heal their developmental shocks, traumas, or stresses and shift the collective consciousness in time to make a difference. Until we elevate the living standards of the human race to a civilized level, can we really be called a human civilization?

Families and societies are small and
large versions of one another.
Both are made up of people who
have to work together,
whose destinies are tied up with one another.

Virginia Satir

CHAPTER TWO

Theoretical Foundations

In the early 1990s we constructed the first draft of our six-level systemic paradigm. It showed how disruptions in the resonance between parents and their children create a fractal pattern of disconnection through these six levels of human systems and delays their evolution. Once we understood that fractal patterns of human behavior are held together through a self-organizing process of energetic resonance, it was easy to see how disruptions to this resonance caused by the transmission of patterns of early developmental shock, trauma, and stress could stall or delay the evolution of individuals, couples, families, groups/organizations, cultures/nation–states, and the entire human race.

Our Heuristic Research on Developmental Systems Theory

About this same time we began developing macro-level DST intervention tools for treating developmental shock, trauma, and stress. Our theoretical leap grew organically out of the heuristic research we conducted while working clinically and as consultants in groups, organizations, and governments. Our experiences as international consultants to the United Nation in Eastern Europe in the early 1990s and as consultants and trainers in Ukraine since 1994 were particularly helpful in understanding the macro-levels of DST.

We discovered not only the parallels in the way each system evolves, but also the similarities in the patterns of dysfunctions that appear in each. Because of these parallels in both evolution and dysfunction, we realized it is possible to use the principles of DST to diagnose where and why a system has stalled by identifying the incomplete essential developmental processes of that system. Once we understood where and why a system got stuck, it became possible to design effective interventions for facilitating the completion of these developmental processes and moving them forward in their development.

In addition to DPW's clinical methods for identifying symptoms of developmental shock, trauma, and stress, DST uses additional methods to diagnose the impact of developmental shock, trauma, and stress on the system. We use self-inventories, structured interviews, focus groups, and process observation to help locate the markers that help identify the impact of developmental shock, trauma, and stress on individuals, couples, families, groups/organizations, cultures/nation–states, and the evolution of the human race.

We found these data-gathering methods useful in identifying the kinds of incomplete essential developmental processes that exist at each stage of a system's development. The data obtained from these methods help the Developmental Process Worker or Developmental Systems Consultant design interventions to help the client, whether an individual, a couple, family, or larger human system.

In our DST model, incomplete developmental processes delay or stall the evolution of all human systems. For example, a child who does not sufficiently complete the essential developmental processes of bonding during the codependent stage of development will experience difficulty in completing the essential developmental processes of separation during the counterdependent stage of development. Each completed set of essential developmental processes in one stage provides the building blocks or foundation for the successful completion of the essential developmental processes at the next stage of individual development.

This same principle operates in couples, families, groups/organizations, cultures/nation–states, and the evolution of the human race. Incomplete developmental processes actually stall the evolution of human consciousness. Moving human systems forward in their evolution requires unique skills to recognize the similarities in development, dysfunction, and intervention in all six levels of human systems.

In the late 1980s and early 1990s, we began consulting with schools, churches, and businesses in the community and again saw the same kinds of problems and conflicts involving incomplete developmental processes. We found ourselves looking at organizations through the same developmental lens that we used in our work with individuals, couples, and families.

We began speculating on how far we might be able to apply our developmental theory. Then in 1992 we had the good fortune to be invited to work as international consultants to the United Nations Centre in Vienna, Austria. Here we worked under the director of Social Development and Humanitarian Affairs and also head of the UN's International Year of the Family. Our assignment was to help found the Bratislava International Centre for Family Studies in

Bratislava, Czechoslovakia. The plan was for us to establish the center, and then the Czechoslovak government would donate the Centre to the UN. The UN would then use the center to train family life educators from developing countries. Our offices were housed in the Ministry of Labor, Social Affairs, and Family inside the Slovak part of the government, and we reported directly to the minister or cabinet head, who reported to his or her counterpart in the Czechoslovak government.

Inside the UN and the Slovak government, we were in a unique position to observe the dynamics of these two large systems. The UN's organization was built on political patronage, and all the heads of divisions were political appointees by their respective governments. This patronage system created a tremendous amount of status quo practices and policies, as appointees maneuvered to maintain their personal positions.

UN positions were given primarily to individuals who had proven themselves as loyal supporters and would do nothing that might possibly discredit the political values of the leaders who appointed them. As good codependents, they were tethered to those who appointed them and unable to exercise individual thoughts or actions. All publications written at the UN had to first be sanitized to make sure they did not contain anything that could be deemed politically incorrect or threatening to the status quo. All decisions at the UN reflected the same mindset. It was a larger and more codependent version of "what will the neighbors think?"

Czechoslovakia, still in its first years of post-communist recovery, was struggling to maintain a government still deeply conflicted by cultural differences. The country was created after World War I by a "shotgun wedding" between two different ethnic groups, the Czechs and the Slovaks. After World War II they were forced to bury their ethnic differences even more while under the USSR's totalitarian rule. The culture and values of people in the Czech Republic were historically and culturally more similar to those of Germany, particularly the Bohemian part. The Czechs were naturally more industrious, more left-brained, and more Western European. The culture and values of the people in the Slovak Republic were historically and culturally more Slavic. Slovaks were more agricultural, more right-brained, and more like the people of Ukraine and Eastern Europe. So we saw from our internal vantage point that the "forced marriage" was cracking a bit at the seams.

About three months into our assignment, Czechoslovakia decided to separate into the Czech and Slovak Republics. Their two very different cultural roots had finally reached a critical bifurcation point. Their forced codependency had made it difficult for their joint government to move forward. We saw how the leaders and citizens on both sides had suffered by living in a "marriage of convenience" that contained many deep incompatibilities. The Czechs perceived the Slovaks as holding them back in their rapid movement toward Western practices in both government and business, and the Slovaks seemed resentful about being forced to move rapidly toward the West when they experienced themselves as more rooted in the traditions of the East.

The Slovaks were much less prepared to handle the challenges of the Velvet Divorce, as it came to be known, because it pushed them into premature independence. Developmentally they resorted to using ego defenses that reminded us of 2-year-olds who suddenly realize they must become self-sufficient. Even though they were not well prepared to handle their autonomy, their attitude toward the Czechs was, "We'll show you that we can do this. We will take care of ourselves and be better off without you."

The dissolution of Czechoslovakia reminded us of a divorcing couple in other ways. The Czechs' alignment with the West gave them more economic resources, so they came out of the divorce in a stronger economic position. The Slovaks, still tied economically to the less industrialized former Soviet Republics to the East, were economically weaker and less self-sufficient.

Symbolically, it was like witnessing an archetypal couple divorce during the 1950s. The Czechs were like the husband, more educated and successful in the business world, who was awarded the house and the new car and paid child support to the family. The Slovaks were more like the wife, a less educated stay-at-home mom, who was awarded custody of the children, got the old car, and went to live in an apartment.

Beginning in 1990, we also became very involved with humanitarian aid projects in Ukraine. In 1994 CICRCL, our tax-exempt nonprofit institute, helped create a sister nongovernmental organization (NGO), ROZRADA, in Ukraine. This Ukrainian NGO, which is legally tied to ours, provides counseling, consulting, and training services to individuals, couples, families, groups, corporations, other NGOs, and the Ukrainian government, particularly through the Ministry of Family, Youth, and Sports.

Since 1994, Janae has made many trips to Kiev to collaborate with our colleague, Dr. Valentina Bondarovskaia, who directs ROZRADA. While much of her work has involved training the staff in practical psychology, Janae also consulted with Valentina and her staff on case management and supervision issues. ROZRADA has also published our books on codependency and counterdependency in Russian.

Our many years of collaboration with Dr. Bondarovskaia and her team provided us with another living laboratory where we were able to apply the principles of DST. The forced "marriage" between the republics of the former USSR was similar in many ways to that of the Czechs and Slovaks, and so was its dissolution. After almost 20 years, most of these republics, such as Ukraine, are still struggling to build a national identity and to break free of the codependency trap that the Soviet Union created. They were forced to become economically and psychologically separate from Mother Russia.

Our experiences with the United Nations, the government of Czechoslovakia, and our work in Ukraine has given us many opportunities to apply the principles of our emerging DST in macrosystems. All these personal experiences have helped us recognize not only the similarities in the development in all human systems, but also the way unhealed developmental shock, trauma, and stress stalls and disrupts their evolution. We feel really grateful that we have had each other to help sort through these amazing experiences and to harvest so much understanding about what helps and hinders the evolution of our consciousness as a species.

Our Quasi-Experimental Research on Developmental Systems Theory

DST also grew out of our quasi-experimental research with MA-level students, which helped us see how and why the evolution of their consciousness was affected by unrecognized and unhealed early developmental shock, trauma, and stress. One of our research projects involved studying effective methods for shifting the consciousness of graduate students in training to be counselors (Weinhold, 2000). The results of this research indicated that several conditions must be present for individuals to shift their consciousness and begin to recognize and heal the effects of any previously unrecognized and unhealed developmental shock, trauma, and stress.

We found Robert Kegan's theory of stages of consciousness (described later in this chapter) extremely helpful in this research project. Barry adapted his model into a written instrument, The SOC Inventory and then validated the instrument through his research. He used this instrument to measure shifts in consciousness in an experimental group of master's-level counseling students who completed his semester-long class in conflict resolution. This class focused on helping students recognize and heal the effects of developmental shock, trauma, and stress that were at the source of their intractable conflicts.

Barry also gave the SOC Inventory to students who enrolled in a control class in which students did not look at the role of unrecognized and unhealed developmental shock, trauma, and stress in their intractable conflicts. Then he did a pre–post analysis comparing the shifts of consciousness between the participants in both classes. The results showed a highly significant shift in consciousness among those in the experimental group when compared with those in the control group (>.001).

For example, many of the students in the conflict resolution class shifted out of *victim consciousness*. They were also more able to think systemically and to understand how experiences in their family-of-origin system were continuing to impact their lives, without perceiving themselves as victims. Barry concluded this research by gathering focus groups with some of the participants from the experimental group, asking them to identify what helped them to shift their consciousness. They reported the following factors:

- Understanding at an emotional, not just theoretical, level the influences of their family-of-origin system on their present conflicts
- The emphasis on applying the theoretical material in the course to their own lives and conflicts
- The personal sharing that the class members did with each other in the class
- The personal sharing by the instructor that allowed them to reflect on their own life experiences in a new way

Barry replicated this experiment several times with very similar results.

Contributions of Other Theories to Developmental Systems Theory

Since DST is a metatheory, in this chapter we present the contributions of other theories to the theoretical foundation of DST, which is anchored in new research from the fields of psychobiology, brain research, bioenergetics, psychodynamic and developmental theories, transpersonal psychology, humanistic psychology, and cognitive–behavioral psychology. We particularly draw on Bruce Lipton's model of fractal evolution and his innovative concepts of cellular consciousness, conscious parenting, and electromagnetic medicine; Porges & Carter's polyvagal theory; and Allen Schore's theory of affect regulation. We also acknowledge the many pioneers who have created and are continuing to expand the field of pre- and perinatal psychology. We combine specific contributions from these individuals and groups in a unique way in this chapter to anchor our research on the LOVEvolution and developmental trauma tracks within a body of scientific knowledge.

Contributions from Family Systems Theories

Systems theorists have typically found family structures a rich research resource. As family therapist Virginia Satir once said, "It is now clear to me that the family is a microcosm of the world. To understand the world, we can study the family . . . to change the world is to change the family" (Satir, 1988, p. 15). Family systems theorists and therapists typically look at a family's structure as a system to determine what is contributing to the dysfunction of its members. Looking at the impact of unrecognized and unhealed shock, trauma, and stress on a family system provides an even broader perspective for identifying the confluence of forces contributing to a family problem. An approach that looks at the effects of unrecognized and unhealed shock, trauma, and stress on a family system reduces even further any tendencies to label or assign blame to individuals in the family.

Systems theorists believe that dysfunction sometimes serves as a stabilizing force in families that have a lot of emotional drama and persistent conflict. The person who expresses repressed feelings, in this theory, acts as a force toward equilibrium to keep the system from breaking apart. Systems theorists believe that it is more effective to identify what is driving the behavior of the members in a system, rather than, for example, focusing on an acting-out teenager, who appears to be the cause of the problems. Then they use whole system interventions to change the behavior of all of the members in the system. Simply using individual interventions will not only feed the family's dysfunction but actually can sustain it. DST draws on many of the principles of general systems theory discussed in the previous chapter plus some of the leading family systems theories.

Bateson, Bowen, Framo, Jackson, and Sager's family systems theories helped us better understand the complexities of the way that unrecognized and unhealed shock, trauma, and stress are processed in family systems. As early as the late 1950s, the Palo Alto group, led by Gregory Bateson (Bateson, Jackson, Haley, & Weakland, 1956, pp. 251–264) began applying cybernetics to the study of family therapy. Their work eventually led to a major paradigm shift in the field of family therapy. Therapists slowly began viewing the individual and each successively more complex social group as interacting systems. With this new perspective, family therapists began to treat the family as a system containing various subsystems. DST utilizes both the systems language and the concept of development as a dynamic system that is constantly changing and evolving in somewhat nonlinear, but often predictable, ways.

In developing DST, we also borrowed from the work of several of the established family systems theorists. The work of Bowen (1978) and Framo (1982), for example, formed a useful model for helping individuals and families sort out family-of-origin issues recycling in their current family dynamics. Bowen was also the first to emphasize the importance of family therapists doing their personal family-of-origin work during their professional training as a family therapist. This practice supports our belief about the ethical need for therapists to recognize and heal the effects of their own developmental shock, trauma, and stress in order to avoid creating countertransference issues with their clients.

Structural family therapists contributed useful definitions about the boundaries and rules present in each subsystem of a family. Their work helped us to better understand and define the interrelated human systems we use in our approach: the individual, the couple, the family, groups and organizations, nation–states, and the human race.

The work of Don Jackson (1965) and Sager and his associates (Sager & Kaplan, 1971) helped us better understand how to integrate the concepts of intrapsychic systems and family systems. The basic assumption of their models is that unconscious and conscious aspects of family members' inner conflicts form an important part of the systemic feedback loop that can be observed in the interaction, communication, and behavior patterns of family members.

The use of dialogue as an evolutionary tool is ancient, tracing its beginnings back to ancient Greece as well as to native and indigenous peoples. We saw Bohm and Krishnamurti dialogues (Krishnamurti, 1986) and their dialogue process as an important communication tool that helps people attune with each other and build stronger and deeper relationships. Our search for contemporary applications of their work led us to dialogue master Peter Senge. He and his book, *The Fifth Discipline* (1990), taught us how to use dialogue as a healing intervention in larger systems.

Gleick's, Wheatley's, and Briggs and Peat's interpretations of chaos theory, a branch of quantum physics, made important contributions to our approach. Gleick's *Chaos: Making a New Science* (1987) and Briggs and Peat's *The Turbulent Mirror* (1989) provided us with both a language and a conceptual model for understanding chaos theory. We found Margaret Wheatley's book, *Leadership and the New Science* (1992), one of the most practical and readable books in applying chaos theory to living systems. We spent more than a year studying chaos theory with a group of other professionals and applying its principles to the helping professions. After working our way through the strange language of chaos theory, we could see how it supported the use of quantum sciences and languages as foundational concepts in DST.

Chaos theorists believe that all human systems contain an inherent order even though they appear chaotic. This order, however, is often visible only over an extended period of time. Looking at family systems over several generations, for example, often reveals identical patterns of loss, trauma, and separation that are most amazing.

While studying this concept in the abstract, I (Janae) had a personal epiphany that illustrated the point very clearly. This epiphany came during a conversation I had with my second son. I shared with him about how I (the second child) was separated from my mother at the age of 11 months when she went to the hospital for my sister's birth, and how this pattern of separation happened again when my son (also the second child) was 11 months old and was hospitalized for 19 days with two different kinds of pneumonia. He ruminated on this piece of information for a moment and then looked at me with both surprise and pain. Then he shared with me that his second son was 11 months old when he left and eventually divorced his son's mother.

Most clinicians do not look at their clients' development from a temporal perspective; seldom do they review a person's lifetime history looking for the timing of the transmission of traumatic intergenerational events. We began to look at singular and clustered developmental markers involving loss, trauma, separation, and dramatic change in our own lives and then in the lives of our students and clients. We gradually learned how to identify the fractal patterns of unrecognized and unhealed developmental shock, trauma, and stress that followed these temporal markers.

Then we looked for the fractal story lines or themes that appear in each problem presented to us, as we searched for the earliest experience, or source, of this patterned behavior. We were pretty amazed to discover that the most common strange attractor, or organizing experience for people's life scripts, was anchored primarily in the circumstances of their birth and then was reinforced in subsequent developmental shock, trauma, and stress that occurred during the following 3 years.

We also found that our most successful interventions for changing these life scripts occurred with systems (individuals, couples, and families) that were open to change. According to chaos theory, the more open a system is to change, the more likely it will transform itself into levels of higher and higher order in a search for expanded levels of autonomy and identity.

So we began looking at the age when our clients most often sought therapy. What we found was that they were clustered around the ages of 29–31, 39–42, 49–53, and 60–62. Janae's long-term interest in astrology, another systems approach for understanding individual evolution, helped us make sense of these particular age groupings. She had read Barbara Hand Clow's astrology book, *The Liquid Light of Sex: Understanding Your Life Transitions* (1991), in which she identified exactly these time periods as key points in personal transformation. Clow describes the specific psychological, spiritual, mental, and karmic lessons and challenges that must be mastered during these transit periods, which helped us understand more deeply both our clients' underlying issues and how best to support them.

Contributions from the Field of Psychobiology

The field of psychobiology, also known as behavioral neuroscience and biological psychology, applies the principles of biology to the study of mental processes and behaviors in humans. It provides a scientific bridge between fields of study and academic disciplines that helps to integrate disciplines in ways that provide a more comprehensive understanding of both psychology and biology. We found that psychobiology helped us correlate psychological and behavioral phenomena with biological events in ways that contribute to our evidence-based model of human development.

Lipton's Fractal Evolution

Lipton's model of fractal evolution uses language from the quantum sciences to describe the most subtle and intricate aspects of human relational experiences at the cellular level. We first heard him speak in 1995 when he presented his then radically new quantum biology approach to midwives, physicians, nurses, psychologists, therapists, and parents at the Pre- and Perinatal Psychology Conference in San Francisco. He got a standing ovation, as many people in the "soft" sciences heard their personal and professional experiences validated for the first time by someone from the "hard" sciences.

We think Lipton's most significant discovery is that cellular behavior parallels that of an individual. Lipton says that if you want to understand the most basic and minute human experience, study the behavior of cells.

The Biocomputer

Lipton believes humans are biocomputers and that we serve as the model for how computers operate. In other words, computer technologies are an external reflection or projection of human's internal biological processes. Lipton said that humans are not "like" computers, *they are computers*, and their cells function as biocomputer chips that help humans function according to the "software programs" that have been installed through our life experiences (2005, p. 62).

Lipton's research showed that the membrane surface of each cell is an organic, or carbon-based, liquid crystal semiconductor or information-processing transistor. The antennae on the surface of the cell can sense or "read" the energy in the cell's environment and convert the information into a biological BIT that is sent to the brain and nervous system. Here it is routed to the appropriate organ systems, which then produce the hormones and other chemicals needed to help the human act. The nucleus of the cell helps us create not only our physical body, but also our thoughts, beliefs, and feelings (1986).

According to Lipton, the nucleus of the cell functions as a "hard drive" containing DNA-coded software that provides data storage. The human biocomputers have use-dependent "software programs" that direct the genes and the mind–body toward either growth or protection. Because humans operate as a binary system, they cannot do both at the same time.

Cellular Perception

In his binary model, the antennae on the surface of cell membranes are the true "gatekeepers" for the body, as they scan the energy in the cell's environment to determine whether it is safe or unsafe. When they perceive that the environment is safe, friendly, and emotionally supportive, they signal the cell receptors to open and receive the information, sustenance, and energy from the environment to promote growth. So as our cells open up, so do we. As we engage with each other in intimate ways, focus our attention and resources on growth and expansion, we generate experiences of LOVEvolution.

In situations where the cell antennae perceive the environment as unsafe, they signal the cell receptors to close and shift into a defensive mode, directing the cell to produce survival hormones and chemicals and focus the body's energy resources into protection and survival. Again, because humans are binary computers, we have no middle ground. Cells and organisms can be in only one mode at a time: either switched on and open or switched off and closed. His model has huge implications for human development, as we will discuss a bit later.

Lipton also discovered that it is *cellular perception,* or the cells' interpretation of the environment, that controls and directs all body activity. As a result, the nervous system can get locked into a continuing state of "false alarm," which then can become a source of chronic stress. This cellular perception causes the cells to generalize ordinary situations as dangerous (as in a shock, trauma, or stress state) and direct the genes to route all energy into protection and safety. This chronic alarm state activates a cellular protection reaction that eventually shifts the physical body into degeneration and causes the appearance of chronic health conditions such as cancer, heart problems, and diabetes. We explain how this process works in Chapter 8.

Chronic Alarm States

Chronic alarm states keep us on the developmental trauma track of evolution. They cause us to withdraw from others, to mobilize our energy for protection, and "head for the bunkers," so to speak, even when we do not need to. When we operate from a protection mode, it disconnects us from what we call LOVEvolution and the unconditional love that is available to us. When the cell receptors are open, our nervous system is calm, relaxed, and open; our cells direct energy toward growth and expansion; we open up to unconditional love; we engage with others; and we move on the path of LOVEvolution.

Lipton also believes that our DNA communicates energetically with our soul, heart, and brain through a process of resonance and synchronization. Our whole being, he says, is wired to attune with the source energy surrounding us that some describe as *God*. Peter Gariaev and his colleagues at the Russian Academy of Sciences support Lipton's premise. They said that the source field contains all the DNA codes—that "the wave is the DNA and the DNA is the wave" (1997, p. 107). From this perspective, unconditional love energy is always available to us, even though we may not be able to receive it.

Survival of the Most Loving

In the epilogue of his book, *The Biology of Belief,* Lipton wrote about the "survival of the most loving." Here he emphasized that the human race can only go to the next stage in its evolution by consciously emulating the behavior of our cells. Humans must join together to create larger and more efficient organisms—communities of like-minded people who are working towards the advancement of human evolution. He said that the survival of the most loving is the only ethic that will ensure not only a healthy personal life but also a healthy planet (2005, pp. 201–202).

Porges and Carter's Polyvagal Theory of Social Engagement

Drs. Steve Porges and Sue Carter's polyvagal theory of social engagement also validates Lipton's binary biological model (Porges, 2003). Their research on the relationship between human biochemical reactions and social development indicated the presence in the nervous system of a *social engagement system* (SES). This part of their binary model operates through five cranial (vagus) nerves that emerge from the brain stem—the most primitive part of the brain. This system coordinates and integrates head turning, looking, listening, and vocal communication, with output from the heart.

These five nerves also regulate sucking, swallowing, salivating, breathing, and vocalizing—the first and most primal of all human experiences. They allow breastfeeding without suffocation, are involved in flexing the muscles of the middle ear, in discerning and discriminating tones and frequencies of the human voice from background noise, in controlling the expressive muscles of the face and eyelids, and are central to eye contact and nonverbal communication.

Porges and Carter particularly looked at a mechanism known as the vagal brake, a nerve that calms and relaxes the heart. A central component of the SES, the vagal brake helps us interact deeply with the larger world. When operating under optimal conditions, the SES allows humans to engage in heartful and creative social interactions that support optimal development and evolution. The function of the SES parallels Lipton's "growth and expansion" model of cell function and our concept of LOVEvolution.

Although Porges and Carter do not name it as such, they also describe something that might be called the *social disengagement system* (SDS). This part of their binary model, which is the equivalent of our developmental trauma track of evolution, activates when humans feel unsafe and disengage from social and emotional interactions, close their hearts, and mobilize their energetic resources to protect themselves so that they will survive.

For example, it is difficult for the SES to function when the deep muscles of people's necks are chronically tense from stress or unprocessed umbilical cord shock, trauma, and stress at birth. Chronic stress and the nervous system's constant false alarm state create anxiety and depression that foster dualistic thinking and mood disorders.

Schore's Theory of Affect Regulation

Allan Schore's theory of affect regulation also contains a binary model of early human development. His model of *affect regulation* is based on the binary concepts of *emotional regulation* and *emotional dysregulation*. Schore is an assistant clinical professor of Psychiatry and Biobehavioral Sciences at the University of California at Los Angeles. His model uses language from quantum science to describe emotional interactions between infants and parents, using terms such as *emotional synchronization, energetic attunement,* and *resonance* to describe times when parents and infants are "in synch" with each other. We describe his model in more detail in Chapter 3.

All four of these concepts—Porges' SES/SDS, Lipton's "safety and protection mode," Schore's concepts of emotional regulation and dysregulation, and our LOVEvolution/Developmental Trauma—are binary models. They confirm the impact of chronic posttraumatic stress reactions on human evolution at a cellular level.

MacLean's Triune Brain Theory

Another source of support for DST comes from Paul MacLean's triune brain theory (1974). He describes the brain as having three main parts: the reptilian, the mammalian, and the neomammalian or neocortex.

The Reptilian Brain

The reptilian brain or brainstem evolved from lizards and snakes. Because reptiles have no instinctive repertoire of protective behaviors, they are not concerned with their offspring and often abandon, or even eat, their own eggs as soon as they emerge from the female. A remnant of our prehistoric past, the reptilian brain operates on stimulus and response. It is useful for making quick decisions without thinking and is responsible for managing basic physiological functions such as circulation, respiration, digestion, and elimination. During a shocking experience, this part of the brain is responsible for freeze and dissociated responses (Porges, 2001).

The reptilian brain is also involved in mating and in territorial behaviors such as defense, aggression, pecking orders, and the emotions of anger and fear. Because the reptilian brain is fear driven, it focuses on survival and takes over brain functioning when it perceives danger.

Behaviorally, it operates automatically and ritualistically and is highly resistant to change. It is also concerned with getting food and protecting us from danger by constantly scanning the environment and looking for signs of danger. This hypervigilant reptilian behavior keeps us in a chronic state of tension and cuts us off from our mammalian potential and self-reflective consciousness. Anxiety can immobilize our limbic and neomammalian brains, which regulate our creative, optimistic, and relational behaviors. Hypervigilant people who struggle with obsessive compulsive disorder, for example, live in a prison where their higher brains are "locked down."

The Mammalian Brain

The mammalian brain includes the amygdala, which associates events with emotion. It also contains the hippocampus, which is active in converting information into long-term memory and into memory recall. Also known as the limbic brain, the mammalian brain began to evolve with the appearance of the first mammals and is practically nonexistent in reptiles, amphibians, and all other preceding species. This horseshoe-shaped organ also analyzes sensory information for emotional content, tagging anything that contains shock-, trauma-, and stress-related cues or signals. Noncharged data are relayed to the hippocampus, which operates as an internal "secretary" that organizes them and integrates the emotional, cognitive, behavior, and relational data into narrative form. These data are used to explain and make meaning of a person's life experiences and then are stored as memories that can be consciously recalled at will.

The limbic system houses the primary centers of emotion and affects moods and bodily functions and is connected to the sense of smell, to relational needs, and to activities involving the expression and mediation of emotions and feelings, particularly those linked to bonding. The emotions of love, sadness, jealousy, and hope have their source in the limbic brain and can be observed in higher warm blooded animals such as cats, dogs, horses, and primates, including humans. Mammals display protective, nurturing behavior toward their offspring because they have an instinctive hunger for tactile contact and energetic connection. These protective, loving feelings become increasingly complex as the limbic system and the neocortex link up. This mammalian hunger for emotional contact maintains the bond between mother and offspring and generates closely knit family groupings that maximize the survival of the young. The limbic system is also tightly connected to the prefrontal cortex.

The Neocortex

The neocortex is associated with abstract thought, imagination, consciousness, and language and governs our ability to speak, think, and solve problems. From an evolutionary perspective, it is the newest part of the brain and is found in the brains of all mammals but not in any other animals. It makes up about 80% of the brain and affects our creativity and our ability to learn and self-reflect. It is responsible for many higher-order functions such as intuition, synthesis, and social engagement.

How Our Three Brains Work Together

When the antennae on the cell membranes perceive danger, the signal first registers in the reptilian brain. Then it is routed on to the autonomic nervous system, which notifies the adrenal glands to mobilize the body for protection. They flood the limbic brain with cortisol and other adrenal hormones, causing a rapid and dramatic change in the brain's operation. The danger stimulus often fires a visual image in the right brain and triggers a flashback memory containing disturbing auditory, visual, relational, and behavioral information and catapults the person into a dissociated state.

At this point, the limbic brain, which operates as an internal "secretary" that sorts the sensory information coming in from the nervous system according to valence, simply cannot keep up. In order to keep functioning, the "secretary" throws the incoming sensory information into "piles," storing it in compartments of dissociated memory for processing into logical memories at a later date. These compartmentalized and dissociated memories, which cannot be consciously recalled at will, create the black hole and the unconscious mind.

In most cases, the split-off material stored in the compartments of the black hole never gets processed. It remains dissociated from awareness until some visual, auditory, olfactory, proprioceptive, or kinesthetic cue activates a memory filed in the "pile." This trigger can activate everything stored in the memory module and create a full reenactment of the original trauma. The feelings associated with the regressed experience seem so real that it is difficult to distinguish present from past. Only when a person is asked when they have felt this way before can they begin to see a connection to similar experiences in their past. This is the heart of regression, the traumatic reenactment process, and also of posttraumatic stress disorder (PTSD), which we describe in more detail later in the book.

The neocortex or neomammalian brain found only in humans is divided into right and left sides or hemispheres. Each side has specialized functions that are connected by a neural bridge known as the corpus callosum. The left hemisphere is responsible for language and analyzes and processes information in a linear, logical, or sequential manner, much like a personal computer. The right hemisphere matures before the left and is directly impacted by early social experiences. It is particularly active during intense states of elation during play and contributes to the development of reciprocal interactions between the mother and infant.

Perhaps the most important role of the right hemisphere is in the attunement process between the mother and infant (Schore, 2003b, p. 13). This interactive right brain attunement process also forms the foundation for empathy (p. 44). Individuals with traumatic attachment histories are unable to perceive the emotional states of others and, therefore, often are not able to feel empathy for others (p. 47). The right brain also plays a dominant role in emotional processing during infancy and the first 3 years of life (p. 229). The process of specializing emotions begins in the right hemisphere at the end of the first year and, therefore, plays a critical role in the attachment and bonding process. From Schore's perspective, "attachment is … the right-brain regulation of biological synchrony between organisms" (p. 41). It is through experiences of brain-to-brain synchronization with the mother that the child eventually learns self-regulation.

Using Lipton's computer metaphor, we might say that a child's right hemisphere gets programmed through the experiences with his or her mother. From the perspective of quantum biology, we might say that the nervous system becomes energetically imprinted. Whatever the metaphor, the right brain plays a major role in reading facial expressions and guiding the young child's response to adult caregivers. The left hemisphere growth spurt does not begin until around age 2 (2005, p. 185). It is involved in the development of verbal language and the development of both guilt and the conscience, as the young child begins internalizing the parents' verbal, moral, and parental values and standards.

A great deal of research is being conducted on the prefrontal cortex part of the brain, which does not develop until after the age of 3. Psychologically, Paul MacLean considered it the neurobiological seat of the self—the conscious, reflective personality of an individual (cited in Mines, 2003, p. 42). Self-psychology includes concepts such as self-actualization, self-awareness, self-development, self-control, self-esteem, and self-disclosure. From a developmental perspective, the self is associated with the emergence of an ego that is eventually surrendered to a higher purpose or spiritual mission. This phenomenon, which usually does not happen until full psychological maturity, often marks a spiritual transition from self-service to the service of others.

MacLean referred to the left prefrontal cortex as the "vault of heaven," "angel lobes," or "holy tissue." He believes that this area has a special purpose, that which makes us human. "Angelic" means that it may be responsible for the kind of direct experiences of "knowing" described by early Christian Gnostics and others able to communicate directly with the world of Spirit. This part of the brain may be where people experience feelings of unconditional love that are part of the LOVEvolution track of our binary theory.

Contributions from the Field of Pre- and Perinatal Psychology

This field focuses on what is now almost universally recognized as the most critical period of human development. At this stage, children are extraordinarily sensitive to their environment, and their biological systems are the most plastic, pliable, and receptive to learning. This makes them exceedingly vulnerable to the irreversible or partially reversible impact on development of early experiences of shock, trauma and stress. At the same time, they are highly resilient. The right brain is highly use dependent, and its development is absolutely embedded in the bonding relationship between the parents and the child. Early interventions designed to repair the effects of shock, trauma, and stress that occurs during the birth process can make a lifelong difference in a child's development (Schore, 2003a, p. 202).

The degree to which children are emotionally and energetically supported during gestation, birth, and the first year of life largely determines how they will develop. Will the flexible, dynamic, and use-dependent structures of the infant's brain and nervous system get hard-wired for growth and expansion or for safety and protection? Early neurobiological interventions during this critical period of development can help mediate the impact of shock, trauma, or stress (Schore

2003a, p. 264), particularly to highly imprinting stressors such as birth. The use of therapeutic interventions early in life, particularly those developed by practitioners of the pre- and perinatal psychology community, can have a lifelong impact on children.

Dr. Thomas Verny, a pioneer in this field and author of *The Secret Life of the Unborn Child* (1988), conducted in-depth research into an infant's psychological, emotional, and social development, from preparation for pregnancy through the postpartum period and lactation. The focus of pre- and perinatal psychology has gradually expanded to include the study and treatment of prenatal and birth shock, trauma, and stress and the creation of a model for healthy, mammalian-based parent–child bonding practices.

Frederic Leboyer (2002), Marshall and Phyllis Klaus (2000), Michael Odent (1994), and David Chamberlin (1998) are all among the early pioneers in this field of study. William Emerson, Stanislav Grof, and Barbara Findeisen have created an extensive body of knowledge in the field through the www.birthpsychology.com website. This new wave of research in developmental psychology has anchored this field in the quantum sciences, which has given us new understanding about how humans develop and relate.

Contributions from Cultural Research in Bioenergetics

Dr. James Prescott served as a health scientist administrator at the National Institute of Child Health and Human Development (NICHD) at the U.S. National Institutes of Health (NIH) from 1966 to 1980. He founded and directed the Developmental Behavioral Biology Program at the NICHD and conducted research on the effects of sensory deprivation on human sexual pleasure and affection, particularly during adolescence.

Prescott's research draws heavily on the work of Wilhelm Reich and Alexander Lowen, who used the principles of bioenergetics to track the flow of energy in the human body. Bioenergetics uses a binary system based on pain and pleasure to look at how the expression or repression of energy shapes people's physiology and psychology. For example, repressed grief often creates an overinflated, high-held chest, mechanical breathing, a contracted pelvis, and a general state of rigidity in the body.

Maternal–Social Deprivation

One of Prescott's most significant contributions to the field of developmental psychology is his redefinition of *maternal–social deprivation*. Drawing on principles from bioenergetics, he identified this deprivation as a complex sensory problem caused by the lack of body touch and body sensation. Prescott said that the deprivation of body touch and body sensation causes somatosensory affectional deprivation (SAD) and disrupts development in the parts of the brain that are responsible for maternal–infant bonding. Schore's more recent research validates Prescott's earlier work.

In an article on the pre- and perinatal psychology website (1997), Prescott claims that the orbito-frontal cortex is responsible for building the primary neuropsychological foundation necessary for basic trust. He adds that the somesthetic (touch) sensory system provides the primary neuropsychological foundation for affection, and the olfactory (smell) sensory system provides the primary neuropsychological foundation for intimacy. In normal development these emotional–sensory systems are combined in rich patterns of complex sensory stimulation in which basic trust, affection, and intimacy are integrated with one another to form an emotional brain capable of love. This *neurointegrative brain* develops, according to Prescott, long before the infant can understand the spoken or written word.

Pleasure and Bonding

All three of these emotional sensory systems are involved in the experience of pleasure and bonding. It is through the emotional senses that the infant knows when he or she is being loved or rejected. According to Prescott, the failure to encode the infant's developing brain with the smell of its mother's body through breastfeeding can have long-term adverse consequences for bonding and for the male–female sexual relationship.

Prescott's research revealed that repressed emotions caused by mother–infant separations cause abnormal brain changes that result in depression, impulse dyscontrol, and violence. He confirmed these findings by studying the effects of the deprivation of human sexual pleasure and affection during adolescence in primitive cultures. He found that peaceful cultures valued the importance of mothering and encouraged loving and affectionate sexual relationships among young adults.

Cultures that deprived children of pleasurable sensory experiences and play produced irreversible mental retardation in the children and intellectual deficits in adults. Prescott's cross-cultural research concluded that cultures that inflict pain on infants and repress sexuality become violent, and that secure maternal–infant bonding is essential for peace in the world (Prescott 2002).

Unfortunately, Prescott's research findings got him caught in a political crossfire. The existence of and results from his NICHD-supported research programs were ignored in a 2004 NIH publication because they did not support the prevailing religious and cultural values of this country, which deny the importance of secure mother–infant bonding and forbid youth to engage in affectional sexual relationships.

Prescott also organized his research findings into a model based on two paradigms: a patrilineal, theistic religion and a matrilineal, Earth religion. One of his most important research findings concerned the impact of each of these paradigms on the development of the brain. Table 2.1 below summarizes Prescott's binary research (2002) and Riane Eisler's (1987) binary cultural models.

Contributions from Psychodynamic and Developmental Theories

These theories emphasize identifying the early antecedents of present intrapersonal or interpersonal conflicts or problems. The core concept is that unhealed developmental shock, trauma, and stress from childhood tend to recur until they are healed. Psychodynamic methods, consequently, help people identify the unhealed developmental shock, trauma, and stress from their childhood and then find ways in the here and now to heal their lingering effects. This process of self-discovery first involves teaching people to understand the conditions of optimal development. This includes understanding the essential developmental processes that an individual needs to complete successfully and correlating the presence of developmental shock, trauma, and stress in their early development with the cause of their current conflicts and psychological problems.

Erik Erikson, Robert Havighurst, and Jean Piaget's developmental theories and research helped us identify the stages of physical development and the cognitive, emotional, and psychosocial processes to be mastered at each stage. The work of Erikson (1959), Havighurst (1972), and Piaget (1951) provided us with foundational material for identifying these stages and the essential developmental

TABLE 2.1

Contrasting Patrifocal and Matrifocal Cultures

Patrilineal / Patriarchal Cultures	Matrilineal / Matriarchal Cultures
Gender inequality	Gender equality
Sexual purity	Sexual liberty
Addictive synthetic drugs	Natural botanical drugs
Authoritarian	Egalitarian
Pain is a moral good	Pleasure is a moral good
Depression–violence	Joy–happiness
Left brained	Right brained
Neuro-dissociative brain	Neuro-integrative brain
Life taking	Life giving

processes that need to be completed in each stage to support full development in the next stage. We discuss this material in depth in Chapters 3 and 4.

Transactional Analysis

Jacqui Schiff, Eric Berne, Dorothy Babcock, Terry Keepers, John Bradshaw, Pam Levin, and Jean Illsley Clark's transactional analysis (TA) approaches provided many ideas and methods of working with adults who were severely affected by early childhood shock, trauma, and stress. In 1970, Schiff published a book titled *All My Children,* in which she described a revolutionary therapy approach called *reparenting,* which grew out of Eric Berne's work on transactional analysis. Schiff reported a great deal of success with the reparenting therapy she and her husband had used, often with chronic schizophrenic clients. Their residential treatment program required 24-hour-a-day care. Most of the people who went through their program went on to become highly functioning adults, many becoming therapists themselves.

Schiff's methods, considered highly controversial at the time, encouraged clients to regress to an infant stage. The interventions were designed to heal clients' developmental shock, trauma, and stress that occurred in early childhood and infancy and included diapering them, holding them, and feeding them from bottles, as well as providing them with effective anger- and rage-reduction tools. Their methods were designed to reconnect their clients with their original developmental shock, trauma, and stress, and to allow them to express their repressed feelings related to the shock, trauma, and stress in a safe, supportive environment. Then they provided them with the support, nurturing, and new information they needed to heal their early developmental shock, trauma, and stress.

Schiff wrote a sequel, *The Cathexis Reader* (1976), which described a set of passive or discounting behaviors that kept people stuck in symbiotic or codependent relationships along with reenactments of early developmental shock, trauma, and stress. The book outlined effective methods for gentle and loving confrontations of these dysfunctional behaviors. Passive people who feel weak and helpless, for example, often discount their own needs and focus on the needs of others, hoping to win some attention or approval from them. In addition, they discount their ability to ask directly for what they want. Being forced to ask directly to get their needs met has been found to be an effective means for helping them heal the effects of their early unrecognized and unhealed developmental shock, trauma, and stress.

As Schiff and her colleagues studied passivity and discounting, they discovered that these behaviors were not just part of the pathology of schizophrenics. They were also very much a part of the everyday life of most people. The Schiffs indicated that these behaviors were the major causes of intractable conflicts. This understanding helped us see how undiscovered and unhealed developmental shock, trauma, and stress can have adverse effects on everybody in unknown ways and are at the source of most intractable conflicts between people at all levels of human systems.

TA practitioners Dorothy Babcock and Terry Keepers (1976) combined the passivity/discounting concept with script analysis in a book for parents called *Raising Kids OK*. Robert and Mary Goulding (1978) were among those who adapted the concept into other types of TA therapy such as Redecision Therapy.

During this period, Schiff became embroiled in political battles over her methods within the International Association of Transactional Analysis, and eventually she was censured by the organization. The censuring effectively stopped the progress of Schiff's treatment modality, although a few of her former students did continue to develop the theory. We have harvested the best of her work and include it as part of DST and DPW, the application of the theory.

Object Relations Theories

Bowlby, Winnicott, Kernberg, Kohut, Mahler, and Cashdan's object relations theory and therapy approaches posit that events during the first year of life dictate the course of all subsequent human development. Bowlby (1969), Kernberg (1976), Mahler, Pine, and Bergman (1975), Mahler (1980), Mahler and Furer (1968), and Winnicott (1965) were pioneers in this specialized field of psychodynamic psychology. Of these theorists, we drew heavily from the research of Margaret Mahler and her colleague, Louise Kaplan, who charted the course of development from the bonding stage of the infant (birth to 9 months) through the separation stage (9 to 36 months). Kaplan's book, *Oneness and Separateness* (1978), based on Mahler's research, provided us with a clear narrative description of these two stages, including what might prevent the successful completion of the essential developmental processes in each stage. Cashdan's book, *Object Relations Therapy* (1988), helped us identify the specific distortions that emerge as a result of developmental shock, trauma, and stress in early parent–child relationships.

With the onset of the addictions and recovery movement in the late 1980s, object relations theory and therapy began to appear in literature containing a broader developmental perspective. John Bradshaw utilized many reparenting concepts in his series of books on recovery and inner child therapy, including *Healing the Shame that Binds You* (1988) and *Homecoming: Reclaiming and Championing Your Inner Child* (1990). Jon and Laurie Weiss described corrective parenting techniques for treating codependency in *Recovery From Co-dependency* (1989). Jean Illsley Clarke wrote two important books applying this evolving theory to parenting practices: *Self-esteem: A Family Affair* (1978) and *Growing Up Again: Parenting Ourselves, Parenting Our Children* (1989) with Connie Dawson. Pamela Levin also wrote several books that further developed reparenting theory, including *Becoming the Way We Are* (1988a) and *Cycles of Power* (1988b).

Our own books, *Breaking Free of the Co-dependency Trap* (2008a), *The Flight From Intimacy* (2008b), and *Breaking Free of Family Patterns* (2006), utilize some reparenting techniques and a developmental approach. The family patterns book describes the process of breaking addictive relationship dynamics using many concepts from object relations theory. We eventually integrated many reparenting and developmental concepts into DST as tools to help people recover their true self by healing their developmental shock, trauma, and stress.

Clarke and Levin's books contributed positive affirmations designed to assist in the healing of early cognitive distortions due to shock, trauma, and stress. These practioners also created lists of the developmental needs of early childhood to help people locate the sources of their adult dysfunctions. We found these lists useful in helping clients in their recovery process and incorporated them into our lists of essential developmental processes to be completed in each stage of development.

We also incorporated Steven Karpman's drama triangle (1968) into DST to illustrate the lingering effects of unhealed developmental shock, trauma, and stress on communication patterns in relationships. From Karpman's description of persecutor, rescuer, and victim roles and how the roles rotate around a triangle, we identified an equivalent set of incomplete developmental processes operating in the parent–child separation process. We extended his model into an optimal family dynamic by identifying the essential developmental processes needed to create the Functional Family Triangle, the opposite of the drama triangle. DST correlates the interpersonal dynamics of the drama triangle with drama resulting from unrecognized and unhealed developmental shock, trauma, and stress that contain symptoms of posttraumatic stress. We describe the specific dynamics more completely in Chapter 7.

Alice Miller and Philip Ney's intergenerational theories taught us a great deal about the psychodynamics of developmental trauma. Much of the reparenting component of our paradigm grew out of the pioneering work of Swiss analyst Alice Miller (1981, 1984, 1986, 1988, 1991). Her books helped us examine the role of early narcissistic wounds on later development. Miller's work clearly explained many of the adverse effects of "standard parenting practices" and documented that the same dysfunctional patterns of behavior repeat themselves from one generation to the next. Her latest book (2005) also helped us better understand the process of the intergenerational transmission of the effects of unrecognized and unhealed developmental shock, trauma, and stress.

Philip Ney (1988) also helped increase our understanding of the intergenerational transmission of the effects of unrecognized and unhealed developmental shock, trauma, and stress. Ney based his model of family dramas on three rotating roles: the perpetrator, the victim, and the observer. He proposed that family members repeat the maladaptive parenting practices that were used on them as a means of better understanding their parents' behavior. Ney also noticed that people who were in an observer role as children remained in that role as adults. Similar to the dynamics of the drama triangle, in Ney's theory the roles rotate among family members.

Ney applied his theory to professionals in the workplace to demonstrate how easy it is to get caught up in countertransference behaviors involving roles therapists played in their own family of origin. Professionals can easily slip into the roles of victim, perpetrator, or observer, preventing them from being effective. DST draws heavily on Ney's theory, using it to demonstrate the recycling of the effects of unrecognized and unhealed developmental shock, trauma, and stress through intergenerational structures. Ney's theory reinforced our belief that it is critical for helping professionals to identify the nature and source of their own unrecognized and unhealed developmental shock, trauma, and stress

Beverly James's attachment-trauma approach was the first book we found that correlated attachment and trauma. In *Handbook for Treatment of Attachment-Trauma Problems in Children* (1994), James provided an integrated blueprint for assessing and working with trauma-related attachment disturbances. She also identified a disturbance in the parent–child relationship that she called *trauma bonds*. Her research and clinical protocols were useful resources for refining the developmental trauma component of DST.

Global Process Work

Our extensive study in 1985 and 1986 with Arnold Mindell provided a significant contribution to our approach. Mindell, a former Jungian analyst, developed an adaptation of Jungian theory he called global process work (1983, 1985a, 1985b, 1987). Mindell adapted much of Carl Jung's work, including his ideas about dreams. Mindell began to realize that people are dreaming all the time. Their waking dreams, according to Mindell, are often means of avoiding unpleasant realities or unpleasant memories of early trauma, while their sleeping dreams provide an outlet for unconscious material to emerge.

The real genius of Mindell's work, however, was his expansion of information theories such as neurolinguistic programming (NLP) into six main information channels and his use of Taoist principles in therapy. The six information channels that Mindell identified are the visual, auditory, proprioceptive, kinesthetic, relationship, and world channel. His form of information theory provides a mechanism the therapist can use to track the source of a problem by noticing which of these six communication channels the client uses when presenting his/her problems and symptoms. Mindell's use of Taoist principles provided a context of "rightness" of all symptoms and problems, as well as the use of client-centered techniques for "following" the client.

In addition, Mindell used the principles of unified field theory from quantum physics to show how problems move from one *field,* or system, to another. According to his theory, for example, an unhealed shock, trauma, or stress that is not identified and healed at the individual field will move out into the relationship field and emerge there as a problem. If not identified and healed at that level of system, it would move out into the next level of the system—the family. Using this theory to examine national and international conflicts, he began to hypothesize about how intractable global conflicts could be the collective manifestation of many unhealed individual, relationship, group, and organizational shocks, traumas, and stresses.

Stages of Consciousness

Robert Kegan's work, summarized in his book, *In Over Our Heads* (1994), also contributed to our theory. He identified five distinct stages of cognitive development in the evolution of consciousness that grew out of Piaget's theories of cognitive development. They include the following:

- **Stage One: Magical Thinking.** People exhibit poor cause-and-effect thinking.
- **Stage Two: Concrete Thinking.** People base their reality on what is visible, tangible, and concrete and are unable to grasp the meaning of abstract concepts such as human rights or justice.
- **Stage Three: Cross-Relational Thinking.** Individuals in this stage of consciousness are able to think abstractly and are able to see the relationships between experiences and events, but they perceive the world as acting upon them.
- **Stage Four: Systemic Thinking.** Individuals in this stage of consciousness can think holistically and systemically and are able to perceive the underlying patterns of thoughts, feelings, and behaviors that recycle and control their lives. They still may lack ways to change this condition.
- **Stage Five: Trans-Systemic Thinking.** Individuals in this stage of consciousness can not only see the relationships between their current behaviors and past family-of-origin issues, they are able to choose new behaviors that allow them to change their life-restricting patterns.

Based on his and other research findings, Kegan estimated that about 70% of the adults in the United States are at stage three or below. He called these people the *Traditionalists*. Those in stage four he calls the *Moderns* and those in stage five he labels the *Post-Moderns*. According to his research, approximately 30% of the adult population is approaching or at stage four and less than 1% is approaching or at stage five. Kegan claimed that most people are "in over their heads" because their consciousness has not sufficiently evolved to cope with the mental demands generated by the complexity of modern life.

This research has been valuable in understanding why so many people remain unaware of the effects of their early childhood experiences on their current behavior. It helped us see that until people have reached systemic thinking or trans-systemic thinking, it is difficult for them to break out of the cognitive trap they find themselves caught in.

We concluded from our research cited earlier in this chapter that it is necessary for individuals to understand how their own family-of-origin system has impacted their life. If they do not understand this principle, they are not going to be able to understand other larger, more complex, and seemingly abstract systems and the impact they can have on their lives. This led to the research that validated our hypothesis that when people understand the impact of their family-of-origin system on their current life circumstances, they can better understand the impact that other complex social/political systems have on them.

Transpersonal Theories of Development

The term transpersonal means "through the mask or the ego" to the deeper realms of the human psyche. Transpersonal theories of development emphasize the need to move around, under, over, or through one's ego defenses in order to evolve. The basic idea in transpersonal theory is that each person has an essential or true self that is beyond the ego. Ego defenses cause people to become attached to certain false ideas, feelings, beliefs, and activities that can get them stuck in their development. Without a larger or transpersonal perspective, it may be difficult to see the way through certain intrapersonal and interpersonal conflicts. The transpersonal therapist may include spiritual practices and concepts such as meditation, yoga, breathwork, forgiveness, karma, past lives, reincarnation, nonattachment, and the higher self.

As we synthesized various theories, we realized that our approach needed a solid spiritual foundation. A spiritual component seems to help people move directly into and through their core issues in a permanent manner. All of the following transpersonal theorists contributed to our understanding and the growth of our approach.

Ken Wilber's transpersonal theory of human development helped us expand our knowledge of development into the spiritual and transpersonal realms. His books, *The Atman Project* (1980) and *A Brief History of Everything* (1996), were very helpful in describing the transcendent and spiritual aspects of developmental psychology. Wilber used the concepts of the stages of human development that are "beyond the ego" and the superconscious levels of awareness to chart the transpersonal realms of development.

In addition, Wilber's work motivated us to study other transpersonal and spiritual approaches, including Christian Gnosticism; the teachings of spiritual masters from Eastern philosophies such as Integral Yoga, Taoism, Hinduism, Agni Yoga, and other teachings of the so-called ageless wisdom traditions. This foundation of ancient wisdom helped guide us as we integrated the spiritual and transformative elements of human development into DST.

Leonard Orr and Sondra Ray's rebirthing and breathwork theory and practice also expanded our knowledge of nonverbal and body-oriented methods for processing unhealed shock, trauma, and stress. Their book (Orr & Ray, 1977) on rebirthing taught us about the power of the breath in helping people reconnect with and heal early childhood shock, trauma, and stress, including that connected to their birth. After reading this book, we trained as rebirthers, an experience that helped us understand the importance of natural childbirth techniques that respect the sanctity of the birth process and the need of the child to be in charge of his or her own birth.

Frederick LeBoyer and Igor Charkovsky's nonviolent birthing methods proved to be very useful in understanding how certain patterns can be set in place at birth. The work of LeBoyer (1975), a French obstetrician; Charkovsky (cited in Verny, 1984), a Russian physician; and the work of the American midwifery movement helped us develop therapeutic methods for assisting people in recreating an ideal birth. Further, our study of pre- and perinatal psychology and primal therapy helped us develop a variety of correlations between adult problems and unrecognized and unhealed prenatal shock, trauma, and stress and the effects of these events on the birth process.

Humanistic Theories

Humanistic theories emphasize relationship dynamics and the communication patterns of the individuals who have relationship problems. Interventions, which typically involve helping individuals better understand each other by using clear, straight communication in problem situations, may involve teaching communication skills as a way to prevent relationship problems. The main premise is that people who communicate effectively with each other are likely to have fewer relationship problems and that the problems they do have are more readily solved because they have a foundation of skills to work with them. The humanistic theories emphasize communications models, which we found useful to integrate into our meta-model.

Late in his career, Carl Rogers became very interested in applying his person-centered theory to the resolution of international conflicts. He hypothesized that the negative stereotypes people project on others cause intractable conflicts and might be replaced by caring and empathic relatedness. He successfully demonstrated this in numerous international settings (Rogers & Ryback, 1984).

In the early 1980s, Rogers began to meet with very diverse, large international groups (sometimes as large as several thousand people) who had longstanding intractable conflicts. For example, he met with a large group of Irish Catholics and Protestants in Northern Ireland. He also led cross-cultural workshops in Brazil, Dublin, South Africa, and Hungary. One meeting in Austria included a significant number of diplomats and other government officials. At this meeting, he modeled how diplomats could increase their capacity for empathic understanding and genuineness (1986).

As we integrated reflective listening into our approach for helping people repair the damage of lost resonance, or as we reenacted early developmental shock, trauma, and stress, we found Rogers' hypothesis to be accurate. When people with dysregulated feelings or behaviors treated each other with respect and could express some empathy toward each other, they were able to better understand their differences. As a result, they can better regulate their feelings and behaviors. Reflective listening is now an essential component of DPW, the application of DST.

Rational–Emotive Behavior Theories

Albert Ellis's rational–emotive behavioral therapy (1995) helped us understand the role of irrational or mistaken beliefs as the source of a conflict or problem. He says that irrational beliefs affect the way people approach others in conflict or problem situations. To help people solve their personal problems and resolve their conflicts, Ellis first looked for the underlying irrational belief, such as "I must be liked by everyone I meet. If I am not, there is something wrong with me." According to Ellis's theory, people trying to resolve a conflict need to first look for their own beliefs rather than attacking the other person's beliefs. Ellis said that people need to develop more situational values that avoid imposing rigid standards on themselves and others. His theory particularly impacted our search for more effective ways to help people reframe their conflicts and traumas and to resolve conflicts of values and beliefs.

Traumatology Theories

A whole new field of cognitive–behavioral research known as traumatology began emerging after the end of the Vietnam War. A number of individuals involved in this research provided critical theoretical contributions to our approach.

Charles Figley (1978, 1985, 1986, 2006; Figley & Leventman, 1980; Figley & McCubbin, 1983; Figley & Nash, 2007), a pioneer in the field of traumatology and author of 19 books, helped create *Traumatology,* the first independent, peer-reviewed, scientific/medical journal in the field. After many years of distinguished service at Florida State University as professor and codirector of the Traumatology Institute, he now chairs the Disaster Mental Health program at Tulane University in New Orleans. His early work with veterans helped legitimize the field and created a body of knowledge on which other researchers such as ourselves could build their work.

Donald Meichenbaum's research on PTSD was extremely useful in understanding the role that PTSD plays in causing intractable conflicts. Meichenbaum, one of the chief contributors to cognitive–behavioral theory, has devoted 30 years of clinical research and study to PTSD (1994) and is recognized as one of the leading authorities in the world on this subject. It was his research on PTSD that helped us link intractable conflicts with developmental trauma. Meichenbaum's book presented a thorough analysis of the elements of trauma and discussed how developmental trauma is stored in the mindbody and later activated as symptoms of posttraumatic stress.

Bessel van der Kolk's posttraumatic stress approach is summarized in *Traumatic Stress: The Overwhelming Experience on Mind, Body and Society* (van der Kolk, McFarlane, & Weisaeth, 1996). His approach also contributed significantly to our understanding of the developmental and biological aspects of human adaptation to trauma, including the nature of traumatic memories. His research and clinical knowledge on the treatment of posttraumatic symptoms, particularly those related to brain function and the mechanisms and processes of traumatic memory, were critical in validating our own clinical experiences. His approach was particularly significant in correlating the effects of unrecognized and unhealed developmental shock, trauma, and stress and regression with experiences of intractable conflict.

An Evolutionary Crisis

At a species level, we are facing an evolutionary crisis. The fact that so many human systems are currently stuck in the counterdependency stage of evolution has taxed the resources of humans and of the planet. We desperately need to shift into the independent stage, where we have a higher level of consciousness available in order to address our problems through a systemic lens.

A critical mass of the population must be able to operate at least at level four of Kegan's stages of consciousness and be moving into stage five where they can begin formulating systemic solutions to the problems of inadequate natural resources. Many people in places of power, such as corporate CEOs and government officials, still operate out of reptilian consciousness and exploit others and work only for their own benefit.

People holding a nurturing humanitarian vision for the planet must convince others that a massive collective shift in consciousness is necessary for us to evolve and perhaps even survive as a species. Lipton sees this evolutionary leap from a biological perspective, arguing that we must move from the reptilian stage of evolution into the mammalian stage. This means we need to collectively give up our oil-addicted lifestyle (oil is a reptilian-era fuel). We must use our mammalian consciousness to protect future generations and to shift to use of renewable energy sources.

There is strong evidence that we may be closer than we realize to the critical mass needed to make an evolutionary shift to the independent stage of human evolution and finally to the interdependent stage. We believe that learning how to identify and heal our developmental shock, trauma, and stress is an important step that will accelerate this evolutionary shift. This shift will ensure that the decisions that are made to protect the future of this planet will involve systemic thinking.

Native Americans were able to do this many centuries ago, so it is not an entirely new way of decision making. For example, the Iroquois Nation, particularly the Oneida Tribe, even today require both the tribal leaders and its members to consider the impact on the next seven generations when making decisions (Oneida Indian Nation, February 18, 2007). This kind of forward thinking is necessary on a global level to move into the independent and interdependent stages of human evolution.

PART TWO

LOVEvolution

The unseen force of the universe
is unconditional love.
It is available to everyone with a heart
open to giving and receiving it.
When your heart is open you evolve.
We call this … LOVEvolution.

CHAPTER THREE

LOVEvolution and the Essential Developmental Processes of the Codependent Stage of Individual Development

LOVEvolution and Its Role in Human Evolution

Unconditional love is the most powerful energy force in the universe. Long known to lovers, parents, pet owners, artists, and musicians, the power of love to change the world is now being acknowledged by cutting edge American scientists such as Bruce Lipton (2005) and Gregg Braden (2004) and Russian scientist Pjotr Gariaev and his colleagues (Fosar & Bludorf, 2001). These scientists described unconditional love as a subtle and invisible energy also known as *torsion wave energy* that fills the 97% of our universe once believed to be empty. Metaphysicist David Wilcock called it *source energy* and said it has intelligence and *consciousness* (2007). In the Far East, religious traditions refer to this energy as the *ground of being,* and various Eastern philosophies and martial arts refer to it as *ki* and *chi.*

The central premise of this book is that when you are able to receive unconditional love from this source energy and give it to others, you are able to evolve. We call this process LOVEvolution. We believe that it wires us for a full mammalian experience and the ability to be both deeply intimate and psychologically separate.

We see *LOVEvolution* and *developmental shock, trauma, and stress* as parallel tracks of development that are directed by cellular consciousness. The developmental shock, trauma, and stress track, characterized by emotions involving anger, helplessness, and hopelessness, wires people's brains and nervous systems for environments high in chaos and for emotional separation. Those with nervous systems wired for this track likely experienced developmental shock during the first trimester of prenatal development or at birth. They also may have experienced shock, trauma, or stress caused by the lack of secure bonding with their mother during the first 6–8 months of life and while separating emotionally from their mother and father between the ages of 6–8 months and 36 months. Early experiences of shock, trauma, or stress impair people's ability to engage socially and emotionally, causing them to close their hearts and to play out dysfunctional drama triangle dynamics with their parents, who are either not connected to each other, are not connected to the child, or both (Weinhold & Weinhold, 2008a, 2008b). We discuss this process in greater detail in Chapters 5, 6, and 7.

The love-based LOVEvolution track, characterized by positive emotions of affection and optimism (LeDoux, 2002), wires people's brains and nervous systems for limbic resonance and emotional intimacy. Those living primarily on this track are capable of sustained experiences of deep emotional and spiritual connection with both parents, even while in the womb. This allows them to engage socially and emotionally so that they can experience what we call the divine triangle or the functional family triangle, in which parents are bonded with each other and with the child. With this strong relational foundation, children are able to individuate from their parents, to keep their hearts open, and to experience the luminosity and pure potential of their spiritual selves.

The divine triangle is a tightly connected family structure in which children are able to complete the essential developmental processes related to bonding and separation. In contrast, experiences of the drama triangle involve a fracture in the emotional connections between 1) the child and the mother, 2) the child and the father, or 3) between the mother and the father, or even a combination of fractures. These relational fractures, which condition children to two-against-one dynamics containing persecutor, victim, and rescuer roles, interfere with completing the essential developmental processes related to bonding and separation. In this fragmented drama triangle, children are most able to get their needs met by playing the victim role.

While these two tracks of development are not hardwired into the brain and nervous system until between the ages of 10 to 14 years old (Huttenlocher, 1984, pp. 488–496), the critical juncture point in these two tracks is between 10 and 12 months (Diamond & Doar, 1989, pp. 271–294). The LOVEvolution track is an optimal or ideal model of human development that advances both individual and collective evolution. The developmental shock, trauma, and stress track stalls individual and collective evolution. Figure 3.1 shows these two evolutionary tracks and how they both bifurcate at about 10–12 months.

The ability to maintain personally relevant intimate bonds with other humans is vital for evolutionary survival (van Lancker, 1991). LOVEvolution is synonymous with our optimal model of human development, with Porges's concept of the social engagement system (SES), with Schore's concept of emotional synchrony,

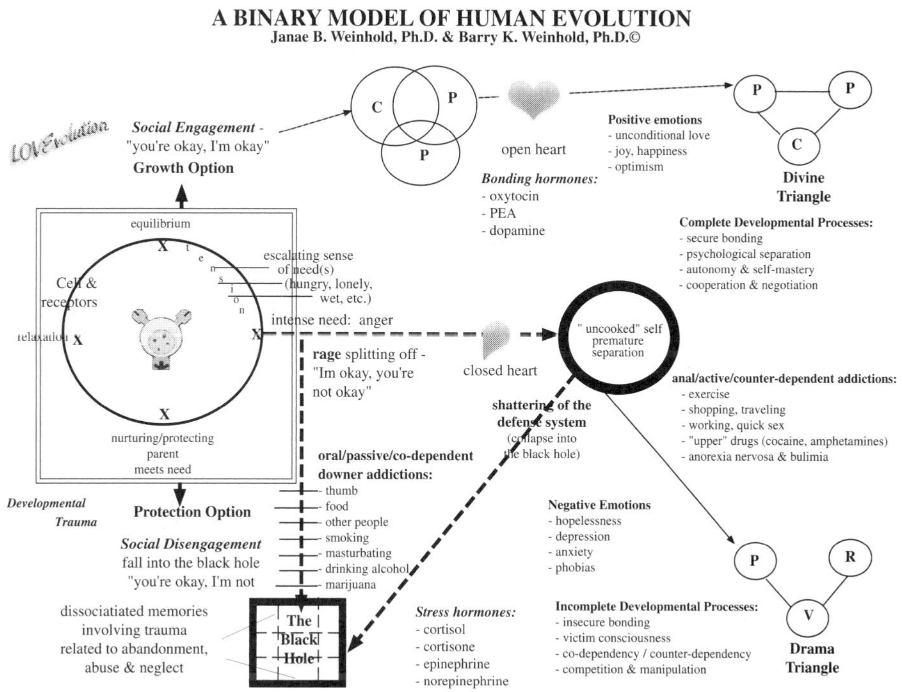

FIGURE 3.1

A Binary Model of Human Evolution

and Lipton's concept of cellular consciousness. All of these terms recognize that humans evolve because of their experiences of unconditional love. When unconditional love is absent or unattainable because of unhealed shock, trauma, or stress, it delays and can even totally stop development.

Our LOVEvolution paradigm also recognizes that evolution occurs when an organism or system becomes so filled with unconditional love that it must divide and create more cells to contain the excess energy. It is possible to conceptualize evolution at the level of the Creator by imagining yourself as pinched-off pieces of God. Or you can think about LOVEvolution as a force flowing between two people who become so expanded by their experience of unconditional love that they want to create something together that symbolically contains energy from their experience of spiritual union. This vessel might be a child or a creative project such as a beautiful home, a garden, a book, a painting, or a shared transformative experience such as a spiritual pilgrimage.

In our paradigm, all energy can be measured and assigned a frequency. Energy coming from anger, shame, judgment, and fear, for example, vibrates at a very low frequency, while the vibrational frequency of unconditional love is very high. By understanding the principle of vibrational frequencies, it is possible to make conscious choices about how to use your energy in relationships. This ultimately determines whether you evolve or devolve.

Energetic exchanges of unconditional love between humans and between humans and animals, plants, minerals, and the earth create shared experiences of deep resonance. Also known as partnership relationships, these shared experiences reinforce and unify our perceptual structure of reality.

Partnership relationships with long-term experiences of shared resonance and unconditional love can help raise the frequency of both parties to a higher level. Individuals who experience such relationships also radiate the energy of unconditional love to others and widen their circle of resonance and emotional attunements. This helps raise the vibrational frequency of everyone who comes in contact with them. Unconditional love energy can also be transmitted through books, videos, and audiotapes. Sharing this resonance with others can help advance evolution.

Understanding the concept of LOVEvolution also helps make meaning of the experiences and events of a person's life. Once you understand how the quality of your relational interactions can either help or hinder your evolution and the evolution of others, you can consciously choose how you want to interact with others.

The principles of LOVEvolution also help you understand that your world is not random and that it seems that way only because of your limited perceptions. The concept of LOVEvolution supports the perception that life and all of creation are unified and organized around biological patterns containing specific geometric structures, values, and beliefs. In other words, LOVEvolution provides a framework and language for understanding not only your evolution, but also that of everyone and everything around you.

One of our most interesting discoveries in reviewing the scientific literature on human development for this book was how many researchers are now using the language of quantum sciences to help bridge the gap between psychology, science, and religion. It was a real pleasure to find some of the distinctions among these fields disappearing and to see the emergence of a unified paradigm describing the structure and meaning of human experience.

Quantum Physics, DNA, and LOVEvolution

Developmental psychologist and visionary Joseph Chilton Pearce (1998) has been working collaboratively with the HeartMath Institute in a new field known as *neurocardiology,* which recognizes the heart is not just a muscle pumping blood throughout the body, but also is a sensory organ. The heart is now seen as an extensive nervous system with a sophisticated information encoding and processing center that this field describes as the *heart-brain.*

Pearce said there is a "brain" in the heart, whose ganglia are linked to every major organ in the body and to the entire muscle spindle system that uniquely enables humans to express their emotions. About half of the heart's neural cells are involved in translating information sent to it from all over the body so that it can keep the body working as one harmonious whole. The other half makes up a very large, unmediated neural connection with the emotional brain in our head and carries on a 24-hour-a-day dialogue between the heart and the brain of which we are largely unaware.

The Institute of HeartMath in California conducted a remarkable experiment to determine the effect of different emotions on DNA (McCraty, Atkinson, & Tomasino, 2003). In this experiment, some human placenta DNA (the most pristine form of DNA) was placed in a container from which they could measure changes in the DNA. One vial of DNA was given to each of 28 participants. Each participant had been trained on how to generate and feel certain feelings, and they each were asked to emit strong emotions. What was discovered was that the DNA actually changed its shape according to the feelings that the researchers emitted.

When the researchers felt gratitude, love, and appreciation in the presence of these vials, in every case the DNA responded by relaxing, and the strands unwound and became longer. When the researchers felt anger, fear, frustration, or stress, in every case the DNA responded by tightening up. It became shorter and switched off many of its receptor codes. If you have ever felt "shut down" by negative emotions, now you know why: your body was physically shut down. In every case, when the researchers emitted feelings of love, joy, gratitude, and appreciation, the shutdown of the DNA codes reversed and the codes were switched back on again.

The HeartMath researchers then followed this experiment by testing HIV-positive patients. They discovered that feelings of love, gratitude, and appreciation created 300,000 times the resistance to the disease in these patients than when they were not exposed to those feelings. Individuals trained in deep love were able to change the shape of their DNA. Braden (2000) said this information illustrates the presence of a newly recognized form of energy that connects all of creation. This energy, which is similar to that described earlier by Gariaev (1997) and Wilcock (2007), appears to be a tightly woven web that connects all matter in the universe. Essentially, we are able to influence this web of creation through the vibrational frequency we emit.

The research of the HeartMath Institute (Pearce, 1998) revealed several other important findings. The first is that about 60–65% of all cells in the heart are neural cells—exactly the same as those in the brain. They function in precisely the same way. They monitor and maintain control of the entire mind/brain/body physical process, as well as the direct connections between the heart and the emotional, cognitive structures of the brain.

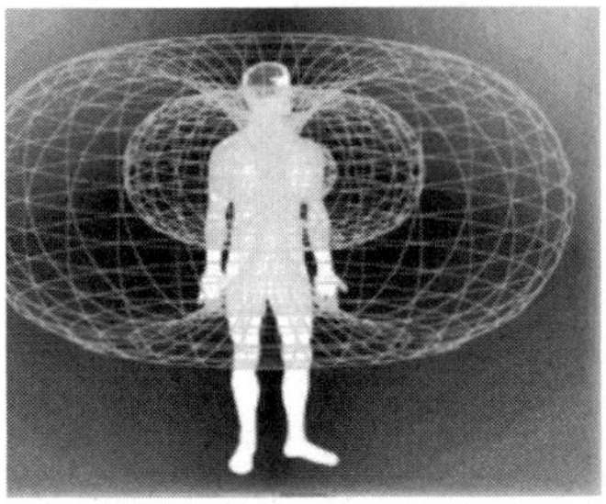

FIGURE 3.2
Electromagnetic Field

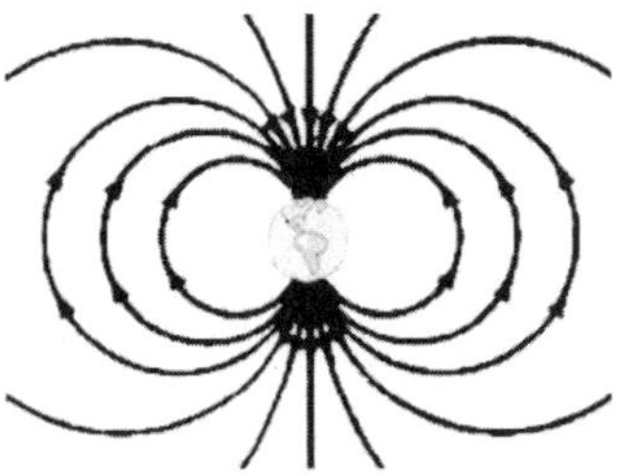

FIGURE 3.3
Electromagnetic Field

Their second discovery was that the cells within the adult human heart have an exceptionally large electrical output. The rhythmic coherence of the beating heart generates some 2.5 watts of electrical activity with each heartbeat. This electrical activity is 50 to 60 times greater than the electrical energy of the brain and is enough energy to light a small electric light bulb.

This also creates a pulsating magnetic field that radiates outward and operates like a protective electromagnetic field around the body identical to the electromagnetic field around the earth. Figures 3.2 and 3.3 show these two electromagnetic fields measured by sensitive instruments.

The electromagnetic field of the heart surrounds the body from a distance of 12 to 25 feet outward and encompasses power waves such as radio and light waves, which comprise the principle source of information upon which the body and brain build our neural conception and perception of the world itself. The electromagnetic field of the heart produces, holographically, the same field as the one produced by the earth and the entire solar system.

The HeartMath Institute's third important finding is that the heart is the major endocrine glandular structure of the body and produces hormones that profoundly affect the operations of body, brain, and mind. Their fourth discovery is that direct and unmediated neural connections exist between the heart and the emotional structures of the limbic brain. More importantly, these neural connections go up through the amygdala into the prefrontal or "angelic" lobes—the newest part of the human brain. Pearce described this system that connects the body, the heart, and brain as the "holographic heart" (1998).

The significant role of the heart permeates virtually all of the most recent research on attachment and bonding. Other developmental researchers such as James Prescott (1997), Bruce Lipton (2005), Stephen Porges and Sue Carter (2003), and Allen Schore (2003a, b) also used binary models anchored in biology, physiology, neurology, and cardiology to explain the subtleties of human behavior. Their research findings parallel and support our own binary model of development in which the evolution of the individual is directed through experiences of LOVEvolution and the devolution of the individual is directed by unrecognized and unhealed experiences of developmental shock, trauma, and stress.

Our Model of Optimal Human Evolution

In this chapter, we look more closely at the LOVEvolution track of our binary model of human evolution. It draws from the work of Jean Piaget (1951), a Swiss philosopher, natural scientist, and developmental psychologist known for his studies of children and his theory of cognitive development, and Carl Jung (1968), a Swiss psychiatrist and founder of Jungian psychology who proposed and developed the concept of individuation.

We see completed individuation as the most important developmental marker in the evolution of the individual. It means that the individual must have achieved secure bonding and attachment in the first year of life and then have successfully navigated the process of becoming a separate, fully functioning human being by age around age 3, which is called the *psychological birth.*

Our model of human evolution contains four stages: codependent, counterdependent, independent, and interdependent. Each stage contains essential developmental processes that must be completed in order to move on to the next. If they are not completed, development in the next stage is delayed, slowing down the evolution process. Table 3.1 shows these four stages and the essential developmental processes for individuals.

LOVEvolution and the positive effects of a reciprocal love dialogue begin with the daily interactions between parents and their children. In this book, we show in much detail the profound effects that consistent experiences of unconditional love have on the development of the human body, brain, and psyche starting with gestation, birth, and early childhood. While it may seem to some a rather "flaky" concept, we ground the LOVEvolution track of our binary model in the recent multidisciplinary research findings that are emerging in the fields of physiology, quantum biology, and developmental psychology. Virtually all of the individuals and groups now conducting this research emphasize the importance of early secure bonding and healthy human relationships for the future of the human race.

Our developmental model is deeply rooted in matrifocal values similar to those identified by cultural psychologist James Prescott (1997) and by anthropologist Riane Eisler in her "partnership" model of cultures (1987, 2003). It is much more difficult for individuals to complete our four-stage model of optimal development in cultures that are based on patrifocal or "dominator" values. Patrifocal and matrifocal values, unfortunately, are still in conflict in many cultures, making it difficult to find solid cultural support for this evolutionary process.

Virtually every person and group who has studied early childhood development now agrees that the template for an individual's physiology, biology, and psychology begins at conception and that the very earliest relational dynamics between the child and his or her parents are crucial in the building of this template. Scientists from many related fields are now joining hands with developmental psychologists and parents to create a new paradigm for understanding the subtle nature

TABLE 3.1

The Developmental Stages and the Essential Developmental Processes of Individual Evolution

Stage of Development and Primary Task	Essential Developmental Processes in Each Stage	Suggested Experiences for Completing the Essential Developmental Processes of Each Stage
Codependent (conception to 6 to 8 months) **Bonding and Attachment**	• Mother receives good prenatal care and support • Experience a nonviolent birth with immediate interventions to heal any shocks or birth trauma • Experience secure bonding/attachment with mother and/or other adult caregivers • Build primal trust with both parents through a consistent resonant connection • Learn emotional resiliency skills • Create a secure internal model of self vs. other • Build healthy emotional communication and social engagement skills with both parents and others • Achieve secure bonding experiences with siblings and extended family • Promote effective communication and social engagement skills with parents and others	• Mother maintains a high-quality diet and reduces environmental stressors to prevent the risk of shock and excess cortisol production during pregnancy • Parents plan for and want the child • Parents build prenatal relationship with the child • Parents use nonviolent birthing practices • Mother nurses and rooms-in with her child at the hospital; prolonged skin-to-skin contact with both parents in first 12–24 hours following birth • Family leave policies allow both parents to stay home without financial stress • Mother receives effective postnatal emotional andphysical support • Mother provides nurturing, respectful touch; eye contact andgazing, singing andspeaking in loving ways • Child gets timely emotional and tactile comfort to help heal developmental traumas caused by disruptions in resonant connection to parents • Child receives unconditional love from both parents • Child is mirrored and validated for his/her essence by both parents • Immediate andextended family members provide consistent nurturing and empathic contact • Parents provide comfortable and protective environment to meet child's needs for safety and survival as he or she begins to crawl or walk
Counterdependent (6–8 to 36 months) **Separation and Individuation**	• Achieve complete psychological separation from both parents • Learn to explore one's environment in safe ways • Learn to trust and regulate one's own thoughts,	• Parents offer timely help to heal any narcissistic wounds or developmental shocks or traumas in both themselves and their child that disturb resonance • Parents give permission and support to the child to safely explore his or her environment • Give the child twice as many "yes's" as "no's" as he or she explores

(continued)

TABLE 3.1 *(continued)*

Stage of Development and Primary Task	Essential Developmental Processes in Each Stage	Suggested Experiences for Completing the Essential Developmental Processes of Each Stage
Counterdependent *(continued)*	feelings, behaviors in socially appropriate ways • Internalize appropriate physical and social limits • Develop healthy narcissism • Resolve internal conflicts between oneness and separateness • Bond with self • Continue to build secure internal working model • Successfully complete the psychological birth process	• Parents arrange the home environment to provide safety for the child to explore • Parents help the child internally regulate his or her emotions, especially shame • Parents help child identify self-vs.-other needs • Parents model for the child appropriate ways to meet his or her needs • Adults help child to quickly reestablish the resonance with his or her mother when it is disrupted • Parents use nonshaming responses in setting limits and giving consequences • Caregivers offer empathy and compassion as the child learns to regulate his or her conflicting emotions, thoughts and behaviors • Caregivers authentically mirror the child's essence • Caregivers support the child in becoming a separate individual and trusting his or her internal impulses • Parents provide positive support for the child's efforts to develop an autonomous self
Independent (3 to 6 years) **Mastery of Self & Environment**	• Master basic self-care • Master the process of becoming a functionally autonomous individual separate from parents • Develop object constancy • Develop trust in core values and beliefs • Achieve secure bonding experiences with nature • Learn effective social engagement skills • Develop secure internal working model of self vs. other • Achieve secure bonding with peers	• Parents rearrange home environment to support mastery of self-care for the child (eating, dressing, and toilet training) • Parents support the child in developing effective internal limits and consequences • Parents teach the child appropriate ways to defer gratification of his or her wants and needs • Parents support the child in learning effective emotional self-regulation and control • Immediate and extended family members offer the child nurturing, supportive, and consistent contact • Parents support the child in learning to trust his or her inner sense of wisdom and guidance • Parents provide child with experiences for safe exploration of nature

(continued)

TABLE 3.1 *(continued)*

Stage of Development and Primary Task	Essential Developmental Processes in Each Stage	Suggested Experiences for Completing the Essential Developmental Processes of Each Stage
Independent *(continued)*		• Parents support the child in developing sensory relationships with nature • Parents provide the child with reciprocal social interactions with other children • Parents teach the child cross-relational thinking, including empathy and respect for others • Parental support the child in developing cause-and-effect problem-solving skills • Adults model partnership solutions to conflicts
Interdependent (6 to 29 years) **Cooperation and Negotiation Skills**	• Learn how to cooperate with others • Learn how to negotiate with others to get needs met • Learn to accept responsibility for personal behaviors and life experiences • Experience secure bonding with peers and other adults • Develop a social conscience • Achieve a secure bonding experiences with the main culture • Develop a secure bonding experiences with the planet • Live out of an authentic adult self • Achieve secure bonding with own children • Understand the influence of incomplete developmental processes on own life and the how to heal developmental shocks or traumas successfully	• Parents model effective cooperative social engagement skills in couple, family, and peer relationships • Teach the child negotiation skills to get his or her needs met in healthy ways • Parents seek solutions to the child's conflicts that honor the needs of all parties involved • Parents teach the child the importance of keeping his or her relationship agreements • Provide adult models that can teach the child empathy and compassion for others • Provide adults who can teach the child intuitive language and thinking skills • Provide the child with nurturing, supportive, and consistent contact from immediate and extended family members • Teach the child how to build sustain-able relationships with other adults and suitable ways to find a find primary love partner • Provide adult input on the values of the child's cultural group and teach the child how to overcome any limits imposed by family and culture • Adults encourage the child to develop an internalized safety parent by allowing him or her to engage in safe risk-taking behaviors • Teach the child how to find personal meaning and a personal mission within the context of the "global family" • Teach the child how to heal his or her developmental shocks or traumas • Parents model systemic and trans-systemic thinking for their children

of parent–child relationships. Most importantly, they are translating their findings into a new language that parents and others can understand and are creating more sophisticated tools that support conscious conception, nonviolent birthing, and enlightened child-rearing practices.

Conscious Parenting

Cell biologist Bruce Lipton and his colleagues in the field of pre- and perinatal psychology are members of this new paradigm. They believe that the energetic structure of an individual's template actually begins prior to conception. Regardless of the exact point, it begins very early—much earlier than once believed. The first stage of our model of individual development, codependency, begins with conception and goes through the age of 6–8 months. During this period, the essential developmental task involves creating a secure bond between the child and the parents.

In Lipton's book, *The Biology of Belief* (2005), his chapter on "Conscious Parenting: Parents as Genetic Engineers," described how parents act as "genetic engineers" during the months prior to conception. In the final stages of egg and sperm maturation, a process of *genomic imprinting* adjusts the activity of specific groups of genes that will shape the character of the child yet to be conceived (Reik & Walter, 2001, cited in Lipton, 2005, p. 172; Surani, 2000).

Lipton's interpretation of the research in this area was that, during the process of genomic imprinting, what is happening in the lives of parents has a profound influence on the mind and body of their child. He agreed with Thomas Verny (Verny & Weintraub, 2002, cited in Lipton, 2005, p. 172) in that "it makes a difference whether we are conceived in love, haste or hate, and whether a mother wants to be pregnant."

An impressive body of research on prenatal development documents the impact of parental attitudes at the time of conception on the subsequent development of the fetus. Studies show that unborn children are energetically attuned to their mother's every action, thought, and feeling. From the moment of conception, the experience in the womb shapes the brain and lays the groundwork for the personality, emotional temperament, and higher thought.

Mothers and fathers, Lipton said, are in the conception and pregnancy business together, even though it is the mother who carries the child. According to Lipton, what the father does profoundly affects the mother, which in turn affects the developing child (2005, p. 173). The essence of conscious parenting is that both parents have important responsibilities for fostering healthy, intelligent, productive, and joy-filled children.

Some parents report actually having transpersonal encounters with their babies *before* they have been conceived. They find themselves drawn into these experiences through vivid dreams, visions, and telepathic encounters that come weeks, months, or even years in advance of physical conception (Chamberlain, 2003). Some parents are even able to begin communing with the soul of the incoming child and negotiate the appropriate time for conception (Robertson, 2005).

Prenatal Bonding

Verny's pioneering research in pre- and perinatal psychology indicates that babies remember everything and are deeply impacted by the events around them. Unfortunately, they are only able to communicate this telepathically, a phenomenon not yet widely understood or accepted. Research from the field of pre- and perinatal psychology also indicates that memory and interactive response patterns begin by the third month of gestation. An impressive body of information from other researchers such as Chamberlain (1998, 1999, 2003), Emerson (1993, 1996, 2007), Verny (1984, 1988) and Hepper (1996) now describes prenatal development in considerable detail.

Because of the significance of pre- and perinatal experiences in forming the personality, they also contribute to the development of the child's internal working model of reality. Prenates who are exposed to environmental toxins taken in by the mother and then transmitted from the mother through the placenta, such as nicotine, alcohol, and prescription or illicit drugs often develop addictions to these same substances as adults (Kellogg, 1991).

A recent study analyzed the umbilical cord blood from 10 randomly selected newborns in U.S. hospitals. These tests detected a total of 287 chemicals, and they concluded "of the 287 chemicals we detected … we know that 180 cause cancer in humans or animals, 217 are toxic to the brain and nervous system, and 208 cause birth defects or abnormal development in animal tests" (Houlihan et al., 2005). The infant's developing brain experiences these substances as threats and begins wiring expectations of danger into his or her cellular defenses. One of the important findings from a cross-section of pre- and perinatal research is the correlation between birth traumas and difficulties in sustaining adult relationships.

Our own breathwork therapy and the experiences of many of our clients support this research. Many of our clients report having birth memories in which they heard exact conversations between adults who were present at their birth, while others said they knew what the adults who were present were thinking. After their breathwork therapy, several clients were able to verify the accuracy of these birth memories with their parents. This anecdotal information helped us validate that newborns are able to tune into the thoughts and feelings of those around them.

Ideally, the bonding process begins prior to conception, and the prospective parents have information about the essential developmental processes related to conception, gestation, birth, and the first 6–8 months of life. Perhaps they conceive using practices of conscious conception and gestation. In this little-known body of knowledge, the mother pays particular attention to her diet and nutritional state prior to conception. She avoids alcohol; drugs of all kinds; and chaotic, conflictual, or stressful environments that activate her adrenal stress response (ASR) and pump cortisol and other stress-related hormones into her bloodstream and into the bloodstream of the unborn child.

Pre- and perinatal psychology pioneer, William Emerson, reported working with clients having problems with aggression and violence. When regressed in therapy, they discovered memories from the time of their conception involving traumatic issues in their family or immediate surroundings. The most frequently mentioned shocks or traumas involved forced sex, including manipulated sex, date rape, and rape; substance abuse; physical abuse; dismal familial, social, or cultural conditions; and personal or cultural shame, such as having been conceived out of wedlock. Other of Emerson's regressed clients reported biological memories related to conception involving encounters as sperm and/or eggs that contained intense aggression, annihilation, death, power, and/or rejection (1996).

Emerson (1996) also reported having clients with implantation memories. Implantation is the biological process whereby the conceptus attaches itself to the uterine wall—a vital and precarious stage of embryological development. Prior to and during implantation, regressed patients reported that they experienced the terror of being near death. Some reported feeling unwanted and that they had no place to go, no place to belong, and "decided" at that moment that the world was a hostile and unsafe place for them.

Once the pregnancy begins, the mother needs to focus as much of her time as possible on her thoughts and pay attention to uplifting things that keep her body producing a constant state of endorphins and hormones. This helps both her and her gestating baby experience pleasure and harmony. As the unborn baby becomes larger, both parents gradually withdraw from the outer world, and they attune more deeply with their child.

The womb is the "first school," and gestating babies are alert, aware, and attentive to social cues involving voice, touch, and music. The parents need to sing and talk to their baby, fill their home with beautiful and inspiring music, rub the baby's body through the mother's belly, and observe his or her cycles of waking and sleeping. They should talk with the baby about the upcoming transition to the outer world and share their excitement and anticipation about his or her arrival outside the womb.

Ideally, parents should wait for their baby to signal his or her readiness to be born, knowing that his or her brain will secrete the hormones that start the labor process. They empower their child to direct the process, and they then follow his or her lead in each moment of the final stages of gestation into the birthing process. They refuse well-meaning advice from grandparents or medically trained people who recommend inducing birth, using anesthesia, and other invasive birth practices unless absolutely necessary.

Instead, they use the tools learned in their natural birthing classes to help them relax and surrender deeply to the birth experience. Having cleared their own birth traumas, they are able to follow their child's birth journey without becoming fearful or getting triggered. They also strive to trust those who are assisting them through the birthing experience.

To reassure their parents and close friends, the parents choose birth facilitators who have access to medical support for backup, in case it might become needed. The parents do not discount the possibility that their child might need the karmic experience of a breech or cesarean birth and make arrangements for those possibilities should they become birthing options. At each step in the birth process, the parents and birth facilitators focus on staying in energetic attunement with each other and the baby and quickly refocus if something takes them out of harmony.

During the birth, invited friends and family surround the couple and infant with a field of unconditional love and support. If anyone in the support circle gets triggered during the birthing process, they quietly leave, isolate their energy from the group, and work on themselves. Ideally, all those in the birthing room focus on sustaining the field of unconditional love to support the couple, child, and those assisting with the birth. This helps both the mother and baby relax through the twists and turns of the birthing process.

Once the child emerges from the womb, the child is wiped clean of the birthing fluids, immediately placed naked on the mother's belly, and the umbilical cord is allowed to stop pulsing on its own. Only then does the father cut it. Both parents talk to the child during this process and acknowledge the cutting of the cord as the first separation from the mother. They both talk to the baby and reassure him or her of their support in adjusting to being outside the mother.

Then the parents and birth assistants give the newborn time to crawl up the mother's belly to her breasts for the first feeding. Videos of this process are amazing, as they show very clearly that the child knows exactly what to do if given the time and opportunity. Marshall Klaus (1995) found that babies who were placed on their mother's chest and received extended eye contact could find their mother's breast and begin nursing within 25 minutes. Skeptics quickly become believers when they see videos of a newborn using her sense of smell to guide her as she slowly climbs her mother's belly to her breast. This process of rejoining with the mother for nurturing and sustenance completes a circuit of connection that moves them from their internal experience of bonding to their external experience of bonding.

Research by Klaus (1995) and his colleagues regarding conditions for optimal bonding called for extended skin-to-skin contact between the newborn and parents during the first 36 hours after birth. This includes suckling during the first hour following birth and arrangements that keep the parents and child together in the same room during this period.

After the child is born, the parents focus on maintaining this state of emotional synchrony. The developmental process of bonding is more achievable if the parents do not have worries about their jobs, finances, and obligations to other children or family members. Stressors like these can distract them from the critical first parenting and can cause fluctuations in the harmonic equilibrium between them and their child.

Unfortunately, not nearly enough parents have financial and social resources that allow them to withdraw from the outside world and focus totally on parenting their child immediately after birth. This is why it is so important to have national family leave policies that permit the mother and father to stay at home for a period of time while their jobs are being held for them and they are being paid. Longer family leave time for both parents would, in our estimation, have a huge impact on advancing human evolution. Most fathers, unfortunately, must return to work within a few days and mothers within a few weeks or months. It is very difficult to make these rapid transitions in caregiving without inflicting at least some developmental shock, trauma, and stress on the child.

The Bonding Cycle

During the first days, weeks, and months after birth, newborns go through many cycles of waking and sleeping that are driven primarily by hunger, the need for pleasure and nurturing, and the need for relief from discomfort and pain. Their extremely sensitive nervous systems respond to even subtle sensations and energy. This is very visible in something known as the "startle reflex" in which infants suddenly brings their legs and arms together toward their chest.

These cycles of waking and sleeping are regulated by the baby's need to relieve tension in the nervous system. When babies feel the first pangs of hunger, they begin making small noises and movements. As the internal tension grows, so do the noises and movements. Eventually the escalating tension reaches a point where they release a very clear cry indicating that they have a need. This cry signals the parents that it is time to provide something to meet this need. Figure 3.4 illustrates the phases of the bonding cycle.

Because babies' nervous systems are still developing, a newborn's cry does not give the parents much information, so they may have to attempt a series of trial-and-error interventions. As the parents and baby attune with each other more deeply and the parents learn to recognize nuances in the child's cries, they are able to meet the baby's needs more quickly and effectively. This helps the child relax more quickly and go into a deep state of equilibrium. Then the cycle starts all over again.

The sleep and waking cycles can be very short in newborns, particularly if they are small—sometimes only two hours. This disrupts the parents' regular sleep cycles so that they often do not get the amount of REM sleep they need in order to maintain their energy and sense of well-being. Outside support for the parents during this time is very important. It can prevent parents from becoming overly fatigued, cranky, depressed, or emotionally unavailable during this important period of development.

Bonding not only involves both parents' abilities to reestablish emotional synchronization after a disturbing event, it also involves the ability to create

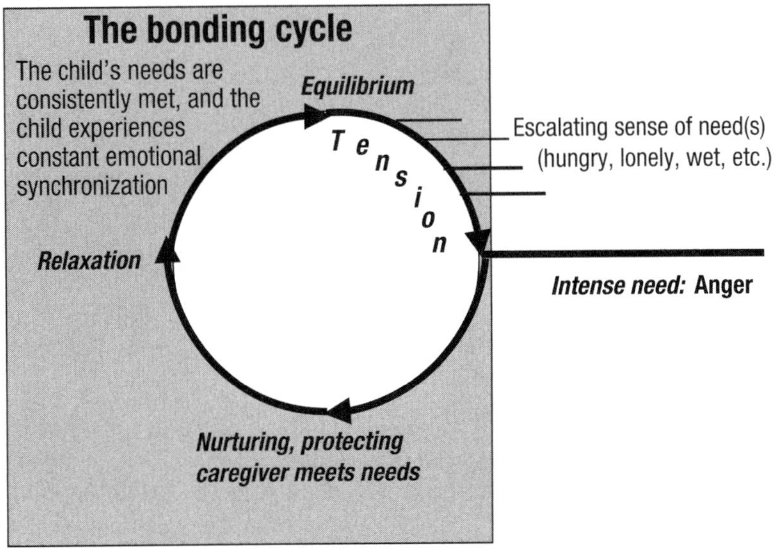

FIGURE 3.4

The Bonding Cycle

positive and upbeat play states. This stimulates the child's endocrine system to secrete "upper" hormones such as oxytocin and dopamine. Periods of positive emotional stimulation create a sense of safety for infants and help develop positively charged curiosity that supports the exploration of novel emotional and physical experiences (Schore, 2003b, p. 40).

One of the recognized causes of shaken baby syndrome is that angry or frustrated parents or caregivers cannot cope with persistent crying. Many newborns cry because they are releasing tension related to birth trauma and may actually be suffering from birth-caused dislocated shoulders, necks, and hips. Dr. G. Gutmann, a German medical researcher specializing in the treatment of traumatic birth syndrome, discovered that more than 80% of the infants he examined shortly after birth were suffering from an injury to the cervical spine and the neck (1987).

Babies who suffer a traumatic birth are more difficult for parents to attune with. Their inability to provide comfort and stop the child's pain often frustrates them and, after extended periods of unsuccessful comforting, can cause them to energetically disengage from the child. Some parents may even perceive their child as not liking them because of their own inability to soothe the child at these times. All of this disturbs the process of emotional attunement and may cause a developmental shock, trauma, or stress.

Schore's Model of Attachment

Schore's research provides a comprehensive lens for understanding the complex natures of both human attachment and developmental shock, trauma, and stress. Schore and some other developmental psychologists use the term *attachment.* We use the term *bonding*. In this book we use these terms interchangeably. Schore's groundbreaking research recognizes the biological perspective of attachment and correlates psychological events with biological processes. His three books on regulation theory (1999, 2003a, 2003b) used the language of quantum physics to describe the nuances of parent–child interactions that, over time, facilitate children's experiences of either growth or protection.

Schore's regulation theory, which parallels the concept of orbital resonance, defines attachment as "biological synchronicity between organisms" (2003b, p. 39), a term that can be applied not only to human and mammalian behavior but also to the cells, as Lipton suggested. Schore's theory described how the exchange of positive emotions between infants and their caregivers creates a safe environment that stimulates the development of the orbito-frontal portion of the right prefrontal cortex of the brain.

The orbito-frontal regions are not functional at birth, but develop gradually through a process of energetic imprinting, and reach a critical period of maturation between the ages of 10 and 12 months. This part of the brain is involved in emotional control. By about this time, children have developed their internal working models of reality. This is critical information for parents, as it affirms the importance of their parenting during their child's first year. If this part of the brain does not develop during its sensitive period, children will lack the ability to regulate their emotions. This loss is the most far-reaching effect of early developmental shock, trauma, and stress (Schore, 2003a, p. 208).

Eckhard Hess's research also indicated that 2 months marks a critical developmental milestone in the occipital cortex of infants' brains that dramatically increases their social and emotional capacities (Yamada et al., 2000). For the first time, they can fully see their parents and make direct eye contact (Lipari, 2000). The mother's emotionally expressive face is now the most potent visual stimulus in the infant's environment, and the intense interest in her face, especially her eyes, leads the baby to track them and to engage in periods of intense mutual gazing. The large pupils in infants' eyes act as a nonverbal communication device that elicits caregiving responses in adults (Hess, 1975). Schore believes that by the age of 2 months, mothers and infants are already exchanging high levels of cognitive and social information through their face-to-face interactions. The intense periods of mutual gazing are part of Schore's model of attachment and affect regulations.

Schore suggested that attachment is the right-brain regulation of biological synchronicity between parents and children (2003b, p. 41). The right hemisphere, which matures before the left, is specifically impacted by early social experiences with the parents, particularly during experiences of intense elation. Its development is critical to achieve right-brain synchrony between the child and parents.

You might think about the internal working model of reality as a computer program for navigating the world. It contains beliefs and expectations about how others will respond to your needs in certain situations and about the amount of power and influence you have in changing your external reality. For example, the internal working model of bonded children tells them that they are worthy of love and respect; that others are trustworthy and dependable; and that the social world is safe, reliable, and consistent. They expect to be loved and cared for and that people will respond respectfully to their expectations. If this need is not met, these children are direct in indicating how they feel and what it is they want or need.

The right hemisphere stores the internal working model database regarding children's relationships with their parents. It also contains mechanisms that help children maintain positive emotions even when experiencing inconsistent care from adults. Schore believes that it is the output from the mother's right brain hemisphere that regulates the infant's right brain mechanisms and that it does this through emotionally synchronized, psychobioligically attuned face-to-face, skin-to-skin, brain-to-brain interactions. This synchronized system controls infants' regulatory, homeostatic, and bonding functions. In the first year of a child's life, the right brain begins its hemispheric specialization for processing emotions. Since the brain is use dependent, without appropriate stimulation a child's right brain may not learn how to effectively process emotions (Rothbart, Taylor, & Tucker, 1989).

According to Schore, the orbito-frontal part of the brain also serves as the emotional director or "senior executive" of the social–emotional brain. It controls the functions of the entire right hemisphere, which manages unconscious processes. It also performs, on a moment-to-moment basis, a *valence tagging* function. Through this function, it is able to examine every byte of incoming data from the cells for its emotional charge to determine whether it is pleasure or pain. When a byte is tagged as "pain," it activates the ASR and mobilizes the child for danger. Bytes that are tagged as "pleasure" open the child to growth and learning. Here we see the overlap of Schore's research with that of Lipton and Prescott.

Schore asserted that children's brains are shaped by their earliest experiences and emphasized that caregiver–infant interactions throughout the first 2 years of life determine whether this control system in the brain develops for growth and learning or for danger and protection. Affect, cognition, and behavior, he said, only evolve in a growth-facilitating emotional environment (2003a, p. 122).

Schore also stated that the right brain is the seat of unconscious emotional regulation and is critical for learning stress-coping skills and effective interpersonal behavior throughout the lifespan. He cited a growing body of interdisciplinary studies suggesting that these interpersonal emotional experiences are critical to the early organization of the limbic system. This part of the brain not only processes emotions but is responsible for organizing new learning and adapting to a rapidly changing environment.

Schore also emphasized that psychology and neuroscience are currently moving away from a longstanding focus on cognitive processes and toward a focus on the importance of emotions, the self, and personality. Perhaps the most significant part of his research on infant attachment is his ability to articulate the core psychoneurobiological processes involved in the emotional synchronization between parents and infants.

He used the term *emotional synchronization* to describe the human experience of deep emotional connection, which is based on the developmental principle of *reciprocal mutual influences*. He recognized that the right brains of bonded parents and children shift into a pattern of resonance. This phenomenon is commonly referred to as being on the same page or wavelength. Schore said that "the self-organization of the developing brain occurs in the context of a relationship with another self, another brain" (1996, p. 60)—that of the mother. Schore's illustration of this relational dynamic is presented in Figure 3.5.

Infants who have the opportunity to experience face-to-face, skin-to-skin, brain-to-brain synchrony by 2 to 3 months of age become particularly sensitive and responsive to this reciprocal attunement. Infants who do not have this experience struggle with relational reciprocity and social engagement, particularly as they grow older.

Myron Hofer described how infants' immature internal homeostatic systems are regulated by the caregiver's more mature and differentiated nervous system. In this symbiotic pleasurable state, the adult's and infant's individual homeostatic systems are linked together and provide "mutual regulation of vital endocrine, autonomic, and central nervous systems of both mother and infant by elements of their interaction with each other" (1990, p. 71).

Creating a solid infant–mother bond also requires reciprocal interaction. A baby mirrors back the parents' loving gaze, causing the endorphin levels in both of them to rise. This completes a closed loop emotional circuit, a sort of "love loop." "This loop creates a dynamic, interactive system which is less about what the mother is doing *to* the baby and more about how the mother is being *with* the baby and how the baby is learning to be *with* the mother," according to Schore (1999).

Psychobiologists such as Hofer emphasize how the caregiver's more mature and differentiated nervous system serves as a regulating mechanism for infants "open," immature regulatory systems. The critical factor involved in bonding is the mother's conscious ability to use her nervous system as an instrument for attuning to the baby and creating this state of emotional synchronization. This involves the mother's ability to follow very subtle cues from the child. Attunement between mothers and children helps children learn to regulate their emotions and bioenergetic systems such as hormone production. It is particularly important in helping children modulate the production of cortisol and other adrenal hormones so that they can quiet themselves after an upsetting experience.

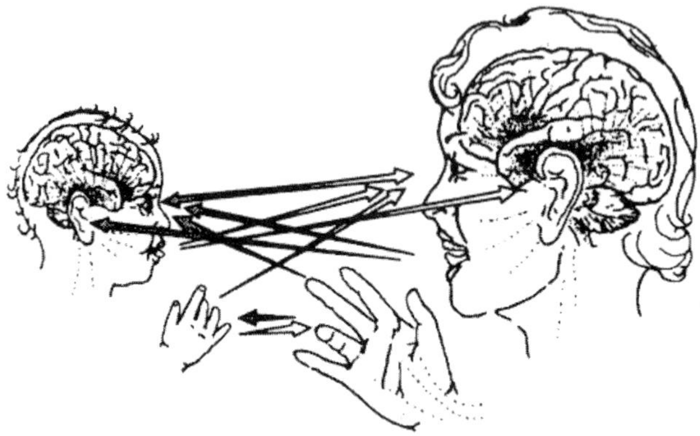

FIGURE 3.5

Emotional Synchronization

Schore (2004) gave this example:

> Your baby is quietly lying on the floor, happy to take in the sights and sounds of the environment. As you notice the baby looking for stimulation, you respond with a game of peek-a-boo. As you play with your child and she responds with shrieks of glee, you escalate the emotion with bigger and bigger gestures and facial expressions.
>
> Shortly thereafter, you notice your baby turns away. The child's sensory system has reached maximum intake and you sense your child needs you to back off so that she can return briefly to a state of calm and restful inactivity. The synchronization between them is more than between their behavior and thoughts; the synchronization is on a biological level—their brains and nervous systems are linked together. (p. 3)

In this process, the mother is teaching and learning at the same time. As a result of this moment-by-moment matching of emotion, both partners increase their emotional connection to one another. In addition, the more the mother fine-tunes her activity level to the infant during periods of play and interaction, the more she allows the baby to disengage and recover quietly during periods of non-play before initiating actively arousing play again.

Neuropsychological research now indicates that these cycles of engaged play, disengagement and restful non-play, followed by a return to play behavior are especially helpful for brain growth

> and the development of cerebral circuits. This makes sense in light of the fact that future cognitive development depends not on flash-cards and videos, but on the attuned, dynamic and emotional interactions between parent and child. The play periods stimulate baby's central nervous system to excitation, followed by a restful period of alert inactivity, which allows the developing brain to process the stimulation and the interaction. (Schore, 2004)

The vital task of infant–parent bonding and the comfort associated with it require the optimal functioning of the right hemisphere of the brain. If right brain functioning is minimized or lost, its impact is not just psychological, it is also biological. It plays a significant role in regulating physiological functions such as the endocrine system and helps people deal efficiently with life challenges (Wittling, 1997). Many new studies link early attachment difficulties with adult cardiovascular disease and cortisol function (Schore, 2003a, p. 265).

When in sync, said Schore (2004), adults and babies both experience positive emotion. When they are out of sync, both experience negative emotions. Many parent–child interactions involving negative emotions may be related to parents getting triggered by the effects of unhealed developmental shocks, traumas, and stresses from their own childhood. All parents have days when they are out of sync with their baby, and the new perspective is that it is not such a bad thing. In fact, it may be quite valuable. Short-term mis-attunement is not a bioneurological disaster, if the adult and child can quickly re-attune. The process of falling out of sync and then repairing the disruption actually teaches children resilience and a sense of confidence that the world will respond to their needs and comfort them if they get hurt or scared.

Mis-attunement becomes a biological disaster when adults do not help the child re-attune. Unfortunately, very few adults have information about the subtleties of human interactions and may not even be able to recognize the difference between experiences of infant attunement and mis-attunement. This is not out of malice, but out of ignorance—it is simply where we are in our evolution as a species. The lack of information about how humans bond with each other is, from our perspective, still the biggest problem facing humanity and certainly the primary cause of developmental shock, trauma, and stress.

The human love dialogues described in this chapter, which involve innumerable cycles of appetite, anticipation, and consummation, also contain our first experiences of rationing, frustration, disappointment, disruption, separation, and limitation. These experiences become interwoven with the hunger for relating to others, particularly the sexual hunger known as *libido,* which develops in the context of the infant–mother dialogue. For this reason, they have tremendous power—perhaps more than any other emotional experience (Kaplan, 1984, pp. 117–118).

Porges and Carter's Polyvagal Theory

Porges and Carter, psychobiologists and codirectors of The Body Center at the University of Illinois at Chicago, conducted research on the evolution of the human nervous system and the origin of brain structures. They have identified physical structures in the brain that regulate the intricate social interactions and communications that Schore described (Porges, 2003).

Porges and Carter discovered that the amygdala, part of the limbic brain, is able to read other people's body movements and intentions. This area also detects familiar faces, voices, and movements. So hand gestures, facial expressions, and vocalizations that appear "safe" activate a person's SES and deactivate the parts of the brain that produce fight, flight, and freeze responses.

In their model, this process occurs through the synergistic functioning of five cranial nerves that comprise the SES. They are responsible for coordinating and integrating body functions and regulating social interactions such as looking, listening, head turning, vocal communication, and facial expression—critical parts of the subtle social interactions that facilitate deeper human connections. In a safe environment, their synergistic operation regulates heart rate and promotes social behavior, communication, and calmness.

When this part of the brain does not perceive familiar and safe social cues, even when they are available, the cranial nerves shut down the relational behaviors—head turning, looking, listening, vocal communication, and facial expression. A biologically different system then activates a second function that we call the *social disengagement system* (SDS). This system also has its unique purpose—protection—and a structured and step-by-step process that puts it in operation. The five cranial nerves first signal the sympathetic nervous system. In turn it activates the ASR to mobilize the fight/flight/freeze responses to help the person protect him- or herself from the perceived danger. Sometimes the brain and cells respond to a perception of danger that is not real. These false alarms can keep the person's body in a chronic state of developmental stress.

One of the most interesting correlations with Porges and Carter's research is a bodywork system known as top-down yoga, which works with the cranial nerves and the SES. Lorin Kiely (n.d.) developed this approach to help repattern the cranial nerves and nervous system and prevent them from responding to perceptual false alarms that mistakenly activate the SDS. He uses subtle neck and head yoga movements to help with this repatterning process. Top-down yoga is an excellent tool for helping people switch from a shock-, trauma-, and stress-based life experience to one that is love based. It also unifies the cerebrospinal and autonomic nervous systems. This activates a conscious and voluntary restructuring of our traumatized brain and nervous system with what is primordial and latent in our evolutionary potential.

The findings of Porges and Carter also paralleled those of Lipton on cellular intelligence indicating that the receptors on the outer walls of cells guide our evolution by either opening up for growth or closing down for protection. Their research also supports Lipton's premise that prolonged or developmental stress creates the perception of danger in the environment, thus shutting down social engagement, delaying social development, and stalling evolution.

Porges and Carter's findings also agreed with Schore's in that they said the first 2 months of infancy are critical in development. They see this as the period when the SES is first put in place. The brains of children will not develop properly if their parents do not look into their eyes or engage in gazing or listening and do not respond to their baby's first sounds with vocal communication. The primary response of the set of cranial nerves will be the SDS and the SES will become a secondary response, rather than the other way around.

Infants who are born with poorly developed cranial nerves often have difficulty in engaging in reciprocal social exchanges with their parents. These children, who may have some form of autism or Asperger syndrome, often frustrate parents who want to engage them and cannot. This social and emotional mismatch can severely disrupt the bonding process and set in motion a downward spiral of sadness, grief, and even anger in the frustrated parents. Porges and Carter have also created processes to help autistic children develop their SES that appear to be highly successful.

By the end of the 2nd month of postnatal development, infants' social and emotional capacities increase dramatically, which correlates with an 8-week milestone in brain development. At this point, the mother's emotionally expressive eyes become the most compelling stimulus for an infant. The child's intense interest in her face, especially in her eyes, leads him or her to track it in space and to engage in periods of intense mutual gazing. The infant's gaze, in turn, evokes the mother's gaze. With the SES active in both mother and child, their locked eyes open a potent channel between them where they experience Schore's emotional synchronization. This parent–infant oneness is visible in their locked nonverbal gaze and mirrored facial expressions, postures, and body movements.

These episodes of social engagement and emotional synchrony are the first signs of social play in a sequence of infant-leads-mother-follows interactions. This highly organized dialogue of visual and auditory signals, transacted within milliseconds, is composed of rapid shifts between states of attention and inattention in each partner's play. In this interactive matrix both partners match states and then simultaneously adjust their social attention, stimulation, and accelerating arousal to each other's responses in what is best described as the "dance of attunement." This dance develops as each partner learns the rhythmic structure of the other and follows in a dance where neither is leading or following. It is a rapid-fire flow of subtle cues and signals that fuses them into a single organism.

The Chemistry of Bonding, Love, and LOVEvolution

Schore's model of attachment also included research findings about the chemistry of bonding and attachment. It indicated that the intimate contact between the mother and her infant function as the result of a reciprocal activation of their hormonal systems and attunement between their hearts and the right hemispheres of their brains. During their mutual gazing interactions, for example, the mother's face induces the production of "upper" hormones, such as dopamine, in the infant's brain while also regulating the levels. The gazing generates high levels of arousal and elation in the child's behavior that are quieted by the mother's soothing and calming behaviors, which also help to regulate the child's oxytocin levels (Schore, 2003b, p. 60).

Oxytocin is known as the "anti-stress hormone" because it counteracts the impact of too much dopamine and high levels of cortisol associated with stress (Last, 2007). This factor is critical in understanding how to help infants reregulate themselves during times of mis-synchronization. Oxytocin creates feelings of optimism, calmness, and connectedness; increases curiosity; and reduces cravings associated with addictions. It also increases sexual receptivity; facilitates learning; repairs, heals, and restores wounds; diminishes pain; lowers blood pressure; and protects against heart disease. It also plays a role in pair bonding (Robinson & Wilson, 2006).

Oxytocin is released in the brain during social contact, but it is especially pronounced during skin-to-skin contact and promotes bonding between people. When the birth and bonding processes are not disturbed by excessive medical interventions, oxytocin acts as one of nature's chief tools for activating the birth process and the bonding instincts. Roused by the high levels of estrogen (a female hormone) during pregnancy, the number of oxytocin receptors in the expecting mother's brain multiplies dramatically near the end of her pregnancy (Palmer, 2002). This makes the new mother highly responsive to the presence of oxytocin. These receptors increase in the part of her brain that promotes maternal behaviors.

Oxytocin's first important surge is during labor, which helps ensure a final burst of antibodies for the baby through the placenta. Passage through the birth canal further heightens oxytocin levels in both mother and baby. Oxytocin not only influences maternal behavior, it also stimulates the milk letdown during nursing. Attempts at nursing during the initial hour after birth cause oxytocin to surge to exceptional levels in both mother and baby.

Mothers who postpone nursing lose part of the ultimate hormone high that is available immediately after birth. Nature designed this powerful initial imprinting as a fail-safe system that helps mothers and babies find and recognize each other in the hours and days after birth. Mothers continue to produce elevated levels of oxytocin through nursing and holding their infants, which provides both with a sense of calm and well-being. Oxytocin levels are higher in mothers who exclusively breastfeed than in those who use supplementary bottles. Under the early influence of oxytocin, nerve junctions in certain areas of mother's brain actually undergo reorganization, thereby hard-wiring her maternal behaviors.

Although the hormone vasopressin is present and active during bonding between the mother and infant, it plays a much bigger role in the father's behavior.

It is released in both parents through physical closeness and touch and promotes bonding between the father and the mother. It also helps the father recognize and bond with his baby and makes him want to be part of the family rather than alone. Vasopressin is also known as the "monogamy hormone." Dr. Theresa Crenshaw, author of *The Alchemy of Love and Lust* (1997, p. 106), said, "Testosterone wants to prowl, vasopressin wants to stay home." She also described vasopressin as tempering men's sexual drive.

If the father is cohabitating with the pregnant mother, vasopressin also causes his brain to reorganize in ways that encourage paternal behaviors. The father becomes more dedicated to his mate and expresses behaviors of protection. Vasopressin reinforces the father's testosterone-promoted protective inclination regarding his mate and child but tempers his aggression, making him more reasonable and less prone to extreme reactions. In this way, vasopressin helps induce a more sensible view of fatherhood, providing stability as well as vigilance for the family.

Oxytocin, dopamine, and vasopressin, which are all involved in the developmental chemistry of parent–child interactions, are co-regulated through their biological and emotional experiences of synchrony. This applies to not only their high states of positive and pleasurable exchanges, but also to their moments of emotional dysregulation.

Pleasurable human interactions involving the SES, birth, breastfeeding, skin-to-skin contact, and sexual activity produce "feel-good" chemicals such as oxytocin and phenylethylamine (PEA) that help soothe, comfort, and lift the spirits. PEA, which is found in cocoa and chocolate, elevates energy, mood, and attention. When we fall in love, we become bonded through rising levels of PEA and oxytocin (Last, 2007, p. 25). Much of the desire for intimacy with other humans is to activate the production of these chemicals and hormones.

The biochemical drive to reexperience the feelings associated with the hormones produced by deep attunement, unconditional love, and bonding is so profound and transformative that, once experienced, it becomes a kind of "holy grail" that people seek for the rest of their lives—either through intimate relationships or through addictions. This desire to experience more "upper" drugs is evident in the almost epidemic use of a drug known as "ecstasy" by teens and adults around the world (Gold & Tabrah, 2000). This yearning for a return to the energetic, emotional, and chemical experience of deep human communion is the most potent motivator of all human behavior. It is also anchored at an archetypal level through many images of the divine madonna and divine child found in cultures around the world. Perhaps this archetype represents a transpersonal human experience imprinted at birth when people's nervous systems were flooded with the "upper" hormones that drives them to want to reexperience the high again.

To believe and to serve was not enough ...
we now find that it is
becoming not only possible
but imperative literally to love evolution.

Tielhard de Chardin

CHAPTER FOUR

LOVEvolution and the Essential Developmental Processes of the Counterdependent Stage of Individual Development

The counterdependent stage of individual development begins around 6–8 months of age, when the child's focus gradually shifts away from the oneness of bonding to exploration and separation, and ends at about 36 months. The essential developmental process for children during the counterdependent stage is the completion of psychological separation from their parents. Carl Jung called this the *individuation process* (Hoeller, 1989), which culminates in what researcher Margaret Mahler termed the *psychological birth* (1968).

As the counterdependent stage of development unfolds, the child ventures further and further from the bonded safety of the codependent stage into more and more psychological separateness. An exploring child who falls down or gets frightened quickly returns to his or her parents for comfort. This stage contains several subphases that are characteristically punctuated by emotional episodes related to the child's emerging sense of self and the desire for autonomy. The latter part of this stage is characterized by utterances of "no" and oppositional behaviors that help children build boundaries between themselves and others. This includes not just the parents but also other authority figures such as older siblings, grandparents, and adult childcare providers.

Table 3.1 outlined the essential developmental processes of the counterdependent stage of our four-stage model of development. Because so many people are stuck in this stage, we present it again in Table 4.1. Not only have very few people had the unique experiences we describe here, many have suffered a lot of developmental trauma during this stage. Developmental trauma at this stage prevents the psychological birth of the individual from occurring, forestalling the full development of an individuated self.

TABLE 4.1

The Essential Developmental Processes of the Counterdependent Stage of Individual Development

Stage of Development — Primary Task	Essential Developmental Processes in Counterdependent Stage	Suggested Experiences for Completing the Essential Developmental Processes of Counterdependent Stage
Counterdependent (6–8 to 36 months) **Separation and Individuation**	• Complete psychological separation process from one's parents • Learn to explore one's environment in safe ways • Learn to trust and regulate one's own thoughts, feelings, behaviors in socially appropriate ways • Internalize appropriate physical and social limits • Develop healthy narcissism • Resolve internal conflicts between oneness and separateness • Bond with self • Continue building secure internal working model • Complete the psychological birth process	• Parents offer timely help to heal any narcissistic wounds or developmental traumas that disturb resonance in both themselves and the child • Parents give child permission and support to safely explore his or her environment • Give the child twice as many "yes's" as "no's" as he or she explores the world • Parents arrange environment to provide safety • Parents help the child internally regulate his or her emotions, especially shame • Parents help the child to identify self-vs.-other needs • Parents model for the child how to effectively meet his or her needs • Adults help the child learn to quickly reestablish the resonance with his or her mother when it is disrupted • Parents use nonshaming responses with the child in setting limits and giving consequences • Caregivers offer empathy and compassion as the child learns to regulate his or her conflicting emotions, thoughts, and behaviors • Caregivers authentically mirror the child's essence • Caregivers support the child in becoming a separate individual and trusting his or her internal impulses • Parents give positive support for the child's efforts to develop an autonomous self

The Essential Developmental Processes of the Counterdependent Stage of Individual Development

Only children with secure bonding have a solid enough foundation to successfully complete the separation process psychologically and emotionally. This secure foundation allows them to gradually move away from the mother and father and toward the unknown world. The more secure children's bonding, the easier it is for them to complete the separation process. Their natural drive to explore the world, however, requires a different kind of support than they needed during the bonding stage.

Separation requires adult supervision, consistent limits and consequences, and experiences (excluding, of course, life-and-death situations) that truly help children learn cause-and-effect thinking. For example, a child learns securely what "hot" means by touching something hot enough to make the appropriate connections in the brain but not so hot as to cause significant injury.

Ideally, children should complete this emotional separation process from their parents by about age 3. Once individuated, they have the self-confidence to rely on their own internal intuition, knowing, and life experiences when making day-to-day decisions. They no longer need to rely solely on others to direct their lives. This is at the heart of the psychological birth (Mahler, 1968). At this point, they have a healthy sense of self that helps them to accept responsibility for their actions, share and cooperate, cope with frustration and stress in appropriate ways, respond effectively to the authority of others, and express their feelings in assertive ways.

As we said earlier, children need good bonding experiences with their mother and father or other adult caregivers during their first 6 to 8 months of life in order to individuate and complete the psychological birth by age 3. Mahler (1968), a researcher and child psychologist, conducted extensive observational research with mothers and their babies to better understand the indispensable ingredients of the essential developmental processes of the first 3 years. She found that holding, singing, and talking to the child; mirroring back the child's essence; patient attention to the child's needs; and nurturing touch were essential for strong maternal–infant bonding. She described this experience as *symbiosis*.

The innate drive for both mother and child to enter a deep, mutual state of emotional attunement is at the core of symbiosis. Mahler and others found that there are degrees of symbiosis, depending on the quality of the relationship between mother and child. She found that the stronger the mutual emotional attunement, the more likely that children were to have the foundation for completing the psychological birth and becoming emotionally separate. Mahler said that this should occur between 2 and 3 years of age. She also said that the separation stage is motivated by children's innate drive to explore the world and to become autonomous. This drive, however, creates an internal conflict for toddlers, who also want to continue the comfort and warmth of the oneness with parents, particularly the mother.

When children begin to separate emotionally, the quality of the bonding relationship with both parents is crucial. If, for example, the mother is depressed, tired, not available emotionally because she is unable to cope with the demands of parenting, or anxious because the child's father is unavailable, this will affect the time and the pace of the separation process. In the presence of such obstacles, children often delay their first moves toward separateness. This delay usually indicates they need more secure bonding experiences before they can venture out further.

If this need for further secure bonding experiences is not completely met, children will eventually move on with their physical development without developing the inner psychological and emotional security they really need. This is the first stage of constructing a narcissistic or false self that performs "as if" in their exchanges with the outer world. Children pretend to not need this inner psychological security and venture further out hoping that someone will create safe boundaries for them. Insecure children learn to fake their independence with a counterdependent attitude of "I'm strong and can take care of myself, I'll show you I don't need you" attitude.

Some children separate prematurely because of the effects of developmental shock, trauma, or stress. Perhaps they experienced intense birth trauma or a milk allergy, or a mother or father is abusive or clings to them too tightly and is overly intrusive in an effort to control every facet of their lives. Developmental shock, trauma, or stress also occurs if the mother demonstrates that she cannot be trusted to provide either the bonding support or the safety for exploring. In such circumstances, children may even prefer strangers as early as 3 months and stiffen against their parents' efforts to hold and comfort them. This protective behavior can cause anxiety in the parents. A mother may wonder, for example, "Why doesn't my child like me any more?" Depending on the mother's self-esteem, she may see the child's attempts to separate prematurely as a threat to her identity as a mother. A father may also feel rejected and withdraw if the child does not respond to his efforts to hold and play with him or her.

Regardless, the movement from bonding into separation is a very delicate process, requiring that both mothers and fathers not only have good information but also emotional and psychological stability. This means that they have healed their own developmental shocks, traumas, and stresses related to bonding and separation. Children's inner struggle between oneness and separateness creates the framework of the journey toward selfhood. We summarize the four subphases of the counterdependent stage of development in Table 4.2 and then offer a narrative description of them in the section that follows.

TABLE 4.2

The Essential Developmental Processes of Each of the Four Subphases of the Counterdevelopment Stage of Individual Development

Counter-dependency Subphase	Essential Developmental Processes	Suggested Experiences for Completing the Subphase
Early Exploration Stage (6 to 9 months)	• Becoming aware there is a world beyond the oneness of mother and father • Differentiating between familiar and strange faces • Introducing short periods of separation between mother and infant • Learning to sit alone • Learning to physically move away from caregivers, first through creeping and then through crawling experiences • Learning to self-regulate emotions when distressed • Learning to build an internal representation of the mother to hold onto until she physically returns	• Exposure to nonfamiliar faces both in the home environment and through excursions outside the home • Comfort and reassurance during episodes of anxiety or discomfort due to disruption in the parent–child attunement in strange environments • Involvement of father or a second bonded parent figure in the child's life during this stage • Sensitive and aware parents who are able to pace the child's exposure to strange faces, experiences, and environments • Looking into the child's eyes and talking directly about changes in the parent–child relationship, such as the introduction to professional childcare, care by family members, or by new people coming to live in or visit the home • Timing the length of separation between mother and child according to his or her temperament • Timely help from parents to heal any narcissistic wounds or developmental traumas in both themselves and the child that disturb resonance • Introducing transitional objects such as stuffed animals, blankets, or soft dolls for the child to carry or sleep with (avoid using pacifiers for this purpose)
Full Exploration Stage (10 to 15 months)	• Mastering the evolutionary shift from creeping and crawling to standing upright • Mastering the challenge of walking unassisted • Mastering the art of falling and returning to standing upright • Learning to say "no" • Learning that mother's absence is not personal or permanent	• Parents give permission and support to safely explore the home environment • Parents give the child twice as many "yes's" as "no's" while he or she is exploring • Parents arrange environment to provide safety • Parents give clear limits and rules for exploring • Parents help child internally regulate his or her emotions, especially shame, when limits are given • Parents help child differentiate between his or her own needs and the needs of others • Father or second bonded parent figure regularly takes child on excursions away from mother, first inside the home and then gradually outside the home

(continued)

TABLE 4.2 *(continued)*

Counter-dependency Subphase	Essential Developmental Processes	Suggested Experiences for Completing the Subphase
Full Exploration Stage (continued)		• Parents model for the child how to meet needs effectively • Adults help the child to quickly reestablish the resonance with the mother when it is disrupted • Parents use nonshaming responses to the child in setting limits and giving consequences • Caregivers authentically mirror the child's essence rather than performance, compliance, or mirroring parents' narcissistic needs
Early Separation Stage (16 to 24 months)	• Coping with emotional outbursts and tantrums caused by the inner conflict between the desire to explore and the fear of separation • Learning that mother is her own person and has separate needs • Learning that mother's love is unconditional but that there are limits to her energetic resources • Learning to cope with the "mother of separation" and recognizing that she is a different mother than the "mother of bonding" • Developing an internal mother representation to cope with her physical absence • Mastering the "splitting" stage in which the child sees the parents as all good or all bad	• Caregivers offer empathy and compassion as the child learns to regulate his or her conflicting emotions, thoughts, and behaviors resulting from inner conflicts related to separation and bonding • Caregivers avoid the use of punishment and shame as tools for diminishing the ego • Caregivers stay emotionally separate during emotional outbursts and tantrums, allowing the child to express these difficult feelings without judgment or shaming • Caregivers support the child becoming a separate individual by offering choices (food preferences, dressing options, which comfy objects to sleep with, his or her own glass for drinking) • Parents give positive support for the child's efforts to develop an autonomous self • Support the child in coping with mother's limits regarding safety, disobedience, and rule breaking • Keeping photos of mother in childcare setting or carrying something with mother's photo on it • Being able to hear mother's voice over a telephone • Being able to watch a short video of mother talking to the child • Focusing by father or second bonded caregiver on supporting the child's feelings when mother is not available and not agreeing with the child's perception that mother is "bad" • Supporting any regressive behaviors that might appear, such as the need for more cuddling or wanting to sleep in their bed for a short time • Maintaining sensitivity to the mother's own cues about when to set limits on regressive behaviors,

(continued)

TABLE 4.2 *(continued)*

Counter-dependency Subphase	Essential Developmental Processes	Suggested Experiences for Completing the Subphase
Early Separation Stage (continued)		as the separation process is a reciprocal and mutual dance and the mother is also separating from the child • Acting in unison to hold the child's psyche during the splitting stage by working out parental conflicts away from the child • Recognizing parents' own tendencies to split when the child is splitting by supporting each other or even getting therapy • Reinforcing limits in a consistent way that looks very black and white • Recognize parents' own narcissistic needs for perfect mirroring from their child and keep those needs separate from their parenting • Utilizing the "Guidelines for Completing the Individuation Process" included in this chapter
Complete Separation Stage (25 to 36 months)	• Reducing the child's inflated ego and limiting behaviors involving euphoria, grandiosity, entitlement, and omnipotence • Achieving object constancy during stressful periods of separation from the parents, particularly the mother • Mastering both/and thinking • Developing solid cause-and-effect thinking • Moving toward cooperative and self-sufficient behaviors • Learning to accept limits without oppositional behaviors • Healing any developmental traumas from previous stages of development	• Providing clear limits regarding the environment and the child's behavior and boundary violations • Reinforcing limits without physical punishment or emotional punishment involving shaming, belittling, humiliating, or name calling • Allowing the child to have his or her feelings about the loss of the inflated ego and loss of perceived adult powers while parents remain empathic and maintain emotional equilibrium • Increasing the role of father and other caregivers in interacting with the child and leading him or her out into the world • Not permitting children to dominate parents who lack experience in setting limits and giving consequences • Assuring child about his or her own capacity for self-care, emotional regulation, and personal sufficiency • Supporting the child during periods of regression when demonstrating "baby" behavior by providing "baby" comfort; this support and comfort must be provided with an open heart and without criticism or judgment • Helping the child heal any signs of unhealed developmental trauma from earlier stages of development

The Essential Developmental Processes of Each of the Four Subphases of the Counterdependent Stage

Mahler (1968) and Stephen Johnson (1987), another developmental psychologist, found that the internal conflict between oneness and separateness gets resolved when children are able to successfully complete the four distinct phases in the separation process just described. As you look more carefully at each of the phases, it may help you recognize things that are keeping you stuck as an adult in the counterdependent stage of development. If you can locate any specific developmental shock, traumas, or stresses related to what you perceive you got or did not get in each of the four subphases of the process, then you can begin to heal them in present time.

The following descriptions of the four subphases of the counterdependent stage of development delineate the essential developmental processes in each. For each essential developmental process, an accompanying set of developmental needs must be met. As you read the following descriptions, ask yourself: "Knowing what I do about my parents, what do I think my experience would have been with them during these phases?" This could help you connect issues you have in your adult life with the effects of unrecognized and unhealed developmental shock, trauma, and stress stemming from the separation stage of development.

The Early Exploration Phase (6 to 9 months)

During the early exploration phase, you became aware that there was a world outside of the oneness between you and your mother and father or other caregivers. At first, you looked at this world from the edge of your mother's lap or over your father's shoulder while being held or burped. You saw your mother smile, and you smiled back. Imitation helped you learn new responses for watching and doing. Also, you first began to notice strangers and may have reacted at first with some fear.

However, if the relationships with your mother and father were strong, supportive, and nurturing, you eventually grew more curious than scared of strangers. If the relationship was weak or you were not yet ready to separate, then the fear may have been stronger and you clung to your parents when strangers approached in order to feel safe.

In the early exploration phase you had no way of holding onto an image of your mother or father when either one was out of physical sight ("out of sight, out of mind"). You may have coped with this fear of loss by trying to keep your mother or father always in view. Eventually you were able to imagine that your parents were with you even when they were not. You could only sustain this for short periods of time at first, but gradually you learned to tolerate longer periods of being physically separated from your parents.

If your mother of oneness was available, nurturing, warm, and secure, you could hold on to memories of these experiences even when she was not present. Your mother may have assisted you in developing these qualities by being predictable and reliable. For example, when she had to leave, she would let you know in advance that you were going to be cared for by a sitter or by your father. She knew the quickest way to destroy your newfound confidence was to sneak away when you were not looking. Also, she knew any prolonged absence of several days while you were very young could leave you feeling abandoned.

During the early exploration phase, you moved closer and retreated many times during a day to confirm that the bond with your mother or father was still intact. You may also have been touched, given a loving smile, a brief snuggle, a bottle, or an opportunity to nurse on your mother's lap. Each time, however, you were lured back to exploring the world because your drive to explore the world around you grew stronger by the day.

Your father knew that his role was to play with you, hold you, and help you separate from your mother. Soon you learned that your father was not just a part of your mother but a separate person. You saw these differences and similarities, and she let you know that she trusted your father, which also helped you trust him. If your mother tried to keep you from your father, then you may have picked this up and feared your father. You also needed other relatives and friends to bond with. Again, you learned to trust people that your mother or father trusted.

One of the essential developmental processes of this phase involved developing a specific smile of recognition for your mother, father, or other caregivers. During this period, it was also time for you to learn to discriminate between your parents and strangers. If the bonding with your mother was strong, you showed more curiosity and wonderment toward strangers. If it was less strong, you might have felt fear and distress around strangers, especially when you were around 8 months of age.

The Full Exploration Phase (10 to 15 months)

During this phase of counterdependency, you began to walk and ventured out even further. Learning to walk was a celebration of your ability to master your world. This skill would lead you to the development of a "love affair with the world." Separation and exploration became almost a full-time occupation coupled with occasional trips back to your mother's lap or your father's knee for needed comfort and reassurance.

Teething and too many "don'ts" may have slowed you down, but elation over new discoveries could distract you. The inborn drive for separateness and wholeness was in high gear by the end of this phase, and you probably had some transitional objects such as a teddy bear, a doll, or a blanket that represented your mother in case she was not immediately available. You may have carried these comfort objects everywhere you went. Eventually, you abandoned these objects when you were able to develop an inner sense of your mother that you could use to soothe or comfort yourself when you needed it.

During this period, you loved the thrill of being mobile. In this expansive period, you found that you could explore a large area in your home and discover all kinds of new things each day. Your excitement often reached a state of euphoria, causing you to often forget about wanting to be close or even eating, unless something scary happened. Because your mother seemed so big and so powerful, you saw her as omnipotent. Because you were not separate from her, you often felt omnipotent as well—able to do grandiose things and entitled to have everything that crossed your path. Life seemed limitless to you.

One of the essential developmental processes for this phase involved learning that there were limits to mother's presence, energy, patience, time, and resources. Because you needed to learn about her limitations gradually, she gave them to you incrementally. When she had to leave you with another bonded caregiver, she stayed away only as long as she knew you could tolerate it.

At first this was just for a matter of minutes. As you grew older, she expanded this to hours. She made sure that you had a reliable person to care for you while she was gone, someone who could support your feelings if you were unhappy about her absence. She also helped you learn how to take care of your own needs and to be self-sufficient while she was gone. She provided you with transitional objects, such as soft animals for comfort, so that you could mother yourself in her absence. She knew that this would help you to develop a "nurturing parent" inside yourself.

Other essential developmental processes for this phase involved learning that your mother's absence was not personal and that she was a separate person with her own needs and interests. She or other caregivers helped you express your feelings of frustration and supported you emotionally when things did not go your way. You also needed a constant adult presence to monitor your exploration and make sure you were safe. Your caregivers helped you when you struggled with two seemingly contradictory fears: the fear of separation (abandonment) and the fear of oneness (engulfment and annihilation).

The Early Separation Phase (16 to 24 months)

Near the beginning of this phase, you realized that you were a person totally separate from your mother. When you first understood this, you may have felt scared and returned to your mother to be cuddled. It may have appeared to others as if you were regressing back to an earlier phase of development, but if you received the comfort you desired, it was likely short lived. Again, your innate drive to become separate prevailed, and you returned to exploring and mastering your world.

Your mother and father kept encouraging your efforts to separate during this phase, while providing you with support and nurturing when you needed it. You likely felt angry and frustrated when you were unable to master certain tasks or when your parents placed restrictions on you. Your parents accepted this anger and frustration as normal and responded empathetically to you. A warm hug and some assurance that you were still loved was all that you really needed. Humiliation, isolation, or punishment only set up further cycles of tension that you needed to discharge. Their repeated reassurances helped you develop a sense of your self, feelings of being loved and accepted, and the ability to stay connected to your inner feelings.

Another important component of this phase is the phenomenon called *splitting*. Sometimes when you mastered a task or returned to your mother, you found a receptive warm reunion. When this happened, you experienced your mother as "good" and everything looked and felt good during these times. At other times, however, you were unable to master a task, or when you needed a warm hug you found your mother busy cooking dinner or talking on the telephone. In these moments you experienced her as "bad," and this feeling generalized to everything about her. Mother became "good mother" when she was available and "bad mother" when she was not available. The healthy resolution to this internal conflict occurred gradually as you learned two important things. First, your mother had a mix of good and bad qualities, and she was basically a good person in spite of this dichotomy. Second, you also had good and bad qualities that were separate from your mother, and this mixture of good and bad qualities was also okay. You gradually realized that you were both okay.

If you did not resolve this internal good/bad split during this phase, you continued to see yourself, other people, and situations in the world as divided into good and bad, black and white, right and wrong. If, as an adult, you can think of only two solutions (either/or) to problems and tend to use black-or-white thinking, you probably did not successfully complete the splitting phase of your early development.

The essential developmental processes for this phase included learning how to resolve your inner conflict between wanting to be separate and wanting to be close. You had to come to terms with the reality that your parents were not always "gods" or perfect parents. And because you were becoming separate, you also had to come to terms with your own human frailties. You learned there were limits to your natural narcissistic urges toward omnipotence, grandiosity, entitlement, and euphoria.

If you did not complete these processes successfully, it is likely that you became stuck at this phase of your development, creating a reality split into polarities of good/bad, all/nothing, or always/never. You also may have maintained your narcissistic urges toward grandiosity, entitlement, euphoria, and omnipotence. As an adult, these may be expressed through behaviors involving manipulation, pride, self-centeredness, an overly inflated ego, addictions to activities and substances that helped you maintain your euphoria, and, if in dire circumstances, rage attacks when faced with limitations.

This period was the most critical in completing your psychological birth. During this time, you were confronted with a decision either to become separate emotionally from your mother or to stay codependent. If you chose to return to the safety of oneness, you developed more codependent behaviors and decided you would rather feel safe and get your needs met by being dependent on others.

However, if you had repeated experiences of emotional, physical, or sexual abuse, neglect, or repeated developmental shocks, traumas, and stresses, you likely decided that oneness and closeness was unsafe and too scary. Out of a need to protect yourself, you might have prematurely chosen to separate emotionally from your mother or father and developed a false self.

This false self helped you to wall off your feelings of vulnerability and fear and your need for closeness by creating defensive behaviors that pushed people away and prevented others from knowing how much you really did need them. It also helped you to appear capable and act strong. You created an internal illusion about your inflated importance with the hope it would prevent not only yourself but also others from seeing your vulnerability and wounds. If these things happened during this phase, you have defensive behaviors similar to those of a 2-year-old when you encounter adult situations involving limits or feelings of vulnerability.

Parents and other bonded caregivers play a critical role in helping the child move through the splitting substage of development toward an internal experience of object constancy. *Object constancy* is a child's ability to maintain a sense of equanimity when someone challenges his or her narcissistic urges. Parents' most difficult task is to avoid participating in the child's perceptual good/bad split. Behaviorally, this split manifests as the two-against-one game in which the child allies with one parent against the other by sharing secrets or taking sides. Here, the child not only tests the strength of the bond between the parents or caregivers but also the adults' psychological maturity.

Adults who have not completed their own psychological birth display splitting behaviors while in the midst of a conflict with their children and get into needless power struggles. When this happens, the adults will find it difficult to validate a child's reality and reflect the child's feelings, making the child's separation process even more difficult. A father with unresolved abandonment issues, for example, may reveal his split by criticizing his wife and making her bad in some way if he feels she is paying more attention to his child's needs than she does to his needs. It is no surprise, therefore, that the most common time for fathers to leave a marriage or file for divorce is when the first child is about 2 years old.

The Complete Separation Phase (25 to 36 months)

If you had loving parents who supported your need for emotional separation between 25 and 36 months, you were able to develop a sense of separateness and identity by the age of 3. Object constancy enabled you to hold yourself as an object of worth while being separate from other people. As a 3-year-old, you had only enough object constancy to feel safe in the world as a separate person if you had accumulated enough internal memories of good-mother and good-self experiences. The struggle to maintain object constancy continues in your life encounters with new problems and crises that threaten your sense of self.

It is a normal part of the human experience to constantly reconcile our yearnings to return to paradise and the bliss of oneness with our intense longings to be separate, autonomous individuals. The resolution of this issue, as you can see, involves a complex set of developmental processes.

For example, when you went to your emotionally present father and complained about your unavailable mother, he needed to know how to respond effectively. If he used your complaining as an opportunity to vent his own feelings about having an unavailable wife, you may have learned to devalue women and overvalue men. Fathers often feel abandoned when their wives become so consumed by taking care of their children's needs that they end up not paying enough attention to the father's needs.

However, if your father took the side of your mother and criticized you for complaining about her, you learned that there was no emotional support available from your father to help you become separate from your mother. You may have felt betrayed and defeated if any of these things happened repeatedly. What your father needed to do was support your feelings without agreeing or disagreeing with your definition of your mother's "badness." ("I see you are really upset that Mommy's gone, and until she comes back I am here to play with you.")

This response does not blame anyone and acknowledges your feelings but can be difficult for men who never learned how to express their own emotions to use. Some fathers feel scared and helpless when they find themselves in the middle of the intense separation struggle between mother and child. They find reasons to work longer hours or have an affair or even leave the marriage altogether. Without the emotional support of your father or another person to help you complete your psychological birth between the ages of 2 and 3, it is very difficult and almost impossible.

The Parents' Role in the Completion of the Essential Developmental Processes in the Counterdependent Stage

In order to support the completion of the essential developmental processes during the counterdependent stage, parents must assume the following basic responsibilities:

- Identify and heal their developmental shocks, traumas, and stresses from their own separation stage of development

- Avoid getting personally triggered by their child's good–bad splits in perception
- Give their child twice as many "yes" as "no" responses while they are exploring their world
- Child-proof the home to allow safe exploration, thus reducing the number of limits that need to be set
- Set appropriate and safe limits without the use of shame or physical punishment
- Show respect and compassion for the feelings of their child
- Take their child's needs seriously
- Meet their child's needs in appropriate and timely ways
- Use "time in" rather than time out to discipline the child

Time-In Versus Time-Out Limits

We would like to call particular attention to the use of time-out as the most common way of disciplining children. While it is a big improvement over corporal punishment, we personally think it is a major cause of developmental shock, trauma, or stress during the counterdependent stage of development.

So we want to say very clearly: Time-outs mostly are designed to serve the needs of adult caregivers rather than the needs of the child. They provide adults with time to reregulate their own emotions after an emotional outburst by their toddler. Its use, however, is a way that adults justify separating from the child. They frame it as time for the *child* to think about and correct their behavior and to reregulate themselves emotionally, when the opposite is true. While time-outs are helpful for the parents, they are absolutely one of the worst things for toddlers. Why? Because time-outs violate the most basic principles of adult–child relationships and the research of Allen Schore and others we have cited.

In Chapter 3 we presented Schore's research about how the output from the mother's (or other caregiver's) right brain hemisphere regulates the child's right brain mechanisms. This creates emotionally synchronized, psychobioligically attuned face-to-face, brain-to-brain interactions. Schore is very clear in his position that the attuned mother–child dyad is the mechanism that controls children's ability to regulate their biological, psychological, and emotional states. The closer in proximity the child is to the adult caregiver, the easier it is for the child to reregulate him- or herself during or after an emotional meltdown. Separating a child from the caregiver when the child is emotionally dysregulated just reinforces the effects of whatever developmental shock, trauma, or stress the child experiences in the process and helps hardwire it even more into his or her nervous system.

When parents correctly understand the cause of toddlers' emotional outbursts, they recognize that meltdowns are an extreme case of emotional dysregulation. The cause of the emotional outburst is usually an inner conflict between the desire to separate and explore and the desire for the parents' love and approval. Toddlers need their parents to understand their feelings of frustration and anger at having natural or imposed limits set on their exploration and their desire to be independent. What children get in a time-out that separates them from the parents is even more distress, which increases their emotional dysregulation.

Many adults, unfortunately, make the situation worse for a 2- to 3-year-old child by saying, "I don't want to be close to you when you are behaving this way. Go to your room until you can get yourself quieted down." This message often comes with a look of scorn, which the child internalizes as, "There is something wrong with me. I feel ashamed of myself, and I don't know how to stop my feelings. I need help." This dynamic creates even more inner conflict and gives rise to toxic shame that is reinforced over time. This is the foundation of shame-based behavior in children.

What children really need is a time-in where they can sit on or by a centered adult and be talked to in a calm, soothing way. This not only helps them reregulate their feelings, it stops the feelings of shame. When this happens, children realize there is nothing wrong with having these feelings, and they can calm down. You can find a printable copy of Time-In Techniques at our website, www.weinholds.org/devtrauma.

Parents are much more empathetic when they understand that emotional outbursts are a symptom of children needing help to reregulate their escalated emotions. Rather than getting angry and feeling frustrated, parents can intervene empathetically in ways that truly help calm both themselves and the child. This normalizes the negative emotions, communicates an acceptance of the child's struggle to become independent and efforts to self-regulate feelings, and restores the resonance in the relationship.

Developmental shock, trauma, or stress caused by the prolonged shaming that is inherent in time-outs is not only too much for toddlers to endure emotionally, it has long-term damaging consequences. Toddlers not only fail to learn how to discharge or regulate their feelings of shame in a healthy way, they learn to blame others as a way of coping. They also learn to project the energy of their shameful emotions out of their body and onto others in order to relieve their inner stress.

Conscious parents and caregivers who have identified and healed their own developmental shocks, traumas, or stresses are more able to help children successfully complete their psychological birth and the essential developmental processes of the counterdependent stage of development by age 3. These children are able to maintain object constancy, go on "internal power," and utilize "I'm okay, you're okay" thinking.

I (Janae) also want to say that I have presented this developmental information to many childcare professionals and early childhood educators at conferences and trainings, and most have been very receptive. There have been a few, however, who insisted on making children completely responsible for reregulating their emotions through the continued practice of time-out. What I eventually saw is that these adults would rather blame, shame, punish, and traumatize emotionally dysregulated children than look at why they got triggered by this child's behavior. I cannot tell you how much it upsets me to see some of these individuals in positions as behavioral experts in the childcare profession using their work as an avenue for transmitting intergenerational cycles of developmental shock, trauma, or stress—and doing so in spite of my very direct efforts to point out the harm of what they were doing.

The Development of Healthy Narcissism

Children need to be seen as real and authentic persons, to be understood, to be able to express their feelings and needs, to be taken seriously, and to have their feelings and needs respected by their parents. These are normal healthy narcissistic needs. If these needs are met adequately during the bonding and separation processes, for example, the child will probably develop healthy self-esteem. One of the initial ways that children can get their narcissistic needs met during the bonding process is through their mother's mirroring of their essence while they gazed up at her face. This is how infants learn who they really are.

Children who are mirrored appropriately during the bonding and separation stages experience healthy narcissism and eventually move on. It is as though the child has "enough"—enough unconditional love, enough nurturing, enough mirroring, enough protection and limits, and enough consequences. This forms the foundation of a person with a strong sense of self, one who then becomes a true humanitarian and is able to serve others or to be in an intimate relationship without losing his or boundaries. This is essential for the successful completion of the separation process (Weinhold & Weinhold, 2008b, pp. 60–63).

If your mother mirrored back her desire for you to be a certain way or expected you to meet her unmet narcissistic needs or to fulfill her own incomplete dreams, this may have twisted or distorted your self-image. You may have stayed fused with her in order to be loved and cared for. Mothers must be able to meet their own needs with other adults rather than through their children. Otherwise, it creates *parentized* children, who operate as a surrogate spouse and activates something known as a *reversal,* in which children try to meet the needs of their parents rather than the other way around. We discuss this concept further in Chapter 6. Reversal dynamics anchored in the counterdependent stage of development make people vulnerable to subsequent reversal dynamics inside larger systems such as the workplace, schools, churches, and governments.

Alice Miller (1981) listed the ways that parents can help their children experience healthy narcissism. As you read this list, ask yourself, "Can I imagine my parents doing these things for me when I was 2 to 3 years old?"

- React calmly and reassuringly to any of my aggressive impulses
- Support my attempts to become separate and autonomous instead of being threatened by them

- Allow me to experience and express my natural feelings and urges such as rage, fear, jealousy, or defiance
- Allow me to develop and follow my natural curiosities safely during each developmental stage, rather than overprotecting me or requiring me to be a people-pleaser
- Be available both physically and emotionally when I became emotionally dysregulated
- Permit me to express conflicting or ambivalent emotions and treat those feelings seriously and with respect
- See me as separate from themselves, as someone with my own needs, feelings, wishes, preferences, dreams, and accomplishments

With this kind of parental support, children can experience healthy narcissism and grow up without being narcissistically wounded and developmentally shocked, traumatized, or stressed during the separation process. The only truly unselfish, genuine people in the world are those who were able to get these healthy narcissistic needs met appropriately at this stage of their development.

Very few people get this kind of support, so it is likely that you have some narcissistic wounds with defenses around them to protect you against any further wounding. Miller (1984) described people who did get their narcissistic needs met in childhood this way:

> Children who are respected learn respect. Children who are cared for learn to care for those weaker than themselves. Children who are loved for what they are cannot learn intolerance. In an environment such as this they will develop their own ideals, which can be nothing other than humane, since they grew out of the experience of love. (p. 97)

LOVEvolution and the Creation of the Functional Family Triangle

Navigating the conflicts that naturally occur during the counterdependent stage of development requires the parents and/or caregivers to use very specific protocols related to splitting and separation. To help children stay on the LOVEvolution track, we offer some suggestions for navigating this delicate process:

- When one parent is not available to the child, the other parent or another bonded caregiver needs to be available to physically and verbally support the child's feelings of anger, grief, fear, and sadness: "I can see that you are upset because your daddy left."

- The available parent or caregiver needs to assure the child that the absent or unavailable parent will return: "I'm here to take care of you while your daddy is gone tonight."
- Avoid making anyone bad during conflicts and focus on supporting the child's feelings: "You seem angry because your daddy left. You don't like daddy when he leaves. It is okay to feel angry when daddy leaves."
- Both parents and other caregivers must create clear communication patterns between both themselves and between themselves and the child to prevent two-against-one or triangulation dynamics: "I can see that you are angry at Mommy because she asked you to put your toys away. Perhaps you want to go to her and tell her how you feel. Would you like me to go with you to talk to her?"

The key to the functional family triangle is building a strong bond among all three members—mother–father, mother–child, and father–child. If a bond in any of these relational links is weak or missing, then the child is conditioned to experience the two-against-one dynamics common in most dysfunctional families.

So what about single-parent families? We know of no research on the effectiveness of bonded caregivers, such as a babysitter or grandparents to fill the missing parent's role and to ensure the child experiences the support of a divine triangle in the family structure. Based on our experience, surrogates (extended family members, teachers, ministers, Scout masters, childcare providers) are often highly effective in creating functional family triangle structures that assist in the individuation process. This is particularly important for boys whose primary parent is a woman and the father is either absent or very emotionally unavailable. Finding someone to fill the absent father role can help facilitate the son's psychological birth. One of the most likely reasons why people seek counseling is for the counselor or therapist to help fill that role.

Daughters who live with a single mother seem to have less difficulty separating from their mothers. However, they may have difficulty in completing their psychological separation from their fathers unless they have bonded with them. Our own observations in working with families who have experienced divorce is that the children experience cognitive delays in developing both/and thinking skills. This delay is particularly true in children whose families have a lot of post-divorce conflict.

The Psychological Birth of the Child: The Most Important Milestone in Human Development

The successful resolution of the conflicting drives between the desire for oneness and the desire for separateness occurs by age 3. This occurs when children's normal, healthy, narcissistic needs are acknowledged and met by caring, self-assured, aware, and psychologically whole parents and adult caregivers.

If you did not have parents who were able to help you complete this stage successfully you developed a false self that was more acceptable than your true self, that made it easier to get along with others in your family. As an adult, you may have retained aspects of your false self that now interfere with intimacy in your adult relationships. More than likely, you also resorted to erecting defenses to prevent people from learning what was really happening inside you. All these behaviors kept you trapped and feeling isolated, blocking intimacy in your relationships. If so, it is difficult to ask directly for help when you need it or for others to assist you in getting your needs met. It also increases the likelihood that you will use the drama triangle to manipulate others into meeting your needs.

People still coping with the effects of unhealed developmental shock during the codependent stage generally develop a deflated victim self that looks weak and helpless, while people with developmental traumas during the counterdependent stage generally have an inflated false self. Those with developmental shock during the codependent stage are more prone to depression, while those with unhealed developmental traumas and stresses during the counterdependent stage are more likely inclined to grandiosity and adrenalized hyperactivity that help them avoid feeling depressed. Because most people experienced some developmental shock, trauma, and stress during both stages, it is fairly common for people to cycle between both depression and hyperactivity.

To complete your psychological birth as an adult, it is necessary to resolve your internal struggle between two seemingly opposite forces: the natural drive toward oneness and closeness and the equally powerful drive to be an emotionally separate, self-determining individual. In couple relationships, the most common sign that this process is not complete is what we call the "dance of intimacy," which involves partners switching back and forth between codependent and counterdependent roles.

If you have not completed your psychological birth, the need for the intimacy of oneness can also bring up intense fears of being engulfed or consumed. This experience can feel like a psychological annihilation and dismemberment of your self. The counterforce of separation can produce intense fears of existential alienation, aloneness, and abandonment by God.

Navigating these intense experiences as an adult requires spiritual courage. Jung identified such experiences as an integral part of *individuation*. Jung saw it as both a psychological and spiritual process that generally is not completed by most people until after mid-life. He said people must move beyond the conventional wisdom in order to discover *gnosis,* or the knowledge of the heart that renders human beings free (Hoeller, 1989).

Jung also realized that humans cannot fulfill their potential if they become too attached to the trappings of the external world. He said people needed to be "in the world, but not of the world" in order to feel free. He urged people to look for their spiritual truths inside themselves and not in established religions. Jung saw this spiritual rebirth as a necessary prerequisite to the completion of the individuation process by adults.

Understanding what happened in your childhood, identifying and healing your developmental shocks, traumas, and stresses and developing new relationship skills will help you complete your psychological birth. You may ask, "How will I know if I have completed it?" You will have a keen sense of who you really are and handle life's challenges and conflicts with a minimum of stress while feeling good about yourself and good about others. You will be able to maintain your object constancy in the midst of most of life challenges. You are comfortable with being both close and intimate and being separate and alone when you want. Triggers from past developmental shocks, traumas, or stresses that used to elicit an emotional response no longer have that effect.

Another benchmark is the ability to ask for what you want and need from others in such a way that they are delighted to give it to you. Only those who have worked on themselves psychologically and spiritually can expect to successfully complete this essential developmental process.

At this point in our individual evolution, most of us have not had sustained experiences of deep emotional attunement and biological synchrony to fully anchor us on the LOVEvolution track. We believe that this is due to the presence of the effects of unrecognized and unhealed developmental shock, trauma, and stress—the topic of the next section of this book.

Guidelines for Completing the Individuation Process

The psychological birth and individuation process requires the support of two bonded caregivers for the child to become emotionally and psychologically separate. Here are some guidelines to help children complete the individuation process:

1. ***When one bonded caregiver is not available to meet the child's needs and the child complains or gets upset, the available caregiver should do the following:***
   - Support the child's feelings.
     ("I can see that you are upset because your daddy left.")
   - Refuse to participate in the child's judgment about the "badness" of the unavailable parent but offer empathy to the child.
     ("It's hard when you don't see your daddy all day. You'd like him to stay here with you.")
   - Reassure the child that his or her needs will be met.
     ("I'm here to take care of you while your daddy is at work today.")

- Inform the child that the missing caregiver will return.
  ("Your daddy will be back at four o'clock to pick you up and take you home.")
- Inform the returning caregiver about the child's reaction to the separation.
  ("Kevin was sad today when you had to leave. He wished that he could be with you all day today.")

2. ***The returning caregiver should do the following:***
   - Ask the child if this is true.
     ("Were you upset today that I had to leave? Did you want me to stay with you all day?")
   - Support the child's feelings and offer closeness.
     ("You were sad and mad today. Do you need anything from me right now?")
   - Express his or her own feelings about separation to the child.
     ("I miss being with you, too. I feel sad when I have to go to work and leave you.")
   - Give the child reasons for the absence.
     ("I have to go to work to earn money to pay for the things we need.")

3. ***When the child has a conflict with one caregiver and brings the conflict to the second caregiver, the second caregiver should do the following:***
   - Support the child's feelings.
     ("I can see that you are upset with your mother. You look angry. Are you angry?")
   - Do not agree or disagree with the judgment the child has about the first caregiver's "badness" but instead offer empathy to the child.
     ("You are angry because your mother made you clean up your toys. You don't like to pick up your toys just because she told you to.")
   - Support the child in dealing directly with the first caregiver to resolve the conflict.
     ("Are you willing to talk to her and tell her how you feel?")
   - Help the child talk to first caregiver.
     ("Do you need any help from me when you go to talk to your mother?")
   - Let the child know that it is not okay to triangulate and have family secrets.
     ("If you are not willing to tell her how you feel, I will tell her that you are upset about your conflict with her.")
   - Let the child know that you will not resolve his or her conflict with the first caregiver and that you are available to support both the child and the first caregiver when they are ready to resolve it.
     ("I do not want to get in the middle of this conflict between you and your mother. I will not go to your mother and speak for you. I will only

let her know that I am aware you are angry with her. If the two of you want to talk about this, I am available to support both of you.")

- Inform the child that if he or she resolves the conflict without you that you would like to know the outcome.
  ("When you and your mother talk about your feelings about having to pick up your toys, please let me know what happens.")

At first, you may feel awkward and unfamiliar using these kinds of responses. This is normal when you are learning a new skill. The truth is, we are all on a learning curve in understanding the kind of support children need to successfully complete the individuation process. Very few people have ever experienced this kind of communication in their lives.

When you do use it, however, you will see how effective it is in helping your children feel respected and understood. These rules also apply to therapists or other helpers because clients are unconsciously seeking help to complete their individuation process. Because they will not say this directly, you must be alert to the dynamics of this process and avoid the common pitfalls. Here are some guidelines about what *not* to do in any situation where the person is trying to individuate:

- Do not contribute to making anyone bad.
  ("He is never here when you need him.")
- Do not take sides.
  ("You are right. He doesn't care about you. He doesn't care about anyone.")
- Do not ignore or discount feelings.
  ("Don't cry. Do you just want to have a pity party?")
- Do not discount the importance of the person's situation.
  ("You are just overreacting. It isn't that bad.")
- Do not create secrets.
  ("I won't tell her you are angry at her.")
- Do not rescue.
  ("I will talk to him and tell him to be nicer to you.")
- Do not play "two against one."
  ("You and I can figure out how to keep her from being so mean to you.")

Using both sets of these guidelines is critical for completing the individuation process, whether it is during the counterdependent stage of development or later in life. If you find yourself using the incorrect responses, you can always go back and change them. It is never too late to use the new responses during a separation experience. Since most of us still have unresolved inner conflicts about wanting to be separate, the communication guidelines above are also useful for resolving conflicts in adult relationships where these same dynamics are present.

These protocols also help support functional family triangle experiences. Through repeated successful trials, the child eventually learns that neither mother nor father are all bad and eventually adopts "I'm okay—you're okay," both/and thinking. The child becomes free to use emotions and inner knowledge to direct his or her life. He or she is emotionally prepared to handle frustration and to move forward to independence, the next stage of development.

When functional family dynamics are not present in the parent–child structure, a dysfunctional family triangle known as the drama triangle develops instead. The dynamics of the drama triangle are the result of unrecognized and unhealed developmental shocks, traumas, or stresses originally from the counterdependent stage of development. These recycling developmental dynamics, which will be discussed in detail in Chapter 7, interfere with people getting their basic needs met in subsequent relationships and are a major factor in the creation of intractable conflicts.

PART THREE

Developmental Trauma

Unrecognized and unhealed developmental shock, trauma, and stress are the primary obstacles to the evolution of the human race.

Barry and Janae Weinhold

CHAPTER FIVE

The Trauma Continuum

In this section of the book, we look at the second part of our binary model of human evolution: the developmental trauma track and the lingering effects of unrecognized and unhealed shock, trauma, and stress. The field of traumatology is still relatively new, so we begin by distinguishing among shock, trauma, and stress and then give an overview of the literature in the field of traumatology. Then we look at the impact of developmental shock, trauma, and stress on individual development during the codependent and counterdependent stages. We conclude this section of the book in Chapter 8 with some paradigm-shifting research that confirms the role of unrecognized and unhealed shock, trauma, and stress as major causes of degenerative conditions such as cancer.

Differentiating among Developmental Shock, Trauma, and Stress

The terms *shock* and *trauma* are used almost interchangeably in the field of traumatology, which makes it very difficult to discriminate between these biological and psychological states and even more difficult to determine their appropriate treatment interventions. In this chapter, we present a framework for understanding the important differences among developmental shock, trauma, and stress and the appropriate interventions for each.

As we stated previously, because experiences of shock, trauma, and stress disrupt human development, we describe them as *developmental shock, developmental trauma,* and *developmental stress.* As we differentiate among these three terms, we also recognize they are part of a continuum. In the Introduction, in Table I.1 we presented an abbreviated version of this continuum. Here in Table 5.1 we present a more detailed version of the trauma continuum.

TABLE 5.1

The Trauma Continuum

	SHOCK	TRAUMA	STRESS
Brain part involved	Brain stem, reptilian brain, ectoderm tissue	Limbic brain	Neocortex
Autonomic nervous system part involved	Parasympathetic nervous system	Sympathetic nervous system	Social engagement system (SES)
Behavioral symptoms	• Whitening of the skin • Staring, reduced blinking • Sudden flattening of affect • Amnesia of events • Lack of affect in describing a charged situation • Paralyzed speech • Cold limbs • Agoraphobia • Need to stand far away from others to feel safe • Unresponsiveness • Bulging eyes • Flaccid muscles	• Reddening of the skin • Rapid eye blinking • Edgy laughter • Fidgeting • Profuse sweating in social situations • Compulsive talking • Hypervigilance • Emotional outbursts • Exaggerated startle response with long duration • Sudden heat in body • Darting eyes • Overresponsiveness • Tense muscles • Difficulty sleeping	• Active, engaged but edgy and anxious • Strained facial expressions • Lack of consistent eye contact • Talking louder • Difficulty being relaxed
Time orientation	Dissociated	Past and present events entwined and confused	In present time
Interventions	*Goal: Help re-embody after dissociation* • Avoid analysis, catharsis, and looking into the past or future • Focus on present time • Track the urge to withdraw • Explore empowering options for restoring sense of self • Encourage the expression of feelings • Use nurturing, comforting, and protective language to hold clients in a	*Goal: Interrupting adrenaline cycle* • Bring body, emotions, and thought into present time • Develop both/and thinking by holding dualities, opposites, and paradoxes • Learn to process intense emotional experiences by feeling, witnessing, and surviving the emotions • Transform traumatic emotional experiences into narrative memories • Use nurturing, comforting,	*Goal: Communicating with clients to help them stay socially and emotionally engaged in present time* • Develop bodily awareness of unconscious and involuntary internal biological states • Develop

(continued)

TABLE 5.1 *(continued)*

	SHOCK	TRAUMA	STRESS
Interventions (continued)	"therapeutic embrace" while they return to their bodies.	and protective language to hold clients in a "therapeutic embrace" while they move through the trauma • Quiet, focusing, stilling awareness practices such as journaling and walking • Time in nature • Identify the fear behind the trauma reaction • Develop comfort with eye contact • Create clear personal boundaries	conscious and voluntary control of internal biological states

Developmental Shock

Developmental shock is a new term in the traumatology literature. It grew out of our heuristic research, and we believe it will make an important contribution to the field of trauma reduction when its importance is more fully understood.

Shock in the Traumatology Literature

In our literature review for this trauma continuum, we found very little information about shock in the traumatology field. The two most helpful sources of information about shock and shock states were in the work of Babbette Rothschild and Stephanie Mines. Rothschild, a specialist in body psychotherapy, has written two books (2000, 2003) that focus on the appropriate interventions to use in treating shock. She also provides training in somatic trauma therapy through her center in California.

Mines's training and her collaboration with William Emerson and the Association for Pre- and Perinatal Psychology and Health (APPPAH) provided her with the foundational experiences for writing her book, *We Are All in Shock: How Overwhelming Experiences Shatter You and What You Can Do About It* (2003). This groundbreaking book helped us immensely in organizing the shock component of our trauma continuum. Much of our synthesis on how to recognize and treat shock comes from these two main sources.

Once we created our developmental shock/trauma/stress continuum, we realized the significance of differentiating between shock and trauma. From an intervention perspective and the "do no harm" ethic of the mental health profession, we recognized how few clinicians understood the difference between them. We also realized that they were likely using interventions that were not only inappropriate but possibly doing harm. Rothschild wrote about what is probably a very common occurrence in the mental health profession in an article called "Applying the Brakes" published online in the *Body Mind Spirit Magazine* (2003):

> Much as we don't like to admit it publicly, it's an open secret among therapists that the road to recovery from trauma can be fraught with clinical missteps.
>
> In the past few years, I've frequently been consulted by highly competent colleagues who were dumbfounded by the speedy decline of clients contending with traumatic memories.
>
> Eight of these clients included a nurse, a businesswoman, a salesman, a therapist and other men and women who'd functioned relatively well prior to therapy.
>
> Yet after attempts to address their traumatic pasts (including rape, mugging, childhood abuse, and household fire), three were hospitalized, two went on disability, and the rest endured debilitating flashbacks, panic attacks, or other symptoms of dysfunction.
>
> All the therapists involved were experienced and well trained. Each one favored a different, theoretically sound, therapeutic modality (psychodynamic psychotherapy, EMDR, body psychotherapy, and cognitive–behavioral). None was irresponsible. So what exactly went wrong?
>
> In each instance, I eventually discovered, traumatic material was addressed before the client was equipped to manage it. These therapists were proceeding in a manner consistent with the usual aim of psychotherapy: helping a client open up. They knew very well how to call the genie of traumatic experience out of the bottle, but as is all too common, they didn't know how to get the genie back in....
>
> I never help clients call forth traumatic memories unless I and my clients are confident that the flow of their anxiety, emotion, memories, and body sensations can be contained at will. I never teach a client to hit the accelerator, in other words, before I know that he can find the brake. (¶ 1–6, 8)

We hope that our trauma continuum will provide a larger framework for discriminating among developmental shock, trauma, and stress and for identifying and implementing more effective interventions in the practice of counseling, social work, and psychotherapy. In Part Four of the book, we discuss effective interventions for treating unrecognized and unhealed developmental shock, trauma, and stress.

The Impact of Pre- and Perinatal Shock

Dr. William Emerson (1996, pp. 125–142), a pioneer in pre- and perinatal psychology, was one of the first to differentiate between shock and trauma. Shock has major impact at both the psychological and biological levels, including the production of adrenal and thyroid hormones. Reenactments of trauma experiences still permit some social engagement because they remain partly anchored in present time. Reenactments of shock experiences, in contrast, shut down social engagement, as they involve dissociation.

Individuals who were more traumatized than shocked during their early childhood experiences are more able to maintain some sense of control and/or power during the reenactment of traumatic events. They are able to use fight or flight defenses to help defend against or modulate the effects of their traumatization. In shock, however, neither fight nor flight responses are available, and the person falls into a freeze response, becomes immobilized, and then dissociates. Dissociation is the critical characteristic that distinguishes shock from trauma.

Emerson also identified two causes of shock—those of commission (an event in which something tangible happened) and those of omission (something that should have happened but did not). Shock can be a single-incident event, such as an abortion attempt, an epidural procedure, a long labor where a child is caught in the birth canal, a c-section, or being circumcised. It also can involve multiple obvious experiences, such as severe neglect, indifference, and a lack of touch or comfort. Unhealed early shock experiences, like developmental traumas, prevent the full development of the mammalian brain and make it difficult for a person to experience healthy love and compassion. It can lead to a lifetime of unhealthy, unsatisfying codependent relationships and self-defeating behaviors.

Because shock experiences register in the brain stem and the cerebellum, they have a huge impact during early embryological development when the structure of the emerging human is being created through a process known as embryogenesis. Embryonic cells have three layers of tissue—the endoderm, the mesoderm, and the ectoderm—that gradually differentiate to form specialized parts of a human.

Ectoderm or outer tissue forms the nervous system, hair, nails, teeth, the lining of the mouth, the skin, skin pigment, brain neurons, and the anal canal. Mesoderm or middle tissue forms the muscles (heart, skeletal, and gut), the kidneys, and red blood cells. Endoderm or inner cell tissue forms the digestive tract, the respiratory system and lungs, the thyroid, and the pancreas. All tissues that derive from the same germ layer are controlled by the corresponding part of the brain (Markolin, 2010, p. 18). This is new information emerging in the field of complementary medicine that is critical in the study of prenatal causes of degenerative conditions.

By the end of the first trimester, all of the physical structures formed from these three layers of tissue are completed. Any developmental shock during this critical period can cause a variety of birth defects in any of these three tissue layers. Common defects occur in the eyes and genital organs or physical anomalies such as ectodermal dysplasias, which involve abnormal development of the skin, hair, nails, teeth, and sweat glands (Odent, n.d.).

Nerves connect the brain to the teeth and transmit electrical messages out to specific organs in the body. Biological dentists, a new specialty group in the field, now have tooth charts that combine dentistry science with Chinese medicine. These charts use the Chinese energy meridian system to show how each tooth connects to specific body organs. This holistic branch of dentistry recognizes the close relationship between dental health and psychology, nutrition, body structure, the craniosacral system, the immune system, and the central nervous system.

We are working on a hypothesis that says the experiences of developmental shock during the first trimester of prenatal development leave energetic imprints in the embryonic tissues that lay the foundation for schizophrenia and degenerative health conditions later in life. We discuss this topic in more detail in Chapter 8.

Between the beginning of the second trimester of prenatal development and 6–8 months after birth, children do not yet have all parts of the brain and central nervous system fully developed and interconnected. However, the process of connecting all these systems begins very early. Stephanie Mines said that, "Because memory is well-established by the third trimester, environmental experiences are constantly being stored, and they are thoroughly shaping the development of the brain" (2003, p. 178).

Acute or chronic experiences of developmental shock during the entire prenatal stage are stored in our energy field and in our body (Rand, 1996, p. 6). Energetic imprints of early shock and trauma are often stored as "miasms," a term created by Samuel Hahnemann, the father of homeopathy (King, n.d.). With the advent of language from the quantum sciences, the concept is now more easily defined as a field of energy stored in the mindbody that influences genetic expression and the appearance of health issues. Some of the most widely known miasms are associated with tuberculosis, syphilis, psoriasis, and cancer. Contemporary homeopaths such as Peter Chappell (2003) have extended this framework to psychotherapy and refer to these energetic emotional patterns as "trauma miasms."

Developmental shock during the prenatal stage of development is most commonly caused by violent incidents such as abortion attempts against the fetus, domestic violence against the mother, exposure to ingested and inhaled toxins such as alcohol and nicotine, and exposure to natural or human-made catastrophes. These extreme events shock the embryo, zygote, or fetus and leave energetic imprints that can disrupt or cause aberrations in prenatal development.

Other intensely emotional events, such as a family crisis during prenatal development, commonly cause mothers to energetically disconnect from their infants. Hormones secreted as the result of their mothers' shocking experiences can also biologically trigger developmental shock reactions in the fetus (Mines, 2003, p.

180). During birth, developmental shock reactions can be caused by medical interventions such as pitocin-induced deliveries, the administration of epidural injections or general anesthesia to mothers, a c-section delivery, umbilical cord trauma, multiple births, or breech presentation.

According to Claire Winstone (2003, pp. 8–24), early experiences of developmental shock can block access to some of the deepest aspects of the self, creating later difficulties with intimacy, self-esteem, and connecting to one's sense of purpose and meaning and spirituality. An embryo, zygote, fetus, neonate, or infant has no language to conceptualize experiences of developmental shock, no sense of boundaries, no protection, and only a limited ability to move and flee to safety. Thc only option wired into a developing human at this juncture is to freeze and then dissociate.

The Biochemistry of Shock

The autonomic nervous system—the parasympathetic, sympathetic, and social engagement system (SES)—work together synergistically to help a person maintain internal balance and homeostasis while experiencing different kinds of activities and body functions. The SES keeps people socially and emotionally engaged, the sympathetic system provides extra energy when it is needed, and the parasympathetic system provides calming after stressful activities.

Very intense physical or emotional events disturb this balance. Extreme events that are experienced as life threatening, contain fear-inducing news, or trap people in a life-or-death situation not of their choosing from which there is no escape overwhelm the autonomic nervous system and drop people into freeze responses where they become immobilized and dissociated.

Freeze states are an extreme defense strategy used only when there is no possibility of fight or flight. The mindbody uses this "feigned death" defense only as a last resort in an attempt to survive until the danger is past. This freeze or immobility state may resemble a form of hibernation or near death, as the blood pressure drops, muscles collapse, and the mind numbs and is unable to store information. As a result, amnesia is very common after such shock-inducing experiences.

Shock and Brain Function

Developmental shock registers in the brain stem and cerebellum, which control autonomic body functions, large muscles, and instinctive survival behaviors. It triggers the parasympathetic nervous system, which normally works to restore a calming, relaxed response, so that it overproduces the hormones that slow down the vital functions. This freeze response is a natural survival mechanism for convincing a predator that its prey is already dead and therefore undesirable. In humans, it allows a person to escape from something through inactivity that often appears as indecision, procrastination, and passivity. The triggering of unhealed experiences of shock may also be a cause of chronic depressive states.

During a shock reaction, people experience lowered vitality, increased depression, dissociation, and a loss of time orientation. Physically they slow down so much that they have a frozen appearance, glassy staring eyes that do not blink, bulging eyes with dilated pupils, a whitening of the skin, cold limbs, flattened affect, and paralyzed speech. People in shock have the urge to move away from others and curl into fetal position, appear immobilized, and experience falling into the black hole. In Part Four of the book, we discuss the appropriate interventions for treating shock.

The Long-Term Effects of Developmental Shock

Individuals who experience developmental shock eventually develop parasympathetic dominance and are at risk of health problems such as weight gain, lightheadedness, low blood pressure, low heart rate, foggy thinking, low blood sugar, obesity, and degenerative conditions such as chronic fatigue syndrome, asthma, depression, Type 2 diabetes, and Alzheimer's (Mead, 2006). Shock, and the internal conflict associated with it, is stored in the body and reactivated by events in daily life until it is resolved. Shock wounds require interventions that engage the most unconscious or shadow aspects of the personality.

Coupling

Like trauma, shock states are activated not only by stimuli resembling the original shock event, but also by many apparently unrelated triggers. Traumatologist Peter Levine refers to this process of generalizing as *coupling* (1997, p. 109). Suppose a woman who was in an auto accident was driving a 2001 blue Ford Taurus sedan. If she begins to have aversion or avoidance reactions to cars that resemble the one she crashed in, she is coupling stimuli in her mindbody. Effective treatment of shock must help clients uncouple stimuli such as blue sedans and the impulse to shift into a protective mode in the presence of such stimuli.

Dissociation and Memory

Dissociation, a psychological defense mechanism that protects infants and very young children against experiences of shock, also contains psychobiological components. It is a state of acute mental and emotional fragmentation in which certain thoughts, emotions, body sensations, and relational memories are partitioned from the conscious mind and compartmentalized in the unconscious mind because they are too overwhelming for the conscious mind to integrate. This subconscious strategy for regulating powerful negative emotions is also known as *intrapsychic splitting,* as these thoughts, emotions, sensations, and/or memories are split off from conscious awareness. Dissociated memory can be split off for either a short or long time. It usually returns to conscious awareness only when triggered by a sensory cue involving a picture, smell, sound, emotion, body memory, or relational dynamic that opens a circuit to the stored memory of an earlier shocking event.

Dissociated memory makes people vulnerable to specific sensory cues such as smells, pictures, sounds, touch, and specific kinds of relational dynamics. When a cue appears in the environment that correlates with a sensory cue anchored in a previous experience of a shock, it triggers the partitioned memory of the original shock and activates a freeze reaction. This immediately causes the person to experience an inner collapse involving a loss of reality and orientation to time.

If a war veteran, for example, comes upon a horrific auto accident while driving, he may immediately access dissociated memories from a shocking war scene. His body reacts as though he were in the past, causing him to act as if he were in a combat situation. The memories of that shocking war scene may also correlate with an earlier layer of shocking memories related to incidents of abuse or neglect during his childhood. Dissociation is a component of falling into the black hole, which we describe in more detail in the next chapter.

The earlier a shock happens in a person's life, the more likely he or she will develop dissociative behaviors (Schore, 2003b, p. 138). In the first weeks and months of life, infants lack sophisticated protective mechanisms and defenses against shock. Their only response is to freeze and dissociate. The bonding process is still developing and somewhat tenuous between the child and caregiver. The internal working model of reality is not yet anchored in infants' right brains, so they are totally vulnerable and without defenses. They may dissociate if their mother or other caregivers are too invasive or overstimulating for them to cope. If they experience some emotional dysregulation, then dissociation becomes a way of attempting to reregulate their emotions.

About the only effective defense against overwhelming emotional experiences is dissociation—not just from the psychological shock, but also from the overwhelming biological reactions happening in their bodies. Infants who adopt dissociation as a mechanism for coping with early experiences of shock may make it their primary response against a broad spectrum of daily stressors. It is possible to identify these children, as they are in a chronic state of appearing withdrawn or "spaced out" and are often misdiagnosed as autistic.

A person who is in the midst of intense conflict may also dissociate. For example, if another person says or does something that reminds you of an unresolved shocking event from your past, the dissociated memories related to the past conflict will activate a freeze response in the present conflict situation, and you become unable to speak or defend yourself. This will cause you to feel confused and withdraw emotionally. It can also cause a regression or dissociation reaction in which you are spontaneously transported to the past and out of your body.

Regression can cause one or both parties to immediately disconnect from their present-time couple conflict and shift their awareness to traumatic events that happened in the past. It can trigger a mutual reenactment of shock that is related to both partners' unrecognized and unhealed shock experiences from the past, and cause them both to shatter internally and either emotionally collapse or escalate. Neither is able to think clearly in the moment about how to effectively resolve their conflict.

Psychohistorian Lloyd deMause has done an extensive study of mutual or collective reenactments of shocking experiences (deMause, 1982). He characterized them as "group fantasies" or group psychodramas that are unconsciously acted out through wars and ethnic and religious conflicts that contain archetypal and mythic elements. His psychohistorical model validates the systemic perspective we use in DST, particularly how unrecognized and unhealed individual shock, trauma, and stress are transmitted both intergenerationally and between small and large human systems.

Developmental Trauma

The literature on trauma does not contain much on developmental trauma, which is a relatively new term that we have used to describe our heuristic research findings. We see developmental trauma as being far more pervasive than the acute trauma that is seen as the cause of PTSD and thus as very important in advancing our understanding of the effects of trauma in general.

Trauma in the Traumatology Literature

There is an enormous body of literature in the field of traumatology. Much of it, unfortunately, not only does not discriminate between shock and trauma but also does not discriminate between chronic and acute trauma.

A *trauma* has traditionally been defined as any experience that overwhelms the psyche and the body's nervous system and creates lasting changes in its hormonal stress response (van der Kolk, McFarlane, & Weisaeth, 1996, p. 4). Traumas connect cellular intelligence, the sympathetic, parasympathetic, and social engagement systems with the heart and right brain. They create heightened biological sensitivities to auditory, visual, sensory, and movement stimuli and relational cues such as facial expressions, voice tone, and body language (Porges, 2003).

Most research on the causes of trauma focuses on acute traumatic events such as accidents, murder, wars, natural catastrophes, human-made ecological disasters, and physical and sexual child abuse. Most traumatologists recognize that exposure to acute trauma, particularly repeated exposure, causes symptoms of posttraumatic stress, leads to developmental delays, and contributes to degenerative illnesses. Most of the current research has not focused on studying the long-term effects of developmental shock, trauma, or stress that is outside these traditional definitions of trauma. In our approach, we go beyond this traditional trauma paradigm.

Our Definition of Developmental Trauma

In this book, we identify developmental trauma as a previously unrecognized form of chronic relational trauma that causes delays in early development during the bonding and separation stages. We believe that the lingering effects of unrecognized and untreated developmental trauma are the major causes of delayed development in all human systems: individuals, couples, families, groups/organizations, nation–states, and the human race. This form of developmental trauma is so widespread and so pervasive in our global society that it has become virtually invisible. Two of our goals in writing this book are to make the world aware of the effects of this form of chronic trauma and to provide tools for healing it so that humanity can evolve.

We expand the traditional definition of trauma by showing how "ordinary" day-to-day events can cause chronic trauma. These events, typically considered "standard practices" by unknowing parents or professionals, begin very early in life. They are so common culturally that they are virtually invisible to the untrained eye. These events include shock or trauma at the time of conception, during prenatal development and birth, and postnatal shocks or traumas during the first 3 years of life.

We also include in our definition common events such as being born before the previous sibling is 3 years of age, separations from the mother that are either too long or too numerous, postpartum depression, prolonged ear infections, family crises, and inattentive or unresponsive caregivers. All of these events disrupt the emotional resonance between the mother and child and prevent secure bonding from occurring between them.

A growing body of research shows three critical factors that influence the impact of shock or trauma in early development:

1. The age of the child at the time of the event
2. The duration of the shocking or traumatic event
3. The amount of comfort the child received from caregivers at the time of the event

When young children are exposed to very intense and/or very lengthy shocking or traumatic experiences with little or no comforting, the more pervasive the event on their subsequent development.

An excellent example of this is a male child born to a first-time mother who experiences an 18-hour labor that also involved breech delivery and umbilical cord trauma. After the birth, the boy is taken aside, circumcised, and moved to an infant nursery. This exact scenario has happened to millions of boys since the 1940s, when circumcision became common and infant nurseries after birth were the norm. Only now are professionals such as pre- and perinatal psychologists recognizing the long-term consequences of these very common birth and perinatal practices.

Infants and young children have upsetting, painful, and disturbing experiences every day. Not all of them, however, are experienced as shocking or traumatic. The factor that determines whether these experiences are just psychological "owies" that are forgotten, or are filed in the nervous system as shock or trauma, is whether or not the child received timely comfort and appropriate emotional support. It is common, for example, for young children to fall off their bicycles and skateboards or to be excluded by friends. As adults, very few remember these kinds of childhood events as traumatic because a caring adult quickly comforted them.

How parents respond to a child's painful experiences also determines whether the child's nervous system stores an event as a shock or trauma (Schore, 2003b, p. 123). When parents get triggered and lose their ability to regulate their emotions, they also lose their connection to their children. In this case, the painful event evokes a shared, intergenerational trauma. For example, if a father loses one of his parents, he would naturally feel shock, trauma, or both. As the father processes his grief about his parent, his child would naturally feel the temporary loss of connection to his father and also the loss of his grandparent, assuming he was bonded with both of them. In these cases, it is difficult for the grieving father to comfort his child and both end up experiencing a mutual shock or trauma state.

The traumatic events that adults *do* recall from their childhood typically involve memories of physical abuse or isolation or feelings of being emotionally misunderstood, rejected, or abandoned. This means that their emotional needs for comfort and assurance were not recognized and not responded to. Children's nervous systems quickly calm down when they are held closely, have their wounds quickly administered to, and are spoken to in loving and assuring ways. In this situation, the children's bodies are able to slow the production of cortisol and quickly restart the flow of the "feel-good" chemicals such as oxytocin, and the crisis is over.

The History of Trauma

The study of early childhood trauma is relatively recent. For many years, it was believed that children's nervous systems were not fully developed at birth but matured along with brain function, memory, language, and motor development. Operating under this assumption, adults believed infants could not feel or remember pain and treated them as inanimate objects—performing surgery on them without anesthesia, beating them unmercifully, and sexually abusing them. Recent research on the development of children's nervous systems indicates quite the opposite is true, as we will describe shortly.

The field of traumatology began with the study of military veterans returning from the Civil War, World Wars I and II, the Korean War, and the Vietnam War (Herman, 1992). Men returning from these combat experiences exhibited symptoms of *shell shock*—glazed eyes, problems communicating and relating, memory loss, and difficulties in returning to their peacetime work. It was not their physical wounds that incapacitated them, it was their psychological and emotional scars. Some acted hysterical, screaming and weeping uncontrollably, while others appeared frozen and immobilized and were mute and unresponsive. After World War I, the condition was categorized as *combat neurosis*. Then the study of trauma waned until veterans began returning from WW II. However, once this war was over, interest in trauma diminished again.

During the 1920s, Sigmund Freud identified the phenomenon of *repetition compulsion* in his patients. He also recognized the significance of early childhood experiences and saw how children developed certain patterns of behavior that they repeated over and over again in latter life.

His concept of the repetition compulsion has become the source paradigm for many subsequent psychologists wanting to make sense out of unconscious repetitive behavior. Freud also associated it with the *talionic response*—the "eye-for-an-eye" compulsion that drives revenge. He was the first to recognize these behaviors as components of what is now known as *traumatic reenactment*—a characteristic of posttraumatic stress.

The big spurt in trauma research in the U.S. began after the return of veterans from the Vietnam War. Many of them joined support groups run by other veterans where they were able to retell and relive their traumatic experiences. Some of these groups included sympathetic psychiatrists, who provided them with professional assistance.

One of the important outcomes of these groups was that they focused public attention on the real legacy of war: lasting psychological damage caused by combat trauma. The assertiveness of these veterans' groups put enough pressure on the Veterans' Administration that it eventually created a legal mandate for psychological treatment programs for PTSD. It was here that the search began for effective tools to treat trauma.

The women's movement of the 1970s paralleled the consciousness-raising that happened in Vietnam veterans' support groups. Women recognized that many of them also had symptoms of combat neurosis. While men were slowly beginning to receive recognition and resources to alleviate their war trauma, many women found their "problem without a name" was anchored in their relationships with Vietnam vets and included domestic violence, rape, male domination, and sexual abuse. This awareness helped spawn the rise of feminism and an effort to educate society about the existence of posttraumatic stress in women with abusive relationships and its impact on their lives and their children's lives.

A couple of important things came out of the women's movement. The first was new language to help articulate the impact of dominating and authoritarian male behavior on women, children, and families. The second was a redefinition of rape to include date rape, acquaintance rape, and marital rape. With the women's movement came the emergence of crisis and domestic violence centers where women and children could get practical, legal, and emotional support for victimization and relational trauma and for symptoms of PTSD.

The children's movement, if it might be called that, began in the 1980s with the emergence of the field of pre- and perinatal psychology. The founding members of this field have continued to build a body of scientific knowledge that supports their premise that humans have consciousness and memory from their very first moment of life.

During the 1990s, the field of traumatology saw the emergence of many new modalities for treating—not just medicating—the symptoms of trauma. Eye movement desensitization and reprocessing (EMDR) involves moving the eyes side to side while recalling elements of a trauma. It was one of the first trauma reduction tools to be widely used. While it was effective in clearing auditory and visual elements of trauma, initially it did not clear the proprioceptive and relational elements of a trauma. Thought-field therapy (TFT), a body-oriented therapy, worked exceptionally well on clearing trauma related to touch and movement. Emotional freedom therapy (EFT), also a body-oriented therapy, involves specific patterns of tapping on the body's energy meridians. Much of the early research on these new technologies was conducted with veterans of the Vietnam War, who helped build a solid research base for their effectiveness in treating symptoms of PTSD. In Chapters 10 through 13 we discuss intervention modalities for treating developmental shock, trauma, and stress.

Trauma and Brain Function

New discoveries from brain research are overturning the concept of the brain as a fixed and inaccessible organ. No longer seen as a self-contained unit with a preset, unchangeable structure set at birth, the brain is now recognized as a flexible, malleable instrument capable of adapting to a broad range of physical, emotional, cognitive, and environmental stimuli. According to Schore, "The human cerebral cortex adds about 70% of its final DNA content after birth" (2004). A new area of brain research focuses on prenatal development and on the treatment of posttraumatic stress symptoms. From this new area of research, the correlation between childhood trauma and subsequent disturbances or social behavior and violence is gradually becoming accepted (Niehoff, 2002).

Developmental trauma registers in the limbic or mammalian brain. It activates the sympathetic nervous system, which stimulates the production of adrenal hormones and causes the fight/flight response, hypervigilance, and hyperactivity.

It creates more aggressive, physical behavior and conflict that can lead to adrenal fatigue and exhaustion contributing to cellular breakdown and disease.

Physically the symptoms include reddening or flushing of the skin, darting eyes and rapid eye blinking, edgy laughter, and hypervigilance designed to prevent exposure to the triggers of stressful or intimate conflicts. Other symptoms include overresponding to stressful situations and hyperactivity, an exaggerated startle reflex, tense muscles, and regressive states that cause confusion between past and present realities. Addictions or compulsive behaviors such as talking, eating, working, exercising, smoking, drinking, and sex are ways that people avoid encountering the emotions they repressed from previous unrecognized and unhealed traumatic experiences. This is usually a defense against falling into a shock reaction and dissociation.

Developmental trauma, as defined in our trauma continuum, is stored primarily in the limbic or mammalian brain, which processes and stores memories related to our relationships and emotions. Structurally, it contains the hypothalamus, the amygdala, and the hippocampus. Early emotional memories are stored in the amygdala as pictures, symbols, or icons rather than narrative language. Severe traumas from wars, natural catastrophes, and collective traumas such as global catastrophes, for example, are also symbolically stored in the amygdala as a form of genetic or race memory that Barbara Hand Clow described as "catastrophobia" (2007, pp. 189–190).

During episodes of PTSD, visual images related to the memory being re-experienced fire in the brain as flashbacks. These images also hold memory traces containing certain visual scenes that get stuck in the brain's processing. Symbolic memories are unavailable to the conscious mind, but emerge in dreams, artwork, body memories, feelings, and events that trigger an image of earlier traumas (van der Kolk, 1988, pp. 273–290).

A second kind of memory, called narrative memory, uses language—words and meanings based on words. Narrative memory, which begins being stored in the hippocampus around age 4 or 5 years, forms the memory found in the conscious mind (LeDoux, 1994, pp. 50–57).

In order to release a traumatic memory from the amygdala, it is necessary to convert the pictures or symbols that are filed in the amygdala into narrative language that is stored in the hippocampus. This transfer of information between these parts of the brain has become a key component of trauma reduction and trauma elimination therapies. It is also a critical factor in helping people to make meaning of their traumatic experiences, which also allows the experience to be integrated into the person's life experience. This follows the adage, "when life hands you lemons, learn to make lemonade."

Trauma also disrupts the circuitry in the corpus callosum, a structure found in mammalian brains that connects the left hemisphere's cognitive function with the right hemisphere's emotional, relational, and symbolic functions. Short circuits in the corpus callosum can impair not only a person's ability to recognize his or her feelings, but also the ability to express them. This impairment creates *alexithymia,* or the lack of words to express feelings (Goleman, 1996). Therapies that involve art and movement with younger children combine the symbolic with the narrative, which helps build new circuitry in the corpus callosum and shift the brain into whole-system functioning.

The Biochemistry of Trauma

Our research on the biochemical processes of both shock and trauma revealed how virtually all human experience is dictated and regulated by the production and release of hormones and other chemicals such as peptides, proteins, and neurotransmitters. From a biochemical perspective, it is clear that the body has a very specific response program, one that can be tracked and monitored, to cope with perceived danger. Once science identified this biochemical response program and removed the mystery from the process, it opened the door to understanding the scientific basis of more subtle human experiences, such as developmental trauma.

Developmental trauma, whether it is acute or chronic, represents the midpoint of the developmental shock/trauma/stress continuum and causes a full mobilization of the body at a biochemical level. The hypothalamus, pituitary, and adrenal glands all secrete specialized hormones such as epinephrine, norepinephrine, cortisol, and cortisone that are responsible for this mobilization. They coordinate the function of the body's organs to generate a protection response. The blood vessels constrict in the digestive tract and force the blood to the arms and legs for fighting or fleeing. In the protection mode, all growth-related functions in the body stop and can eventually compromise the body's physical survival because of reduced reserves of vital energy.

Cortisol, also known as the "fear hormone," is responsible for aggression, hyperarousal, and anxiety. It is associated with depression, addictions, a weakened immune response, obesity, diabetes, osteoporosis, and a suppressed libido. Excess amounts of cortisol are believed to be causes of clogged arteries, heart disease, high blood pressure, and the breakdown of muscles, bones, and joints. Developmental trauma causes excess amounts of these hormones to be released into the body, and it is considered as a major factor in chronic and degenerative diseases (Lipton, 2005, pp. 151–152). Cortisol and its related hormones are also responsible for the flight reactions and the hyperactive behavior commonly associated with trauma.

The rapid-fire biochemical processes that occur after being triggered often create an internal feeling of collapse often described as "shattering." This psychobiological experience involves the breakdown of psychological defenses, more commonly known as a nervous breakdown, as the brain shifts from the more complex and sophisticated neocortex part of the brain to the limbic brain and eventually to the cerebellum and old brain. During this process, people confuse past events with present-time events and encounter dissociated memory and split-off feelings and beliefs related to past events involving shock and trauma. This psychological collapse also overwhelms the SES and sympathetic parts of the autonomic nervous system, activates the SDS, and contributes to the re-experiencing component of PTSD (van der Kolk, McFarlane, & Weisaeth, 1996, pp. 369–370).

During life crisis experiences, small amounts of cortisol from the adrenal glands provide a quick burst of energy to ensure survival, heighten memory, boost immunity, lower sensitivity to pain, and help maintain the biological homeostasis of the body. Although cortisol is a critical part of the body's response to stress, it was designed only for short-term use. Once the crisis is over, the body's natural relaxation response allows blood pressure, heart rate, digestive functioning, and hormonal levels to return to their normal state.

Unfortunately, in our fast-paced culture, some people's trauma response gets activated so often that they have difficulty in normalizing it. This creates higher and more sustained levels of cortisol in the bloodstream that are now associated with the negative effects of developmental trauma. These effects include impaired cognitive performance, suppressed thyroid function, blood sugar imbalances such as hyperglycemia, decreased bone density, a decrease in muscle tissue, higher blood pressure, lower immunity, inflammatory responses in the body, and increased abdominal fat.

Abdominal fat is associated with more health problems than fat deposited in other areas of the body. Some of the health problems associated with increased stomach fat are heart attacks, strokes, higher levels of "bad" cholesterol (LDL), and lower levels of "good" cholesterol (HDL).

The most important part of the biochemical experience of trauma, however, is the experience of escalated emotional states. When people are unable to reregulate themselves emotionally, they respond in one of several ways. Cortisol may drive them to act out fight responses by becoming aggressive or hyperactive, or to act out flight responses and avoidance.

It may be difficult to believe, but virtually all of this dramatic internal biochemical activity is invisible to other people. With training, however, it becomes possible to recognize these subtle physiological and behavioral symptoms. These include changes that are associated with shock and trauma—the size of the pupils in the eyes, skin color, and the ability to communicate as we describe in Table 5.1. More severe responses to trauma can include explosive behaviors such as crying and screaming. Implosive behaviors such as vomiting and fainting are symptoms of shock rather than trauma.

The Impact of Developmental Trauma on Young Children

Violata and Russell (1994) conducted a Canadian meta-analysis of 88 published research studies on the effects of nonmaternal care on the development of infants and young children. They found that when infants and young children, particularly boys, spend more than 20 hours a week away from their mothers, it can seriously affect their social–emotional development, behavioral development, and maternal attachment. Their study found no support for the belief that high-quality childcare is an acceptable substitute for parental care.

Women, unfortunately, are returning to work relatively soon after giving birth. National estimates from U. S. Census data reveal that among first-time mothers employed and giving birth between 1996 and 2000, 60% had returned to work by 3 months after delivery (Bureau of Labor Statistics, 2005). Schore was very clear about the impact of early disruptions in the mother–infant relationship that cause emotional dysregulation.

> Although short-term dysregulations are not problematic, prolonged negative states are toxic for infants, and although they possess some capacity to modulate low-intensity negative affect states, these states continue to escalate in intensity, frequency and duration. (2003a, p. 77)

The cultural lack of awareness about social and emotional needs of young children contributes to what we believe is cultural neglect. This has serious implications for our national policy of federal and state support for childcare that encourage new mothers to work.

The countries in Western, Central, and Eastern Europe have universal parental and maternal leave policies that are much more supportive of infants and families. Their leave periods average around 10 months (Kammerman, 2000, p. 97), and they typically provide some form of wage replacement or income supplement for parents (Waldfogel, 2001, p. 29).

Other research on the impact of developmental trauma indicates that many 2- to 4-year-old children who are not exposed to extreme adversities involving maltreatment or deprivation are stressed because of their social experiences (Nelson & Luciana, 2008, p. 73). Children this age show a rise in cortisol levels when they are enrolled in full-time childcare, but not on the days when they are at home. We find it interesting that the interpretation of this research finding focuses on the stressful nature of peer relationships during this period of development, as though these interactions might be the primary cause of the children's elevated cortisol levels. Our interpretation of this information looks at developmental shock, trauma, and stress from too much time away from the mother, too many different adults providing care in the childcare facility, care by emotionally unsupportive adults, and too few adults supervising too many children.

This same research study indicated that long hours in childcare facilities strain children's sympathetic and parasympathetic nervous systems. Over the course of the day, cortisol levels climb, and they were the greatest in the children least skilled in social interactions, particularly those rejected by peers or rated as less socially competent and less capable of regulating their emotions.

This same study indicated that facilities where adults provided sensitive, responsive, and individualized care, children had little or no evidence of childcare-induced cortisol elevations. We interpret this finding as an indication that childcare environments that provide care equivalent to that provided by children's mothers does not stress them emotionally.

The findings of this study about the impact of childcare on children's development contradict those of the Canadian meta-analysis. This kind of confusion among experts makes it even more difficult for parents of infants to make decisions about new mothers returning to work. These questions, which involve delicate choices between the social and emotional needs of the infant and the larger needs of the couple and family, are never easy.

Unfortunately, childcare professionals and early childhood educators are only just beginning to understand the importance of children's social and emotional needs. I (Janae) began training people in these fields in the late 1990s and found that the biggest obstacle to upgrading the profession was the impaired social, emotional, and mental health of the providers and educators themselves. While there were childcare providers who attended my presentations, workshops, and trainings and implemented some of my suggestions, many still showed tremendous resistance to changing how they care for young children.

My biggest complaint about the childcare and early childhood profession is their insistence on using time-out practices to isolate very young children when they become emotionally dysregulated. This is absolutely the worst thing they could do for the child and is a primary cause of elevated cortisol levels in preschool-age children, particularly those between the ages of 2 and 4. Asking children who are energetically separated from caring adults to reregulate themselves is not only impossible for most young children but also totally unethical. I developed a set of time-in practices that I handed out at my presentations and posted on our website. While some saw the logic in this, many ignored the principle.

I finally concluded that adults use time-outs as a way to reregulate themselves and to separate themselves from the children who trigger them in some way. Once I discovered this, I began encouraging stressed childcare providers to create backup support within their facility so that they could take a time-out from the children and the stressful environment and calm themselves. During our discussions, they were able to recognize how their personal stress increased the children's levels of stress and actually made the problem worse.

The "custodial" model of childcare so popular a generation back that focused on the physical care of children has gradually changed into an "educational" model that focuses on brain development and cognitive learning skills. The emerging "social and emotional" model is too confrontive to many in the field, as it asks them to look at why they treat children the way they do. This self-reflection requires that they examine the experiences of their own early childhood and look for correlations between their personal issues with children who trigger them and their unrecognized and unhealed developmental shock, trauma, and stress from the past. Most are still unwilling to take this step.

Parents and professionals also lack awareness about children's social and emotional needs during custody hearings and in the establishment of visitation rights when parents divorce. Ken Magid's research (Magid & McKelvey, 1989, p. 335) showed that at different ages there is a limit to the amount of time that children can cope with being physically separated from a bonded parent or caregiver. If parents exceed these limits, they risk causing developmental shock, trauma, or stress in their children. Table 5.2, which Magid developed as a guideline for determining parental visitation for divorced parents, shows his recommendations for the preferable and acceptable limits for children at different ages. The most common effects of overly long separations are a breakdown of trust, a feeling of abandonment, and other emotional problems such as depression.

Identifying Developmental Trauma

The spectrum of age-related responses to developmental shock, trauma, and stress, we discovered, plays a very significant role in determining an adult's personal style of resolving conflict. Those who experienced shock experiences in the first year of life were more likely to have freeze responses during conflict. Those who experienced trauma during the second year of life often used flight responses during conflict, while those who experienced stress during the second and third years of life typically reacted with fight responses during conflict.

Our heuristic research on this particular correlation provided us with foundational information for developing our developmental model of conflict resolution, which we describe in our book, *Conflict Resolution: The Partnership Way*

TABLE 5.2

The Limits of Parental Separation

Age of child	Preferable limit	Acceptable limit	Harmful limit
Under one year	2 days	7 days	More than 7 days
1 – 2 years	3 days	10 days	More than 10 days
3 – 5 years	1 week	3 weeks	More than 3 weeks
6 – 9 years	2 weeks	4 weeks	More than 4 weeks
10 – 13 years	4 weeks	6 weeks	More than 6 weeks
14+ years	6 weeks	9 weeks	More than 9 weeks

(Weinhold & Weinhold, 2009). The following inventory will help you determine if you have any hidden effects of unhealed developmental shock, trauma, or stress in your background.

Self-Inventory: Identifying Developmental Trauma

Directions: Read the statements below and use 1–4 in the blank to indicate your self-assessment of how true each item is: 1 = Almost never, 2 = Occasionally, 3 = Usually, and 4 = Almost always

___ 1. I have trouble feeling close to the people I care about.
___ 2. I feel like other people are more in charge of my life than I am.
___ 3. I seem reluctant to try new things.
___ 4. I have trouble regulating my weight.
___ 5. I am easily bored with what I am doing.
___ 6. I have trouble accepting help from others even when I need it.
___ 7. I work best when I am under a lot of pressure.
___ 8. I have trouble admitting my mistakes.
___ 9. I tend to forget or not keep agreements I make.
___10. I have trouble handling my time and money effectively.
___11. I use intimidation or manipulation to settle my conflicts.
___12. I feel personally attacked when someone has a conflict with me.
___13. I have a difficult time giving and receiving compliments.
___14. I have a short fuse when I feel frustrated with others or myself.
___15. I tend to blame others for causing the problems I have.
___16. I feel like I have a huge empty place inside of me.
___17. It is hard for me to have positive thoughts about my future.
___18. Inside I feel like a tightly coiled spring.
___19. When I get anxious, I tend to eat or drink too much.
___20. I feel empty and alone.
___21. I tend to question the motives of others.
___22. I feel unloved by others.
___23. I have a hard time defining what I want or need.
___24. When I get into a conflict, somebody else gets his or her way.
___25. I tend to overreact to certain people and/or situations that bug me.
___26. I feel like I am on an emotional roller coaster.
___27. I have trouble sticking with any spiritual practices I start.
___28. Important people in my life have abandoned me emotionally or physically.
___29. I have trouble concentrating on what I am doing.
___30. When I think about my childhood, I draw a big blank.

___31. I have trouble experiencing the intimacy I want in my relationships
___32. I have trouble falling asleep and staying asleep.
___33. I tend to "walk on eggs" around certain people or situations.
___34. I avoid places or situations that remind me of experiences from my past.
___35. I have recurring bad dreams about what happened to me in the past.
___36. My thoughts seem to have a life of their own.
___37. I have trouble paying attention to what others are saying.
___38. I tend to avoid situations and people that could cause me conflicts.
___39. I experience big gaps in my memory about my childhood.
___40. I have a hard time knowing what I am feeling inside.
_____ Total Score

Interpretation:

If your score was between:
40–82 = Some evidence of developmental trauma
83–120 = Moderate evidence of developmental trauma
121–160 = Strong evidence of developmental trauma

Further analysis:

Look at the content of items where you scored 3–4 for clues to unhealed developmental traumas.

Posttraumatic Stress Disorder

When we are exposed to present-time events or experiences that contain cues or signals reminding us of past traumas, this can activate symptoms of posttraumatic stress. It includes regression; confusion between past and present events; flashbacks; hypervigilant avoidance of certain situations; sleep disturbances; problems with concentration; and physical symptoms such as sweating, nausea, and increased heart rate. These symptoms are identical to either acute trauma or the subtler developmental trauma. If not cleared, these traumas eventually cause physical, emotional, mental, and relational distortions.

Developmental trauma that is not cleared from the brain and central nervous system at the time of the original traumatic event is stored in the limbic brain and central nervous system, where it may be triggered in present time by auditory, visual, or perceptual cues or stimuli. Triggering catapults a person's time–space orientation from the present to the past and causes an experience of developmental regression.

For instance, a woman who was in an automobile accident as a small child may experience an automatic physical reaction when she hears the screeching of tires and crushing of metal. She may start trembling; feel a sense of panic and danger; and be flooded with images, feelings, beliefs, and reactions related to her own car crash. Even though she knows in her adult mind that she is not in the midst of an automobile accident, both her brain and her body react as though she were in danger.

Psychologically, she begins acting as if she were the age she was at the time of the accident. If she had unhealed trauma prior to this accident, the sound of screeching tires and crushing metal not only triggers memories of her childhood accident, it may also trigger earlier memories of trauma or shock.

Biologically, her brain will also regress from the neocortex into the limbic part of her brain. As she does, her behavior will also change. Initially, she may use her neocortex to think or talk about the accident. If this does not help her reregulate herself emotionally, then she may fall into a deep emotional state and begin to cry. When this does not help her become emotionally reregulated, she will go into shock and fall into her reptilian brain–based survival responses (Schore, 2003b, p. 138).

This woman is suffering from a PTSD, which has symptoms that range on a continuum from mild to severe. Those with less severe or fewer symptoms may have what is known as *subclinical* PTSD, meaning that they do not meet all the criteria for a clinical diagnosis, but they still display some of the characteristics of the disorder.

Our heuristic research revealed the presence of both clinical and subclinical symptoms of PTSD in people who had experienced developmental trauma. The criteria for making a diagnosis of PTSD are identified in the *Diagnostic and Statistical Manual of Mental Disorders* (*DSM-IV,* American Psychiatric Association [APA], 1994). It defines PTSD as a set of behaviors resulting from exposure to a traumatic event and involving any of the following conditions:

- The person experienced, witnessed or was confronted with an event or events that involved actual or threatened death or serious injury, or a threat to the physical integrity of self or others. *Vicarious traumatization* occurs when a person witnesses the serious injury or death of others.
- The person has intense fear, helplessness, or horror. In children this can be expressed as disorganized or agitated behavior.
- The person has clinically significant distress and impairment in social, occupational, or other important areas of functioning.

PTSD can be categorized as acute, delayed, chronic, or intermittent/recurrent.

The *DSM-IV* delineates the standard clinical symptoms of PTSD:

Re-experiencing the traumatic event in one of the following ways:

- Sudden flashbacks of memory of the trauma at unexpected and unwelcome times
- Enduring memories of the traumatic event or events

- Recurrent distressing dreams or nightmares about traumatic events
- Suddenly feeling that the event is happening now
- Intense distress when exposed to events that symbolize or resemble a part of the original event

Avoidance of things that remind one of the traumatic event or a general numbing reaction. The symptoms can include:

- Compulsive efforts to avoid thoughts or feelings of the trauma
- Compulsive efforts to avoid activities or situations that remind one of the trauma
- Amnesia for an important part of the trauma
- Marked disinterest in work, relationships, or recreation
- Feelings of detachment or estrangement from others
- A restricted range of feelings, including anger and love
- A sense of doom about the future

Hyperarousal symptoms as evidenced by any of the following:

- Difficulty falling or staying asleep
- Irritability or outbursts of anger
- Difficulty concentrating
- Hypervigilance
- Exaggerated startle response
- Physical symptoms such as vomiting, nausea, or increased pulse rate

These criteria and descriptors were gathered and systematized by professionals who had studied the impact of acute events such as rape, murder, domestic violence, or accidents on human behavior. As we began studying trauma and were trained in EMDR and other trauma reduction therapies, we discovered that many of our clients had similar undiagnosed symptoms of PTSD.

When we gathered more information about our clients' life histories as part of our heuristic research, we discovered that these people had not experienced or witnessed acute traumatic events. This led us to look more closely at their histories, so we began soliciting very detailed information about their early developmental experiences. Clients who did not have any memory of their early childhood were asked to interview their parents, siblings, extended families, and neighbors to get more information.

The information that many of these clients with symptoms of PTSD shared with us about their birth and the first 3 years of their lives revealed high levels of previously unrecognized and unhealed developmental trauma. This research helped us understand why they displayed so many of the symptoms of PTSD and was an important step in our discovery of developmental trauma.

Vicarious and Secondary Trauma

Vicarious traumatization occurs when a person witnesses a trauma that is happening to someone else or hears or sees reports of traumatic events. Much of the literature in this field focuses on the vicarious traumatization of professionals such as therapists, police officers, firemen, emergency services personnel, and members of the military who encounter extreme trauma involving gross torture, violence, murder, or dismemberment.

Following the 9/11 disaster in New York City, researchers found that more than 90% of New York schoolchildren were suffering from symptoms of vicarious traumatization as a result of witnessing the event over and over again on television. The extensive amount of research and literature on this topic has now established secondary or vicarious trauma as an important area of study in the field of traumatology.

The principles of vicarious traumatization can also be applied to the field of developmental traumatology. Older children are often traumatized when they witness their younger siblings being emotionally neglected by parents who are overwhelmed by their responsibilities. Witnessing their younger siblings' subtle reactions to the loss of emotional synchronization with their parents often triggers the older children's memories of this same experience of emotional disconnect they experienced earlier in life. We had many clients report that this vicarious retraumatization unconsciously triggered their unprocessed feelings when they witnessed their younger siblings being neglected, which often activated a set of instinctive caretaking behaviors. This often caused them to step into surrogate parent roles to help their younger siblings.

Parentized children, those who end up taking care of their parents rather than vice versa, often sacrifice their own childhoods and grow up to become professional caretakers such as teachers, therapists, and ministers. The parentizing process can also involve children caretaking their overwhelmed parents by assuming some of their daily responsibilities in hopes that the overburdened adults will be able to take care of them. Parentized children may take over shopping for food, cooking for the family, and providing essential care for younger children.

Witnessing others who are being traumatized causes powerful unconscious reactions in the psyche. From a systemic perspective, witnessing is a major cause of conflict in couples, families, organizations, cultures, and civilizations. People are also unconsciously attracted to those who have similar kinds of developmental trauma. As a group they project the dynamics of their traumas onto collective authority figures such as presidents, prime ministers, religious leaders, and corporate CEOs and create camps of "us" and "them." This often escalates into an emotional response at a collective level and can provoke economic, racial, political, and religious wars.

Developmental Stress

Developmental stress is also a relatively new term that we created to describe the effects of early childhood stress. In the literature there is almost no research that identifies developmental stress as a cause of posttraumatic stress. This, in our opinion, is a big hole in the research literature and ignores one of the most important causes of posttraumatic stress.

Stress in the Traumatology Literature

Stress in the traumatology literature is typically associated with posttraumatic stress and the ASR and not recognized as its own discrete category. It is typically lumped together with trauma. Because there is already an abundance of information on both stress and trauma in the literature but they are not distinguished, we are addressing these two topics separately in this chapter as separate parts of the developmental trauma continuum.

In our trauma continuum, we recognize developmental stress as a unique and separate category of dysregulated behavior that involves the neocortex part of the brain and the SES part of the autonomic nervous system. It has distinct behavioral symptoms and involves awareness that is anchored in present time.

Stress is simply the body's adrenal response to taxing demands. *Distress* causes concern or anxiety, is experienced as exceeding our normal ability to cope, and feels unpleasant. It can be short or long term, typically decreases the ability to perform tasks, and if long term can lead to mental and physical fatigue.

Eustress is a term for positive stress that helps to motivate, to focus attention and energy, and feels exciting. It improves the performance of tasks, is short term, and is experienced as within our normal ability to cope. Stressors are difficult to categorize objectively because people react differently to similar situations. Having a child, taking a holiday, getting married, beginning a new job, buying a home, retiring, moving, and receiving a promotion all seem like eustressors because they imply positive events.

However, they can also be *distressors*, as there are negative aspects to each of them. An event can also switch from being a eustressor to a distressor, or vice versa, depending on how it unfolds in a person's life. What both distressors and eustressors have in common is that they activate the ASR and prepare the mindbody for higher levels of activity.

The Biochemistry of Stress

As soon as the mindbody perceives the need for additional energy, the brain activates the sympathetic nervous system. It tells the hypothalamus to produce a hormone commonly known as CRF. This hormone tells the adrenal glands to secrete substances that increase the heart rate, breathing, muscle responses, mental alertness, and the body's metabolism. As soon as the crisis is over, the parasympathetic nervous system kicks in with hormones to quiet the sympathetic nervous system and calm the person. This partnership between the sympathetic and parasympathetic nervous systems is nature's way of helping people stay in balance and connected to those around them.

Behaviorally, stressed people are moderately active and socially engaged, but may act edgy and anxious. They may have strained facial expressions, be unable to maintain consistent eye contact, talk louder, and have difficulties in relaxing or sleeping, but are still experiencing reality in present time.

Stress and Brain Function

Stress activates the brain's neocortex and the sympathetic nervous system, which stimulates the production of adrenaline to cope with a short-term crisis. At the beginning of a developmental stress reaction, people attempt to get physical and emotional support in a relational way. This activates the SES, which then overrides the sympathetic and parasympathetic nervous systems and strengthens socially engaging behaviors involving the use of facial muscles to help the person return to balance.

With the SES active, the person is able to make nonverbal cues such as smiling, head nodding, eye contact, eyebrow and eyelid lifting, and verbal cues such as speaking calmly and empathically. Both the verbal and nonverbal cues help the person stay engaged with others to be able to problem-solve, express emotions, and use cognitive functions to identify and modify their behavioral patterns. In Chapter 9 we discuss appropriate intervention modalities for working with developmental stress states.

A mother is she who can take the place
of all others
but whose place no one else can take.

Cardinal Mermillod

CHAPTER SIX

Developmental Shock, Trauma, and Stress in the Codependent Stage of Individual Development

The terms *developmental shock, developmental trauma,* and *developmental stress* provide a framework for understanding how very early relational events impact not only the development of individuals, couples, and families, but also all their social systems. These new terms, rooted in the fields of pre- and perinatal psychology, developmental psychology, and traditional traumatology, have the potential to alter the path of human evolution. Once people comprehend the meaning of these terms, they can no longer accept the myth that infants cannot feel and do not remember, nor continue to treat them as inanimate objects. The real tragedy of this archaic myth is that it has discouraged parents and other adults from bonding with children and supporting them during the most critical periods of their physical, social, and emotional development.

Developmental Shock, Trauma, and Stress: New Classifications

The concepts of developmental shock, trauma, and stress challenge us to think outside the box in identifying early childhood experiences that constitute shock, trauma, or stress. Parents typically believe that the way they are parenting their child is "normal"—it's what everybody does. The truth is that they likely approach parenting their children the way they were parented as a child. These "normal" parenting events, particularly those between the time of conception and the first 6–8 months, shape a child's experience for life. How children are parented during the crucial bonding stage of development has the biggest impact on their subsequent development.

The key factor in these early parenting events is that they often involve emotional and energetic disconnections between the mother and infant that are too long, too frequent, or both. They cause infants to become emotionally and biologically dysregulated and trigger them into states of developmental stress, trauma, and shock. If not relieved quickly and appropriately, these states impact children's developing brains and nervous systems, alter their biological response patterns, and ultimately reduce their ability to form secure adult relationships. We focused on this aspect of developmental shock, trauma, and stress in Chapter 3 and now want to look at other dimensions of these concepts.

Our definition of developmental shock, trauma, or stress differs from that used by Bessel van der Kolk (2005, pp. 401–409), clinical director of The Trauma Institute in Brookline, Massachusetts. While we support his goal of calling more attention to the lasting effects of early trauma, he does not differentiate among shock, trauma, and stress states, and he currently does not include the more subtle early relational components in his definition of developmental trauma. Rather, he defines developmental trauma as a form of *complex trauma* caused by early experiences of multiple, acute, and prolonged developmentally adverse traumatic events of an interpersonal nature, such as physical abandonment and severe neglect, sexual or physical abuse, war, and community violence. These exposures typically occur within the child's caregiving system and include rather obvious physical, emotional, and educational neglect and child maltreatment beginning in early childhood (van der Kolk, 2005, pp. 401–408).

Leaders in the treatment of childhood trauma have spearheaded a project with colleagues nationwide to support the introduction of a new diagnosis in the *DSM–V,* due to be released in 2012, that more completely accounts for the components of acute developmental trauma. They say that in the absence of a diagnosis that accurately captures the pervasive nature of disturbances related to early childhood trauma, children tend to receive a hodgepodge of labels for any number of symptoms—posttraumatic stress, attention deficit, conduct, and mood disorders, which are then treated as separate conditions. And very few of these diagnostic labels really take into account the presence of unrecognized and unhealed developmental shock, trauma, and stress.

"Approaching each of these problems piecemeal, rather than as expressions of a vast system of internal disorganization, runs the risk of losing sight of the forest in favor of one tree," said van der Kolk. "What you call someone has large implications for how you treat someone, even though you may be describing the same phenomenology [using different terms]." He noted, for instance, that because of the emotional dysregulation that traumatized children frequently display—as well as self-harming behaviors they may adopt as a coping mechanism—they are often misdiagnosed with bipolar disorder and treated exclusively with drugs and behavior management (van der Kolk, 2005, p. 402).

While this group of traumatologists appears to be more focused on more obvious and acute episodes of traumas, we have deliberately focused on the subtle, "ordinary," and relational issues that cause chronic episodes of developmental shock, trauma, and stress. Complex developmental trauma can be viewed as a spectrum of events that ranges on a continuum between these two opposite poles. We believe that most people are able to recognize the extreme end of the trauma continuum and its impact on development. Unfortunately, few recognize the role of developmental shock, and virtually no one sees the developmental stress end of the continuum. Our trauma continuum focuses on subtle, "ordinary," relational events as causes of developmental shock, trauma, and stress. We believe that they have a pervasive impact on parenting practices, couple relationships, and family structures, and that the functionality of these systems drives the evolution of the human race.

Prenatal Shock, Trauma, and Stress

The concept of cellular consciousness is now being widely used in the field of pre- and perinatal psychology. *Cellular consciousness,* according to Australian physician Graham Farrant and his colleague Terry Larimore (1997), is the complete memory that we each carry in the cells of our bodies regarding our earliest experiences, including not only conception but also the separate experiences of being a sperm and an egg.

Bruce Lipton's use of a similar concept has been revolutionizing research in the field of pre- and perinatal psychology and validating how these very early periods and experiences influence the development of embryos and prenates in ways that are only now being understood. Lipton described how human beings, from conception throughout life, process incoming environmental information and store the results in the membranes of their cells. He called these stored cellular memories "learned perceptions" (Lipton, 2001).

Neuroscientist Candace Pert (1997) is also proving in her laboratory what pre- and perinatal practitioners have suspected for years. Her research indicated that the potential for domestic violence and sexual abuse are first imprinted into our genes during conception and gestation. This coding at the cellular and molecular level takes the form of a positive charge (growth, love) or negative charge (protection, fear). This imprint is then awakened and reinforced by subsequent relational experiences and emerges fully in what we call the drama triangle, where people engage in the perpetrator, rescuer, and victim roles in their relationships, particularly during such cultural rites as dating, marriage, and childbirth. According to Pert, the failure rate of traditional treatment programs for physical or sexual violence is often the result of the misconception that behavioral therapists can "educate" or "train" someone to call forth a loving response from what is clearly a mindbody program that is operating in the fear-and-protection mode.

Farrant's research on cellular consciousness (1988) identified categories of memory that parallel the process of conception: the sperm awaiting ejaculation, the sperm's journey to and fertilization of the egg, the egg's welcoming of the sperm in, and the implantation. His regression therapy work with clients revealed not only that shock and trauma can happen during any of these phases, but that the zygote and then fetus can retain prenatal memory of shock and trauma related to not being wanted, twin loss, abortion attempts, and plans for adoption.

According to Farrant, if the sexual act in which a baby is conceived is hostile, fearful, ambivalent, or just part of having a good time with no commitment to one another on the part of the adults involved, both the egg and the sperm will carry this cellular imprint. If a fertilized egg has a difficult time implanting—attaching to the lining of the uterus—this is also imprinted at a cellular level. Whatever the imprinting, it is possible to see the child acting out the experience symbolically during early play.

Farrant's research led him to view conception as a complex union of the egg, the sperm, and the soul. He was also able to link various physical ailments to the reports of specific experiences within those first 10 days between conception and implantation and identified a discernible pattern of life problems that he associated with certain kinds of conception experiences. Farrant's work opens a line of prenatal research that connects with Brodie's findings on the long-term impact of shock and trauma on the mindbody. We discuss this further in Chapter 8.

Leah LaGoy, another pre- and perinatal psychologist, says that birth trauma can trigger memories of conception and gestational shock and trauma and deepen their imprint. LaGoy (2007), who has studied the "vanishing" or "lost twin" syndrome, discovered that it is very common for pregnancies to begin as twins. Elizabeth Noble (2003, p. 1) said she believes that about 1 in 8 pregnancies begin as twins, but only 1 in 70 actually deliver twins. She said that 80% of twin pregnancies result in the loss of one or both babies. LaGoy's doctoral dissertation focused on the in utero loss of a twin on the surviving twin's capacity to experience life, ability to trust, capacity to form relationships, and fundamental belief structures. Her research findings confirmed her hypothesis that the trauma of twin loss impacted the ability of the surviving twin's ability for attaching not only with the mother but to engage fully in life.

If one considers conception, implantation, early twin loss, and umbilical cord experiences in terms of attachment, she said that babies being put up for adoption will already have experienced a tremendous amount of attachment trauma before they were born. Adoptees have often been gestated in wombs of mothers who are experiencing isolation, fear, general disconnectedness, and even hostility (LaGoy, 1993).

Children can recall their experiences of pre- and perinatal shock and trauma, said LaGoy, if they are given the chance. Those who suffer from early shock and traumas are likely to suffer from developmental delays, pediatric illnesses, feeding issues, sleeping problems, temperament issues, difficult behavior, and learning disabilities (1993).

Clinical researcher William Emerson said that pre- and perinatal shock and trauma should be treated as early as possible, because unresolved emotional issues affect the spiritual and psychological development of children. Early shock and trauma, he said, determine how children will perceive their subsequent experiences. If treatment occurs early on, during gestation or the first year, then childhood experiences can be freed from prenatal influences, and children can live the rest of their lives unencumbered by the bonds of early shock or trauma.

Emerson found that children who had no shock or trauma, or whose shock and trauma had been healed, were more spiritually evolved, manifested higher levels of human potential, and were developmentally precocious. They exhibited higher self-esteem and intelligence test scores and were more empathic, emotionally mature, cooperative, creative, affectionate, loving, focused, and self-aware than shocked and traumatized children who did not receive early treatment (Emerson, 1993).

Circumcision Trauma

Circumcision began as a religious sacrifice or rite of passage marking a boy's entrance into adulthood. It had various meanings, depending on the culture: it was a form of sympathetic magic to ensure virility, a means of suppressing (or enhancing) sexual pleasure, an aid to hygiene where regular bathing was impractical, a means of marking those of lower (or higher) social status, and a means of differentiating a circumcising group from their noncircumcising neighbors. It was also used to discourage masturbation or other socially prohibited sexual behaviors, to increase a man's attractiveness to women, a symbolic castration, a demonstration of one's ability to endure pain, or a male counterpart to menstruation or the breaking of the hymen.

In some warrior cultures, circumcision was designed in large part to destroy the mother–son bond and prepare the boy for warriorhood. In this case, male genital mutilation was an introduction to violence and barbarism. Feminists such as Anne Pyterek (n.d.) believe that the continued use of circumcision over the millennia contributes to the widespread presence of misogyny around the world.

Mothers who understand the sensitive pre- and perinatal period of development and their responsibility to protect their infants feel horrified by the act of circumcision. Pyterek questioned in an online essay:

> How could a betrayal so huge, so profound, NOT take root in the tons and tons of societal garbage heaped upon the heads of little boys and produce such misogynous crap as wife-beating, witch-hunting, prostitution, pornography, mother-blaming, rape, sexism,

> endless perversions of every kind, and just general cold, unemotional, not-able-to-talk-about-his-feelings kind of guys? (¶ 5)

She, like other educated mothers, knows that male circumcision causes incredible shock and disrupts the mother–infant bond during the crucial period after birth.

French obstetrician, Frederic LeBoyer (1980), said:

> Once we remember that all that takes place during the first days of life, on an emotional level, shapes the pattern of all future reactions, we cannot but wonder why such a torture (circumcision) has been inflicted on the child. How could a being who has been so aggressed in this way while totally helpless, develop into a relaxed, loving, trusting person? Indeed, he will never be able to trust anyone in life. He will always be on the defensive, unable to open up to others into life. (¶ 3)

The United States is the only country in the world that continues to circumcise male infants for nonreligious reasons. Somewhere between 60% and 80% of all newborn males are still being circumcised in this country, even though in 1983 the American Academy of Pediatrics stated that there is no known medical justification for this practice (Wallerstein, 1985, pp. 123–132).

A nurse anonymously posted the following on The Compleat Mother magazine website (Circumcision Resources Link, n.d.):

> I work as an RN in an OB unit and 99% of all newborn boys here are circumcised. I've been a nurse 15 years, and it still makes me nauseated imagining the pain these poor, helpless, newborns must be in. I would love to strap these docs in an oversized circumstraint and stick their penises in a meat grinder and see how they feel. One effect I've noticed after circs is the almost state of shock these little ones go into: they're sleepy and won't nurse, and cry when you change that bloodied vaseline gauze. (¶ 31)

I (Janae) can validate this nurse's observations. My oldest son was 5 weeks premature and weighed only 5 lbs. 2 oz., so his circumcision was delayed for a week until he grew a bit. I was present in the physician's office while he was taken to a room in the back, where I could hear the unbearable wail he unleashed during the circumcision process. That evening he refused to nurse because, as I now know, he was in a deep state of shock. Circumcision certainly fits Hamer's definition of a biological-conflict-shock, as no warning is given to the infant and there is no escape from the experience. Because usually little or no immediate comfort is given to the child other than a pacifier, the experience certainly is filed in the brain as life threatening. It would be interesting to use CT scans on 6-month-old circumcised boys to see if they show signs of a lesion in their brains as Hamer (2000) found in adults who had experienced inescapable shocks. We talk more about Hamer's work in Chapter 8.

In 1997 up to 96% of infants in some areas of the United States still received no anesthesia during circumcision. Even if an anesthetic is used, those currently in use for circumcisions are not effective during the most painful parts of the procedure (Lander, Brady-Fryer, Metcalfe, Nazarali, & Muttitt, 1997). Most parents are not aware that their boys are circumcised without any anesthetic. If circumcision is required for religious reasons, it should be done with a local anesthetic and not just the customary wine that is given during many religious circumcision rituals. Female circumcision is still practiced in the U.S. by some immigrants from Muslim countries, where it is widely practiced and usually done by women in the family before girls reaches adolescence.

Scientific studies have consistently shown that circumcision also disrupts a child's behavioral development. Studies performed at the University of Colorado School of Medicine revealed that circumcision is followed by prolonged, distressed non-REM (rapid eye movement) sleep. Because of the infliction of unbearable pain on their neural pathways, circumcised babies withdraw into a type of semi-coma that lasts for days and sometimes even weeks in order to recover from the shock (Glazov, 2001).

Psychiatrists' clinical findings revealed the presence of serious and sometimes disabling long-term somatic, emotional, and psychological consequences of infant circumcision in their adult male clients. These consequences resembled complex PTSD and emerged later during adult psychotherapy focused on the resolution of perinatal shock and trauma. Adult symptoms associated with circumcision shock include shyness, anger, fear, powerlessness, distrust, low self-esteem, relationship difficulties, and sexual shame. Long-term psychotherapy dealing with early trauma appears to be effective in healing these consequences (Rhinehart, 1999).

Breaks in the Bonding Cycle

It is quite common now for very young children to be cared for by strangers who are not securely bonded to them and may not be interested in, or even capable of, synchronizing with them emotionally. When young children are separated from their parents for periods that are too frequent, too long, or both, their young nervous systems are unable to cope and they suffer bonding breaks.

Figure 6.1 shows what happens when parents are not able to attune with children and provide them with emotional regulation and experiences of synchrony. When infants are unable to attune with their caregivers, it overwhelms their autonomic nervous systems and they go into shock and collapse into a dissociated emotional state that looks as though they are falling asleep. They fall into what many describe later as a black hole or abyss, where they lose contact with what is going on around them, and they fear they will not survive.

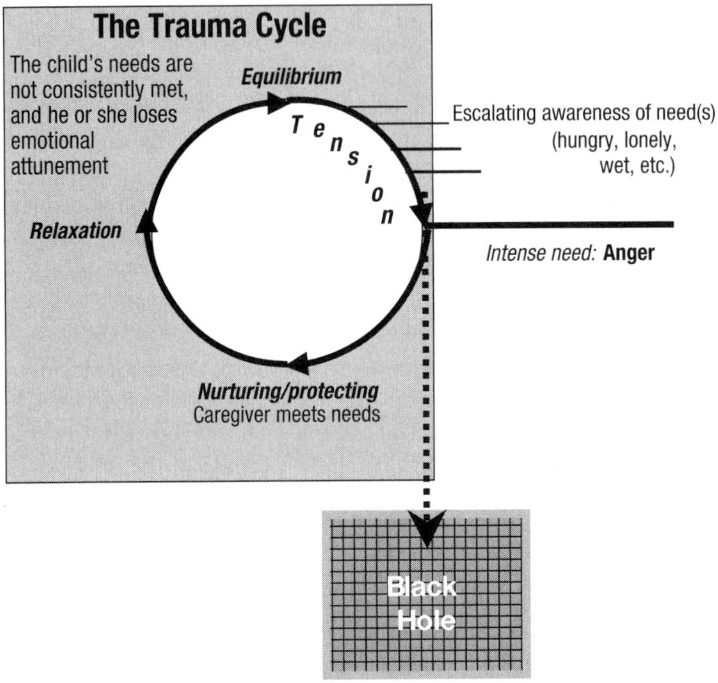

FIGURE 6.1

Breaks in the Bonding Cycle

The black hole is a dissociative state of consciousness where memories of overwhelming events involving the loss of caregiver attunement are split off from the conscious mind and stored. Young children typically have only a few dissociative memories stored in their black holes but may accumulate a very complex and compact system of dissociated memories as they grow older.

After several episodes of falling into the black hole, children learn a variety of coping mechanisms to help them to avoid it. They will use their thumbs, fists, soft blanket, or pacifier as substitutes for the missing nurturing, love, and emotional attunement. This disrupts their fall into the black hole and helps them reregulate their emotions. Oral mother substitutes used during the bonding stage of development serve an important function in a shocked or traumatized child. They are a substitute for the physical comfort and emotional synchronization that they needed from the mother. Because the emotional component is missing, however, the substitute never completely satisfies the deep yearning to attune with her.

In a desperate attempt to experience emotional attunement and autonomic nervous system regulation, the child often continues to utilize more and more of the mother substitute or to try other kinds of substitutes to see if they will create the inner feelings of relaxation and peace that the connection with the mother brings. These early behaviors lay the foundation for adult oral or "downer" addictions such as smoking, eating, masturbating, using drugs such as alcohol and marijuana, and attaching to others in a codependent way. If the child is not able to slow or prevent falling into the black hole because of a lack of emotional response from the mother, he or she may go into a long-term shock state of weight loss and unresponsiveness that characterizes a "failure-to-thrive" baby.

Because infants perceive themselves as the center of their world, they also internalize a belief that it is their fault that their adult caregivers abandoned, abused, or neglected them. This judgment against the self creates a belief of "you're okay and I'm not okay" or "I'm flawed in some way that makes me unlovable." This dynamic is illustrated in Figure 6.2.

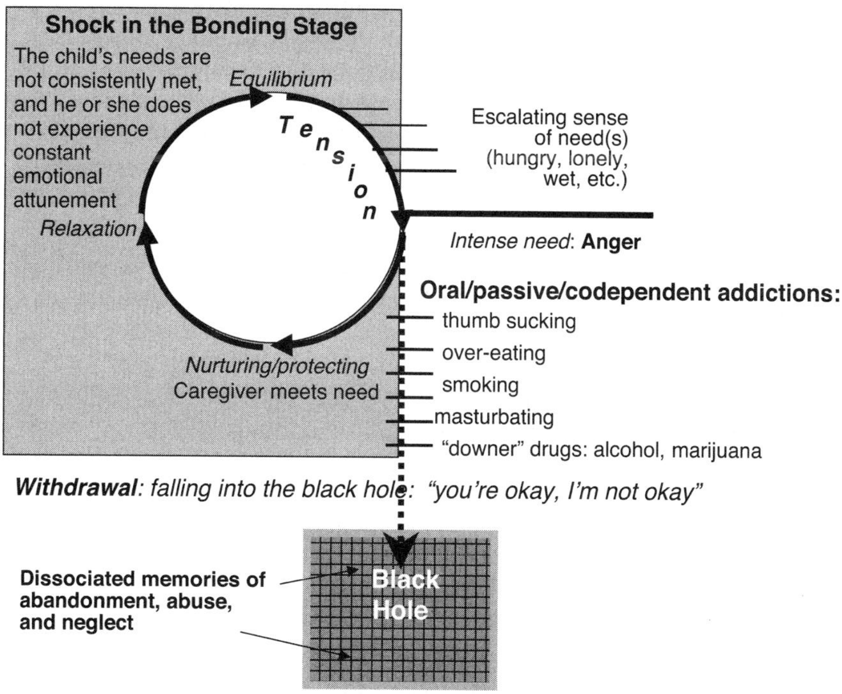

FIGURE 6.2

Breaks in the Bonding Cycle

Shocks that occur during the codependent stage of development have a tremendous impact on how children's brains and nervous systems develop. Because they mature according to how they are used, the brains and nervous systems of shocked infants begin hardwiring for the devolutionary developmental trauma track. Relationally, these children develop insecure attachments and display anxious, ambivalent, and avoidant personality disorders. They grow up with codependent behaviors, a deflated sense of self, and a variety of oral addictions. They are typically attracted to partners and friends who have counterdependent behaviors.

Common Causes of Developmental Shock in the Codependent Stage

Children's cellular memory, brains, and nervous systems become permanently imprinted with specific cues and signals experienced during subtle but shocking events. These cues and signals become highly sensitized triggers that instantaneously activate the body's ASR. Eventually, these biologically based behavioral response patterns create developmental stress that becomes hardwired into children's brains, bodies, character, and relationships. We believe that adult mental health is rooted in these early emotional and relational experiences, particularly related to the amount of unconditional love that is or is not available.

The most common causes of developmental shock during the codependent stage of development include the following:

- The inability of parents or adult caregivers to attune with children and create consistent experiences of emotional synchronization and unconditional love
- Emotional coldness, unresponsiveness, or remoteness by the mother or other early primary caregivers
- Persistent disregard of the child's basic emotional needs for comfort, stimulation, and affection, particularly during times of developmental stress
- The inability of the parent to help the child quickly reregulate his or her emotions
- Persistent disregard of the child's need for physical touch, particularly skin-to-skin contact
- Repeated changes of primary caregivers that disrupt or prevent bonding during the first 6 months, especially during the first 2 months
- Premature, repeated, and/or overly long periods of separation from the mother during the first 6 months, particularly the first 2 months
- Undiagnosed and/or chronic or recurring painful illnesses such as colic or chronic ear infections during the first 6 months
- Extended periods of crying in which the parents are not able to provide comfort

- Betrayal by trusted adult caregivers who use children to meet their own needs for love, touch, emotional support, security, and protection
- Inconsistent or inadequate childcare
- Chronic maternal depression or physical illness
- Premature birth and life-saving medical interventions
- Physical separation from the mother at birth
- Maternal use of drugs and alcohol during gestation and nursing periods
- Invasive medical procedures such as ultrasound or amniocentesis during the gestational period
- Drug-induced births

Intergenerational parenting patterns are also primary causes of developmental shock. Research on the neurobiology of attachment indicates that the early experiences of female infants with their mothers influence how they will respond to their own infants when they later become mothers. This early mother–child imprint serves as the psychobiological mechanism for the intergenerational transmission of both supportive and maladaptive parenting styles. According to Schore, it is a primary influence on mothers' ability to respond to their children's needs for emotional attunement and relational synchrony (2003a, p. 195). If a mother was left in intense emotional dysregulation for long periods as an infant, she is likely to be unresponsive to her own child during prolonged periods of crying and screaming. This intergenerational pattern of neglect can be very difficult to identify and treat because the source of it is buried so deep in the psychobiological wiring.

The Reversal Process

Perhaps the most common cause of developmental shock, trauma, and stress that begins in the codependent stage is an intergenerational phenomenon known as the reversal process. This involves parents and other caregiving adults unconsciously using their relationship with their children as a way to avoid locating and healing their own childhood shocks, traumas, and stresses.

For example, her child's loud and relentless crying triggers a woman whose mother was unresponsive to her as an infant. Her lack of response to her child's crying is a way of burying her own traumatic memories of having an unresponsive mother. Responding to her child's crying with comfort and nurturing would require encountering the dissociated memories stored in her own black hole and all the emotions connected to them. This option seems like such an overwhelming challenge that it is just easier to repeat the mother–child disconnect pattern and traumatize her child (Weinhold & Weinhold, 2008a, p. 65).

Unfortunately, parents are quite frequently triggered by their intimacy with their children. Lloyd deMause (1982) discovered that the symbiosis between parents and their children often triggers the parents' own unhealed developmental shocks, traumas, and stresses that occurred at the same age as their child. He said that they emotionally regress to the age of their child, encounter their own developmental shocks, traumas, or stresses, dissociate or regress, and then are unable to attend to their child's needs.

The parents' experience of re-encountering their own developmental wounds has an upside and a downside. The upside is that it can reveal to them some of their own childhood shocks, traumas, and stresses. The downside is that they typically do nothing to heal these experiences and instead pass their own shock, trauma, and stress on to their children, contributing to intergenerational cycles of suffering, living on the developmental trauma track and devolution.

Parents may also unconsciously try to avoid their own developmental issues by manipulating their children into taking care of them through unconscious role reversals. In order to numb the intense emotions that erupt when they get triggered by their children, the parents may turn to alcohol or drugs or disengage from the bonding process altogether. They also may choose to avoid their feelings by returning to work and turning the care of their infant or child over to a babysitter or putting them in childcare.

While they do not realize it, parents are often emotionally regressed to the age of the child for whom they are caring, leaving no adult emotionally present to care for the child. Children experience their parents' regression as abandonment. This then causes children to disengage from their parents and activate their protection behaviors. Children often decide that the only way to survive in a reversal situation is to ignore their own needs. They believe that by taking care of their parents' needs their parents will eventually be more available to meet their needs. This reversal pattern is quite common in eldest children.

Another way that parents transmit their developmental issues onto their children is unconsciously using them as projective objects. In this case, the parents are unable to see their children as separate human beings and instead view them as an extension of themselves. Parents project their own unfulfilled wishes and dreams onto their children and expect them to become the doctor, lawyer, sports figure, musician, artist, or the notable person that they had hoped to be. This reversal programs the child to try to carry out the parents' unfulfilled dreams in order to earn their love. Parents also project their fears and other unrecognized and unhealed shocks, traumas, or stresses they do not wish to confront onto their children.

Another way that parents play out their unrecognized and unhealed developmental issues with their children is expecting them to provide what they needed as a child and did not get. Parents also expect their children to give them perfect narcissistic mirroring, constant reassurance, and expressions of love, rather than focusing on their children's emotional needs and supporting them in healthy self-development.

Children experience developmental shock, trauma, and stress because so few parents are aware that they regress and reverse roles. The reversal process is very difficult to identify and heal, because parentized children look well-behaved and obedient to the outside observer.

However, the children almost always know when their parents are into reversals with them. They believe that if they do not sacrifice themselves, however, their parents will not take care of them and they might not survive. This pervasive, powerful, narcissistic programming dominates in the United States, where culturally people feel entitled, that their needs should come first, and that others should sacrifice their needs in the process.

Caring for young children can be a great growth stimulus for conscious adults who are able to identify their own developmental issues, take responsibility for meeting their own needs for love, protection, and safety, and who arc capable of deep emotional attunement. If this childhood reversal program is not modified in the family, children carry it forward into other adult relationships. If it is not healed here, it will show up in the family of the next generation. If not healed at that level, it will continue to collectively imprint the function of organizations and nation–states. We believe that healing the effects of this reversal process is essential for advancing human evolution at all levels.

The Biochemistry of Developmental Trauma

The body's biochemical state is determined by whether or not a person is socially engaged and experiencing emotional synchrony. When people are in shock, trauma, or stress, the body is either physically shut down or flooded with stress-related hormones. Schore identified direct correlations between infant PTSD and child, adolescent, and adult stress disorders (2003a, pp. 207–208). The most difficult part of this developmental stress, particularly for small children, according to Schore, is the child's difficulty in regulating his or her emotions when the care-giving adult fails to act as a regulating mechanism. This is not only a primary cause of developmental shock, trauma, and stress, it also is responsible for damaging the long-term growth of parts of the brain that regulate emotions (Schore, 2003a, pp. 207–208).

Schore also said that even subliminal and low-intensity stressors can trigger terrifying and painful emotional experiences from the past that have been imprinted into the circuits of the nervous system (2003a, p. 208). Identifying and healing very early experiences involving the loss of a socially engaged and emotionally regulated adult caregiver is difficult because the memories associated with it are stored in the hardwiring of the brain and nervous system. It requires some unweaving the warp and woof of a shocked and traumatized brain and central nervous system in order to clear the blockage.

When the mindbody is flooded with stress hormones, it interferes with the ability to think clearly. In a conflict situation, people first draw on their most sophisticated resources in the neocortex part of the brain—logic, reason, problem solving, and social engagement/fighting. If this fails, they go to the next level of sophistication in the limbic brain: fleeing. If neither of these is effective, then people fall into the most primitive brain response: freezing. In this moment, they are immobilized in a state of shock. This evolutionary ranking of responses to a conflict situation is part of Porges and Carter's polyvagal theory (Porges, 1995).

The Lasting Impact of Developmental Shock, Trauma, and Stress during the Codependent Stage

In our book, *Breaking Free of the Co-dependency Trap* (2008a, pp. 8–9), we discussed extensively the impact of developmental trauma during the codependent stage of development. Here are some of the most common adult behaviors that indicate possible bonding breaks:

- Being "addicted" to people
- Feeling trapped in abusive, controlling relationships
- Having low self-esteem
- Needing constant approval and support from others in order to feel good about yourself
- Feeling powerless to change destructive relationships
- Needing alcohol, food, work, sex, or some other outside stimulation to distract you from your feelings
- Having undefined psychological boundaries
- Feeling like a martyr
- Being a people-pleaser
- Being unable to experience true intimacy and love

The following is a list of very common behaviors that children display after exposure to early experiences of developmental shock, trauma, or stress (Cook, Blaustein, Spinazzola, & van der Kolk, 2003). Some of these same traits also apply to adults.

1. *Attachment problems:* uncertainty about the reliability and predictability of the world, distrust and suspiciousness, social isolation, interpersonal difficulties, difficulty attuning to other people's emotional states and points of view
2. *Biochemical disturbances:* hypersensitivity to physical contact, analgesia, somatizing the trauma in the physical body, increased health and medical problems
3. *Affect or emotional dysregulation:* easily aroused high-intensity emotions, difficulty de-escalating, difficulty describing feelings and internal experience,

chronic and pervasive depressed mood or sense of emptiness or deadness, chronic suicidal preoccupation, overinhibition or excessive expression of anger

4. *Dissociation:* distinct alterations in states of consciousness, amnesia, depersonalization, and de-realization
5. *Impulse control problems:* poor modulation of impulses, self-destructive behavior, aggressive behavior, sleep disturbances, eating disorders, substance abuse, oppositional behavior, excessive compliance
6. *Cognitive disturbances:* difficulties in regulating attention, problems managing life situations, problems focusing on and completing tasks, difficulty planning and anticipating, learning difficulties, problems with language development
7. *Poor self-concept:* a lack of a continuous and predictable sense of self, low self-esteem, feelings of shame and guilt, generalized sense of being ineffective in dealing with one's environment, belief in being permanently damaged by a trauma
8. *Narcissistic disturbances:* unwillingness to admit mistakes; needing to be the center of attention, grandiose and inflated self-image; drug, alcohol, or food addictions; cut off from feelings; lack of empathy; feelings of entitlement

Again, these problems fall along a continuum from mild to severe. The critical point in this discussion is that "subtle and ordinary" trauma creates the same symptoms and problems as acute trauma that is "extreme and dramatic" and that all serve as the foundational experiences in determining a person's ability to form and sustain healthy relationships, to succeed in the world, and to experience positive mental health.

I've built walls,
A fortress deep and mighty,
That none may penetrate.
I have no need of friendship;
Friendship causes pain.
Its laughter and its loving I disdain.
I am a rock,
I am an island.

"I Am a Rock", Simon and Garfunkel (1965)

CHAPTER SEVEN

Developmental Shock, Trauma, and Stress in the Counterdependent Stage of Individual Development

Between the ages of 6–8 months and 36 months, the triune brain and autonomic nervous system become much more connected and integrated. During this period, children learn to walk and talk, which gives them many more resources during times of stress. They have developed fight and flight responses to protect them when they perceive danger and help them avoid falling into shock. During this period, they may also have developed coping mechanisms such as thumb or pacifier sucking or attachment to a blanket or doll in order to comfort themselves and self-soothe.

The most important developmental task during the separation stage of development is helping the child to become emotionally and psychologically separate from both parents and able to operate from internal power or locus of control. This separation also involves separating the child's developing ego from the parents' adult egos and tempering the naturally narcissistic rage that comes with adults setting limits and giving consequences. While this process may provoke temper tantrums in the 2- to 3-year-old child, the failure to complete this part of the separation work during the counterdependent stage of development cannot begin to compare with the narcissistic rage exhibited by a developmentally delayed adolescent or a 30- or 40-year-old adult.

By adulthood, people have many more weapons available in their arsenal to use when someone or something attempts to limit their feelings of entitlement, euphoria, grandiosity, and omnipotence. If you challenge the most extreme of these folks, those with a really "short fuse," they might try to punch you out, attempt to kill you with a knife or gun, or use more sophisticated social and psychological tools to help them to discharge their narcissistic rage. This phenomenon came to mind when we visited Alaska and saw that most of the stop signs had bullet holes in them. "No limits for us," they seemed to say.

Incomplete Developmental Processes during the Counterdependent Stage

Around the age of 6–8 months, toddlers begin to physically crawl and then creep away from their parents. They also learn how to push away from too much physical closeness and begin to use the flight and fight responses when given limits. On the trauma continuum, emotionally overwhelming experiences during this stage tend to fall more into the category of developmental trauma and to involve the sympathetic nervous system and the limbic part of the brain.

The biggest daily challenge in parenting toddlers is enduring the upset they experience when faced with the physical and social limits that their parents impose on them. These and the natural limits they face everyday frustrate toddlers who are having a love affair with the world and are wanting to see how far they can push their passion to explore. Setting and enforcing behavioral limits gradually deflates their natural narcissistic urges involving entitlement, euphoria, grandiosity, and omnipotence. It is important for caregivers to set these limits with compassion, understanding, and empathy, as they typically activate strong feelings of frustration, anger, guilt, and shame.

Toddlers need the assistance of attentive, sensitive, and understanding parents or adult caregivers to help them learn how to regulate these emotions, which are an integral part of the separation stage. In Chapter 6 we discussed how important it is for parents and other adult caregivers to help children reregulate their emotions and repair any mis-attunements during the bonding stage. It is just as important to support children's emotional reregulation during the separation stage. Sensitive and cooperative adults must support toddlers in their transition between symbiosis and the psychological birth, and this can be a bumpy ride.

Toddlers are naturally ambivalent and oppositional in this stage of development, so adults must be both consistently loving and consistently firm to help them navigate this bumpy journey more easily. The most effective way to help toddlers regulate their emotions during this stage is for adults to keep their cool and not split or get triggered. Having been through this stage with our children and grandchildren, we understand the challenge behind these words and offer it as an ideal to work toward. The presence of calm adults also helps toddlers create healthy internal models of their adult caregivers.

Consistent love and affection during the bonding process helps build trust in the parent–child relationship, forming the foundation for the self-regulation of emotions. Trust is not innate but a product of repeated experiences of going in and out of attunement with the mother and other adult caregivers. Children learn to trust that adults will re-attune with them and help them reregulate their emotions. Once they have developed this trust, they carry this internal sense of security with them when they move into the separation stage (Tronick, 1989, pp. 112–119).

If toddlers fall down and get an "owie," they trust they can return to the soothing comfort of an adult's lap and calm down. Then they quickly slide off the lap and return to exploring their world. Wilting and fatigued toddlers are also able to instantly recharge during this emotional refueling stop and return only when another limit deflates their narcissistic urges (Mahler, 1980).

Mothers of bonding often do well at attuning with their infant. While they may be skilled in repairing bonding disruptions quickly and effectively, they may not be so effective as mothers of separation. A mother of bonding may feel abandoned or even resent the fact that her darling baby who once loved to cuddle is now more interested in exploring the world than being on her lap.

In the counterdependent stage, a mother must undergo a major shift in her relationship with her child. She must move from being the mother of endless "yes's" of infant care to the mother of frequent "no's." Her need to monitor, limit, and restrict her toddler's exploratory and experimental behavior and administer consequences can put her in an uncomfortable policeman role. If parents or adult caregivers are not able to understand the difficult inner world of toddlers and the frustrations that they express through their angry outbursts, they may not be able to respond as lovingly as they did during the bonding stage when toddlers seemed more compliant and interested in oneness.

Developmental neuropsychological studies show that by 10 months of age, 90% of maternal behavior consists of giving and receiving affection, playing with children, and other positive caregiving functions. In sharp contrast, mothers of 13–17-month-old toddlers express a negative prohibition to their toddler on the average of once every 9 minutes. In other words, the mother's role changes drastically in this short period from being a positive and unconditionally loving caregiver to being a negative and conditional socializing agent. Mothers must somehow find effective ways to persuade their toddlers to inhibit their desires for unrestricted exploration, to reduce their need to have temper tantrums, to control their bladder and bowel functions, and to curtail many activities that toddlers enjoy immensely (Rothbart, Taylor, & Tucker, 1989, pp. 59–80).

In addition, separation anxiety intensifies during this stage because toddlers understand for the first time that their mothers are separate persons with separate needs and interests. Toddlers sometimes use narcissistic rage and temper tantrums in an effort to control their mothers so they will not abandon them. This strong opposition, unfortunately, can trigger mothers into reenacting their own unhealed developmental issues involving their own incomplete struggle to become separate. If the mother retreats or becomes escalated in this power struggle, the toddler can feel emotionally abandoned.

Stir into this drama the fact that very few parents have identified let alone healed the developmental issues from their own toddler stage, and you have a recipe for conflict. If parents and other adult caregivers are carrying the effects of unrecognized and unhealed developmental shock, trauma, or stress related to their own separation, their own toddlers' oppositional behavior and temper tantrums can easily trigger them into a reenactment. Rather than welcoming their stressed toddlers back to their laps for comfort, these adults may want them out of their sight. Mothers may have difficulty reregulating their feelings that trigger the reenactment of their own unrecognized and unhealed developmental shock, trauma, or stress. Over the years of my parenting and grand parenting, I (Janae) adapted one of the country sayings I grew up with to an adage for parents: "Never get in power struggles with skunks or 2-year-olds."

So what do frustrated mothers and toddler caregivers typically do? They use time-out methods to isolate the toddler. While a time-out is useful for adults to reregulate their emotions, it is absolutely the *worst* option for toddlers. In order to help calm their stressed nervous systems and to control their narcissistic urges, toddlers need comfort and closer connections with adult caregivers. The forced separation from a time-out can trigger deep emotions in toddlers that, if not modulated, can lead to low self-esteem later in life. This is where shame enters the picture.

Shame is seen as an *attachment emotion* (Lewis, 1980, pp. 59–80) because it is a reaction that toddlers have when they are unable to re-attune with their mother or repair their dysregulated feelings. The shame is caused by the toddlers' belief that something is wrong with them because the mother does not respond in the loving way she used to. They internalize the disapproving scowl on her face or her harsh tone of voice as a rejection ("I am bad"). The now emotionally escalated mother causes her toddler to become even more upset and filled with the toxic shame of rejection.

According to Schore, toxic shame is "the primary social emotion" (1991, pp. 187–250) that emerges around 14–16 months of age. By this age, toddlers are usually exploring and attempting to master their environment while also staying in their mother's vicinity so that they can share with her the great excitement of what they have discovered or mastered. This period offers mothers a chance to give lots of validation and praise for these accomplishments. Unfortunately, if toddlers also bring their frustrations and anger to their mothers to be reregulated, these encounters are also likely to bring limits, restrictions, and negative looks. This just creates more stress and emotional dysregulation in toddlers.

Guilt and shame are quite different. Guilt implies that you did something bad or inappropriate and involves conditional negative messages such as, "You're doing a bad thing and need to stop it." Shame contains an unconditional negative message saying, "You are a bad person," which the child does not associate at all with his or her problematic behavior. Because it is so deeply personalized and causes internal splitting, shame disrupts children's learning of "both/and" and cause-and-effect thinking abilities.

In his book, *Healing the Shame That Binds You,* John Bradshaw (1988) wrote, "I had one of those life-jolting discoveries that significantly changed everything. I named the core demon in my life. I named it 'shame'" (p. vii). He added, "Toxic shame is unbearable and always necessitates a cover-up, a False Self. Since one feels his True Self is defective and flawed, one needs a False Self, which is not defective and flawed. *(Once one becomes a False Self, one ceases to exist psychologically.)*"

Bradshaw listed the following characteristics of toxic shame (p. 10):

- It becomes a core identity that provides you with a sense of being flawed and defective and also powerless to change.
- It causes you to hide your inner feelings and thoughts from others, and it means you must guard against letting other people see these inner thoughts and feelings.
- It causes people to constantly guard against exposing these qualities to themselves.
- It is experienced as an inner torment or a sickness of the soul.
- It produces shame about shame, so you are ashamed to have toxic shame and will not admit shame.

In order to hide shame, people project it on others in an almost instantaneous knee-jerk reaction. As soon as they feel shamed, they seek release by quickly shaming someone else. This dynamic is at the heart of projection.

Bradshaw also identified three ways that people learn shame. The first involves identifying with shame-based role models, particularly parents. The second way is through abandonment traumas involving abuse or neglect and role reversals that force children to abandon their own needs and take care of their parents' needs. This causes children to override their own needs and feelings and to deny their natural instincts to become a separate individual. In this trauma, they may feel ashamed for even having needs, feelings, or instincts. The third way that toxic shame happens, according to Bradshaw, is through experiences of profound betrayal that violate children's sense of primal trust. Many people are not able to grieve this deep kind of loss through psychotherapy, bodywork, and/or breathwork until they reach adulthood and are stronger psychologically.

The encounters with caregivers that once brought children comfort and joy as infants quickly become the principal source of shame for toddlers. If these encounters also involve being isolated through time-outs, they can generate more toxic shame than young toddlers can handle. Repeated experiences of isolation can cause acute developmental trauma in toddlers. It not only contributes to low self-esteem but prevents the completion of the most important developmental process of the separation process: the psychological birth and individuation.

Intense and prolonged experiences of feeling shame, without any support to help toddlers to reregulate their emotions, can cause them to regress, in the unconscious hope that they will receive the kind of comfort they did during the codependent stage. Eventually they realize the futility of using this strategy for getting help in regulating their feelings. So they either give up and disengage or try another strategy—becoming more aggressive.

Toddlers who feel a lot of shame during the exploratory process are likely to conclude that it is too scary and dangerous to develop a separate self. They may decide that their exploratory behavior is "bad" and the source of their shame. They may also internalize their caregiver's negative reactions about their counterdependent behavior and judge themselves negatively. When something later in life triggers a shame response, such as getting negative feedback from a boss or a spouse, people often regress and re-experience the feelings they had as a toddler.

The painfulness of adult shame reactions is often greater than the situation calls for because it involves dissociation or regression and the reenactment of their unrecognized and unhealed developmental shock, trauma, or stress. An experience of shame-induced dissociation can be so intense that it is not just uncomfortable to experience, but can actually feel life threatening. The fear of annihilation is exactly why toddlers begin building narcissistic defenses to protect themselves from ever feeling blamed and shamed again.

Toddlers do give their mothers and caregivers many signals showing that they are in distress. In addition to emotional outbursts, they may hang their head, avert their mother's gaze, and avoid physical contact. If mothers and other adult caregivers fail to notice these signs of withdrawal and internal emotional dysregulation, toddlers just give up trying to become separate or do a split and declare angrily, "I will show you I don't need you." With empathic support and proper attention to these cues, parents can help toddlers learn to control these powerful emotions.

In order for toddlers to become separate individuals, they must learn how to tolerate the loss of their illusion about being omnipotent and learn to control their infantile rage at having limits. They need not only the understanding support of their mothers, but also the empathic support of their fathers. Without the support of both parents, the individuation process will not be completed on schedule and will continue to press for completion later in life. Infantile rage that does not go through this reduction process will likely erupt in adulthood when other people or life circumstances impose limits on their behavior.

All the recent researchers of shame "emphasize that loss of ability to regulate the intensity of feelings is the most far-reaching effect of early trauma and neglect, that this dysfunction is manifest in more intense and longer-lasting emotional responses, and that defense mechanisms are forms of emotion-regulation strategies for avoiding, minimizing or converting affects that are too difficult to tolerate" (Schore, 1994, p. 85).

The Development of the False Self

If toddlers do not have enough emotional and social support to pursue individuation, they develop an artificial or a false self designed to please their parents and protect themselves from feeling shame and from falling into the black hole. They hope that this ploy will help them maintain the comforting intimacy and symbiosis with their mother and prolong the safety of the codependent stage. Unfortunately, this also forces them to abandon their inner urge to develop a separate self. As a result, they are likely to recreate these same kind of self-limiting codependent relationships in their adult life. They continue to monitor their ideas, feelings, and behaviors to make sure they do not think, do, or say anything that might threaten their symbiotic adult relationships.

Defense mechanisms learned during the separation stage of development that form the foundation for attachment disorders in early childhood can become serious personality disorders as people grow older. Defiant and oppositional behavior that persists beyond the age of 3 is an indication that the unrecognized and unhealed effects of developmental shock, trauma, and stress have begun to be hard-wired into children's brains and personality structures.

Once toddlers begin developing language, they learn to use the fight response to disengage during a trauma to try to protect themselves. They learn to distance themselves from intimacy and closeness by adopting an "I'm okay, and you're not okay" stance. They may develop a whole array of "upper" defenses that not only help maintain this separateness but also support the false self. Figure 7.1 illustrates the process of premature separation, the false self that emerges, and some of the most common addictions that support counterdependent behaviors. These defenses help children avoid events and emotions that could trigger traumatic memories related to separation.

As the defenses against the need for emotional intimacy solidify over the course of a person's lifetime, they can turn into full-blown narcissistic disturbances. The massive number of narcissistically defended adults has become a global problem. Because so many people did not experience healthy narcissism and go through the developmental process of ego reduction, they still act like entitled, grandiose, euphoric, and omnipotent 2- and 3-year-olds. Adult temper tantrums get played out through child abuse, domestic violence, wars, and a full range of other revenge-seeking and protective behaviors. Furthermore, the upper addictions associated with separation trauma—drugs, work, quick sex, traveling, and over-consuming––serve as inadequate and unsatisfying substitutes for the deep emotional connection that they missed with their mother and also the experience of union with the Divine. Unfortunately, it often takes people a long time to discover that this is the source of many of their problems.

The physical and psychological armoring characteristics of narcissism and other avoidant defense mechanisms can eventually become a prison. Initially

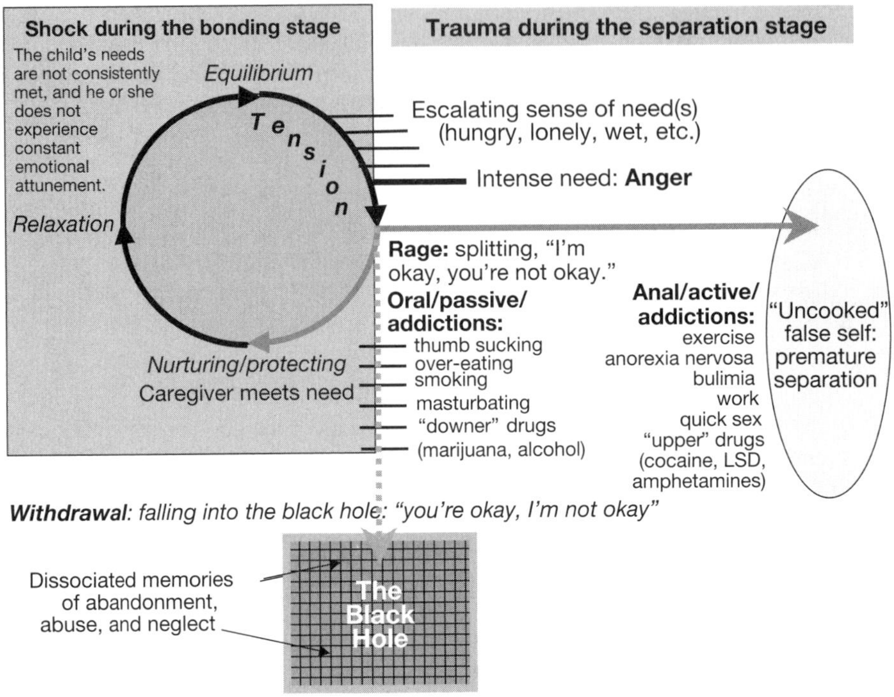

FIGURE 7.1

Trauma during the Separation Stage

created as protective mechanisms, they can become so wired into the brain and personality structures that they require a dramatic, life-altering event to break through them. These "cosmic two-by-four" events not only shatter the defense system, they often trigger the very early and very dissociated memories that initially caused the individual to build a false self. These "wake-up calls" shatter the false self and drop the person into the black hole. Figure 7.2 illustrates this dynamic.

The shattering of the narcissistically wounded false self in an adult is a very painful experience that typically involves an experience of shock. It is commonly known as a "nervous breakdown" or a "spiritual emergency" and opens up dissociated memories and all the pain associated with them. When people fall into shock, they need a lot of comfort and emotional support for some period of time afterward. While breakdowns of the false self are painful and often force people to halt their normal activities, they can also be very growthful times. They

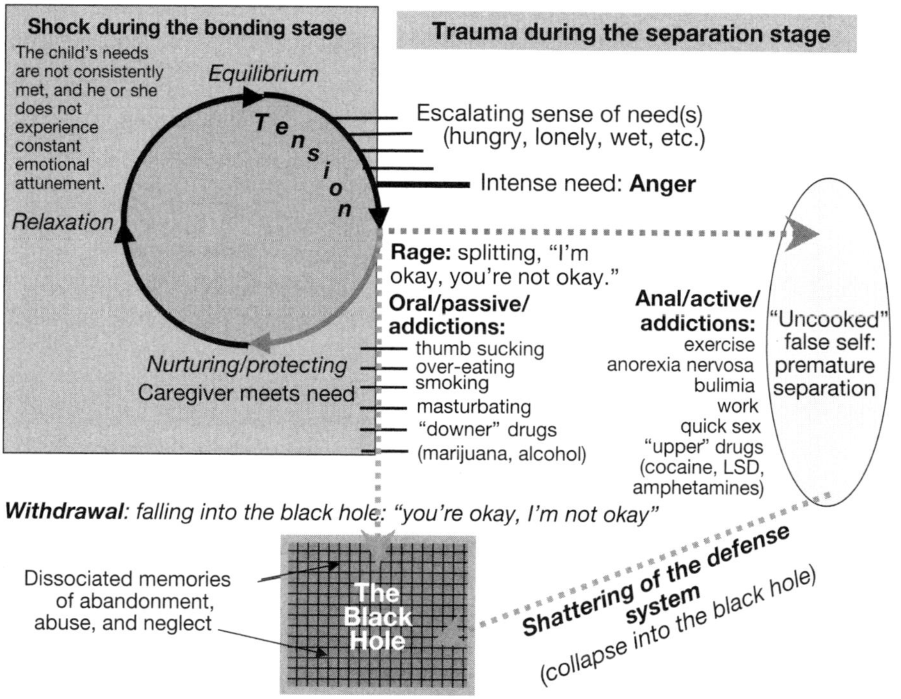

FIGURE 7.2

The Shattering of the False Self

provide people with a time-out from the world, creating a window of opportunity for reviewing their beliefs and behavior patterns and for reevaluating their life choices.

The biochemistry associated with emotional losses involving developmental shock, trauma, and stress and the activation of the autonomic nervous system involves a very unique set of chemicals and hormones that are produced through the ASR. They include cortisol, serotonin, norepinephrine, and corticotrophin releasing factor (CRF). Once we began studying the biochemical aspects of shock, trauma, and stress, we saw how precisely these unconscious and intricate emotional states are orchestrated in the mindbody. This part of our research also helped us understand why it is so difficult for people, particularly children, to modify their behaviors when in these states, as it requires consciously overriding a host of biological processes that are normally unconscious.

We believe that the biochemical transition between emotional dysregulation and emotional regulation is the most difficult challenge small children face when shuttling back and forth between conflictual divorced parents. The biological adjustment associated with leaving each parent can cause spikes in the production of shock, trauma, and stress hormones and cause both depressive and hyperactive behaviors. It can take them several days to detoxify from high levels of cortisol, so shifting biochemical gears can cause a few bumpy days.

In order to facilitate the reregulation of children's biochemistry in these situations, parents or adult caregivers must stay calm and present during these periods and provide calming and soothing tones of voice, nurturing touch, eye gazing, and even some physical activity with their children. It is difficult for most adults to identify this kind of developmental trauma because its cues often are so subtle.

Being in the presence of an emotionally escalated child can trigger adults into a regression and a reenactment of memories associated with their own unrecognized and unhealed developmental shock, trauma, or stress. They can regress or dissociate into a past reality where they feel overwhelmed. Because they are absorbed by their inner reactions from the past and no longer conscious in present time, regressed adults are unable to recognize the subtle signs of their child's traumatic reaction to loss and separation. In this traumatized state, dissociated adults are unable to help their children reregulate their emotions.

A common example of this would be divorced parents with a small child whom they drop off and pick up for visitations. If both parents came from divorced families, they are more likely to get triggered by their child's emotional upsets because they may have experienced similar difficult transitions between their own parents.

We believe that posttraumatic stress is a major factor in much of the abuse adults direct at infants who are emotionally distraught and will not stop crying. This is why adults shake, hit, or throw babies. In many such cases, the adults feel overwhelmed by the child's emotions and their inability to comfort the child. They may become very dysregulated, dissociate, and desperately try to avoid falling into the black hole.

Learning to recognize the subtle symptoms of unrecognized and unhealed developmental shock, trauma, and stress requires reading books about developmental psychology and working on one's own attachment histories in personal therapy. We have found that the ability to personalize the information about the effects of unrecognized and unhealed developmental shock, trauma, and stress expands people's capacity for empathy with self and others. They become more capable of attuning with their children and responding to their social and emotional needs. Perhaps the most important skill that emerges from personal awareness about previously unrecognized and unhealed developmental shock, trauma, or stress is that people can learn how to reregulate their emotions when they are triggered into a regression by an emotional memory of an earlier developmental shock, trauma, or stress.

Alongside the fear of encounters involving unrecognized or unhealed developmental shock, trauma, or stress is often an attraction to and fascination with trauma and violence. The natural learning style of humans is to repeat behaviors until they recognize the pattern in them. Freud called this the *repetition compulsion*. We seem to be drawn to what we fear so we can heal our developmental shock, trauma, or stress. We think this may be why so many people enjoy watching violence in movies and enjoy having the wits scared out of them. While people may appear addicted to violence, they may be attempting to understand and heal the developmental shocks, traumas, or stresses from their early childhood through catharsis. On the other hand, when young children, who have not completed their psychological birth, witness violence at home or on TV, they experience it as though it is actually happening to them. They have the same biological and physiological reactions as though they were personally experiencing it.

The Drama Triangle and Victim Consciousness

When people are not able to complete the essential developmental processes of the counterdependent stage in their families, a relational dynamic known as the *Karpman Triangle* (Karpman, 1968) appears. It involves three interchangeable roles: persecutor, rescuer, and victim. The *drama triangle*, as it is also known, involves a series of psychological games among these three roles that allow people to get their needs met only when they are being a victim. Rather than asking directly for what they want or need, victims manipulate others into giving them what they want or need without having to ask. The primary perceived payoff that perpetuates the triangle is the competition for the Victim role: getting something you want or need without having to ask for it directly. In enmeshed families that discourage individuation and the creation of a self, asking for things directly is labeled as "selfish" and used to shame people into maintaining codependent family structures and sustaining the drama triangle.

Dysfunctional drama triangle experiences within the family leave a cognitive imprint on children. This imprint helps create the belief that they can only get their needs met by becoming victims and being passive and dependent on others. No one asks directly from others to get their wants and needs met. Usually this means you have to blame, shame, or persecute others for not noticing that you have needs they should be meeting or rescue them by doing something for them for which they did not ask, and then expect them to do the same for you without your having to ask. This we call the need/obligate system.

The need/obligate system works hand in glove with the drama triangle. When someone perceives a need you have (victim) and provides it for you without you asking them for it (rescuer), then you are obligated to do something for them in return. If you don't do this to their satisfaction, they will criticize you (persecutor) and say that you were selfish and took advantage of them (victim) by getting your needs met while they did not get their needs met. At this point, you can become the victim, or you can become the rescuer and repay your obligation, or you can become angry with them for criticizing you, becoming the persecutor. Again, the goal of the game is to get wants and needs met without asking directly in order to maintain the need/obligate system.

Rather than developing a strong sense of internal power and self-directedness, children who grow up with the drama triangle dynamics and the need/obligate system learn to focus on the needs of others and fail to complete their individuation. They learn to take their cues from others and display passive, other-directed behaviors that are characteristic of the victim role. They remain developmentally stuck and cycle back and forth between the incomplete developmental processes of their codependent and counterdependent stages of development. Figure 7.3 shows that there is no direct communication link between the persecutor and the rescuer. This is because they are both focused on getting their payoffs. For the persecutor, the triangle offers an opportunity to be justifiably angry and to vent usually unacceptable emotions in a righteous way.

For the rescuer, the triangle is an opportunity for getting approval, for looking to one-up by helping others whom they perceive as weaker and for meeting ego needs to be seen as competent and important. People who enter the helping professions often have a desire to help others that ultimately serves to increase their own self-esteem. If that happens, they often burn out because they work too

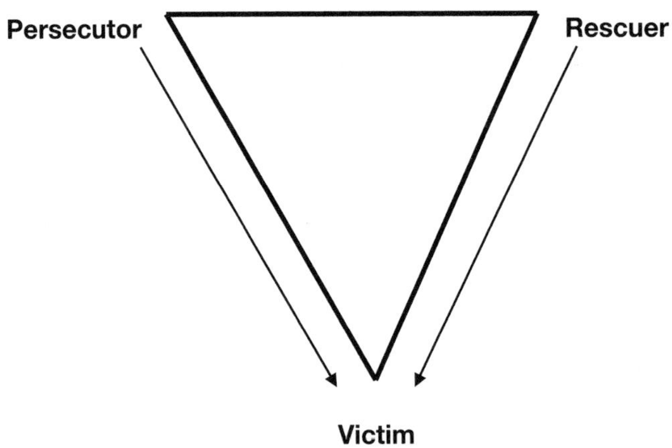

FIGURE 7.3

The Drama Triangle

hard rescuing their clients. Ultimately, the big payoff is playing out the roles long enough to get to be the victim.

The merry-go-round nature of the drama triangle allows the game to go on indefinitely. Even though the dynamics seem benign, this game and the communication style it uses are very difficult to eliminate. Most people do not ask directly for help from others to get their wants and needs met because they fear the other person will refuse and they will feel rejected. This rejection could trigger painful emotional memories connected to earlier unhealed developmental shocks, traumas, or stresses that they would rather avoid.

The first step to changing this pattern requires making a commitment to give up the victim role and to be willing to ask directly for what you want and need 100% of the time. The second step is refusing to rescue others by letting them ask first before you help them or asking their permission before you help them. When you take these two steps, you can eliminate the drama triangle from your relationships.

While it sounds easy, it often is not, because people still want you to play the game with them. When you refuse, they feel rejected and then get angry with you or talk about how they feel hurt. These are just ploys to keep you re-engaged in the drama. Unfortunately, it is very difficult to withdraw from a group that uses the drama triangle as a way of creating pseudo-intimacy. Once you actually stop playing the game, the group turns on you and persecutes you for not wanting to play their game. Within a short time, the group makes you bad and quickly replaces you with a more cooperative player.

How to Recognize a Rescue

The drama triangle can begin from any of the three positions or roles. Individuals who work in the helping or healing professions typically act out the rescuer role. Because counselors tend to attract clients whose issues match their own, the counselor's own posttraumatic cues often create a drama that both the client and the counselor can unconsciously act out together. This professional pitfall involving the loss of boundaries between the client's issues and the therapist's issues is known as *countertransference*. Counselors and other professional helpers can easily become engaged in mutual dramas that can re-traumatize the helper and the client. For this reason, it is critical that those in the helping professions work diligently to clear themselves of their own unhealed developmental shock, trauma, and stress issues.

The following behavioral dynamics of the drama triangle are characteristic of the rescue position:

- Doing something for someone that you really do not want to do but feel some obligation to do

- Being a caretaker and meeting other people's needs without being asked
- Consistently doing more than your fair share of the work in a counseling or helping situation
- Feeling so uncomfortable with receiving that it is possible to only be in the giving role
- Trying to fix other people's feelings or talk them out of their feelings
- Speaking up for other people instead of letting them speak up for themselves
- Not asking for what you need and attending only to the needs of others
- Feeling rejected when your help is graciously refused
- Trying to help others without an explicit contract (this does not include acts of kindness and compassion where help is legitimately needed)

Children who experience developmental trauma during the counterdependent stage usually have a more developed sense of self than those who experience developmental shock or trauma during the codependent stage. Older children, who have more defenses for protecting themselves, are more likely to use the "I'm good, and you are not" false self and one-up defenses.

For example, a 1-year-old child's mother goes to the hospital to have another child. The 1-year-old decides that the mother has abandoned her, decides that the mother is not trustworthy, and refuses to bond with her when she returns home several days later. This split into "I'm okay/you're not okay" or one-up defenses not only encourages inflated self-esteem, it supports the child in playing out the persecutor and rescuer roles in the drama triangle.

Splitting behaviors also indicate that people lack object constancy, the ability to hold themselves as objects of worth when feeling rejected or unworthy. They split against themselves and feel unworthy. This might happen when someone says unkind or unpleasant things to them or they fail to meet their own or other people's expectations. Splitting behaviors also form the foundation for lose–lose and win–lose styles of conflict resolution in adulthood.

The Lasting Impact of Developmental Trauma during the Counterdependent Stage

The following section details some of the psychological effects of unrecognized and unhealed developmental traumas during the separation process.

Ego Defense Mechanisms

Ego defense mechanisms are the most common way that people try to avoid feeling the emotions associated with their unrecognized or unhealed developmental traumas during the separation stage. In addition to entitlement, euphoria, grandiosity, and omnipotence, people with these kinds of unhealed developmental traumas use a number of narcissistic defense mechanisms to try to avoid re-experiencing their feelings:

Denial involves the repression of feelings and memories associated with traumas. It is perhaps the most primitive and best-known defense mechanism. People simply ignore unpleasant facts and filter out data and content that does not fit their self-image, prejudices, and preconceived notions of others and of the world.

Displacement involves getting angry with people who remind you of someone else you are angry with. An example is a boy getting in a fight with another boy who reminds him of his abusive father. It can also involve *identification with the aggressor,* in which a person does trauma-inducing things to others that their parents or other adult caregivers did to them.

Dissociation is a state of acute mental disintegration in which certain thoughts, emotions, sensations, and memories are split off from conscious awareness and compartmentalized because they are too overwhelming for the conscious mind to integrate. Dissociated people often appear "spaced out."

Regression is a return to earlier infantile thoughts, behavior, or stage of functioning in the face of unacceptable impulses or painful memories. Regression experiences that are in service of the ego, however, can help break down defenses that separate people from finding and recovering lost parts of themselves.

Reaction formation involves acting in a manner opposite from a person's unconscious beliefs. A homosexual who joins a gay hate group would be an example of reaction formation. In order to protect themselves from facing their unconscious beliefs, people hate and shame others who act out these unconscious urges or beliefs.

Projection is very similar to a reaction formation in that people will recognize unwanted parts of themselves in others but deny it in themselves. They often are not even aware of those parts of themselves, because they have split them off from their awareness. They keep their focus on others to keep the focus off themselves.

While approximately 40 other ego defenses have been identified, these are the most common mechanisms found in people who suffered developmental trauma during the separation stage. People who feel desperate will do everything they can to protect themselves from re-experiencing feelings connected to unhealed developmental shocks, traumas, or stresses. All defense mechanisms are desperate attempts that people use to avoid feeling their feelings, and ultimately this keeps them stuck in recycling intractable conflicts.

The narcissistic wounds stemming from unhealed developmental shocks, traumas, or stresses cause people to erect defense mechanisms. They do not want others to know that they are wounded, and they try to hide their wounds from others as well as from themselves. They are also very careful to avoid feeling the pain related to these wounds. The narcissistic defense mechanisms listed above help people avoid the following emotions and situations.

Effects of Unhealed Developmental Trauma

Shame attacks involve a feeling of being publicly exposed and feeling helpless to defend or protect oneself. This experience elicits an immediate, almost desperate attempt to shore up the defenses by immediately attempting to shift the shame to someone else. This defense helps to quickly discharge the fear of falling into the black hole.

Narcissistic rage is another desperate defense used to avoid falling into the black hole. It may involve a violent emotional outburst unconsciously designed to block the dreaded feelings related to unhealed developmental traumas from the separation stage. People who have a short fuse can "go postal" if challenged or faced with limits of any kind. These people make others feel like they need to "walk on eggshells" to avoid doing or saying anything that might set them off.

Barriers to intimacy are additional by-products of developmental trauma or stress during the separation process. People who felt betrayed or emotionally abandoned by their parents during this stage are reluctant to let down their guard and experience real intimacy in their adult relationships. They close off their hearts and are not willing or able to give and receive the unconditional love that would help shift them to the LOVEvolution track. It is difficult for them to be intimate because they are always fearfully guarding against another betrayal or abandonment, which unfortunately actually acts as a magnet to attract it again.

Intractable conflicts are also related to unrecognized and unhealed developmental traumas anchored in the separation process. An intractable conflict continues to recycle in a person's life without any resolution. Without healing the source of the conflict, unrecognized and unhealed developmental shocks, traumas, and stresses, there is little hope of resolving them. These conflicts also get reenacted at the collective level through wars and ethnic or religious conflicts. Collective intractable conflicts such as those in the Middle East have existed for hundreds or thousands of years and still boil over into wars and ethnic skirmishes.

Addictions and self-medication are also very common ways that people use to avoid their feelings. Prescription drugs, street drugs, and alcohol are all attempts to ward off unwanted feelings of shame and rage that have never been brought under self-control. Addictive substances and activities such as alcohol, drugs, cigarettes, sex, work, and food serve as transitional objects for people who have not completed their psychological separation. These objects are always available when the fears or anxieties about being out in the world without enough love or support get too great. The first step in eliminating an addiction is mourning the loss of the available mother and recognizing that substitutes do not really replace the feeling of connection to mother, even for a short time. Healing requires one to build an "inner mother" to help provide self-nurturing and comfort.

People use addictions of all kinds to avoid the feelings that catapult them into the black hole. The worst fear of people with narcissistic disturbances is that they will have to feel those terrifying feelings that they felt when they were a toddler.

Conduct disorders are the result of a lack of impulse control and acting out narcissistic and abandonment rage. The *DSM–IV* (1994) has updated these characteristics in their diagnosis of a conduct disorder. This diagnosis applies to anyone under 18; for those over 18 it is usually called an *antisocial personality disorder* (pp. 645–650). Either diagnosis requires a persistent pattern of three or more of the symptoms in the following list during the past 12 months and at least one in the past 3 months:

Aggression to people and animals:

- often bullies, threatens, or intimidates others
- has used a weapon that can cause serious physical harm to others
- often initiates physical fights
- has been physically cruel to people
- has been physically cruel to animals
- has stolen while confronting a victim
- has forced someone into sexual activity

Destruction of property:

- has deliberately engaged in fire setting
- has deliberately destroyed others' property (other than by fire setting)

Deceitfulness or theft:

- has broken into someone else's house, building, or car
- often lies to obtain goods or favors or to avoid obligations
- has stolen items of nontrivial value without confronting a victim

Serious violations of rules:

- often stays out at night despite parental prohibitions, beginning before 13 years of age
- has run away from home overnight at least twice while living in parental or parental surrogate home
- is often truant from school, beginning before age 13

It is clear that the effects of unrecognized and unhealed developmental shock, trauma, and stress play an important role in shaping children's brains and creating adults' internal working models of reality. Bruce Perry's research indicated that children who live with parents who are withdrawn and remote, neglectful, and passive or depressed suffer from delayed brain development. According to Perry, these neglected kids desperately need positive adult attention to compensate for the lack of attention or negative attention they received early in life from their parents or family members (Perry, 1996).

Other research has confirmed that once the internal working model of the world is formed in early childhood, it persists into adulthood virtually unchanged. Krause and Haverkamp (1996) summarized the research this way: "Existing research does suggest that the bond between parent and child is likely to remain in effect across the life span and plays an important role in later life parent–child relations" (pp. 85–86).

Narcissistic personality disorder is caused by severe unhealed developmental trauma in the separation stage of development. The *DSM–IV* (1994) identified its essential feature as "a pervasive pattern of grandiosity, need for admiration, and lack of empathy that begins in early childhood and is present in a variety of contexts" (p. 658). A diagnosis requires the presence of at least five of the following criteria:

- Has a grandiose sense of self-importance (e.g., exaggerates achievements and talents, expects to be recognized as superior without commensurate achievements)
- Is preoccupied with fantasies of unlimited success, power, brilliance, beauty, or ideal love
- Believes that he or she is "special" and unique and can only be understood by, or should associate with, other special or high-status people (or institutions)
- Requires excessive admiration
- Has a sense of entitlement (i.e., unreasonable expectations of especially favorable treatment or automatic compliance with his or her expectations)
- Is interpersonally exploitative (i.e., takes advantage of others to achieve his or her own ends)
- Lacks empathy; is unwilling to recognize or identify with the feelings and needs of others
- Is often envious of others or believes that others are envious of him or her
- Shows arrogant, haughty behaviors or attitudes

Many people would meet some of these criteria, falling short of a full diagnosis, but as a result of unrecognized and unhealed developmental shocks, traumas, and stresses suffer from failure to learn how to regulate their narcissistic urges during the separation stage of development. All personality disorders are very difficult to change through psychotherapy and seriously limit people's lives.

Intergenerational effects are common in people who carry unrecognized and unhealed developmental shock, trauma, or stress. Traumatized parents inadvertently traumatize their children, who then traumatize their children, and so it goes down the chain. Our developmental systems theory (DST) shows how pervasive the effects of this unfortunate truth actually are.

Child abuse and neglect are also examples of intergenerational effects of unrecognized and unhealed developmental traumas. A nationwide study (Straus, 1980) indicated that between 3.4 and 4 million children have been physically beaten by a parent before they leave home. Their study indicated that as many as 1.8 million children had parents threaten them with a knife or gun.

This study covered only those cases of known abuse, and we estimate that only about 10% of abuse in the family ever gets reported. In addition to these incidents of intentional child abuse, many parents unconsciously abuse their children in the name of good parenting. In order to discipline them, they slap, punch, hit with a stick or belt on the bare skin, bruise, cut, scald, burn, torture, beat, and actually maim their children all under the guise of being a good parent.

Parents also abuse their children emotionally, which does not leave visible marks, but may be even more widespread in families than physical or sexual abuse. Parents often justify emotionally abusing their children because it "is for their own good," when, in fact, they are attempting to avoid their own unhealed developmental shock, trauma, or stress. This is the theme of Alice Miller's book, *For Your Own Good: Hidden Cruelty in Child-Rearing and the Roots of Violence* (1984).

The emotional methods that parents use to discipline their children include the use of lies, subterfuge, manipulation, ridicule, shame, scorn, coercion, humiliation, isolation, abandonment, threats of violence, and threats of or actual withdrawal of love. Some parents also abuse their children by habitually ignoring their relational needs. Physical and emotional neglect appear to be the most damaging forms of developmental traumas in early childhood.

We can only imagine how much intentional and unintentional sexual abuse is present in families. Susan Forward (Forward & Buck, 1978) writes that the families where incest is present "come from every economic, cultural, social, racial, educational, religious and geographical background." This fact is also documented in the research of Lloyd deMause (deMause, 1991).

Domestic violence is also anchored in unhealed developmental traumas related to the counterdependent stage of development. The American Institute on Domestic Violence (2001) published the following facts about domestic violence:

- 85–95% of all domestic violence victims are female.
- More than 500,000 women are stalked by an intimate partner each year.
- 5.3 million women are abused each year.
- 1,232 women are killed each year by an intimate partner.
- Domestic violence is the leading cause of injury to women.

- Women are more likely to be attacked by someone they know rather than by a stranger.

Other domestic violence statistics are just as disheartening:

- Women are more likely to be attacked by someone they know rather than by a stranger. As many as 324,000 women each year experience intimate partner violence during their pregnancy (Gazmararian et al., 2000, pp. 79–84).
- The most rapid growth in domestic relations caseloads is occurring in domestic violence filings. Between 1993 and 1995, 18 of 32 states with three-year filing figures reported an increase of 20% or more (National Center for the State Courts, 1996).

Domestic homicide statistics, unfortunately, only indicate successful homicides. The number of attempted homicides is likely much larger. This is particularly significant in homes with children. These children spend their lives in unsafe environments that foster living on the developmental trauma track of evolution. Growing up in environments with a consistent potential for violence has a huge impact on the brain development of infants and young children. The following are several relevant statistics about the impact of domestic homicide:

- Pregnant and recently pregnant women are more likely to be victims of homicide than to die of any other cause (Frye, 2001), and evidence exists that a significant proportion of all female homicide victims are killed by their intimate partners (Nannini, Weiss, Goldstein, & Fogerty, 2002).
- In 2000, 1,247 women were killed by an intimate partner. In the same year, 440 men were killed by an intimate partner (Nannini et al., 2002).
- In 2000, intimate partner homicides accounted for 33.5% of the murders of women and less than 4% of the murders of men (Horon & Cheng, 2001).
- Homicide is the leading cause of death overall for pregnant women, followed by cancer, acute and chronic respiratory conditions, motor vehicle collisions, drug overdose, peripartum and postpartum cardiomyopthy, and suicide (CDC, 2003).

Hate crimes are another category where we see the effects of unrecognized and unhealed developmental traumas in our society. The Southern Poverty Law Center compiles a quarterly record of the hate crimes that have been reported to law enforcement officials. Following are some incidents of those they reported in a recent issue of *Intelligence Report* published by the center (2009). They indicated that between 6,000–10,000 incidents are reported to the FBI and that these incidents represent only a fraction of the 191,000 hate crimes a 2005 federal government report (FBI, 2005) estimated occurs annually.

- Pasadena, CA, April 20 2009: Patrick Mason, 42, and Steven Sumner, 45, were charged with first-degree murder and a hate crime for allegedly killing a black man.
- Denver, CO, April 23, 2009: Allen Andrade, 32, was convicted of first-degree murder and a hate crime and sentenced to life in prison for the summer 2008 slaying of Angie Zapata, a transgender teen he met on an online social networking site. The jury's decision reportedly marked the first time a state hate crime statute resulted in a conviction in a transgender person's murder.
- Miami Beach, FL, May 21, 2009: An Orthodox synagogue was set afire. Mike Baracamonte, 49, was charged with burglary and arson.
- Wichita, KS, May 31, 2009: Scott Roeder, 51, an anti-abortion extremist who was involved with the anti-government "freemen" movement in the 1990s, was charged with first-degree murder and aggravated assault for allegedly shooting to death abortion provider, Dr. George Tiller.
- Cape Girardeau, MO, May 31, 2009: An Islamic center was vandalized. Nicholas Proffit, 31, was charged with two counts of felony property damage under the state hate crime law.
- Magnolia, TX, April 17, 2009: Reported Aryan Brotherhood of Texas member James Stallings was convicted of capital murder in the September 2007 shooting death of Gregory Wilkomm, a 52-year-old disabled man.

School violence is another place where the effects of unrecognized and unhealed developmental trauma appear in our culture. Many young people who have not learned how to contain their narcissistic rage bring it with them to school and project it on their classmates and teachers. It appears as bullying, intimidation, and threats of violence, as well as fights and injuries involving knives and guns.

Even though the problem of bullying behavior in schools has been around for a long time, very little has been done to address the problem. Children are afraid to tell adults about it, and even if they do, they say that no one comes forward to help them. Teachers and administrators often have difficulty in distinguishing true bullying behavior from normal peer conflicts and teasing.

Many teachers also believe that children should learn to solve their own problems and are reluctant to intervene. Many children do not tell about being bullied because they are warned not to tattle or the bullies will retaliate. These victims of violence and aggression often feel isolated, fearful, and alone. Following are some interesting facts about bullying behavior and the victims of bullying based on our research and the research of others (Weinhold, 2006a):

- More than 80% of middle school students reported bullying someone in the past 30 days.
- More than 90% of all students surveyed felt that being bullied caused social, emotional, or academic problems.

- About 60% of victims report being bullied by boys, but 40% are bullied by girls.
- Bullying is most severe in grades 7–9, with grades 4–6 next.
- Almost 69% of all students surveyed believe schools respond poorly to bullying and victimization.
- Ridicule or teasing, verbal harassment, and practical jokes are the most frequently reported forms of bullying. Physical attacks are reported less frequently.
- About 44% of teachers believe disruptive behaviors are getting worse.
- Each month, 250,000 students report being physically attacked at school.
- One out of five high school students reported avoiding the restrooms out of a fear for their safety.
- About 10% of all students drop out of school because of repeated bullying.
- Both bullies and victims have long-term problems related to their bullying experiences. Sixty percent of males who were identified as bullies in the eighth grade had a criminal record by age 23.
- Everybody plays a role in allowing bullying behavior to go on, and everybody has to play a role in eliminating the problem.

Workplace violence is a very common way for the effects of unhealed developmental traumas to show up. According to Bureau of Labor Statistics Census on Fatal Occupational Injuries (CFOI), 564 workplace homicides occurred in 2005 in the United States out of a total of 5,702 fatal work injuries (Bureau of Labor Statistics, 2005).

Verbal threats are the most common violent act in the workplace. A study by the Society for Human Resource Management showed that more than half the companies in the United States have experienced some sort of workplace violence, with verbal threats being cited by 41% of respondents as the most common form (2002).

Road rage is another rapidly growing social problem anchored in unrecognized and unhealed separation trauma. Road rage consists of a wide variety of aggressive acts that drivers take out on other drivers. They include speeding, tailgating, flashing headlights, yelling at other drivers, running stop signs or traffic lights, passing on the right, and weaving in and out of traffic. However, according to a study published by the American Automobile Association (AAA) in 1997, of those who were charged with road rage by the police, 37% used firearms against another driver, 28% used other weapons, and 35% used their car as a weapon against another driver. And the numbers continue to increase (Bodack, 1998).

Air rage is a relatively new category involving airline passengers acting out their entitlement issues. When these passengers are given limits, they often erupt in violent protest. Figures provided by the International Transport Workers' Federation (2000), an umbrella organization for the unions, said air rage incidents have increased from 1,132 in 1994 to 5,416 in 1997. Most statistics are likely to underestimate the problem, as they rarely include incidents of threatening behavior that do not include physical violence.

The Quest to Heal Unrecognized and Unhealed Developmental Shock, Trauma, and Stress

Most adults living with the long-term effects of unrecognized and unhealed developmental shocks, traumas, or stresses have little or no awareness of them. We have had clients who show signs of obvious abuse, abandonment, and neglect in their lives but report having wonderful parents and very happy childhoods. Yet they suffer from low self-esteem and relational patterns involving abuse, neglect, and abandonment, both with themselves and with others. Helping them break through denial and self-limiting beliefs is a first step toward recognizing their unhealed developmental shock, trauma, and stress and uncovering the deep wounds from childhood that they still carry.

With some developmentally focused therapy, clients learn to connect the dots between their adult struggles and their childhood traumas. As this connection happens, they slowly come to understand that some of their "normal" childhood experiences were actually traumatic. When they receive support in expressing their feelings and recalling these experiences, they are able to identify their previously unrecognized and unhealed developmental shock, trauma, and stress.

Dependencies are difficult to break until people feel their sadness about the loss of resonance and unconditional love from their mother and accept that there will never be a "perfect mother" person who is always available for them. Then they are able to find people who are emotionally available to give nurturing and unconditional love and comfort when they ask for it. It is still important to feel their feelings and comfort themselves using their inner nurturing mother.

People who have unrecognized and unhealed developmental shock, trauma, or stress from the codependent stage often try to cover their bonding wounds by seeking out a series of special people such as gurus, bosses, teachers, ministers, politicians, and/or partners on whom they project "perfect parent." In these relationships, the person projects their infantile need for blissful bonding as a way of meeting their need for attunement and resonance.

The intense need to attach to another person and re-experience bliss through an addiction to a "perfect" person is a key element of codependency. If we look at what is right about this behavior, it shows that people instinctively know they must heal their dependency needs in order complete their codependent stage of development. Then it is much easier to complete the separation process. The research is very clear that the more bonded a person is, the easier the task of separation is (Kaplan, 1978).

Those with unrecognized and unhealed separation trauma from the counterdependent stage of development attempt to satisfy the need for symbiotic bliss in exactly the opposite way. They seek safer methods to protect themselves from feeling invaded, such as seeking high levels of activity, many rules, or high standards of behavior or cleanliness that help them maintain strong boundaries. Through these dysfunctional adaptive behaviors, they believe they are healing their core developmental shocks, traumas, or stresses. Unfortunately, these ways do not work. In Chapters 9 and 10, we describe numerous effective and easily learned interventions designed to help clients identify and heal separation traumas.

Developmental Trauma and Personality Disorders

Althea Horner is one of many psychodynamic psychologists who bring together attachment theory, cognitive theory, and object-relations theory. Their major focus is studying the development of a cohesive, reality-related, object-related self. This self develops within the context of the mother–child relationship, with the mothering person as the mediator or central force of this organization. While we are not great proponents of diagnoses and the medical model of pathology, we find her model of object-relations development and associated pathologies useful, as it emphasizes the importance of early childhood development. Figure 7.4, which we have adapted from her work, shows how personality disorders have their roots in the codependent and counterdependent stages of development.

We must say that the knowledge of the mother's immense role in not only the development of the individual child but of culture and civilization is not new in the world of literature. William Ross recognized it in 1885 when he wrote in his poem, *The Hand That Rocks the Cradle is the Hand That Rules the World* (Magill & Tilghman, 1965).

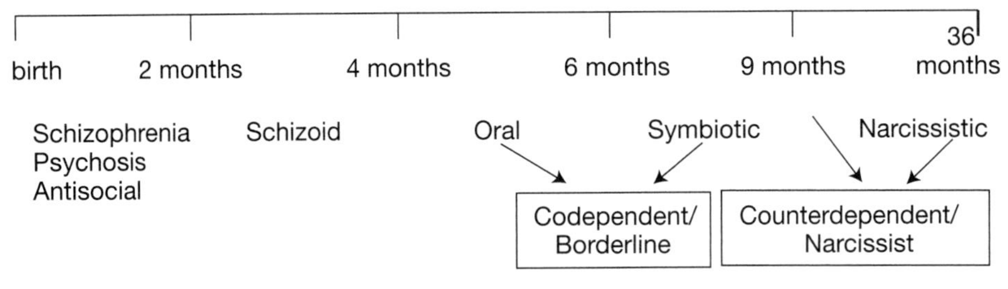

Source: Adapted from *Object Relations and the Developing Ego in Therapy* (p. 37) by A. Horner, 1979, New York: Jason Aronson.

FIGURE 7.4

Developmental Trauma© and Personality Disorders

In the world of art, this very same knowledge has been transmitted for thousands of years. The Egyptians highly valued family life, and Isis was the paragon of motherly virtues. They revered her as the archetypal mother and the patron goddess of childbirth and motherhood. Isis was considered the transmitter of civilization—a belief that was often conveyed through many variations of Isis offering her left breast to her son, Horus, in which the milk from her breast is drawn as a dotted line going into Horus' mouth. At a personal level, this symbology indicated that Isis was giving Horus much more than her milk. At an archetypal level, it portrays women as the purveyors of culture and the advancement of civilization. For this reason, the image of Isis and the infant Horus had a huge influence on the iconography of Mary and the infant Jesus Christ in the Gnostic or early Christian Church.

Unfortunately, the patriarchal forces at work during the last several thousand years have relentlessly attempted to repress and even eliminate the power and influences of the archetypal feminine and the life-giving forces associated with it. Based on our own research, we believe that this struggle may be finally ending and that humanity is moving into a balance between matrifocal and patrifocal values. Obviously, we believe that helping people recognize and heal the lingering effects of developmental shocks, traumas, and stresses will assist this evolutionary process.

If you want to know what
your experiences were like in the past,
examine your body now.
If you want to know what your body
will be like in the future,
look at your experiences now.

Ancient Buddhist Wisdom

CHAPTER EIGHT

The Impact of Developmental Shock, Trauma, and Stress on the Mindbody Connection

We have personally experienced the connections between developmental shock, trauma, or stress and degenerative conditions through Barry's two encounters with cancer. He was able to completely heal both episodes using mindbody tools, nutritional programs, and learning to reduce stress in his life. We find it gratifying that science is making the same connections, drawing similar conclusions about the impact of stored emotions on health, and looking more seriously at the mindbody connection.

Research on the Impact of Shock, Trauma, and Stress on the Mindbody Connection

Mindbody medicine is not new, at least not in Eastern traditions such as Chinese and Ayurvedic medicine, which date back 2,000 years or longer. In the West, mindbody medicine is known as complementary and alternative medicine (CAM). It includes alternative medical systems, mindbody interventions, biologically based treatment, manipulative and body-based methods, and energy therapies. In the historical gap between the practice of Eastern healing traditions and the emergence of CAM, Western scientists separated the body and the mind. Medical scientists focused on body-related issues, and mind-related scientists formulated concepts related to psychoanalysis, cognition, and behavior.

Many contemporary CAM practitioners and researchers are now bridging the gap between mind and body. Cancer researcher Candace Pert (1997) holistic physician Bradley Nelson (2007) and psychologist Daniel Goleman (1996) all have presented strong cases that confirm the connection between emotional states and physical health. Their common conclusion is that the mindbody stores repressed emotions in bodily organs and tissue and that this phenomenon contributes to declines in physical health.

In Chinese medicine, disease is caused by an imbalance in the body. Nelson asserted that the most common type of imbalance that humans suffer from is trapped emotions. He said that they lower immune function and make the body more vulnerable to disease, distort body tissues, block the flow of energy, and prevent normal function of organs and glands (2007, p. 21). Nelson posited that trapped emotions cause two kinds of problems. The first is visible in exaggerated and unhealthy emotional responses to small and innocuous stimuli that throw people off balance and contribute to self-sabotaging behaviors. This is the same response when one is triggered by the memory of an earlier unhealed developmental shock, trauma, or stress.

The second involves toxins from emotions that are trapped in the body tissues and organs. These toxins are released into the body as a protective measure during a shocking, traumatic, or stressful incident and, if not released through some healing of the incident, stay trapped there and eventually morph into degenerative diseases. His treatment protocol uses applied kinesiology to identify these trapped emotions, and then he releases them with simple procedures involving a magnet. Our approach uses the trauma elimination technique and other interventions to release trapped emotions that are mentioned in Chapter 9 and described in Chapters 10 through 13.

Pert's revolutionary work firmly established the biomolecular basis for emotions and explained how the mind and body form a dynamic information network. She provided a solid scientific foundation verifying that emotions and their biological components carry information linking the material world of molecules with the nonmaterial world of the psyche (Pert, 1997).

Goleman viewed emotions as a type of intelligence not measured in typical IQ tests. Emotional intelligence, he said, involves a set of skills such as impulse control, self-motivation, empathy, and social competence in interpersonal relationships (1995, p. 34). He identified specific social and emotional skill sets for intimate relationships and the workplace (2006), for schools, and for ecological living (2009). Goleman recognized that emotional states and temperament may be determined by neurochemistry and that they can be altered. Most importantly, his description of how society benefits from experiences of empathic social engagement is in synch with our developmental paradigm.

The Impact of Developmental Stress and the Chronic Exposure to Adrenaline

To better understand our stress/trauma/shock continuum, we want to look first at the impact of developmental stress on the mindbody. Drs. George Chrousos and Philip Gold at the National Institute of Child Health and Development (NICHD) have pioneered much of the research in this area (2002). They discovered the complex interplay between the nervous system and stress hormones known as the hypothalamic–pituitary–adrenal (HPA) axis. Their theory explained the interplay between the nervous system and stress hormones that activates stress-related conditions such as depression, Cushing's syndrome, anorexia nervosa, and chronic fatigue syndrome.

They call this connection the *stress circuit,* by which signals from the brain trigger the release of hormones as a response to stress. Here's how it works. In response to a perceived stressor, the hypothalamus releases a hormone known as CRH that in turn acts on the pituitary gland, triggering a release of another hormone ACTH. ACTH then signals the adrenal glands to release a number of hormonal compounds.

These compounds include epinephrine (or adrenaline), norepinephrine, and cortisol. It is these three hormones that enable the body to react to a perceived threat. Epinephrine increases blood pressure and the heart rate, diverts blood to the muscles, and speeds up reaction time. Cortisol releases sugar in the form of glucose from the body reserves to power the muscles and the brain into action. Normally, cortisol shuts down the stress reaction after the perceived threat has passed by causing the hypothalamus to stop producing CRH.

As described in Lipton's fractal evolution theory, while the body is in a protective mode to cope with the perceived threat, the three stress hormones, the HPA axis, switch off the hormones that are responsible for growth, reproduction, metabolism, and immunity. In the short term, this is useful in mobilizing the body systems that have to respond to the threat. However, a problem can occur if the stress hormones fail to shut down after the immediate threat has passed and continue circulating through the blood stream for long periods of time. Generally, this is the result of either the effects of a stressful lifestyle, where the stress hormones are deemed necessary to continue that lifestyle, or the presence of unrecognized or unhealed developmental shocks, traumas, and stresses from childhood. (Lipton 2005, pp. 147–150).

According to Chrousos and Gold (2002), HPA hyperactivity resulting from developmental stress can inhibit reproductive functioning in anorexia nervosa and in starvation that shows up in trained ballet dancers, marathon runners, or triathletes. HPA hinders the production of male and female sex hormones. They found, for example, that men who run more than 45 miles a week produced high levels of ACTH and cortisol in response to the stress of extreme exercise. Women with extreme exercise regimens also ceased ovulating and menstruating. They also found that women, on the average, have higher cortisol levels, and they suggested that this may be why women are more vulnerable than men to depression, anorexia nervosa, panic disorders, obsessive compulsive disorder, and autoimmune diseases like lupus and rheumatoid arthritis (Chrousos & Gold, 2002).

Much of Chrousos and Gold's research on stress focused on the long-term effects of stress-related hormones on early childhood development, including prenatal development. That is what we are calling developmental stress. They concluded that the HPA axis may be permanently altered as the result of extreme stress at any time in the life cycle but said the effects of developmental stress on young children are more severe. They found that major developmental stresses during early childhood strengthen the biochemical feedback loop between emotions and behavior. With each major stress, this feedback loop becomes stronger and stronger. By adulthood, individuals may have developed extremely sensitive stress circuits that cause them to overreact hormonally to comparatively minor threats.

Chrousos and Gold also found that prolonged exposure to stress-related hormones, particularly during prenatal development, put children at risk for retarded growth. This can put them in developmental stress states that they are biochemically and biologically unable to switch off, impairing their immune systems and making them more susceptible to degenerative health conditions. From a life-spectrum perspective, they become adults who are shorter than average in height and are more likely to have their life spans shortened by 15 to 20 years, unless interventions break the hormonal stress feedback loop. Developmental stress is also correlated with weight gain. Overeating at night is common among people who are under constant stress.

Adrenaline's components—epinephrine, norepinephrine, and cortisol—are among the most addictive substances in human physiology. Chemically, they are very similar to cocaine and are part of the ASR caused by developmental shock, trauma, and stress. Unrecognized and unhealed developmental shock, trauma, and stress can cause the brain and nervous system to constantly secrete a chronically low level of adrenaline. This is because the mindbody becomes hypervigilant, always on guard to protect against any danger of retraumatization.

The initial surge of epinephrine is usually pleasurable. As a result, some people become "adrenaline junkies" and seek continued experiences that give them a rush. We have seen this phenomenon in our city with the opening of a regional chain of The Rush fitness centers. Their website (n.d.) advertises them as "high energy clubs … designed to keep you 'pumped up' throughout your workout" and "the excitement that will thrill you, the energy that will empower you and the enjoyment that will inspire you."

One of the differences between epinephrine and cortisol is the speed at which they work. Epinephrine levels rise quickly to meet an emergency. They drop just as quickly when the emergency is over. Cortisol builds up more slowly and works on a larger scale. It is also slower to return to normal. Often the cortisol is just getting started while the epinephrine level is retreating. These two stress hormones work together just fine as long as the stressful situation is not prolonged. When the threat is over and a recovery period follows, they go back to normal. That is the way this system was intended to work.

However, in today's hectic, fast-paced society things do not often happen that way. Many of us are hurried and overextended, and our minds and senses are daily bombarded with information from advertisements, neon signs, billboards and road signs, and the sights and sounds of radios, televisions, mobile telephones, cell phone towers, and high-frequency electrical lines.

In addition, 24-hour news coverage informs us of floods, earthquakes, terrorist attacks, child disappearances, and other stressful and traumatizing events. Just a few minutes of a typical newscast has been found to raise the stress levels of viewers. Add to this the flood of daily emails, high workload, concern over finances and the world economy, gas prices—the list goes on. This information overload regularly keeps our bodies supercharged with epinephrine. It is possiblc to spend much of your day and night in a stress state without even knowing it.

Continually going in and out of a state of rising and falling epinephrine keeps the cortisol level increasing. The higher your cortisol level, the longer it takes to recover from the rush. When epinephrine goes back to normal while cortisol is still high, the dark side of these stress hormones surfaces, and anxious feelings and negative thoughts emerge. This all occurs just as the body is relaxing. This biochemical process is called the adrenaline rush and crash cycle. To get out of the crash cycle as quickly as possible, people then look for something to do that improves their mood.

The primary concern is that long-term elevated levels of cortisol in the blood stream affects the functioning of the whole body. We believe that unrecognized and unhealed developmental shock, trauma, and stress are major causes of a chronically elevated cortisol level and the large number of stress-related disorders, such as cancer, cardiovascular and autoimmune conditions, diabetes, obesity, emotional illnesses from depression, anxiety, panic attacks, and phobias. When the HPA axis is running continually at a high level, it suppresses the ability of the immune system to fight infection. High cortisol levels as the result of high stress makes the body more susceptible to degenerative health conditions by switching off protective white blood cells. Conversely, too little of the HPA hormones has been found to lead to the development of autoimmune conditions, where the immune system attacks the body's own cells. Obviously, more study of this relationship is needed.

Prenatally, long-term elevated levels of cortisol may cause changes in the developing brain cells and even lead to schizophrenia. Psychiatrist Dolores Malaspina's research (2006) linked prenatal adversity such as maternal infections, obesity, and malnutrition with the prevalence of schizophrenia. Malaspina's research on 100,000 women who were pregnant and living in Israel during the 1967 Six Day War revealed a very high risk for schizophrenia for fetuses who were exposed to the war stress in the first trimester: The risk was up to four times as high for children of women who were pregnant at the time of the war. In addition, she found that the incidence was dramatically higher for children of mothers who lived in the areas that received the direct shelling (Malaspina, Harlap, Fennig, Corcoran, & Susser, 2003).

This developmental stress could be caused by minor episodes of emotional dysregulation or developmental shock or trauma or, more likely, from both. It often goes undetected but is visible in how we live our daily lives. The Self-Inventory for Identifying Addiction to Adrenaline in the following section is designed to help you and your clients identify the everyday lifestyle experiences that could be related to an addiction to your own adrenaline. In our fast-paced lives, we often ignore these effects of developmental stress until they result in the breakdown of one of our major organ systems. This self-inventory will help you determine how much of an addiction to adrenaline you are coping with.

Self-Inventory for Identifying an Addiction to Adrenaline

Directions: Place a number before each question that best indicates the degree to which this is true in your life. (1 = Almost Never, 2 = Occasionally, 3 = Usually, 4 = Almost Always

____ 1. I talk fast.
____ 2. I drive fast.
____ 3. I eat fast.
____ 4. I read while I eat.
____ 5. I read in the bathroom.
____ 6. I believe that doing one thing at a time is inefficient.
____ 7. I drink more than three cups of coffee a day.
____ 8. I talk on the phone while preparing meals.
____ 9. I love time-efficiency devices such as cell phones, computers, instant messaging, microwaves, and food processors.
____10. I am better at starting relationships than making them work.
____11. I work more than 60 hours a week.
____12. I find it difficult to leave work at the office.
____13. I smoke cigarettes.
____14. I feel anxious when I am out of touch with my work setting.
____15. I feel that sleeping is time wasted.
____16. I find it difficult to relax when the workday is done.
____17. Lying on the beach doing nothing seems more like torture than relaxation.
____18. I find accomplishing many things at once immensely satisfying.
____19. I don't spend as much time as I'd like with my family.
____20. I don't spend as much time alone as I'd like.

____21. I feel driven to get more done.
____22. I schedule my time so tightly I am frustrated by the inevitable interruptions.
____23. I get upset when others are late.
____24. I have difficulty waiting in lines.
____25. I get angry when the traffic light changes and the person in front of me takes too much time getting moving.
____26. I get frustrated with slow drivers.
____27. I skip meals because I get busy with more important things.
____28. I eat on the run.
____29. I hurry my children because they aren't moving fast enough.
____30. I love computers because they are fast, efficient, and accurate.
____31. I have trouble with people who are slow, inefficient, and talk too much.
____32. I believe that living faster means living better.
____33. I hate to make two trips carrying in the groceries.
____34. I do things in a hurry, even though doing it quickly may mean I have to do it again.
____35. I seek out high-intensity experiences.
____36. I resist reading directions, preferring to jump in and get started.
____37. I find that a level of danger is a necessary ingredient for feeling fully alive.
____38. I have trouble slowing down because I fear that something or someone might gain on me.
____39. I feel I must keep myself "revved up" to keep from becoming bored or depressed.
____40. I find people boring if they don't live high-intensity lives.
____41. I find it difficult to take time to just think and dream.
____42. I find it difficult to "shut down" my mind, even away from work.
____43. I keep a notepad or recording machine with me to jot down important thoughts.
____44. I panic just thinking about the possibility that my computer may crash.
____45. My fear of computer viruses rivals or surpasses my fear of AIDS.
____46. I miss taking time to "enjoy the sunsets and smell the flowers."
____47. I like multiplex theaters because I can check out another movie if I get bored with the first.
____48. I like reading *USA Today* because it is quick and easy to learn a little about a lot of things.
____49. I find it difficult to read a book from cover to cover, even when I am enjoying it.
____50. I have many partially read books lying around.
____51. I read mostly business-related material and feel slightly guilty if I read just for pleasure.

____52. I feel dependent on the constant stimulation, pressure, and excitement I get in life.
____53. I find myself accepting civic and business obligations even after I feel overloaded.
____54. I am missing important times with my children, partner, or family because I am too busy.
____55. My preferred forms of exercise or recreation are demanding and/or competitive.
____56. I become anxious or depressed when I can't work out.
____57. I feel my life is moving too fast.
____58. I have had stress-related illnesses such as back problems, high blood pressure, ulcers, or "nervous stomach."
____59. I dream of hitting the jackpot via lottery tickets, sports betting (horse or dog racing, weekly football pools, etc.), or playing the slots.
____60. I like to watch scary movies and TV shows.
______ Total Score

Scoring: Add the numbers in the left-hand column and record your total score. See the interpretation to determine what your score might mean.

Interpretation: Each person must decide the meaning of the scores when analyzing personal lifestyle. For one person, missing their child's first concert may be enough to make a change. For another, it may require a serious heart attack. The following interpretation guidelines will help you in your lifestyle analysis.

60– 90 = Low risk of adrenaline addiction
91–120 = Some risk of adrenaline addiction
121–150 = High risk of adrenaline addiction
151–180 = Very high risk of adrenaline addiction
181–240 = Danger; extremely high risk of adrenaline addiction

Source: From *The addiction to adrenaline inventory,* by J. Diamond, 1989, self-published paper. Reprinted by permission of the author.

If you or your client's score was more than 120, it indicates not only a risk of addiction to adrenaline, but also a strong likelihood of experiences involving unrecognized and unhealed developmental shock, trauma, or stress. Knowing that these behaviors are related to developmental stress may motivate you or your clients to change some of these small daily habits that could be doing long-term damage to your mindbody. In Part Four we discuss the appropriate interventions for treating developmental stress and trauma.

The Role of Shock in Causing Degenerative Health Conditions

A German physician named Ryke Hamer, formerly of the Universities of Munich and Tubingen in Germany, conducted what we believe to be the most significant and pertinent research on the effects of shock on the mindbody. Dr. Hamer described his paradigm in his groundbreaking book, *Summary of the New Medicine* (2000), which is unfortunately out of print. The most current information on his work can be found on his official English language website in an updated article titled *Five Biological Laws* (Markolin, 2010). Please consult http://learninggnm.com for more detailed information on his approach.

Hamer's research began on a very personal note with the tragic shooting and eventual death of his son, Dirk. Then Hamer's wife subsequently developed breast cancer and died. It was after her death and after he was diagnosed with testicular cancer that he made the connection between these tragic events and his and his wife's illnesses.

As a medical doctor, scientific researcher, and head internist of an oncology clinic in Munich, Hamer was in a position to conduct research on his hypothesis that a physical or emotional event within 1 to 2 years of the onset of a cancer diagnosis can create a *biological-conflict-shock,* which he calls a DHS (Dirk Hamer Syndrome, after his son who was killed). This DHS manifests in a visible physical event in the brain that then causes measurable changes in organs and tissues of the body. Hamer said that a DHS is always the first step in the development of so-called cancerous growths, ulcerations, necroses, and functional disturbances in specific organs of the body.

Hamer's Research Findings

After 20 years of research and therapy with more than 31,000 patients, Hamer finally established firmly, logically, and empirically how a physical or emotional event involving a biological-conflict-shock results in what traditional medicine would describe as "cancerous activity" in the body that leads to a cancer diagnosis within 1 to 2 years after the event. He also established that once the conflict/shock is resolved through psychotherapy, the body reverses this process and spontaneously heals itself. This reversal causes a remission phase in which the damage is repaired and the individual returns to good health.

Hamer said that a biological-conflict-shock is not an abstract Freudian term. It is a real-life internal experience of an inescapable conflict/shock that is both biological and psychological and is experienced as very acute, traumatic, and usually isolating because it is not easy to discuss or mull over with others. This biological-shock-conflict event also does not allow a person any time to prepare for it. Even a few seconds of preparation, Hamer said, could lessen the impact of the event—as, in Hamer's case, the unexpected death of a loved one.

Typically, the shock is life threatening, contains fear-inducing news, and traps a person in a life-or-death situation not of his or her choosing from which there is no escape. Biological-conflict-shocks exist throughout the animal kingdom. If an animal experiences a biological-conflict-shock, it is usually related to a concrete event. It can be choking on a morsel of food, having an obstruction in the intestine, or facing a life- or procreative-threatening injury.

Biological-conflict-shocks have special meaning for humans because we have the capacity for symbolic thinking. Therefore, after experiencing the kind of biological-conflict-shock that Hamer had experienced, the shock registers first in the dermal layer of the brain. Then at the precise point in the dermal layer where the shock registers, a set of concentric rings form. He calls these rings a *Hamer Focus* or *HH.* These rings are visible in a computerized tomography (CT) scan. The organ that is controlled by that specific part of the brain then begins to change. This change can manifest as a tumor, as tissue loss, or as a loss of function.

Hamer's research also indicated that even getting a diagnosis of cancer can cause the brain to register another HH that affects a different emotional center in the brain than the one affected by the initial shock. An example of this effect showed up in two recent large randomized trials that indicate labeling someone as a "cancer patient" and doing cancer screenings contributes to doubling the lifetime risk of getting prostate cancer (Brawley, Ankerst, & Thompson, 2009, pp. 264–273). One of the authors, Dr. Otis Brawley, the top medical official at the American Cancer Society, pointed out that men who are given the label of "cancer patient" suffer many emotional conflicts related to the negative consequences of this diagnosis, such as possible loss of sexual functioning, impact upon the ability to earn a living, and cost or availability of health insurance. He also estimates a 50% overdiagnosis of prostate cancer and calls for an end to unnecessary prostate screenings.

Hamer said that the organ in the body where a tumor begins to grow is related to an unresolved emotional conflict that gets triggered during the biological-conflict-shock event. When we have an unexpected conflict/shock that does not get resolved, the emotional reflex center (the HH center) in the brain that corresponds to the unexpressed emotions, such as anger, frustration, or grief, slowly breaks down. Each of the emotional centers in the brain is connected to a specific organ. When an emotional center in the brain connected to a particular organ breaks down, it begins sending inaccurate information to the organ or tissues it controls, causing it to create deformed cells in its tissues—cancer cells.

Hamer further discovered that the nature and content of the unresolved conflict determines which mindbody program gets initiated following the conflict/shock. The types of tumors that subsequently develop have symbolic meanings that reflect the nature of the unresolved internal conflict/shock. Emotional conflicts involving swallowing, for example, symbolically express "I can't accept this, I can't swallow it," and are related to cancers of the esophagus. A person's inability to obtain sustenance; to express feelings of uncontrollable anger; to accept experiences involving a loss of territory, a layoff at work, or a dismissal; or a separation from a child or partner all involve conflicts that have biological analogies that are expressed symbolically in different organs of the body.

Hamer's Five Biological Laws

Hamer founded German New Medicine after extensive research and a therapeutic practice as an oncologist dating back to 1979. His paradigm contains five biological laws that he claimed totally invalidate the concept of "diseases."

The First Biological Law: A Redefinition of Disease. In his first law he redefines diseases as *significant biological special programs of nature* (SBS) created specifically by the body to assist an individual who has experienced an unexpected, highly acute conflict/shock or DHS. That shock is registered immediately in the psyche, the brain, and the corresponding organ connected to that part of the brain.

Through CT scans Hamer determined that the impact of the unexpected conflict/shock immediately creates sharp concentric rings in a very specific and predetermined area of the brain he calls the HH. The exact location and the size of the HH in the brain are determined by the nature and intensity of the conflict. The exact location of the HH in the brain is determined by a person's perceptions and feelings related to the unexpected conflict/shock. The moment the conflict/shock happens, a signal is sent to the organ or tissue that is connected to that part of the brain and an SBS is created to protect this organ or tissue from the possible effects of the conflict/shock. He also discovered that a single biological conflict/shock can have multiple elements that impact more than one brain area and consequently different organs or tissues. This multiple impact phenomenon is mistakenly called metastasis.

The Second Biological Law: The Two Phases of Healing. His second biological law described two phases to the whole SBS process, provided the conflict is resolved. The first phase he called the *conflict active phase* and the other the *conflict healing phase.* Interestingly, he found that the conflict active phase can cause cell proliferation in the organ if that is needed to facilitate the healing of the effects of the conflict/shock on the organ or tissues. If less tissue is needed to assist in healing the effects of the conflict/shock, the affected organ or tissue will produce a cell reduction or meltdown. According to Hamer, each of these natural healing responses is mistakenly diagnosed as a symptom of cancer.

Hamer found that when the conflict active phase begins and the person becomes aware of the conflict, the normal day–night rhythm is instantly interrupted in a way that affects the whole organism. It throws the autonomic nervous system into a hypervigilant state leading to sleeplessness, lack or appetite, a fast heartbeat, elevated blood pressure, low blood sugar, and nausea. This state also causes the blood vessels to constrict, which leads to cold hands and feet, cold skin, chills, shivers, or cold sweats.

At the brain level, the concentric rings form and become sharply visible on a CT scan. At the organ or tissue level, signals from the brain either create a proliferation of new cells or a cell meltdown that follows the evolutionary development of the human brain. All organs and tissues controlled from the old brain (brain stem and cerebellum), such as the colon, the lungs, the liver, the kidneys, or the breast glands, always experience a cell proliferation or tumor growth. Organs and tissues controlled from the cerebrum (cerebral medulla and cerebral cortex) such as the bones, lymph nodes, ovaries, testicles, or the epidermis of the skin, always experience tissue loss. As the conflict active phase advances, so do the symptoms.

In the conflict healing phase, the person feels a great relief from the stress of the conflict/shock. The autonomic nervous system switches into a calming stage where the person feels tired but has a good appetite. Rest and a healthy diet help the healing and repair process. At the brain level, water and brain fluids are drawn to the related brain area, creating some edema in order to protect the brain tissue during the repair process. This may cause temporary symptoms such as headaches, dizziness, or blurry vision.

The conflict healing phase is composed of two parts. First, the individual returns briefly to a state resembling the conflict active phase with symptoms of nervousness, cold sweats, shivers, and nausea, and the swelling of the organ reaches its maximum. This is followed by a release of the fluids through urinary excretion. The second part of the healing phase shows up in the brain with the appearance of new brain tissue to assist with the repair process, and the tumors in the organs or tissues slowly degrade. Then the HH changes into a white ring configuration on a brain scan. According to Hamer, many people are misdiagnosed and mistakenly treated for a reccurrence of their cancer during this part of the healing phase.

The tumors related to the old brain that developed during the conflict active phase decompose with the help of microbes such as fungi or TB bacteria. If these microbes are not available, the tumor stays in place, but no further cell division occurs. The cerebrum-controlled tissue loss that occurred during the conflict active phase gradually replenishes and refills with new cells. This process occurs in both parts of the conflict healing phase. If there is a reenactment of the conflict/shock during this conflict healing phase, it will prolong or abort the healing and repair process, leaving the organ or tissue not completely healed. In addition, Hamer said that chemotherapy or radiation treatments will interrupt the natural healing process even if the conflict is resolved.

Hamer refered to a "hanging healing" as a situation where the healing cannot be completed because of repeated relapses of the conflict/shock. We would call this a repeated reenactment of the original conflict/shock. He also uses the term *tracks* to describe the group of trauma-based sensory cues that we call *triggers*. EMDR therapists refer to them as *memory components* and gestalt therapists use the term *gestalt* to indicate a unified group of elements. These tracks/triggers/

gestalts/memory components contain a unique group of sensory, situational, and relational components that relate to the original conflict situation, such as the location, weather conditions, relational dynamics, sounds or smells, and so forth. If a person is in the healing phase and a track/cue/trigger associated with the original conflict/shock gets activated, the conflict–organ related symptoms immediately re-emerge. This reactivation might cause symptoms of a common cold, night sweats, skin rash, asthma attack, or diarrhea. The function of a track or trigger is to serve as a warning signal to avoid the same events that relate in some way to the original conflict/shock.

Hamer suggested that recurring symptoms such as colds, asthma attacks, migraines, skin rashes, seizures, hemorrhoids, bladder infections, or other chronic conditions indicate that the conflict/shock has not been resolved and likely is being interrupted by repeated reenactments of the original conflict/shock. According to Hamer, these reenactments can create chronic conditions such as arteriosclerosis, arthritis, Parkinson's, multiple sclerosis, Crohn's disease, and ulcerative colitis.

The key to truly healing these conflict/shocks is reconstructing the original conflict/shock event and clearly and precisely identifying all of the significant tracks or sensory, situational, or relational triggers contained in the original event. This is also a primary goal of our DPW clinical approach for treating developmental shock, trauma, or stress.

In Chapter 9 we describe in more detail how DPW therapists help their clients reconstruct original incidents involving unhealed developmental shock, trauma, or stress and all the potential triggers (or hot spots), and then use the TET protocol and other DPW interventions to help heal them.

Once this is done, the client no longer gets triggered into reenacting the original developmental conflict/shock. If a client gets triggered into a reenactment of the original developmental conflict/shock, it means that the therapist and the client have not yet identified and healed all of the tracks or triggers contained in the original conflict/shock situation.

The Third Biological Law: The Pattern That Connects. Hamer stated that whether or not the body organ or tissue responds to the related conflict with cell proliferation or with tissue loss is predetermined by a biological pattern that correlates with the evolutionary development of the human brain. This is the core of his third biological law. This law shows the correlation between the psychological conflict/shock, the brain, and the organs or tissues within the context of the embryonic (ontogenetic) and evolutionary (phylogenetic) development of the human organism. This law shows that the location of the HH in the brain and the cell proliferation or tissue loss following a DHS are not accidental, but are connected to three separate germ layers that follow a genetic plan of human development.

These three germ layers are the endoderm, the mesoderm, and the ectoderm. This is based on the basic biological principle that "ontogeny recapitulates phylogeny." Hamer was able to show that some organs, such as the colon, are derived from only one germ layer. Others, such as the heart, liver, pancreas, and the bladder, are derived from multiple germ layers, which are controlled by widely separated parts of the brain. He called these *morsel conflicts*. Figuratively, they translate into conflicts involving not being able to contact a person; encountering an offending remark that is difficult to digest; or encountering things that are not possible to possess, things that were lost or taken away, or things that we can't get rid of. In addition, this part of the old brain is connected to conflict/shocks such as life-threatening conflicts; those dealing with loud, annoying noise; feeling excluded in some way; having to flee your home; having an unexpected hospitalization; and experiencing ugly conflicts with the opposite gender.

Conflict/shocks linked to endoderm tissues involve the lungs, the organs of the alimentary canal, the prostate, and the uterus. Conflict/shocks linked to the old brain mesoderm include the skin, the breast glands, the lining of the abdominal cavity and abdominal organs, and the skin that covers the heart. In the mesoderm tissues, the issue of laterality has to be taken into account because of the crossover correlation from the brain to the organ. For example, a right-handed woman with a conflict with her child would have her right hemisphere affected and her left breast would show the tissue damage in the conflict active phase.

Conflict/shocks that are derived from the new brain mesoderm involve the bones, cartilage, tendons and ligaments, connective tissue, fat tissue, the lymphatic system, blood vessels, muscles, the striated heart muscle, the adrenal cortex, the kidneys, the spleen, the ovaries, and the testicles. Hamer found that conflicts linked to the new brain mesoderm tissues relate predominately to "self-devaluation conflicts," such as the failure to perform a task, failing an exam, being put down or demeaned by somebody, the profound loss of a loved one (including a pet), a near-drowning incident, making a wrong decision, an injury involving heavy bleeding, or feeling completely overwhelmed. If something blocks the completion of the process in the healing phase, the person might develop symptoms that are mistakenly diagnosed as lymphoma, adrenal cancer, osteosarcoma, ovarian cancer, testicular cancer, or leukemia. If the healing process is interrupted by reenactments of the original conflict/shock, chronic conditions such as varicose veins, arthritis, or spleen enlargement may appear.

The ectoderm or third germ layer, controlled by the cerebral cortex, connects to the second or epithelial skin found in the mouth, the rectum, and the lining of certain organs. The kinds of conflict/shocks that correlate to this germ layer involve sexual rejection or frustration, not feeling like you belong, a fright or scare within your home, fear of losing your home or actual loss of it, a fear of getting angry, feeling stuck or not being able to escape something dreaded, a fear of heading in a dangerous direction, a fear of being threatened from behind, and other conflict/shocks involving the sensory system.

Hamer also recognized the importance of laterality and gender in the ectoderm or third germ layer in his paradigm. For example, a left-handed man with a separation conflict with his mother will be affected in the left hemisphere and that will manifest as a skin rash on the right side of the body during the healing phase.

During the healing phase, certain so-called "cancers" may appear that involve the breast, bronchial system, larynx, cervix, and non-Hodgkin's lymphoma. Chronic conditions such as skin rashes, hemorrhoids, colds, bronchitis, laryngitis, jaundice, hepatitis, cataracts, goiters, hypoglycemia, diabetes, visual and hearing impairments, and sensory-motor paralysis may occur because reenactments of the original conflict/shock disrupt the healing process. According to Hamer, all of these conditions will eventually clear when the conflict healing phase is complete, and any hanging conflicts due to reenactments of the original conflict are healed.

The Fourth Biological Law: The Role of Microbes in Healing. Hamer's fourth biological law described how microbes help heal the effects of an SBS on body organs and tissues. He applied this law through each of the three germ layers. The endoderm and old-brain mesoderm produce fungi and TB bacteria. During the healing phase, fungi such as candida albicans or TB bacteria help decompose the cells that served a biological purpose during the conflict active phase. During this decomposition process, the remnants of the microbial healing process are eliminated through the stool (colon-SBS), the urine (kidney-SBS, prostate-SBS), and the lungs (lung-SBS). They are typically accompanied with night sweats, discharge (potentially mixed with blood), swelling, inflammation, fever, and pain. These are typically misdiagnosed as infections.

Bacteria (but not TB bacteria) support organs and tissues controlled by the new brain and cerebral cortex. During the healing phase, Hamer said that these bacteria help refill and replenish the tissue lost during the conflict active phase. These bacteria include staphylococcus and streptococcus that help rebuild bone tissue and replenish cells. Should these bacteria be absent because of overuse of antibiotics, Hamer said that the healing will still happen, but not at the biological optimum. He also insisted that microbes do not cause degenerative conditions, but rather play a beneficial role in the healing phase. He stated that this makes the concept of the immune system meaningless and discounts the common premise that it is the primary defense against degenerative conditions.

The Fifth Biological Law: The Biological Healing of Shock. Hamer's fifth biological law merely restated his premise that every degenerative condition is part of an SBS created to assist the organism in resolving or healing a conflict/shock at the biological level. He summarized this law as follows:

> Blinded, we brought upon ourselves this senseless, soulless and brutal medicine. Full of wonder, we can now understand for the first time that Nature is orderly (we already knew that), and every occurrence in nature is meaningful, even in the framework of the

> whole, and that the events we call diseases are not senseless disturbances to be repaired by sorcerers apprentices. We can see that nothing is meaningless, malignant or diseased. (Markolin, 2010, p. 37)

This statement is completely aligned with the principles and philosophy of DPW and DST. We believe, like Hamer, that the body has a tremendous capacity to heal itself if provided with the tools to do so. We train DPW therapists to offer these tools to clients who are interested in healing previously unrecognized and unhealed developmental shocks, traumas, and stresses.

The Reno Integrative Medical Center has been conducting research in this country about Hamer's theories since 2006. They concluded the following:

> After having received some initial training and applying these concepts to our patients for several months we were confronted with an abundant amount of empirical evidence supporting Hamer's ideas. Our most basic assumptions regarding cancer had been incorrect! This paradigm turns conventional medicine and even much of alternative medicine on its head, but once an understanding of the process is grasped, it points the way in terms of choosing various diagnostic or therapeutic interventions. (Reno Integrative Medical Center, 2008)

Training in Hamer's approach is offered in Canada and in Europe but not currently in the U.S. You can find information on these trainings at the New German Medicine website listed in your references.

Traditional Medicine's Rejection of Hamer's Research Findings

Our initial excitement in discovering Hamer's groundbreaking German New Medicine, which identified both the emotional causes of cancer and the use of psychotherapy to heal it, lasted only a short time. The English language websites describing his work also told about the rejection of his research by not only the German medical community but also by most of Western Europe. Wikipedia's (n.d.) information about him said that his license to practice his German New Medicine was revoked in 1986 by a court judgment in Germany and reconfirmed in 2003. As he continued to treat patients, Hamer was investigated several times on allegations of malpractice and the death of patients. He was jailed for 12 months in Germany from 1997 to 1998 and served a prison term from September 2004 to February 2006 in Fleury-Mérogis, France on counts of fraud and practicing medicine illegally. He subsequently lived in voluntary exile in Spain until March 2007, when he allegedly moved to Norway.

The rejection of both Hamer and his many years of research clearly indicate not only how his approach threatens the traditional medical paradigm, but the length to which the traditional medical establishment will go to suppress it. His political persecution and imprisonment rivals that of other geniuses, such as Nikola Tesla (Burgan, 2009), Royal Rife (Rife, 1931), Wilhelm Reich (Reich, 1948), and Robert O. Becker (Becker, 1998), whose paradigm-shifting research threatened the status quo.

The Role of Developmental Trauma in Causing Degenerative Conditions

An American physician, W. Douglas Brodie, independently discovered many of the same mindbody connections as Hamer, although they differ greatly on the concept of "disease." Brodie's work confirmed our belief that unrecognized developmental trauma from childhood is a major cause of disease. After working with cancer patients for more than 30 years, he discovered a set of personality traits consistently present in all cancer-susceptible individuals. Many of these personality characteristics correlate with our research on chronic stress caused by untreated developmental shock, trauma, stress, and unresolved emotional conflicts.

Brodie described the following characteristics as part of his "cancer personality" profile (2001):

1. Being highly conscientious, dutiful, overly responsible, and hardworking. (These characteristics describe parentized children who were forced to take care of their parents' needs and deny their own needs. We also found in our research that people with this personality trait experienced developmental shock, trauma, or stress during the codependent or bonding stage of development.)
2. A strong tendency to carry the burden of others and worrying excessively about others. (These are also characteristics of parentized children and people with codependency-related developmental shocks, traumas, or stresses.)
3. People-pleasers who try to make others happy. (This is also characteristic of those with unhealed developmental shocks, traumas, or stresses during the codependent stage.)
4. A tremendous need for approval and acceptance. (This is a classic symptom of the long-term effects of unhealed developmental shock during the codependent stage.)
5. A history of a lack of emotional closeness with one or both parents. (This is another sign of the long-term effects of unhealed developmental shock, trauma, or stress from the codependent or counterdependent stages.)
6. A tendency to harbor long-suppressed toxic emotions and difficulty expressing them. (This is also a classic symptom of people coping with the effects of unhealed developmental shock, trauma, and stress.)
7. Adverse reactions to developmental shock, trauma, or stress, typically to an especially stressful event beyond the individual's ability to predict or control

that happens about 2 years before the onset of cancer. The "last straw" reaction to this event comes after years of suppressed reactions to developmental stress. (This precisely describes people coping with the long-term effects of unhealed developmental shock, trauma, or stress.)

8. An inability to resolve deep-seated emotional problems anchored in childhood, the presence of which the individual is often totally unaware. (This correlates with our research on the long-term impact of unrecognized and unhealed developmental shock, trauma, and stress.)

Brodie understood that chronic developmental stress suppresses the immune system just as much as episodes of shock or trauma. He saw patient after patient with the same patterns of developmental stress and underlying personality traits that he associated with cancer.

Brodie's Six Developmental Stages of Cancer Growth in the Body

Brodie carefully described six stages of cancer development. His work clearly showed how events involving unrecognized or untreated developmental shock, trauma, and stress within the previous two years are strongly related to the onset of cancer.

Stage One: An Inescapable Shock or Emotional Trauma. According to Brodie, the conditions that produce cancer start with some kind of inescapable shock or emotional trauma. Again, he said this "last straw" event happens within 2 years of the onset of the cancer. This event affects deep sleep and the melatonin production in the body.

Melatonin is necessary for inhibiting cancer cell growth and is the primary hormone responsible for regulating the immune system. During this stage, a place in the emotional reflex center of the brain slowly breaks down, creating a dark spot on the brain visible via an x-ray. Brodie also found that each part of the emotional center is connected to a specific organ in the body, and when this center begins to break down, so does the organ or body part associated to it.

Stage Two: Stress Suppresses the Immune System. Elevated cortisol levels begin to suppress immune functioning. The immune system also receives subconscious messages from the affected emotional center of the brain to slow down and even stop working altogether. The experience of the trauma or shock often feels like an emotional death to the brain, and so it sends messages to the immune system to give up the fight.

This causes somatids, which are subcellular microbes akin to DNA molecules known to prediagnose degenerative health conditions by up to 18 months, to react in the blood cells. Normally these somatids are limited to three stages in their life cycle, but when the immune system is impaired or suppressed they change into 16 stages that begin to create viral, bacterial, and yeast-like forms.

Stage Three: Stress Causes Cell Glucose Levels to Rise. Over time, the elevated stress hormones deplete the adrenaline levels, causing glucose (sugar) levels to rise in normal cells. Adrenaline serves to remove and convert glucose from the cells into energy for the body. When adrenaline is depleted, glucose levels increase sharply within the cells, leaving less room for oxygen to be taken in from passing blood. This is why so many cancer patients become weak and lethargic.

Stage Four: Fungi Enter Cells to Feed on the Glucose. Here the pathogenic microbes (the somatids) establish themselves in the weakened part of the body and feed on the high glucose levels in the cells. The fermentation of the glucose causes highly toxic waste products to be released into the body that further rob the cells of oxygen and energy. This lack of oxygen and cell energy causes normal cells to mutate during cell division, creating rogue cancer cells. The body's tissue and cells become highly acidic due to the waste products caused by the actions of somatids. Over-acidification of the body is due to fermentation of the excess stress hormones in the body. This can also be caused by poor diet, a lack of exercise, a high stress lifestyle, or the effects of unrecognized and unhealed developmental traumas. Viruses, bacteria, yeasts, mold, candida, and cancer cells thrive in a highly acidic environment.

Stage Five: Fungi and Cancer Form a Symbiotic Relationship. The somatids help the yeast-like fungus to form a symbiotic relationship with newly created cancer or tumor cells. This fungus feed on the high levels of glucose in the cells to produce new somatids. The yeast-like fungi also feed on the glucose in the cancer cells, giving them energy to grow and reproduce. This eventually causes the cancer cells to form a mass or a tumor. The fungi prevent the cancer cells from reverting back to normal healthy cells as they produce more of an acidic condition in the body, which provides an environment that stimulates their growth.

Stage Six: Stress Stimulates Tumor Cell Growth or Metastases. The elevated stress hormones, norepinephrine, and epinephrine levels in the body stimulate cancer cells to produce chemicals. Here Brodie's paradigm disagreed with Hamer's, as it stated that stress hormones make it easier for cancer cells to travel to other parts of the body through a process called metastasis. Hamer would say that the diagnosis of cancer creates another inescapable shock experience that begins a new cycle of cancer and is actually a misdiagnosis.

Brodie died in 2005, but his colleagues still carry on his work at their clinic in Reno, Nevada. He, too, was ostracized by his colleagues in the medical profession but did not suffer the severe harassment that Hamer experienced. While Brodie was able to communicate with the cancer patient's conscious and unconscious minds, he realized that it was his relationship with his patient that carried the most healing potential (Walker, 2002).

Developmental Shock, Trauma, and Stress and the Mindbody Paradigm

Our understanding is that developmental shock, trauma, or stress from unrecognized and unhealed childhood events influences the biological environment and contributes to the growth of cancer or other degenerative health conditions. This understanding matches that of Brodie, Hamer, and other innovative researchers. The key has been their willingness and ours to look "outside the box" for the mindbody and systemic causes of these health conditions and to describe the healing process. Hamer's research looked mostly at the effects of acute experiences involving shock, while Brodie's focused more on the chronic effects of developmental trauma and stress. Hamer, in his use of the term "an inescapable shock," does not recognize that acute or chronic trauma or stress could also produce this kind of event. Hamer's work also is aligned with our understanding of the natural mindbody healing process that the client or patient is undergoing. While they are philosophically and theoretically aligned with each other in acknowledging that some highly disturbing event occurs within 2 years of a cancer diagnosis and seems to be a cause of this health condition, they differ on what constitutes a disease itself.

Both perspectives are on the cutting edge of both complementary and allopathic medicine and support our developmental paradigm. Brodie's recognition of the long-term impact of unresolved and unhealed developmental shock, trauma, or stress on the mindbody during early childhood reinforces our own heuristic research findings on the effects of unrecognized and unhealed developmental shock, trauma, and stress on physical and emotional health.

The work of both Hamer and Brodie has been invaluable in helping us to formulate the appropriate psychological interventions for healing the mindbody conflicts associated with developmental shock, trauma, and stress. We believe that developmental shock, trauma, and stress can cause all degenerative health conditions. For example, diabetes is caused by very high glucose levels in the cells that could have been produced through Brodie's six-stage cancer process. Heart diseases such as hypertension are also due to the long-term effects of unrecognized and unhealed developmental shock, trauma, and stress. While diet and exercise play a role in all three of these degenerative conditions, we believe the underlying cause is unrecognized and unhealed developmental shocks, traumas, and stresses. These events create food cravings that help feed the fungal infections and decrease cell energy, making it more difficult to exercise.

Dedicated pioneers such as Hamer and Brodie have opened the door to a new paradigm for preventing, understanding, and curing degenerative conditions, as well as better understanding the mindbody connections to all health problems. We see how their biological research parallels and validates our psychological research on the effects of unrecognized and unhealed developmental shock, trauma, and stress as causative factors in illness and degenerative diseases. The synthesis of their research with our own helped us validate our clinical understanding of how the long-term effects of unrecognized and unhealed developmental shock, trauma, and stress can cause degenerative health problems. Their research findings also provide support for our treatment model, DPW.

Case Example

Although I (Barry) didn't know it at the time, I had an inescapable shock in 1983 that triggered a collapse of my immune system and caused me to get cancer in 1985. Two years prior to my diagnosis of the early stages of colon cancer, I experienced the sudden loss of my wife, Barbara, in a skiing accident. At the same time of the diagnosis, I was also experiencing high levels of stress at work where I was asked to advocate for a young female professor who was being unfairly removed from her job because of campus politics. (She eventually sued the university and won a large settlement). Later, upon reflection of the possible connections between these events, I realized that both the death of my wife and the removal of this female professor were related to issues about the "death of the feminine."

I married Janae in November 1984, and she became an enormous resource in helping me heal deeper layers of the shock of Barbara's death. Barbara's demise also triggered very early memories of being abandoned by my mother a week after my birth. I knew somehow that Barbara's death was connected to the loss of my emotional connection with my mother at a very early age. Many a night Janae held me as I cried about my losses.

My first shock came when I was first taken to my mother after I was born. I had black hair all over my body (a common occurrence), and she told the nurse, "This is not my baby, there must be some mistake. He looks like a monkey." I know this actually happened because every time my mother met a pregnant woman, she would retell this story of my birth. I must have heard the same story told dozens of times before I left home for college.

The second shock happened when my mother could not produce milk to nurse me. She didn't seem to understand that it takes a while before the milk actually comes in. I believe that she also suffered from postpartum depression and perhaps even psychosis because of her beliefs that she was a failure as a mother. When she was unable to produce milk to nurse me after one week, she turned me over to a babysitter and went back to work. I also have a body memory of someone, likely my mother, trying to drown me when I was very young.

The shock of these early abandonments by my mother was so great that I became a failure-to-thrive infant. I weighed 6 pounds at birth, and at 8 weeks I only weighed 5 pounds. They even fudged the weight in my baby book by writing over "5 lbs." to try to make it into "8 lbs." A careful look with a magnifying glass clearly showed the write-over.

I believe that my paternal grandmother saw what was happening and intervened. Between the ages of 6 weeks and 10 months, I lived with her and my mother visited me on weekends. I got enough love and nurturing care from my grandmother that I bonded with her and began to thrive again while living at my grandmother's house.

I did not have access to the information about my infancy prior to Barbara's death because my family had conspired to keep secrets about events that happened around the time of my birth. It was after her death that I finally learned the truth about the family secrets. This helped me understand why my mother was so emotionally fragile after I was born and how it caused my early shock and trauma. Barbara's death was the last straw in my defenses against feeling the emotions related to these early experiences. Finally I was able to consciously process these abandonments and truly begin healing them.

My diagnosis of cancer in 1985 was also a shocking experience. I went into a deep depression, making me fear that maybe my life was over. I considered my options very carefully. Did I want to undergo surgery or chemo or radiation? Or did I first want to see if less invasive methods could be successful? I chose the latter and began working with a nutritionist who helped me make changes in my diet and use nutritional supplements and other noninvasive treatments to support my immune system.

My first task was to clear the candida from my body. Since then, I've learned that candida is very common with cancer and, if eliminated, often stops the cancer in its tracks. This protocol involved adopting a very strict diet that did not involve any sugar or yeast-producing foods and drinking a strong tea made from a tree bark. The diet forced me out of my comfort zone, but I stuck with it and began to feel better almost immediately. After the candida cleanse, I adopted a mostly alkaline vegetarian diet and continued to do holding work with Janae. Within a few months, cancer symptoms were gone.

I had done some re-parenting therapy with my therapist–contract mother that involved early baby work that included holding and deep attunement work. I knew however, that it was important to continue to do holding work with Janae and address other psychological patterns in short-term therapy that were connected to the cancer. This helped Janae and I deepen our partnership relationship, and I committed to doing regular spiritual practices such as yoga and meditation to counter the developmentally-related stress in my demanding lifestyle.

There were many times in my relationship with Janae that I got triggered into reenactments of the early shock and trauma experiences with my mother. At times I would just freeze and become unable to speak or move. Sometimes I could track myself falling into shock and was able to ask Janae to hold me until I could get grounded in my body again. Sometimes she would recognize when I began falling into the black hole and reach out to touch me. Our abilities to recognize the behaviors associated with developmental shock and trauma have been critical in helping me heal much of this very early developmental shock, trauma, and stress.

My self-care regime worked very well, and for close to 22 years I stayed cancer-free. However, a series of inescapable shocks caused a recurrence of the cancer in the spring of 2006. The shocks were the death of my mother and then my father's immediate diagnosis of terminal cancer all occurring within 3 weeks of each other in January 2006. I recognized the symptoms and knew immediately that the cancer was back.

These rapid-fire events triggered deep emotions that shut down my immune system. During this same period, I was also experiencing a lot of stress from directing the Kindness Campaign, a community- and school-based violence prevention program. I also was experiencing high stress levels while supporting my dad in recovering from his esophageal cancer. In the process of researching alternative cures for cancer for my dad, I found there were many more highly effective dietary and nutritional resources for beating cancer than were available 22 years earlier.

I also knew that I had to reduce my lifestyle stress, so I resigned as director of the Kindness Campaign and closed down its local operation. Then I began using on myself the alternative cancer cures I had found to help my dad. This program began with clearing the candida, which had taken hold again. Fortunately, there were more effective treatments to get rid of the candida, and it only took 2 weeks using ThreeLac, a potent candida killing powder. I also discovered Bill Henderson, a local person who had thoroughly researched alternative cancer cures after his own wife died of "the treatment for her ovarian cancer." After what he believed was an unnecessary death, he became determined to find gentler and more effective ways of curing cancer. His book, *Cancer-Free: Your Guide to Gentle, Non-Toxic Healing* (2005), gave me lots of alternative treatment ideas to use with my dad and on myself.

Using the protocol that Henderson suggested in his book, my dad moved from stage IV cancer to being cancer-free in about 3 months. Following the same protocol, I became cancer-free in about the same length of time. My dad died about a year later at almost 93 years from a fall—not from his cancer.

I continue to be free of cancer symptoms and carefully watch my stress levels. I do yoga everyday, do 1 hour of meditation, and carefully watch my stress levels. I have become aware that I am very sensitive to stress and recognize that crossing over a stress boundary will immediately elicit a powerful reaction in me. For this reason, I maintain a stress-free lifestyle, which continues to challenge me.

I still find pieces of developmental shock, trauma, and stress to work on that correlate with my "cancer personality" traits. For example, my empathic nature makes it easy for me to take on other people's problems, which also causes me undue stress. I accept my cancer experiences as teachers that continue to provide me with opportunities for healing my experiences of developmental shock, trauma, and stress.

PART FOUR

Developmental Process Work: A Systems Approach for Healing Developmental Trauma

You can only stomach or face
as much shadow as
you have light within you to bear it.

Gordon Davidson

CHAPTER NINE

Developmental Process Work

Developmental Process Work (DPW) is the clinical model we created for helping individuals, couples, and families shift from the trauma track of development to the LOVEvolution track. Theoretically, DPW fills a gap in the field of epigenetics, which uses language from quantum sciences such as energy medicine, biology, psychology, and computing. Rather than working with solid matter, these sciences work with electromagnetic forces, molecules, and fields of vibrating energy.

Developmental Shock, Trauma, and Stress: New Classifications

Traditional Eastern energy medicine modalities such as acupuncture, qi gong, and Reiki focus on healing through the body. DPW's primary focus is healing through the therapist–client relationship by replicating the same face-to-face, brain-to-brain, heart-to-heart experience of the mother–child attunement. Drawing on the work of Allen Schore, DPW-trained clinicians first learn how to experience this attunement in the client role to heal their own developmental shock, trauma, and stress. Once they are able to experience and sustain this field, they learn to create and sustain it with clients to help them also heal their developmental shock, trauma, and stress

Drawing on Bruce Lipton's work in epigenetics, DPW trainings help therapists first clear and repattern the DNA blueprints set at the time of their conception, and then heal any damage to them caused by developmental shock, trauma, and stress. From an epigenetics perspective, DPW's relational approach helps clients modify their cellular perception of early relational shock, trauma, and stress so that they can directly control the activity and expression of their genetic blueprints. This process provides clients with a master key that unlocks a mechanism by which their thoughts, attitudes, and beliefs create the conditions of our body and the external world.

The primary goal of DPW is helping people heal the lingering effects of their experiences of developmental shock, trauma, and stress so that they are able to receive unconditional love from source energy and give it to others. The ultimate goal is facilitating the full mammalian experience envisioned by Lipton that allows people to be deeply intimate with each other, while also psychologically separate and individuated in the way that we envision.

We often begin the process of helping clients shift from the trauma track to the LOVEvolution track by having them identify and resolve internal and/or interpersonal recurring or intractable conflicts that contain the hidden effects of shocking, traumatic, or stressful experiences from the first 3 years of life. Many of these tools are described in our book, *Conflict Resolution: The Partnership Way* (Weinhold & Weinhold, 2009).

As a clinical modality, DPW helps identify the impact on the mindbody of shock as described by Hamer's German New Medicine on his official website, http://learninggnm.com/, as well as the long-term effects of chronic or developmental trauma and stress such as described by Brodie (2001). The long-term effects of developmental experiences of shock, trauma, or stress cause chronic mindbody imprints in the brain, nervous system, and organs that may first emerge as episodes of illnesses and then later as degenerative health conditions.

DPW emphasizes the role of the client–therapist relationship as a major component in helping clients shift from the trauma track to the LOVEvolution track because the very early events involving shock, trauma, and stress originate with the mother–child relationship. For this reason, the therapeutic environment must be very safe, emotionally supportive, and trust building so that clients can reprocess both the biological and psychological components of their developmental shock, trauma, and stress. Therapists must have cleared enough of the lingering effects of their own developmental shocks, traumas, and stresses in order to interact from an empathic, heart-centered space. In this space, it becomes possible for clients to really experience the unconditional love that is part of the LOVEvolution track.

In this empathic and loving therapeutic crucible, clients are able to identify their unhealed developmental shocks, traumas, and stresses and resolve the intractable conflicts associated with them. Then clients are able to complete any essential developmental processes not completed in the codependent and counterdependent stages of early childhood. Most importantly, clients are able to experience the emotional resonance of a healthy, conscious relationship while they are doing their deep therapeutic work.

Theoretically, DPW is a developmental–constructivistic (McAuliffe & Eriksen, 2000), consciousness-expanding, growth-oriented approach to therapy. It provides clients with a hopeful framework for helping them complete the four essential developmental processes of childhood, adolescence, and early adulthood: bonding with primary caregivers, separating psychologically from primary caregivers, developing independence and mastery skills, and learning to negotiate and cooperate to live interdependently. Rather than helping clients adjust to or cope with lives limited by the lingering effects of unhealed developmental shock, trauma, or stress, DPW focuses on helping them clear the effects of this shock, trauma, or stress from their nervous system, change their core beliefs, express any repressed emotions, re-pattern their intimate relational dynamics, and form loving, lasting intimate relationships. You probably know adults—perhaps your parents or even some of our national leaders—who continue to behave in childish or immature ways that reveal how stuck they are in their psychological development and spiritual evolution.

DPW emphasizes two essential components in the client–therapist relationship. The first involves the therapist's ability to attune with clients in safe and healthy ways that recapitulate a safe, trusting mother–infant relationship. The presence of clear boundaries, therapy goals, and treatment approaches helps make the therapeutic relationship safe and facilitates the deep healing of the lingering effects of developmental shock, trauma, or stress. The second component is using the therapeutic relationship as a tool to help clients experience the unconditional love and emotional support that is essential to completing their individuation process.

One of our rules of thumb is that DPW therapists must be further ahead in their shift to the LOVEvolution track of development than their clients, which means that effective therapists must continually be healing the lingering effects of their own developmental shocks, traumas, and stresses. Unfortunately, this is not a widely recognized professional value or practice, which causes a lot of clients to feel frustrated and turned off by the therapeutic process. When clients do not progress, they often believe it is their fault, rather than that of their therapist who has not done enough of his or her own personal work.

Therapists who have not cleared the lingering effects of their own shocks, traumas, and stresses create both ethical and psychological risks that can not only harm their clients through countertransference, but can also cost them their professional credibility and even their license. Rightly or wrongly, many clients are taking back their power by filing grievances and lawsuits against their therapists if they feel they have been harmed in some way.

The Principles of DPW

DPW uses philosophical principles that specifically support clients' movement toward a more whole, individuated expression of themselves in which they are able to fully experience their aliveness. Its developmental orientation makes it solution-focused, operating largely outside a medical model. Giving clients diagnoses of mental illness implies the need for a medical intervention in the same way that physical diagnoses do for health issues such as cancer, diabetes, heart disease, cystic fibrosis, or other degenerative health conditions.

DPW avoids using people's problems or behaviors as an identity or a label. For example, the statement "I am an alcoholic" (an identity or label) is quite different from "I have an addiction to alcohol" (a behavior). Identifying a person as an alcoholic fosters internal shaming and judgment that encourages him or her to split internally, particularly from his or her own true nature. The second statement helps the client embrace wounded parts of the self that engage in dysfunctional behavior (drinking alcohol). Then it is easier for the client to find solutions to the problems.

From a mental health perspective, the statement "I am a borderline" (an identity or label) is quite different from the developmental perspective of "I have an addiction to oral substances and people because I experienced a trauma in my relationship with my mother when I was between 4 and 8 months old." The developmental perspective immediately elicits a heartful, empathic, and compassionate response. This atmosphere of unconditional love helps both the client and the DPW therapist stay focused on the wounded infant's experiences of shock, the unmet developmental needs associated with them, and the ultimate goal of the therapy: moving them toward the LOVEvolution track.

DPW also discourages clients from identifying with their wounds because this creates feelings of dependency, powerlessness, and helplessness. Although clinical labeling can provide clients with a vision for change or transformation, it more often encourages self-limiting, self-fulfilling prophecies. This philosophical principle of DPW encourages the fusion of the higher self with the lower self and supports clients in finding the courage to overcome problems and addictions that control their lives. It is empowering to say to a client, "Together we will discover and use the resources within you so that you can help yourself overcome the problems you are facing."

In DPW, the "diagnosis" of the problem is also the "prescription." The diagnosis identifies the problem as a short-term issue that can be resolved, rather than as a condition that defines the client's identity. Furthermore, the very act of defining the problem creates potential solutions to it. For example, diagnosing someone with PTSD indicates the need for trauma-elimination therapies that stabilize the overstimulated sympathetic nervous system and diminish symptoms such as reexperiencing and reenacting. This clinical approach also circumvents the medical model's tendency to prescribe medications to calm the nervous system and dull the senses.

Here is another example of how a DPW developmental diagnosis becomes the clinical prescription or intervention. When a client struggles with seeing the world as black/white or all/nothing, medically oriented psychotherapists might start looking at diagnostic categories such as borderline, narcissism, or schizoid personality disorders. Developmentally oriented psychotherapists, who recognize this as a symptom of splitting behavior during the counterdependent stage, would begin exploring the client's developmental history around the age of 2. This is the period when children naturally experience splits in their thinking. Developmental therapists would look for traumatic, shocking, or stressful events that disrupted this phase of development and work on clearing them from the client's mindbody. Rather than focusing on the clinical diagnosis, DPW therapists focus on identifying and healing the relational shock, trauma, or stress in the past that still anchors the splitting behaviors in present time.

Other important principles of DPW are as follows:

- Clients have an innate template that guides them toward wholeness. The therapist's job is to help them discover this innate template and experience unconditional love that is part of the LOVEvolution track.
- All human behavior is an attempt to discover this wholeness and to experience unconditional love as part of LOVEvolution no matter how unskilled or dysfunctional their attempts appear to be.
- Because all human behavior is an unconscious attempt to heal or correct something, there is always something "right" about it. Everyone is already in some phase of the healing process. This principle helps people reframe the meaning of their experiences and prevents internal shaming, judging, and splitting.
- The primary barriers to conscious evolution in intimate relationships are incomplete developmental processes left over from childhood containing unmet developmental needs. These incomplete developmental processes emerge later in intimate adult relationships as intractable conflicts.
- All current intractable conflicts, health issues, and relationship problems are the result of incomplete developmental processes caused by unrecognized and unhealed developmental shocks, traumas, and stresses from early childhood.
- Intractable conflicts are anchored in experiences of developmental shock, trauma, and stress that occurred during the first 3 years of life. These early events are reinforced during subsequent life experiences and cause cycles of intractable conflict that often cause degenerative health conditions.
- The primary tasks of intimate relationships, including therapeutic relationships, are to provide a safe place for people to clear the long-term effects of developmental shock, trauma, and stress from their childhood, to resolve intractable conflicts at their source, and to complete the incomplete essential developmental processes cooperatively that each partner brings into the relationship.
- The client is always in charge of the therapy process and dictates the speed at which it moves. This not only empowers clients and keeps them out of the victim role but prevents therapists from playing the persecutor and rescuer roles in the drama triangle.
- It is possible to slow down a client's healing process, but it is not possible to speed it up. Hurrying clients can do two counterproductive things. First, it can cause them to skip important developmental steps so that they have to recycle the issue. Second, it can overwhelm their nervous systems with too much information too fast and re-traumatize them. This is a breach of professional ethics to do no harm.
- Illnesses, body symptoms, and repetitive behaviors provide important information related to the reenactment of emotional, mental, and psychological issues.

This is true particularly of reenactments involving Hamer's biological-conflict-shock and Brodie's chronic trauma, which we described in Chapter 8. Working with developmental shock, trauma, and stress issues fosters mindbody awareness and can also clear dissociated memories that can cause illnesses.

- Therapists must attune to their clients' energy and pace the work from this emotional synchrony. This puts the power in the hands of clients and keeps the therapist in a facilitative role rather than a directive role.
- The therapist functions as a protector whose foremost task is to provide a safe, nurturing, and empathic space. This provides clients with a safe place where they may recall and heal their developmental shocks, traumas, and stresses and shift from the trauma track to the LOVEvolution track of development.
- Therapists attract clients who have similar experiences of developmental shocks, traumas, and stresses. This mutual attraction can help both parties heal the hidden effects of their developmental shocks, traumas, and stresses. It means, however, that ethical therapists must be actively involved in identifying and healing their own developmental shocks, traumas, and stresses and always be working to heal them if they emerge in their clinical work. This prevents therapists from projecting their unhealed developmental shocks, traumas, and stresses into the therapeutic relationship. In this phenomenon, known as *countertransference,* the boundaries blur between the therapist's unresolved personal issues and the client's therapeutic issues. In this situation, both the client and the therapist can typically feel as though they are lost or in a fog.

The Goals of DPW

The goals of DPW are to help clients:

- shift from the developmental trauma track to the LOVEvolution track of development;
- have an authentic, safe experience of emotional resonance with a healthy adult;
- identify the role of developmental shock, trauma, and stress in their relationships and in any body symptoms or in any health problems they might be having;
- resolve any internal conflicts that might be contributing to their biological and psychological issues;
- rebuild their social and relational fabric torn by the lingering effects of developmental shocks, traumas, and stresses;
- learn to work cooperatively with someone whom they trust and with whom they feel safely intimate;
- learn how to change their patterns of reenactment of developmental shock, trauma, or stress in their intimate relationships in a cooperative, partnership way;
- desensitize themselves to specific triggers from hidden, unhealed developmental stressors, shocks, and traumas and to diminish symptoms of posttraumatic stress;

- reprocess or change distorted cognitions, thoughts, and beliefs about themselves in situations where cues trigger memories of shocking, traumatic, or stressful events;
- heal internal splits in the psyche so that they are able to shift from either/or into "both/and" thinking, which allows more complex ways of perceiving their life experiences;
- strengthen and deepen their ability to create and sustain intimacy and to develop an individuated self;
- move into the independent and interdependent stages of human evolution;
- recognize and clear intergenerational patterns of shock, trauma, or stress and dysfunctional behavior;
- create a circle of healthy adult relationships that provides ongoing social and emotional support; and
- learn how to resolve intractable relationship conflicts at their source.

DPW as a Systems Approach for Counseling Individuals, Couples, and Families

Our unique systems approach sees individuals, couples, and families as interlinking, interlocking, and interacting systems. We believe it is essential to work systemically to heal developmental shock, trauma, and stress because they are relationally transmitted from one generation to the next and from one level of system to the next. As we discussed in Chapter 2, the patterns of shock, trauma, and stress are transmitted from one level of human system to another via fractal patterns of recapitulation containing such symmetry and precision that it sometimes is astonishing.

For me (Janae), I see my mother's suicide when I was 13 as an intergenerational fractal pattern of mothers abandoning their children. I saw this fractal pattern of shock, trauma, and stress continue to reenact through three generations. I compare this event to a very large rock that was dropped into the center of our family "pond." While it made a very big "splash" at the time, I am able to see this event still rippling through my own life and the lives of my children and grandchildren. Because I was present when this "rock" dropped, I know the origin of these now faint ripples and recognize this intergenerational fractal pattern in the struggles my children have had in creating and sustaining intimate relationships.

Because of my own family history, the family systems component of DPW has been critical for helping my clients unravel their patterns of shock, trauma, or stress and to see the influence of their parents and grandparents' relationships on them in present time. The concept of repetitive fractal patterns not only helps them feel more connected and empathic toward the suffering in their families, but it also helps them to depersonalize experiences that feel deeply personal and painful. In turn, this helps them be more compassionate toward themselves and others involved in this process.

The Transpersonal Nature of DPW

The transpersonal component of DPW acknowledges the presence of soul and spirit elements in the healing process and recognizes that the true power of healing comes through transpersonal experiences of receiving and giving source energy. As we stated in chapter 2, transpersonal therapies move the client beyond ego defenses into the deeper realms of the psyche. The role of the DPW therapist is to personally access these realms during therapy sessions and to simultaneously assist the client in accessing them. DPW is *soul work* and must be used with the utmost respect for the divine nature of both the client and the unseen forces that help guide the healing process.

As we have used DPW over the years, particularly on ourselves, we discovered that many psychological issues were also karmic issues. This was evident as we became more skilled in helping people identify the fractal patterns of traumatic reenactment that brought them deep and profound spiritual lessons about forgiveness, accepting "what is," recognizing persecutors and perpetrators as great teachers, and in embracing everything that life experience brings to them. Clients who were the most willing to frame their conflicts, traumas, and betrayals as opportunities for expanding their consciousness made the greatest progress in finding happiness and serenity in their lives.

Training DPW Systems Therapists

Professionals trained in DPW first learn basic skills in individual counseling and then move on to more advanced training that involves working with couples and families. DPW therapists receive a strong theoretical foundation in psychodynamic, object relations, attachment, systems, and process theories.

They also receive a broad spectrum of skill training in various techniques drawn from pre- and perinatal therapy, traumatology, object relations therapy, gestalt therapy, psychodrama, person-centered therapy, transactional analysis, cognitive–behavioral therapy, Jungian therapy, movement therapy, art therapy, bodywork and process therapy. In addition, they may learn various transpersonal techniques such as meditation, prayer, yoga, and breathwork therapy.

Much of the skill development comes through experiential training in which counselors' or social workers' first work focuses on using our Partnership Way tools to resolve the biological, psychological, emotional, and spiritual conflicts associated with their own unhealed developmental shocks, traumas, and stresses. Then they learn how to integrate these skills with shock, trauma, and stress reduction and elimination techniques and anchor them both into their personal and professional paradigms.

DPW-trained therapists who work with complex systems such as organizations, cultural subgroups, and nation–states are called *developmental process consultants* (DPCs). They receive additional training in chaos theory, cross-cultural psychology, large-group dynamics, and cross-disciplinary team building. This broad background in both theory and training provides the solid practical and theoretical foundation needed to work effectively with larger systems.

Our approach for training DPW therapists employs a developmental–constructivist model (McAuliffe & Eriksen, 2000, p. 50), which is based on the following assumptions:

1. Individuals actively construct their own knowledge out of whatever learning experiences they are having.
2. Individuals come to each learning situation in a particular stage of cognitive development that shapes the meanings they create from their learning experiences.
3. The process of learning involves deconstructing what individuals previously accepted as true knowledge and reconstructing newer and more complete knowledge.
4. The learning process never offers a complete and final answer on what is true knowledge—only a more complete representation of true knowledge.

Simply put, individuals construct meaning from the information that they encounter in our trainings, and then they assimilate it according to the current level of their consciousness. As their consciousness evolves, so does their ability to construct and assimilate newer and more complex knowledge. Developmental–constructivist learning theories are drawn from those created by Piaget (1971), Rogers (1986), Dewey (1963), Bandura (1986), Freire (1994), hooks (1994), Kegan (1994), and Kolb (1984).

Our approach asks facilitative educators to interact with students in ways that transform the consciousness of both the teacher and the learner. This task is not about just teaching skills or transferring information. The teacher/facilitator becomes deeply engaged with learners in a reciprocal relationship and serves more as a "guide on the side" than "the sage on the stage."

When designing learning environments and activities that are student-centered rather than teacher- and content-centered, constructivistic educators determine the learners' readiness, their unique learning styles, and their current stages of consciousness. A reciprocal learning environment needs to be interesting to the learners and stretches them slightly beyond their current levels of social, emotional, and cognitive development.

Developmental–constructivistic learning experiences shake up learners a bit, raise doubts about the completeness of their current knowledge, and open them to new perceptions and understandings. A reciprocal relationship also provides students with social and emotional support that makes it safe for them to have transformative learning experiences.

The source of knowledge (epistemology) in a developmental–constructivist approach grows out of mutual interactions between the teacher and the learner. Learning happens in the context of discovery in which there are no predetermined "right" answers. The interactive teaching–learning process itself reveals the answer that is appropriate for the learner's current level of understanding and consciousness. This is in contrast to learning environments that utilize a context of justification where predetermined "right" answers are presented to be learned. There, knowledge is typically viewed as part of *a priori*, or predetermined truth or knowledge, and the teacher's task has been to impart this truth or knowledge to the learner. Traditionally, theories have been used to validate or justify a preexisting truth, rather than to present a hypothesis to be tested.

Developmental–constructivistic educators enter the classroom without a priori truth to impart. They partner with students in a mutual search for a more complete understanding of the truth. Although teachers may have a more complete understanding of the subject matter than the students, they anticipate that students will bring them new perspectives during the discovery learning process. This is a radically different context for the teaching–learning experience, one that we use in this book in our various suggested activities and exercises.

As McAuliffe and Eriksen (2000) pointed out, "Such methods are infused with the themes of valuing experience, promoting active learning, engaging in reflective practice, expecting learners to participate in their own education, offering and receiving feedback, promoting equalitarianism, and inviting dialogue" (p. 21). A developmental–constructivistic approach requires teachers who are secure enough in their own life development to recognize that their approach to the subject being studied may be incomplete.

McAuliffe and Eriksen (2000, pp. 22–38) offered five general guidelines for teachers who wish to implement a developmental–constructivistic approach such as the one we use in DPW training and in our classes, training seminars, and workshops.

1. *Personalize Your Teaching*. We personalize the content we present in our training classes and workshops by asking people to identify their developmental shocks, traumas, and stresses and to work on the conflicts associated with them, rather than role-playing hypothetical situations. This gives them personal experiences of applying the skills we teach in our classes to the effects of real-life shocks, traumas, and stresses and the intractable conflicts caused by them.

During our trainings, we sometimes disclose our own internal and relational conflicts involving developmental shocks, traumas, and stresses and from time to time have presented one of our current relationship conflicts in front of our group. When students have conflicts arise between them during class sessions, we use these as opportunities for helping trainees recognize the elements of reenactment of earlier shocking, traumatic, or stressful events and heal the effects of their developmental shocks, traumas, and stresses at the source.

In addition to modeling and self-disclosure, we also make ourselves available to the students inside and outside of class time. Sometimes we give the students a choice of instructional methods that we could use in order to better match their learning styles. We also ask students to create their own personal theory of counseling so they can take what they learn in class and use it to construct a theory that is personally relevant to them. This theory should be constructed so it can grow and change as their personal understanding of DPW grows and changes.

2. *Vary the Structure of the Class*. We utilize a variety of materials and instructional methods in our classes to help tap into students' unique learning styles. We seldom utilize identical instructional methods in back-to-back class sessions. Sometimes we break the class into dyads for an exercise followed by large-group sharing, and other times we might show a video and conduct a large- or small-group discussion of the content of the video. We also utilize student-led reports and small group projects that make each student responsible for presenting his or her part of any project.

3. *Promote Experiential Learning*. When students engage with us in experiential learning, our reciprocal relationship dramatically increases the ability for all involved to absorb and assimilate information. Even if we provide students with information such as an idea, concept, or theory, we always offer at least one experiential exercise to help them apply it to their own life experiences, allowing them to integrate the information more fully. Some of the experiential activities are designed to stretch learners so that they can look at the information they were given in a new way. For example, we talk briefly about the importance of being centered when entering a conflict situation. Then we guide them through an experiential exercise to help them physically and energetically experience what it is like to be either centered or uncentered, helping them better understand the differences between the two.

4. *Emphasize Multiple Perspectives*. Because we believe it is particularly important to teach students how to heal traumas that emerge as conflicts of values and beliefs, we often discuss divergent values in training. This diversity of values adds immense richness to our classes and invites learners with divergent values to openly dialogue with each other about them.

Our trainings emphasize the dialogue component of developmental–constructivistic learning as an important tool for resolving conflicts of values and beliefs. We identify actual values conflicts that exist among the students during experiential activities and then use them as real-time examples for resolving conflicts of values and beliefs. During demonstrations, it is always interesting to witness a conflict that began as one of values and beliefs deepen and reveal an intractable conflict underneath it.

Once this deeper level of shock, trauma, stress, and conflict emerges, the energy often shifts in both the people who are in a dialoguing demonstration and in those who are witnessing. The room suddenly becomes more silent, the pair involved in the dialogue changes their body language, and the witnesses almost stop breathing. It is as though everyone recognizes that something sacred or scared (notice how similar these words are) is happening, and everyone in the room is suddenly engaged in resolving the conflict. Once the pair involved in the demonstration move through the emotions involved in the conflict, those witnessing the conflict often sigh in relief, as they also experience the resolution inside of themselves. This example illustrates how dialogue can be utilized to bring a diversity of views and a sense of true democracy into the learning environment. It also allows students to help create new common ground that encourages a deeper understanding of value conflicts and how to resolve them.

5. *Encouraging Metacommunication.* We encourage students to self-reflect and then metacommunicate about their learning experiences. Metacommunication involves the ability to witness thoughts, feelings, and behavior, such as "I noticed that I was feeling a bit scared to put forth my idea because my voice had an edge to it when I spoke up in class." An important marker for identifying how effectively students are functioning in a developmental–constructivist environment is their ability to self-reflect and metacommunicate about their learning experiences.

We emphasize self-awareness as a central component of our trainings. Many of our classroom activities involve learners reflecting on their experiences and sharing them with each other, either one-on-one or in small- and large-group exchanges. In the papers trainees write, we ask them to reflect on their training experiences, particularly how they are integrating them into their lives.

We also model self-reflection during our training experiences. Frequently we engage learners in a form of dialogue in which we metacommunicate about something happening internally or about something that is happening in the classroom. Our process-oriented approach makes it easy to use and model self-reflection as an important skill for DPW-trained mental health workers.

Essential Skills of DPW Therapists and Professionals

If you are a DPW professional who is involved in healing developmental shocks, traumas, and stresses in individuals, couples, and families, you need the following set of basic skills:

1. *Contracting skills.* You must establish a clear contract with your clients, whether they are individuals, couples, or families. Both you and your clients need clear outcome goals for both the duration of the overall counseling contract and for each

counseling session. Begin by asking: "What would you like from our session today? Let's see how that fits with your overall therapy contract. What specifically would you like from me today related to your goals?"

The contracting component of DPW solicits client participation in the intervention, which prevents you from acting out the rescuer role in the drama triangle. Contracting also empowers clients, creates safety for them, defines clear boundaries, and teaches them important negotiation skills.

2. *Visioning skills*. Visioning is a critical component of DPW. A clear therapy contract requires that you help the client create a vision of the desired outcomes. The more complete the vision, the more likely it will happen. We encourage working with clients' sensory systems by helping them to use images, asking them to imagine how it will feel, how it will smell, and what their relationships will be like if they make the changes they are seeking. Without specific, behaviorally based goals and a clear vision of a positive outcome, counseling rarely produces lasting positive change. Without a clear vision, the energy of the individual, couple, or family often stagnates or dissipates. This not only prevents the successful completion of therapy goals and objectives, but also stalls their evolution and keeps them stuck on the developmental trauma track.

When doing visioning, it is important that the client does not create a negative therapy vision, one that focuses on eliminating certain negative behaviors. Negative visioning ends up reinforcing the behavior or situation that is causing the problem. An example of this is "quitting smoking" or "giving up alcohol." Both of these goals focus on the undesirable behaviors and lack a positive vision such as "health" or "wellness."

An example of the power of a positive therapeutic vision is the concept of LOVEvolution. Contrasting what life on this track of development might look like with life lived on the developmental trauma track opens clients' minds to the end of suffering and helps them recognize they have choices when they experience challenges in their lives. The path of LOVEvolution can become the road more traveled.

3. *Empathy skills.* DPW therapists must first identify their own intractable conflicts and heal the effects of their own developmental shocks, traumas, and stresses. This process opens their hearts and moves them toward the LOVEvolution track of development, which makes them more emotionally available and supportive in their work with clients. We believe that doing one's own personal work is the best way to develop empathy and compassion for the wounds of others.

By doing their own healing work, therapists are more able to experience the right brain–to–right brain synchronization with their clients that is necessary for helping them process their wounds and learn to regulate their emotions. Through this personal healing, therapists learn how to create this same space for their clients, who then learn the essential emotional self-regulation skills they missed growing up in their family of origin.

4. *Process skills*. The most important skill needed to use DPW effectively is to attune with clients so that they can follow their process as it unfolds. This includes:

- learning how to create a "therapeutic embrace" with clients that allows them to do deeper work;
- recognizing when the energetic field between the DPW therapist and the client changes;
- discerning what caused this change in the energetic field;
- developing effective tools for restoring the equilibrium in the shared client–therapist field;
- giving positive support and validation for the client's presenting problems;
- helping clients reframe presenting problems so that they can use them to grow;
- recognizing when clients are in the process of reenacting a shock, trauma, or stress memory in the therapeutic relationship and directing the reenactment to a new outcome;
- acknowledging to clients the presence of reenactment patterns in the therapy process so that they can separate the present/past time elements of the issue;
- reflecting back shadow aspects of clients' reality that appear to be unseen by them;
- making appropriate interventions to clear the effects of shock, trauma, and stress from the mindbody;
- using trauma elimination techniques to desensitize the client to their symptoms of developmental shock, trauma, or stress;
- reprocessing distorted cognitions or beliefs;
- healing intrapsychic splits within the client's self; and
- helping clients repair damaged relationship dynamics.

5. *Assessment skills.* Clinicians need system-specific inventories to assess clients' current functioning level. You can find examples of the individual assessment inventories in Chapter 11, the couple inventories in Chapter 12, and the family inventories in Chapter 13. Intake data from these assessment tools need to be combined with oral intake information from the client in order to determine the client's symptoms of unhealed developmental shock, trauma, or stress and their incomplete developmental processes.

6. *Intervention skills.* The diagnostic profile created in the previous step becomes a map for implementing behaviorally based interventions. These interventions help clients resolve intractable conflicts; identify patterns of shock, trauma and stress; clear their mindbody of symptoms of these early childhood experiences, and move them forward in their individuation. These interventions also help clients heal their lives from the effects of developmental shocks, traumas, or stresses and complete their essential developmental processes so that they can move forward in their evolution.

7. *Evaluation skills.* Both qualitative and quantitative tools must be used to evaluate the effectiveness of interventions. These include pre- and post-test quantitative measures, such as the Coolidge Axis II Inventory (1999), and the Psychosocial Stressors Scale from Axis IV and Global Assessment of Functioning Scale from Axis V of *DSM-IV* (1994). Feedback forms and exit interviews with clients will also provide post-intervention qualitative data that can be fed back into the design portion of the intervention process to ensure more effective clinical work.

8. *Cross-disciplinary team-building skills.* The systemic nature of DPW requires the skills for working in cross-disciplinary teams. Most traditional education, unfortunately, trains people as specialists with limited information and experience in other disciplines. DPW-trained therapists may be required to collaborate with school officials, social service agencies, and the legal system. DPW counselors and social workers often serve on staffing teams that review the whole system of a client, requiring knowledge of the language and structure of a number of non-counseling disciplines.

9. *Large-group process skills.* DPW therapists who do organizational consulting or work with national or international groups or organizations also need large-group skills. In addition to public speaking and dialogue facilitation skills, they must be able to understand and facilitate group dynamics and to synthesize and summarize complex group issues. These skills are best learned through working with groups of increasingly larger size via mentors or as a cotrainer.

10. *Cross-cultural skills.* DPW counselors and social workers need skills in working in a variety of cultures in order to gain specialized cross-cultural skills. The term cross-cultural can apply to ethnic, racial, religious, social, economic, and political groups within a community, state, or nation, and between nation–states. It can also apply to corporate cultures involving top managers, middle managers, and employees.

This skill set also includes communication competencies in clarifying values and beliefs as well as specialized language and cultural customs. These are best learned through immersion experiences in various cultures and training offered by groups or organizations that specialize in these areas.

DPW as a Systemic Method for Treating Mindbody Illnesses and Degenerative Health Conditions

The training of the DPW therapist also involves understanding the mindbody connections between biological-shock-trauma and illness and degenerative health conditions. Chapter 8 described the work of several pioneering medical practitioners and researchers who understand this connection. Clients who have body symptoms or an illness can use them as doorways for discovering any hidden developmental shocks, traumas, and stresses that are connected to that symptom or illness.

We teach our trainees how to correlate intractable conflicts with body symptoms and illnesses. This process can involve the use of a number of different clinical interventions, depending on the client and the symptom and/or illness manifested. A useful intervention is asking the client to amplify or forbid symptoms or behaviors to see if this evokes emotions, movement, thoughts, or beliefs. Other interventions involve looking for regressive or dissociative behaviors related to acute or chronic developmental shock, trauma, or stress and any incomplete developmental processes that are delaying their individuation.

Experiences involving unresolved intractable conflict often contain patterns of reenactment of unhealed developmental shock, trauma, or stress, both in the individual and in the client's family-of-origin system. Following are some of the questions that we use to help people identify the source of their intractable conflicts:

Questions to Identify the Source of Intractable Conflicts:

1. Have you felt this way before?
2. What is the earliest memory you have of feeling like this?
3. What is the most painful or intense memory you have of this kind of feeling?
4. What is your most recent experience of feeling this way?

Questions to Help Identify What Is Unfinished about a Conflict:

1. What is unfinished about this experience for you?
    - What words were you not able to say?
    - What feelings were you not able to feel?
    - What movements were you not able to make?
    - What goals were you prevented from fulfilling?
2. What are your unmet needs remaining from this conflict or trauma?
    - What did you need during this conflict that you did not get?
    - From whom did you need it?
    - How can you get this need met right now?
3. How are you splitting (good–bad, right–wrong) in this conflict?
    - Who do you see as right and who is wrong?
    - Are you withdrawing into yourself?
    - Are you pushing others away and making them "bad" and yourself "good" or vice versa?
4. Which of the relational dynamics best describes this conflict?
    - I'm okay/you're not okay.
    - You're okay/I'm not okay.
    - I'm not okay/you're not okay.

How DPW Therapists Can Prevent Burnout

A clinical practice filled with clients who are in crisis or experiencing posttraumatic symptoms can be extremely stressful for therapists. Many helping professionals face the risk of burnout, a syndrome illustrated by the following statement made by a counselor:

> I love my work, but lately I find it contaminating my personal life. I have nightmares about the horrible things I hear from my clients. My sex life has deteriorated. I'm irritable and distractible. I'm afraid for my kids and overprotect them. I don't trust anyone anymore. I don't know what is happening to me. (Courtois, 1993, pp. 8–9)

Counselors and social workers who experience vicarious traumatization via their clients typically respond in one of two ways. They may try to avoid the traumatic content that their clients bring to them and begin withdrawing and emotionally disengaging from their clients, or they may overidentify and engage in sympathetic enmeshment with their clients (Wilson & Lendy, 1994).

Programs such as Helping the Helpers (Stamm, 1995) provide tertiary prevention services for professionals with clients who have experienced human-induced victimization (child abuse, family violence, criminal assault, sexual violations) or catastrophic natural disasters. These professionals often suffer from vicarious traumatization, or countertransference, that appears as burnout and compassion fatigue.

Emergency disaster workers such as firefighters, policemen, and rescue workers employ specific debriefing protocols after a crisis. You can also protect yourself by implementing some of the following self-care suggestions:

- Recognize that countertransference is highly likely when working with traumatized clients. Keep your eyes open to any signals and symptoms of vicarious traumatization.
- Create a balance between work and play in your life.
- Seek regular professional supervision, case consultation, and therapy if you are experiencing symptoms of burnout.
- Limit your caseload.
- Monitor the size of your caseload and particularly the number of trauma cases.
- Engage in self-care activities such as regular vacations, exercise, meditation, and regular massages.
- Bring inspirational objects into your office such as plants, pictures, artwork, and music.
- Recognize your limitations and adopt a positive outlook on life. Look for the healthy or "healing in progress" aspects in your clients' stories.
- Join a study group or attend conferences to learn more about how to deal with shock, trauma, and stress in your clients.

- Work on healing the effects of your own unhealed developmental shocks, traumas, and stresses. You may need individual therapy to help you uncover any hidden sources of developmental conflict, shock, trauma, or stress and to help you heal these wounds. If you have intractable conflicts that keep repeating themselves in your life, it is highly likely that you have hidden shock, trauma, or stress that needs to be uncovered and healed.
- Learn all you can about treating PTSD.

DPW Interventions to Heal the Seven Major Effects of Developmental Shock, Trauma, and Stress

We have identified seven major areas of the mindbody that are impacted by experiences of developmental shock, trauma, and stress and numerous interventions that we use to clear them. We list them here in summary form as an overview. In Chapter 10 we discuss in detail the areas of impact of these interventions, and describe more completely how to selectively use these tools to heal the major effects of developmental shock, trauma, or stress.

1. **Tools for Clearing Sensory System Distortions Caused by Shock, Trauma, or Stress** (visual memory, auditory memory, proprioceptive memory, kinesthetic memory)
    - Trauma elimination technique (TET)
    - Levine's somatic exeriencing (SE)
    - Castellino's prenatal and birth process therapy
    - Mines's TARA approach
    - Rothschild's somatic trauma therapy
    - Shapiro's eye movement desensitization & reprocessing (EMDR)
    - Emotional freedom therapy (EFT)
    - Breathwork
2. **Tools for Clearing Mindbody Memories Involving Shock, Trauma, or Stress**
    - Trauma elimination technique (TET)
    - Sensory integration therapy (SIT)
    - Emotional freedom technique (EFT)
    - Breathwork
    - Weinholds' corrective parenting techniques
    - Activities for identifying and clearing body symptoms of developmental shock, trauma, or stress
    - Levine's somatic experiencing
    - Bioenergetics

- Yoga
- Top-down yoga
- Tibetan yoga
- Movement therapies
- Body therapies
- Expressive arts
- Art and play therapy with young children
- Energy and herbal medicine
- Biofeedback
- Diet and nutrition
- Aerobic exercise
- Relaxation activities
- Social engagement activities

3. **Tools for Changing Distorted Cognition and Beliefs Related to Shock, Trauma, or Stress**
    - Trauma elimination technique (TET)
    - Belief-changing exercises and activities
    - Reframing techniques
    - Betrayal clearing exercise
4. **Tools for Reregulating Emotions Involving Shock, Trauma, or Stress**
    - Trauma elimination technique (TET)
    - Emotional freedom technique (EFT)
    - Breathwork
    - Opening the heart exercise
    - Centering
    - Meditation
    - Betrayal clearing exercise
    - Empathy and compassion training
5. **Tools for Healing Splits within the Self and Reclaiming Dissociated Self Parts Caused by Shock, Trauma, and Stress**
    - Gestalt techniques
    - Psychodrama techniques
    - Completion process with your parents exercise
    - Reclaiming projections exercises
    - Active imagination techniques
6. **Tools for Healing Splits within the Self and Reclaiming Dissociated Self Parts Caused by Experiences of Shock, Trauma, or Stress**
    - Trauma elimination technique (TET)
    - Emotional freedom technique (EFT)

- Breathwork
- Identifying and clearing body symptoms of developmental shock, trauma, and stress
- Corrective parenting therapy
- Somatic experiencing
- Bioenergetics
- Yoga
- Top-down yoga
- Tibetan yoga
- Meditation
- Centering
- Opening the heart exercise
- Betrayal clearing exercise
- Empathy and compassion training

7. **Tools for Modifying Distorted Self–Other Relational Dynamics Caused by Developmental Shock, Trauma, or Stress**

   - TET
   - Completion process with your parents
   - Weinholds' corrective parenting techniques
   - Emerson's relational shock resolution therapy
   - Levine's somatic experiencing
   - Mines's TARA approach
   - Castellino's prenatal and birth process therapy
   - Rothschild's somatic trauma therapy
   - Empathy and compassion skill training
   - Partnership conflict resolution skills
   - Reclaiming projections exercises
   - Weinholds' creating conscious, committed partnership relationships model
   - Reclaiming projections exercises
   - Couple sculpting exercise

Case Example: DPW as an Integrative Clinical Model

We have shared previously in this book how our personal experiences and our relationship have contributed enormously to guiding our research on healing the effects of developmental shock, trauma, and stress and to the creation of DPW as a clinical model for healing them. Neither of us has ever been in a relationship with so much intimacy, which has been both a blessing and a challenge. Issues that we never encountered in our prior 20-year marriages to other people surfaced in ways that initially surprised us. This was partly because we were unwilling or unable in our previous relationships to go deeper into the conflicts, which we later recognized made us somehow look healthier in those relationships than we actually were. Once our own conflicts emerged and we went looking for the underlying symptoms of developmental shocks, traumas, and stresses, we were confronted with a lot of new self-awareness.

Characterizing our relationship as a "laboratory" seemed to have an effect on both our research on developmental shock, trauma, and stress and on the creation of DPW. It was as though our intentions to personally heal our own developmental shock, trauma, and stress and to use what we learned to help other people actually deepened our relationship. Over time, we found ourselves in the most amazing process of discovery and learning of our lives that eventually united our personal and couple experiences with many bodies of research and information.

We found ourselves in a dance between our inner worlds and the larger world, with each internal experience revealing a nuance of developmental shock, trauma, or stress that also opened us to something in the outer world we had not yet studied or integrated into our clinical work. In retrospect, we see that our commitment to live our model and to understand it from inside of us also contributed to this dance.

I (Janae) often felt as though my own healing process served as an unfolding map for understanding, identifying, and healing developmental shock, trauma, and stress. The first year of my marriage to Barry was the most energetically expansive experience of my life. In retrospect, it was the beginning of my personal experience of LOVEvolution, for it surely has opened me to receive Source energy so that I could give it to others. It also created a very deep and trusting bond between Barry and me that helped me personally shift from the developmental trauma track to the LOVEvolution track of development. Barry's inherently nurturing qualities and his ability to create and sustain deeply attuned spaces has helped me both access and heal my many experiences of developmental shock, trauma, and stress.

The sense of my personal process serving as a map for DPW became even stronger once I began teaching a series of four graduate-level courses in DPW at the University of Colorado at Colorado Springs in the 1990s. These classes helped me see my personal, relational, theoretical, and clinical holes. One of the most interesting observations I made as I witnessed my own process of discovery and healing was that it was not a linear set of experiences that unfolded in a predictable sequence. While each new awareness was clearly connected to something I already knew about myself, it happened in a way that felt intuitive and guided me from within.

Over time I was able to organize these nonlinear experiences into a coherent structure that revealed the divine perfection in all that has unfolded in my life. I am going to briefly share pieces of this structure as a way of illustrating how DPW unfolded as an integrative clinical modality. In what I share below, you can see how it helped me live more fully in my body and to experience my life from a heartful place.

I have always known that I was a wanted and planned child. My brother was 3½ years older than me. I learned when I was an adult about my parents' struggle to space their children without effective birth control methods other than, as my grandmother once said, "sending them [the men] to the barn." In spite of my very difficult birth, I had 3 really good months with my mother before she realized she was pregnant again. She must have loved me a lot and doted on me during those first months, because I grew up feeling stronger and more secure than my younger two sisters—neither of whom were planned.

I was only 11 months old when my mother went to the hospital to have my sister. During the week that she was gone, my mother's mother kept me. I grew up thinking about this grandmother as the "meanest grandma in the world" because of her cold, hard, angry personality. In regressive recall, I remembered lying alone upstairs in a crib during this time and crying and crying for my mother. During my recall, I had vivid pictures of the flowered wallpaper on the walls of that bedroom. At some point I fell into a deep shock state and must have been dissociated for a long period of time. After my mother returned home from the hospital, according to stories she told when I was older, I refused to have anything to do with her. She would call my name, hold out her arms to me, and try to hold me, but I either pushed or looked away and refused to respond. This abandonment experience, coupled with 10 days in a nursery after my birth, set me on a path of premature separation and counterdependence.

Barry and I attended our first pre- and perinatal psychology conference in San Francisco in 1995. For the next 2 years, we both immersed ourselves in pre- and perinatal psychology and then attended our second conference in 1997. It was actually breathwork in 1996 that brought me my first memories of being born with the umbilical cord wrapped around my neck. My body memories were so strong that I knew them to be true, in spite of what my skeptical and chattering mind said. We purchased several videotapes on pre- and perinatal psychology, some showing William Emerson doing birth re-facilitation therapy with infants and their parents. One of his videos was on umbilical cord trauma, which I studied intensely. While it was really difficult to watch the first few times because I got so triggered, this video helped me understand not only about my birth but also a lot about my personal psychology.

According to Emerson, babies born with the cord around their neck go through labor feeling as though they are going to die. As they move down through the birth canal, the cord cuts off their oxygen. Then they pull back and feel like a failure. They often hear the words "failure to progress" from caregivers who surround the laboring mother, which become forever imprinted in the baby's brain. These words seemed to have had immense power over me until a wise therapist helped me differentiate between my failure to progress as a baby and the labor's lack of progression.

Emerson called the psychological dynamic caused by umbilical cord trauma *completion ambivalence,* as the experience creates a terrible dilemma for the child.

On one hand, tremendous muscular and gravitational forces are pushing to expel the child. On the other hand, the umbilical cord increasingly cuts off the oxygen to the baby's body. The struggle metaphorically becomes, "If I don't get out of here, I'm going to die. But I can't get out of here, because if I do, I'll die. Okay, so I will just stay in here. But if I do, I'll die."

After digesting the video, I began a sort of life review of all the projects that I had started in my life and never managed to complete. I also saw how much effort it took to really complete things even when I made up my mind. I completed my undergraduate degree in 3 years and three summers and can remember very distinctly how I was ready to give up my goal during the second summer.

It was interesting how my father helped me overcome my resistance by sharing one of his folksy homilies about how every farmer had to do some job that he didn't like in order to make his operation work. For him, he hated digging postholes. Without postholes, he couldn't put in posts; without posts, he couldn't build fences; without fences, he couldn't raise cattle and hogs; without cattle and hogs, he couldn't butcher meat for his family or have a source of easy cash when finances were tight. At some level he seemed to understand that I had undertaken a really big challenge. In his wisdom, he gave me the choice to continue working toward my goal or not, and I believe that his detachment about it helped free me from parts of my birth dilemma pattern.

Of my two brothers and two sisters, I was the most outspoken and defiant. No matter what my parents, particularly my mother, would say, I opposed her. I was so defiant that she began washing my mouth out with bar soap in an effort to establish her authority. No problem … I just learned to like both of the kinds of soap she used! In retrospect, I could see that my birth trauma had set me on a lifetime of conflict with my mother, and it played itself out in numerous ways before her suicide and final abandonment when I was 13.

It is only natural that I would test my mother-abandonment program on Barry many times. He, of course, brought his own mother-abandonment program into our relationship, so we had a lot of healing work to do. Much of it we did inside our relationship, which was both challenging and rewarding.

I eventually discovered a lot of evidence of not only the psychological impact from my umbilical cord trauma, but also the physiological impact. As a child, I had a lot of sore throats, infected tonsils, and respiratory infections. In my 50s, I also found a misalignment of my cervical vertebrae at the place where the cord had been so tightly wrapped around my neck. It helps explain why I had an aversion to wearing things that were snug around my neck.

The perinatal period of my development was also very traumatic for me. After having a near-death experience from umbilical cord shock, I experienced a forceps delivery, followed by a hangover from the anesthesia given my mother to knock her out. I was taken down the hall to a nursery and kept there most of the time during our 10-day hospitalization. My mother had decided not to breastfeed any of her children, mostly because of the pressure from her own mother to use the "modern" practice of bottle feeding. So I had minimal contact with my mother during this period and virtually no comfort to help me recover from so much birth shock and trauma.

The loss of connection to my mother at birth and then again at 11 months when she went to the hospital to deliver my sister created a large vacuum of *mother need* that Barry has helped me recognize and heal. It was a brilliant therapist in Colorado Springs with whom we both did *baby therapy* who helped me really understand developmental shock, trauma, and stress at the most personal level. The hours I experienced of her holding and comforting me as I recalled the shock and trauma of my first year of life not only helped me rewrite my *mother script programming,* but also was life altering.

My mother separation pattern played out again when I was 13 with her carbon monoxide suicide that also took my 5-year-old brother. My older brother and two younger sisters and I managed to upright ourselves after this tragedy and move forward in our development. This experience also helped me understand in a very concrete way that I had the skills and strength to survive the collapse of my reality and helped move me from victim consciousness into survivor consciousness. I believe it was also this event that motivated me to become a therapist. I wanted to understand what drove my mother to such desperation, without realizing that my desire to know would draw similar experiences to me.

My former husband threatened to kill himself several times before we were divorced, as he knew this was a big trigger for me. Between my experiences of psychologically separating from him and from my mother, I learned many skills for navigating the "in-between worlds" of altered states. I learned how to facilitate conscious death rituals for parts of me that needed to die and to use these experiences as opportunities for profound transformation. I really learned not to be afraid of death, either for myself or for others. I really accepted that people are always in charge of both their own lives and their deaths.

It was deeply transformative bodywork with a number of gifted practitioners that helped me shift the trauma patterns anchored in my physical body. In my 60s, I was gifted with a genius Hungarian bodyworker who helped me connect the dots between a lifelong pattern of scoliosis and a prenatal pattern known as *large baby–small mother*. Symbolically, it represented being born into a world not large enough to support and appreciate me.

I was amazed to discover that my strong will to re-pattern my physical structure, when combined with the able hands of a skilled bodyworker, could actually create a new way of experiencing life. I did not anticipate, however, that the emotional components of this part of my re-patterning work would emerge with such intensity. It was a bout of walking pneumonia in 2008 in which I came close to dying that I cleared what I hope are the final pieces of my birth shock and trauma memories.

Unfortunately, I passed on almost all of my own patterns of developmental shock, trauma and stress to my two sons and have also witnessed them being passed on to my three grandchildren. It has been painful to witness the intergenerational transmission of these family patterns and has challenged me to accept that they also are in divine order at a soul level. As I've been able to heal my own developmental shock, trauma, and stress, it has slowly changed my relationships with my sons.

I grant Barry the honor of being my greatest teacher at a soul level. His steadfastness during the many rounds of clearing our developmental shock, trauma, and stress has been amazing to experience. I had read about Carl Jung's individuation process, but it has been profound to experience it, map it, and then write about it with a devoted partner. This very personal perspective on LOVEvolution and individuation from "inside the fish bowl" helped me understand just how many times it is necessary to repeat the four stages of development in order to become fully individuated. While we did our work together in increments, in retrospect it feels like we have "eaten an elephant—one bite at a time."

I believe we have been able to sustain the intimacy in our relationship because of our deep soul connection and common vision about helping the world evolve. Sometimes we've felt that we've been clearing not just our own traumas but also those belonging to the collective as well.

At some point in our relationship, we discovered that we shared a common mind. Now this may sound odd and a little codependent, but something wonderful happens when we get in synch with each other on a specific issue or topic. Things that neither of us can generate separately appear—new perspectives, leaps in awareness, paradigm shifts. We do it so effortlessly that sometimes we look at each other in amazement after one of our creative bursts and wonder aloud, "Now where did *that* come from?" Sometimes we talk with our friends about "mental-course," and then laugh, knowing how much synergy we can generate when we each get in balance and attune with each other.

I am aware that, as I have cleared each piece of shock, trauma, or stress with Barry, my sense of identity has become clearer and my sense of personal power increased. It was between 1997 and 2000 that I generated a burst of creative work regarding developmental shock, trauma, stress, and DPW, and that is when I began the first draft of this book. You can see that it has had a long gestation time and that it has cycled through several rounds of my completion ambivalence. Sharing my story with you also affirms that all bad things can become good things, that there are no mistakes in life, and that the world is flowing according to divine but invisible order.

We do not need books about psychology
in order to learn to respect our children;
what we need is a revision
of the theories of child-rearing.

Alice Miller

CHAPTER TEN

A Systems Approach for Healing Developmental Shock, Trauma, and Stress in Individuals

Most experiences of developmental shock, trauma, and stress are caused by neglect in early childhood rather than abandonment and abuse. It is virtually impossible to recognize the presence of emotional, physical, spiritual, or psychological neglect because nothing happened, whereas abandonment and abuse are easier to recognize and recall, because something happened. Obviously, people do remember the incidents involving acute shock, trauma, or stress from growing up in an abusive family, living in a war zone, losing a loved one, or surviving natural disasters or terrorist attacks, although they may forget or distort important details of the incidents.

DPW as a Systems Approach for Healing Developmental Shock, Trauma, and Stress in Individuals

Because developmental shock, trauma, and stress impact the brain, personality, character structure, and body, therapeutic modalities must have the capacity to access the depth of the long-term effects of developmental shock, trauma, or stress. They must be able to access much deeper layers of the mindbody, even down to the miasmic or energetic level. Our work with people healing symptoms of long-repressed developmental shock, trauma, or stress tends to be slower, more complex, and deeper. It is like peeling off the layers of an onion and processing the unhealed developmental shock, trauma, or stress stored in each layer. This process gradually builds trust in the therapeutic relationship, strengthens clients' egos, and helps solidify their sense of self. By the time we reach the "core of the onion," the issues emerge that are related to developmental shocks, traumas, or stresses from the critical first 3 years of development.

Although we have tools that help clients get to their core developmental shocks, traumas, or stresses rather quickly, we found some limits that require honoring. For example, moving faster than clients' nervous systems can process and assimilate the information in each memory layer can re-shock, re-traumatize, or re-stress them and slow down the healing process. For this reason, we focus on staying attuned and synchronized with our clients at each step of the healing process. This not only helps stabilize and anchor clients at an emotional level, it also provides a sense of safety and security that helps strengthen and heal the fractures in their personality and character structures.

Training DPW Therapists to Utilize a Systems Approach to Healing Developmental Shock, Trauma, and Stress in Individuals

First, it is important for the DPW therapist to see the individual as a system. The biological human is composed of a nervous system, a digestive system, a circulatory system, a skeletal system, a respiratory system, and a reproductive system. Each of these systems is a subsystem of the total human system. Furthermore, each of these subsystems is composed of other subsystems. The circulatory system, for example, consists of veins, arteries, and the heart. The heart, in turn, is composed of cells, and the cells are composed of cellular subsystems. For the body to be healthy, all subsystems must function effectively and cooperatively. If the heart does not function properly, the other subsystems (and the human) would be radically affected.

This set of systems principles is key for DPW counselors to understand in working with individual clients. In the DPW paradigm, any problem that clients bring to you should be approached from this perspective.

The Core Skills of a DPW Therapist for Utilizing a Systems Approach in Counseling Individuals

In this chapter we describe 12 core skills for counseling individuals. They provide the foundation needed for learning more advanced DPW skills.

Core Skill 1: Attunement

In counseling the individual, attunement involves behaving in an attentive manner toward the client both verbally and nonverbally. It is important to access the current mental status of your clients and determine whether they are regressed or in present time or experiencing symptoms of shock, trauma, or stress. Later in the chapter we offer some guidelines to help you diagnose their mental status and decide how to intervene.

Generally, examples of appropriate nonverbal attunement with clients parallel Schore's mother–child model that includes face-to-face, heart-to-heart, right brain–to–right brain contact. In a therapy session this would have the therapist seated facing clients, maintaining good eye contact, matching their sensory language, following what they are saying, and surrounding them energetically while in a relaxed state. It also means not going off on tangents or stopping the reciprocal flow of communication to give advice or direction.

Research shows that matching a client's way of accessing information is an effective way to attune. If a client says, "I am clear (visual) that it wasn't my fault," you might match that by saying, "You don't see (visual) why people are blaming you." Eye movements can also provide visual clues. People look up when accessing information visually, side to side when accessing in auditory ways, and down when feeling something emotional. The key to letting them know you are with them is matching their verbal and nonverbal behavior (Dilts & Green, 1982).

Core Skill 2: Information Gathering

In individual counseling, open-ended questions help gather more information than closed ones. An open-ended question allows the client to respond in several ways; a closed question lends itself to yes–no responses. An example of an open-ended question would be: "Tell me about your relationship with your husband." A closed question would be: "Do you get along with your husband?" Minimal encouragers also aid in information gathering. A minimal encourager prompts the client to provide additional information, as, for example, in "Tell me more" or "Could you give me an example of that?"

Core Skill 3: Structuring

In counseling individuals, structuring the nature, limits, and goals of the session can make better use of the time. It lets the client determine (1) where he or she is, (2) who the counselor is, (3) whether or not the counselor can or cannot be of help, and (4) the goals and expectations for the session. Structuring also clarifies:

1. Time limits. Example: "We have agreed to a one-hour appointment today."
2. Role limits. Example: "I see my role as helping you explore your problems and concerns and helping you find solutions that are personally satisfying."
3. Process limits. Example: "I will help you by identifying incomplete developmental processes that might be related to your problems."
4. Action limits. Example: "I will ask you to try out new ideas outside the session and report back to me."

The counselor or social worker should involve the client in the structuring process by asking open-ended questions such as, "What motivated you to come see me?" and "How may I be of help to you?" It is also important to develop a written contract with the client that you work toward fulfilling. You can periodically use the written contract to check your progress. The initial written contract can also be renegotiated if the work moves in different ways than the client first thought.

Core Skill 4: Information Giving

There are times in counseling individuals when a counselor or social worker must give information to the client. In these "teachable moments," facts or data about the client's experiences may expand his or her meaning regarding the presenting issues. The three main purposes of information giving are to (1) identify alternatives, (2) evaluate alternatives, and (3) correct erroneous information. In giving information, it is important to be accurate and to reveal information gradually, only when the individual indicates readiness to hear it.

Core Skill 5: Reflecting Content

As a skill for counseling individuals, reflecting content is a way to (1) convey to clients that you understand them, (2) help clients crystallize thoughts and feelings by asking them to restate something in a more concise manner, and (3) check your own perceptions to make sure they are consistent with what the client is working on. Although the focus is on content, the counselor also recognizes the client's feelings. For example, if a client says, "I don't know about him—one moment he is as nice as can be and the next he is a real jerk," the counselor might say, "He seems like a pretty inconsistent guy who is hard for you to be with. His erratic behavior keeps you pretty confused."

Core Skill 6: Reflecting Feelings

The counselor or social worker can help individual clients become more self-aware and self-understanding through the three aspects of the skill of reflecting feelings: (1) listening for the unspoken feelings, (2) using careful timing, and (3) reflecting the feeling. In identifying feelings, listen for what the client is not saying. Look for clues in nonverbal behaviors, such as the client's breathing, a sigh, a blush, a stammer, or swallowing. Verbal clues include the use of feeling language and tone of voice. Good timing requires that the counselor or social worker wait for an appropriate moment before reflecting, being careful not to cut off an internal flow or disturb the focus of thought. It is also important not to lag behind the client. Reflecting feelings requires the use of a feeling word when the client may not have said one. If a client says, "I wish I could talk to my dad like this," the counselor might say, "Perhaps you have been a little afraid to be so open with your dad."

Core Skill 7: Summarizing Content and Feelings

At times in individual therapy, the counselor or social worker wants to recapitulate, condense, or crystallize the essence of what the client said and felt. Although this skill resembles reflection of content and feeling, it is more comprehensive and covers more than what the client actually expressed. Summarization can be used at the beginning of a session to review aspects of the previous session or at the end of a session to review what has happened. This technique can also be used when a client rambles, is unclear, is at the end of a discussion on a particular topic, or is in conflict.

Core Skill 8: Self-Disclosure

Unless counselors and social workers have cleared their own developmental shock, trauma, or stress, they will find it difficult to help others. There are times when it is appropriate for counselors and social workers to share personal thoughts, feelings, and experiences that relate to a client's situation. At a basic level, self-disclosure also involves listening to the client, reflecting content and feelings, and summarizing what the client says, feels, and needs.

Core Skill 9: Confrontation

In an individual session, a counselor or social worker may notice a discrepancy between what the client is saying and the way that he or she behaves. For example, if a person is talking about a sad topic and then laughs, the discrepancy almost always has some significance. It often indicates an unresolved internal conflict involving a need to express feelings or a desire to avoid or deny expressing feelings. Mentioning these apparent discrepancies often helps the client gain insight into the problem. Confrontation is most effective when done empathically, as this shows respect for the client and validates him or her as a worthwhile individual. The counselor or social worker's tone of voice, posture, and gestures all contribute to the success of any confrontation.

Core Skill 10: Interpretation

Interpretation in a counseling session with an individual involves helping the client create a new frame of reference for viewing his or her problems to better understand a situation. This advanced skill relies on the counselor or social worker's mastery of reflecting content and feelings. The accuracy of the interpretation and the client's readiness to receive it determine whether the client can utilize it. The therapist identifies the essence of what the client shares, summarizes it, and adds new information for the client to consider. For example, a client with a record of absenteeism states, "I really feel bad about missing so much work." The therapist could respond with an interpretation: "So you are worried about your absenteeism. You know how the company views absenteeism, and you are probably afraid you may get fired the next time it happens."

Core Skill 11: Behavior Change

In counseling individuals, eliciting behavior change is an advanced skill that requires mastery of all the preceding skills. Each of the four stages in the process contains different skills:

1. Identifying and clarifying the problem require attunement, information gathering, structuring, reflection of content, and reflection of feelings.
2. Establishing workable goals requires the use of information gathering, information giving, summarization, and self-disclosure.
3. Establishing criteria for effectiveness of the action plan may require the use of confrontation and interpretation as well as reflection skills, so both the client and counselor will know when the objectives of therapy have been achieved.
4. Implementation requires summary skills, reflection skills, confrontation, interpretation, and closure skills—in short, the skills needed to help the client make desired changes.

Core Skill Twelve: Closure

One of the most common problems in counseling individuals is closure. Inexperienced therapists report that termination is typically a difficult time for them in the counseling process. Closure skills enable the counselor and the client to accomplish the following:

1. Bring a particular issue or problem to some resolution.
2. Bring a session to an end.
3. Terminate work with a client.

In the first instance, it is sometimes necessary for the therapist to ask, "If we stopped now, would there be anything we missed? Is this resolution complete for you?" A specific contract with the client makes it easier to reach a mutual decision about whether resolution is complete in terms of meeting the goals of the contract. Without a contract, the therapist should summarize what has been covered, ask probing questions, and reflect content and feelings to complete the closure. Some therapists are timid and avoid closure, while others may be too aggressive and close a topic prematurely. Summarizing skills are also useful in closing a session. It is usually helpful to ask the client to summarize what he or she will take away from the session and to evaluate the outcome of the session based in light of the contract.

Final termination may require several sessions to complete and usually involves self-disclosure and interpretation of the current status of the client as well as a thorough review and summary of the therapeutic contract. Some therapists write a formal evaluation of the treatment so that if the client returns to therapy or goes to another therapist a comparison can be made to the current level of functioning.

Specialized DPW Skills

In addition to the essential core skills, the DPW therapist needs to operate from the goals and philosophical principles presented in chapter 9 and to learn specialized skills that build on the 12 core skills. DPW provides a clinical lens for identifying clients' patterns of early childhood experiences that involve the long-term effects of unhealed developmental shock, trauma, and stress. It also uses developmental interventions for healing the effects of these shocks, traumas, and stresses when they surface as intractable conflicts. The counseling session uses a process model that follows the client's signals and cues until the underlying issues emerge.

DPW focuses on uncovering the distorted dynamics in parent–child relationships anchored in the prenatal, birth, infancy, and early childhood periods to find the sources of current intractable conflicts and relationship problems. Developmentally based inventories help clients identify shocking, traumatic, and stressful experiences from early childhood that are contributing to their adult symptoms of shock, trauma, stress, recurring intractable conflicts, and illnesses and degenerative diseases. DPW also helps clients identify their internal working model of reality, and it helps them identify and repattern distorted relational dynamics that might be impairing their ability to create and sustain healthy relationships.

DPW uses behaviorally based treatment goals that stress the need for safe counseling relationships involving empathy, genuineness, compassion, and unconditional love. It also identifies the roots of current relational difficulties in past relationship disturbances, usually those of early childhood. It helps clients revise their internal working model of reality by creating new patterns of self–other relationship dynamics using the emotional resonance present in the counselor–client relationship.

In addition to responding effectively to clients' verbal cues and nonverbal behavior in order to attune with clients, it is necessary also to be skilled in following the flow of information in their sensory system during a counseling session. This skill utilizes channel theory and information from neurolinguistic programming (NLP; Bandler & Grinder, 1979), as sensory shifts often indicate the release of information from the unconscious mind. Channel and information theory recognizes two levels of processing: internal and external channels. The internal level of processing is divided into four sensory channels:

1. Auditory
2. Visual
3. Proprioceptive (sensory experiences, including emotions and physical reactions)
4. Kinesthetic or movement

The external channel is divided into two channels:

1. the relationship channel (two persons)
2. the family channel (three or more persons)

The primary task of the DPW therapist is to follow the flow of communication as it moves through the client's sensory system during the session and respond to the client in language that mirrors the sensory channel that the client is using to talk about his/her problem. For example, when the client is recalling a past trauma through the visual channel ("I have this picture in my mind of the time my mother hit me and knocked me down"), the counselor might respond, "I can see how traumatic this must have been for you. Your face looks sad right now. Are you feeling sad?" At this point, the client closes her eyes, lowers her head, and she begins to shed tears. The shift from the visual channel to the proprioceptive channel has allowed her to access and express emotions that are associated with this trauma.

At this point, the intuitively guided therapist can continue to work on the emotional level or switch to the relationship channel by saying, "This experience with your mother must have had a lasting effect on your ability to trust not only her, but also other women."

Dividing the sensory system into internal and external channels provides a clinical structure for working with issues systemically. The internal channels relate to individual issues and processing, while the relationship and family channels show the external context in which they operate. Since developmental shock, trauma, and stress happen in the context of relationships with parents and extended family members, channel theory provides verbal and nonverbal mechanisms that therapists can use to help clients to connect their internal experiences with their external world.

During a DPW session, the therapist also assesses which intrapsychic parts of the client are visible and conscious and which are invisible and unconscious. The visible or conscious parts of the client's thought process emerge in the client's presenting issues and are usually stated as though they have conscious ownership of that part ("I am angry when she yells at me like that"). This response indicates that the client is more identified with parts that use fight and flight responses to stay defended and protected. An example of the presence of an invisible or unconscious part would show up in a statement like, "I get yelled at a lot by my mother." This statement shows little ownership of the conflict and represents a victimized and frozen or dissociated response to the problem.

The therapist helps clients approach the edge between the conscious and unconscious parts of their awareness and helps them to work in this very sacred and vulnerable place. The therapist's intention is to help clients to identify both the split-off or unconscious intrapsychic parts involved in their unhealed shock, trauma, or stress. The split-off part might be an inner protector part, an assertive adult part, a nurturing parent part, or a child part that fears failure. The client also could be speaking as the unprotected child part needing adult support and parental nurturing or as the powerless child part needing to feel capable and strong. The next step is helping the client connect these unconscious parts to an earlier experience involving unhealed developmental shock, trauma, or stress.

Once this determination is made, the therapist again needs to affirm the client's presenting problem and support the parts of the self that are conscious. This, again, involves using language that matches the client's channel:

Visual channel = visual language
"I see why you might have this perception."
Auditory channel = auditory language
"I hear what you are saying."
Feeling channel = emotional language
"I can feel how sad you are about this."

The exercises at the end of the chapter outline more specifically some of the steps in conducting a DPW session with an individual. Chapter 11 also contains a transcript of an actual DPW counseling session with an individual that demonstrates many of these steps.

Therapeutic Distinctions for Treating Developmental Shock, Trauma, and Stress in Individuals

We discovered through our own experience that certain therapeutic interventions are appropriate for working with developmental shock, that a second set works best with developmental trauma, and that a third set is effective in coping with developmental stress. In the section that follows, we describe some of the therapeutic considerations to keep in mind when treating each of these conditions. Healing the effects of unhealed developmental shock, trauma, or stress on the mindbody requires tools that specifically focus on visual, auditory, emotional, sensory, and relational components, as well as the physical body and beliefs about the self.

Therapeutic interventions practiced in a DPW context support clients in gradually moving into layers of the mindbody to identify and clear imprints caused by unhealed developmental shock, trauma, and stress. It includes following clients' process, identifying their conscious and unconscious processes and working at the edge between these two realities, and amplifying sensory and behavioral cues. This context applies whether treating developmental shock, trauma, or stress.

Treating Shock

The primary goal in treating shock is helping clients re-embody after an experience of dissociation and to mobilize the regulating and balancing action of the parasympathetic nervous system. Because clients are functioning in the oldest part of their brains, they are have little access to language and are unable to socially engage. For these reasons, it is important to avoid analysis, catharsis, and asking the client to look into the past or future and instead to focus on what is happening in present time. Asking them questions that help them focus on the here and now is helpful. Even asking them to take a couple of deep breaths can be useful, because in a dissociative state their breathing usually slows down.

Therapists can support clients by helping them track their urges to withdraw further into dissociation, using nurturing, comforting, and protective language to hold clients in a *therapeutic embrace* while they gradually return to their bodies. This is the heart of our corrective parenting work, which we describe later in the chapter. It is also important to help clients withdraw from shock states, to explore empowering options for restoring their sense of self, and to gradually encourage their expression of feelings. This work must be slow and very incremental and follow the pace in which clients' nervous systems are able to process overwhelming memories and experiences.

Treating Trauma

The primary goal in treating trauma is helping clients interrupt the adrenaline cycle and modulate the responses of the sympathetic nervous system. During therapy sessions, the use of nurturing, comforting, and protective language holds clients in a therapeutic embrace while they move through clearing the multiple dimensions of a traumatic experience or memory. Outside the therapy setting, music, quiet, focusing, and awareness-stilling practices such as journaling, walking, and spending time in nature are excellent ways to quiet the sympathetic nervous system and to detoxify the body of any excess cortisol. These kinds of interventions help bring the mind, body, and emotions into present-time reality and to clear the confusion between past and present events that are a normal part of trauma-induced regressions. As clients are able to experience in the present, it becomes possible to identify fears behind the trauma reaction and to process any intense emotional experiences by feeling, witnessing, and surviving the emotions. Over time, clients are able to transform traumatic emotional experiences into narrative memories; to develop both/and thinking by holding dualities, opposites, and paradoxes; to develop comfort with eye contact; and to create and maintain clear personal boundaries.

Treating stress

The primary goal in treating stress is communicating effectively with clients to keep them socially and emotionally engaged in the therapeutic process. This is particularly important during the first phase of therapy, as it gives clients time to feel safe and attune with the therapist. It also prevents moving the therapy process too quickly before clients have effective tools for braking the potential slide into more primitive brain states associated with trauma and shock. Another goal of stress-related interventions is helping clients develop bodily awareness of unconscious and involuntary internal biological states and helping them gain voluntary and conscious control of their internal biological states.

Once they recognize the first cues of stress, they can consciously use stress-reducing tools to redirect the autonomic nervous system's impulse to slide into trauma and shock states. It is very common for people who have had an excess of shock and trauma to have such highly sensitive nervous autonomic nervous systems that a stressful situation or issue that is mostly about feeling discomfort can quickly escalate into a safety issue and trigger a trauma reaction or into a survival issue that causes a collapse into a shock reaction. Teaching clients how to discern the difference between comfort, safety, and survival issues is a critical clinical task in treating developmental shock, trauma, and stress.

In this next section, we describe in more detail interventions to use in treating shock, trauma, and stress. Table 10.1 delineates which interventions are best suited for shock, for trauma, and for stress. A few interventions can actually be used with all three states. As we stated in Chapter 9, you will need to address seven different components to developmental shock, trauma, or stress in your treatment plan. The seven different components are described with the suggested clinical interventions we have found useful in healing the effects of that component.

Clinical Interventions for Treating Developmental Shock, Trauma, or Stress

In this section, we identify seven components of unhealed developmental shock, trauma, and stress and suggest specific clinical interventions for healing each of them. We describe our own tools in detail, while others are mentioned only briefly because they usually require additional training outside the scope of DPW. We recognize that this is a partial list of tools and modalities and that another author is writing a book containing a more comprehensive list (Shapiro, 2009).

Tools for Clearing Sensory System Distortions (visual, auditory, proprioceptive, and kinesthetic memory) Caused by Developmental Shock, Trauma, or Stress

- **TET: Trauma Elimination Technique**. This is the primary tool that we have created to help clear the sensory system of distortions caused by developmental

TABLE 10.1

The Shock, Trauma, and Stress Intervention Continuum

SHOCK	TRAUMA	STRESS
Levine's somatic experiencing	Trauma elimination technique	Trauma elimination technique
Emerson's shock resolution techniques	Sensory integration therapy	Betrayal clearing exercise
Castellino's prenatal and birth process therapy	Eye movement desensitization and reprocessing (EMDR)	Weinholds' corrective parenting technique
Mines's TARA approach	Levine's somatic experiencing	Weinholds' model for creating conscious, committed partnership relationships
Rothschild's somatic trauma therapy	Emerson's relational shock clearing therapy	Sensory integration therapy
Weinholds' corrective parenting technique	Mines's TARA approach	Eye movement desensitization and reprocessing (EMDR)
Energy and herbal medicines	Rothschild's somatic trauma therapy	Levine's somatic experiencing
	Weinholds' corrective parenting technique	Empathy and compassion training
	Sculpting exercises	Gestalt techniques
	Emotional freedom technique (EFT)	Reframing
	Tapas acupuncture technique (TAT)	Bioenergetic exercises
	Rebirthing breathwork	Psychodrama techniques
	Holotrophic breathwork	Reclaiming projections exercise
	Somatic experiencing	Completion process with your parents
	Bioenergetic exercises	Belief-changing exercises and activities
	Movement therapies	Reclaiming projections exercises
	Expressive arts	Active imagination exercises
	Sculpting exercises	Partnership conflict resolution skills
	Art and play therapy with young children	Rebirthing breathwork
	Meditation	Holotrophic breathwork
	Diet and nutrition	Yoga
	Energy and herbal medicine	Top-down yoga
		Tibetan yoga
		Movement therapies
		Body therapies (rolfing, massage, craniosacral work)
		Sculpting exercises
		Art and play therapy with young children
		Energy medicine
		Biofeedback
		Diet and nutrition
		Energy and herbal medicine
		Exercise
		Relaxation activities
		Aerobic exercise
		Social engagement activities

trauma and stress. After becoming trained in several trauma treatment modalities, we developed TET by synthesizing elements of Tapas Fleming's (n.d.) Tapas acupressure technique (TAT), Francine Shapiro's (1997) Eye Movement

Desensitization and Reprocessing (EMDR), and Roger Callahan's (2001) thought field therapy (TFT). We use TET as an adjunct to our DPW, which focuses on clearing and repatterning the relational elements of developmental shock, trauma, and stress. We found that the combination of TET and DPW treat all seven elements of developmental shock, trauma, and stress.

Our experience in using TET revealed that it not only clears trauma from present-life experiences, but also from other realities such as past lives, when people are consciously seeking this level of clearing. While this may seem like a very simple tool, it is quite powerful. For this reason, prior to using this technique with clients, we strongly suggest that readers use it on themselves first, preferably with a therapist or trusted colleague or friend.

Step 1: Learn the TET holding pose (See Figure 10.1).

a. Use one hand to hold three points on your face. Touch the points lightly. Touch your thumb lightly just above and adjacent to the inner corner of one eye place the end of your ring (fourth) finger just above and adjacent to the inner corner of the other eye. Place the end of your middle finger on the indentation in the middle of your forehead about a half inch higher than your eyebrows.
b. Place your other hand palm down with fingers together at the back of your head just below the bump at the bottom of your skull (the occipital ridge), centering it at the midline.
c. Once you have learned this pose, go directly to Step 2.

Step 2: Identify the trauma you want to work on. The earlier the trauma you identify, the better the results, although start where your have a clear memory

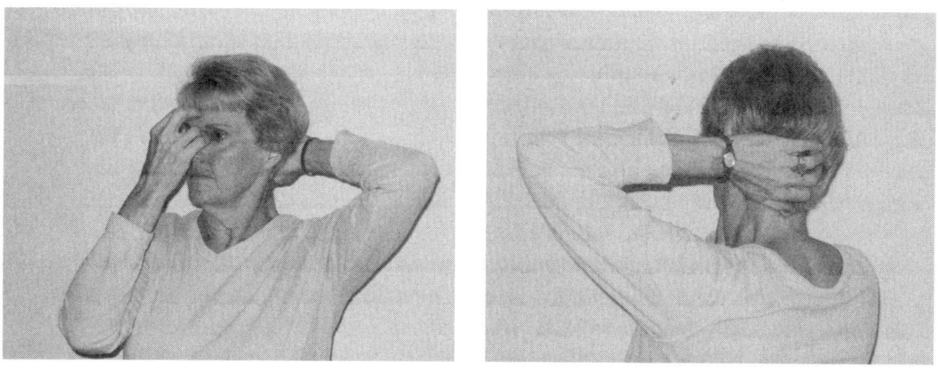

FIGURE 10.1

The TET Holding Pose

of the trauma situation. Identify a single incident or isolated memory of a trauma, rather than one that recurred over time.

- Focus your attention on a picture about this particular trauma.
- Notice what thoughts accompany this picture.
- Identify the belief about yourself that goes with this picture.
- Notice what emotion you feel when you see this picture.
- Feel your feelings, think your thoughts, and remember the belief you had about yourself in this situation.

Step 3: Simultaneously hold your picture, thoughts, belief, and feelings while doing the TET holding pose. Remain in this pose until you feel something happen internally. This can be different for each person. It may be a subtle shift of energy, a feeling of relaxation, a deep sigh, or a change in your breathing. Hold this pose for one minute or until you feel a shift, whichever comes first.

Step 4: Notice where you have been holding tension in your body related to the picture/thoughts/belief/feelings. Focus your attention in this place in your body while continuing to hold the TET pose. Again, remain in this pose until you feel a shift or for one minute, whichever comes first.

Step 5: Return to your picture of the trauma you began with and zoom in close to review it as if with a magnifying glass, looking for *hot spots* or things about the picture that still upset you.

Step 6: Zoom in on a hot spot where you still have a reaction to some part of the picture. Again focus on the picture/thoughts/belief/feelings. Do the TET holding technique until you feel a shift. Focus on the *storage place* in your body where you hold tension related to this memory while using the TET holding technique for one minute or until you feel a shift.

Step 7: Continue returning to the original picture and reviewing. Repeat this process until no more hot spots remain in your picture.

Step 8: Do the process one more time to see whether when you review the picture of the trauma you have a different response to it. You should be able to see the trauma but not have the reactions you first had to the incident. You may sense a calmness or peacefulness in your mindbody.

Step 9: Drink a glass of water immediately after completing a session. Be sure to drink another eight glasses in the next 24 hours to help the toxins released by the TET procedure to leave your body.

- **EMDR: Eye Movement Desensitization and Reprocessing** (Shapiro & Forrest, 1997) is a psychotherapeutic approach developed by Francine Shapiro to resolve symptoms caused by exposure to a traumatic or distressing event and to treat PTSD. It involves moving the eyes side-to-side or using alternate lateral cues while reliving a trauma. While it is effective in clearing sensory elements of trauma, it does not clear the intrapsychic splitting and relational elements of trauma.

- **EFT: Emotional Freedom Therapy** (Craig, n.d.) is a body-oriented therapy developed by Gary Craig that involves specific patterns of tapping on the body's energy meridians. EFT includes more emphasis on clearing the emotional aspect of trauma but also addresses the role of trauma in disease.

Tools for Clearing Mindbody Memories Involving Developmental Shock, Trauma, or Stress

- **TET** (described previously)
- **SIT: Sensory Integration Therapy** is designed to correct sensory integration dysfunction, a neurological disorder involving difficulties with processing information from the five classic senses (vision, auditory, touch, olfaction, and taste), the sense of movement (vestibular system), and the positional sense (proprioception). As a result of unhealed developmental shock, trauma, and stress, sensory information is accessed normally but is perceived abnormally. This is not the same as blindness or deafness because sensory information is sensed but tends to be analyzed by the brain in an unusual way that may cause pain or confusion.

  The most common form of sensory integration therapy is a type of occupational therapy that places a child in a room specifically designed to stimulate and challenge all of the senses. During the session, the therapist works closely with the child to provide a level of sensory stimulation with which the child can cope and to encourage movement within the room. Sensory integration therapy is driven by five main principles (Schaaf & Miller, 2005):

  - *Just Right Challenge.* The child must be able to successfully meet the challenges that are presented through playful activities.
  - *Adaptive Response.* The child adapts his or her behavior with new and useful strategies in response to the challenges presented.
  - *Active Engagement.* The child will want to participate because the activities are fun.
  - *Child Directed.* The child's preferences are used to initiate therapeutic experiences within the session.
  - *Desensitization.* A child with lower or hyposensitivity may be exposed to strong sensations such as brush strokes, vibrations, or rubbing. Play may involve a range of materials to stimulate the senses such as play dough or finger painting.
- **EFT: Emotional Freedom Technique** (described previously)

- **Breath Work**
  - **Rebirthing Breathwork** (Orr & Ray 1977), also *called pranic breathing, conscious breathing,* or *transformational breathwork,* is a branch of alternative medicine postulating that specialized breathing techniques may have therapeutic benefits. Leonard Orr created rebirthing breathwork, so named because he began having memories of his birth during his early experiments with connected breathing. The client makes a connected breath without a pause between inhale and exhale of the breath or between the exhale and inhale of the breath. The inhale part of the breath is very deep, filling both the belly and the top of the lungs. Total relaxation during the exhale part of the breath is critical for avoiding unpleasant body sensations like stress, tension, or even muscle cramps.

    We teach a version of this tool as part of DPW for counselors who want to help clients to process and reregulate their emotions. It also helps people experience what it is like to at least temporarily shed a level of developmental stress they are carrying around in their hypervigilant search for possible developmental shocks, traumas, or stresses to avoid.
  - **Holotropic Breathwork™** was developed by Stanislav Grof, MD, together with his wife Christina (n.d.), as a substance-free means of discovering the healing power of human experience in nonordinary states of consciousness. It is a safe and simple way to trigger experiences of nonordinary consciousness that open us to psychic depths and spiritual understanding. It can help people recover memories of developmental shocks, traumas, or stresses from their personal history, experiences from their birth, and archetypal and cosmic phenomena that become available to them in holotropic awareness. It can help people reregulate their emotions and transcend the constraints of their ordinary thoughts and habits.

- **Weinholds' Corrective Parenting Techniques** are methods that we have not published previously, where we contract with clients to provide nurturing comfort and holding while they process memories of developmental shock, trauma, or stress experiences, particularly those involving their mothers during the first 6 months of life. See Chapter 11 for a good example of how they might be applied. In this technique, which we learned through our own therapy experiences, Janae acts as a surrogate mother and Barry as a surrogate father to help clients reconstellate these experiences and restore and deepen their capacity for deep attunement and emotional resonance. This intervention is particularly helpful in changing clients' distorted self–other relational dynamics.

  The physical containment and comforting help clients restore the connection inside them broken by a lack of consistent and sustained experiences of deep attunement and emotional resonance and allows them to recreate this secure place in therapy with their mother. After doing this work, when clients are triggered in their current relationships, they can find this space inside themselves and can recreate the feelings connected to this secure bonding experience when they need to.

Clients who experienced disconnects or invasive interactions with their mothers can benefit from nurturing holding and comforting while processing the effects of developmental shock, trauma, and stress. This enables them to reintegrate any split-off parts that they lost in building defenses against feeling the feelings associated with these early experiences. The holding work creates a safe place for clients to experience the deep sadness that helps them heal the internal splits they created for protection.

We have selectively used this intimate intervention with a very small group of clients, mostly therapists, to help them reclaim parts of themselves that were split off in early dissociative experiences. This intervention requires extensive clinical training that involves therapists going through their own corrective parenting therapy, followed by ongoing clinical supervision.

- **How to Identify and Clear Body Symptoms of Developmental Shock, Trauma, or Stress**

This is an activity that we created to help clients identify and clear any body symptoms of developmental shock, trauma, or stress.

1. Do an energetic body scan: Start at the top of your head and go down to the bottom of your feet noticing what parts of the body you are aware of and what parts you are not aware of. Notice where the body awareness is the strongest and the weakest. Also notice areas where there is tension.
2. Identify a chronic body symptom (it can be a rash, joint problem, digestive problem, allergy, weight issue, weakness in the body, or any other area of the body where you experience stress or tension: dis-ease).
3. Try to amplify the symptom by increasing it in strength. Notice how successful you are in amplifying the symptom.
4. Then try to forbid the symptom or try to cause it to diminish in intensity. Notice how successful you are at causing the symptom to diminish in intensity.
5. Now draw a picture of the symptom that represents how you see or experience it.
6. Create a dialogue on paper with the symptom. Ask some of the following questions and wait for the answer to come to you. Then write down word for word what comes to you.

   - What is your purpose for being in my body?
   - What are your feelings and needs?
   - What would you like me to do to help you fulfill your purpose of being in my body?

- What could I do or say that would help you know I have learned the lesson you are here to teach me?

7. Discuss what you learned from this dialogue with your counselor or a partner.

- **Somatic Experiencing®** is a short-term naturalistic approach developed by Dr. Peter Levine (1997, 2005) for resolving and healing trauma. It is based upon the observation that animals in the wild utilize innate mechanisms to regulate and discharge the high levels of energy arousal associated with defensive survival behaviors. These mechanisms provide animals with a built-in immunity to trauma that enables them to return to normal in the aftermath of highly charged life-threatening experiences.

  While humans are born with virtually the same regulatory mechanisms as animals, the function of these instinctive systems is often overridden or inhibited by the rational portion of our brains. This restraint prevents the complete discharge of the stress hormones from our bloodstream and does not allow the nervous system to regain its equilibrium. The undischarged survival energy remains stuck in the body and the nervous system. The various symptoms of trauma result from the body's attempt to manage and contain this unused energy.

  Somatic experiencing uses the awareness of body sensation to help people renegotiate and heal their traumas rather than relive them. With appropriate guidance with the body's instinctive felt sense, individuals are able to access their own built-in immunity to trauma, allowing the highly aroused survival energies to be safely and gradually discharged. When these energies are discharged, people frequently experience a dramatic reduction in or disappearance of their traumatic symptoms. Levine's therapeutic work is available to both professionals and nonprofessionals.

- **Bioenergetics** (Nicholls & Ferguson, 2002) is a set of body psychotherapy tools that helps people identify places in their bodies where the energy is blocked and release the chronic tension that is stored in these blocked places due to developmental shocks, traumas, or stresses. After identifying a developmental trauma, it is necessary to release the body memories connected to it. Where appropriate, a skilled DPW therapist can help a client to release body memories very quickly and easily. We use bioenergetics tools in our training workshops.

- **Yoga** (Feuerstein, 1996) is a system of physical and mental practices that originated in India. It includes a number of variations, such as Hatha, Karma, Bhakti, Nada, Raja, Tantra, Bikram, Kundalini, Kriya, and Iyengar. Most of these schools emphasize bringing the mindbody into balance through the use of the breath and different poses or asanas to help strengthen the body and manage stress.

- **Top-Down Yoga** (Kiely, n.d.) practices are helpful to release body memories of developmental shock, trauma, or stress. Top-down yoga is particularly useful as a self-help technique for managing developmental stress and finding more balance in one's life. You do not need to be athletic or spiritual to benefit from these simple psychophysical exercises. There are no convoluted positions to master and no theory necessary for its application. The practices focus on relaxing the eyes, ears, throat, chin, jaw, and the vagal brake, which plays a role in social interactions that require reciprocal engagement and disengagement strategies.

    You can do it at any fitness level, well or sick, and gain immediate benefits. You perform it on yourself, by yourself. It encourages taking back control of your mindbody and experiencing the joy of being proactive in your self-care management. We find it useful because it works with the vagus nerves in the neck where, according to the work of Stephen Porges (2001) and Sue Carter, people hold body memories of past developmental shocks, traumas, or stresses. We teach some of these techniques at our training workshops.

- **Tibetan Yoga** is also known as the Five Tibetan Rites (Kelder, 1985). Reportedly more than 2,500 years old, it is based on a series of five movements that are each repeated 21 times. Practiced over a period of time, the rites rejuvenate the body and help keep it in energetic balance. We utilize this form of yoga and sometimes teach it to our trainees or clients.

- **Movement Therapies** (Sandel, Chaiklin, & Lohn, 1993) help clients release stuck places where they have stored body memories connected to a developmental shock, trauma, or stress. This tool is often part of our training workshops for DPW therapists.

- **Body Therapies (Rolfing, Massage, Craniosacral work)** (Levine, 1999) all work to realign the body's bones, muscles, and connective tissue. Some, such as craniosacral therapy, also work with the cerebrospinal fluid. These deeply transformative therapies are very useful for restoring the body to its natural state after shocking, traumatic, or stressful experiences have distorted it.

- **Art and Play Therapy with Young Children** (Landreth, 2002) can be very useful to access unconscious processes related to shock, trauma, or stress. There are various kinds of art and play therapy, and we employ an assortment of tools from these modalities in our trainings.

- **Energy and Herbal Medicine** (Hurley, 2006) interventions include homeopathic remedies such as Bach Rescue Remedy and Perelandra products (Wright, n.d.), flower remedy therapies such as aromatherapy, and herbs such as valerian, hawthorne, and kava kava, which are some of the more well known. Because homeopathics and herbs are powerful substances, they are best used with the support of trained professionals.

- **Biofeedback** (Lehrer, Woolfolk, & Sime, 2007) involves the use of sensors that are stuck to a person's head and/or hands. The sensors are attached to an electronic device that emits different frequencies that alter brain-wave signals. The relaxation frequencies are typically in the alpha and theta ranges of 5–11 Hz. A wide range of technological devices is now available for home biofeedback use.

- **Diet and Nutrition** (Izzo, Sica, & Black, 2007) are critical components of a stress-reduction regime. Food intake should be rich in a variety of whole grains, vegetables, and fruits, with a minimum of processed foods, alcohol, caffeine, and tobacco. Ideally foods should be produced organically, as nonorganic foods often contain toxins that cause the body to have a trauma reaction.

- **TAT (Tapas Acupuncture Technique)** was created by Tapas Fleming (n.d.). Trained in Chinese medicine, she discovered her TAT trauma treatment protocol while using acupuncture tools to treat food allergies. She discovered that the body physiologically reacts to toxic foods exactly the same way that it does to an emotional trauma. She realized that the treatment she had developed for treating food allergies could also be used by mental health professionals for the direct treatment of traumas.

- **Aerobic Exercise** (Cooper, 1982) is most effective when it becomes part of a regular regime. Some of the most invigorating include swimming, tennis, hiking, and classes at gyms or exercise facilities. Just 10 minutes of exercise three times a week can build a base for beginners, gradually building up to 30 minutes or more every other day.

- **Relaxation Activities** (Lehrer, Woolfolk, & Sime, 2007) include well-known practices such as deep breathing exercises, listening to inspirational and calming music, walking or sitting in nature, and taking short naps. Thomas Edison is renowned for his catnapping technique. Legend has it that he would sleep in his chair, holding ball bearings in the palms of his hands. After an appropriate amount of rest, he would relax enough to drop the balls, waking himself up (Hardwick, 2008).

  Meditation has been used for thousands of years in Eastern cultures to quiet the mind; disengage the sympathetic nervous system; and reduce heart rate, blood pressure, and adrenaline levels. Twenty minutes once or twice a day over a long period of time can have a dramatic impact on not only the mindbody, but also on consciousness.

- **Social Engagement Activities** (Porges, 2001) include formal and informal support groups. A support group is a gathering of people who share a common condition or interest for specific issues such as weight loss, bereavement, addictions, and health conditions; informal and unfacilitated support groups such as men's, women's, parents', and couples' groups; facilitated therapy groups; and extended family networks. Support group members typically share their personal journeys with each other emotional and offer comfort and moral support, and they may provide tips and advice based on their own experiences.

Many support groups now take place online, which is very convenient for helping people who have rare or unusual conditions to connect and support each other. Social support is a critical component of shock, trauma, and stress treatment programs, as it provides emotional connections with other people when they feel isolated from friends and family. Social engagement activities help people resist the urge to withdraw into regressive and dissociative states associated with recent traumas and shocks.

Tools for Changing Distorted Cognition and Beliefs Related to Developmental Shock, Trauma, or Stress

- **TET** (described previously)
- **Belief-Changing Exercises:**
  - **Changing Your Personal Law** is an exercise that we developed to help people uncover unconscious beliefs about themselves that were formed as part of a developmental shock, trauma, or stress and are still causing them to create unpleasant experiences in their lives. Start by identifying your personal law, which is the bottom-line most negative belief or thought you have about yourself. It is the basis of self-hatred and usually shows up in the self-talk that you engage in when you make a mistake or do something that does not turn out the way you want. Following is an example of an exercise on how to begin to unravel these unconscious beliefs and make plans to change them.

    1. Write down exactly what you say to yourself. The words you use are important.
    2. Working with a partner, your job is to convince him or her that what you wrote down is true.
    3. Your partner's role is to listen to you, ask questions to help clarify what you mean, and then to rate you from 1–100 on how convinced they are that what you told them is true. The partner gives an actual percentage.
    4. This time try to convince your partner that this is not true of you while your partner rates how convincing you are. Again, the partner gives a percentage.
    5. Look at the two percentages and subtract the higher one from the lower one to get your actual score.
       (This represents how difficult it will be to change your belief).
    6. Switch roles and repeat this process.

- **Reframing Techniques** (Seligman, 1998) are communication tools that help clients assign a different meaning or context to a life experience. We use them to help clients change distorted beliefs they have about what happened to them during their childhood and put them in a different context. For example, a client who was adopted might enter therapy believing that her birth mother rejected her because she was unlovable. After reading books we suggested that were written by mothers who relinquished their babies, the client began wondering whether her birth mother still thought about her and grieved her loss. We had two adoptee clients who sought and eventually met their birth mothers after they read these books. Afterward, both women experienced a deep gratitude to their birth mothers for relinquishing them and giving them the adoptive parents and the lives they had led with them.

- **Betrayal Trauma Clearing Exercise** (Weinhold & Weinhold, 2009): If clients experienced a break in primal trust with their parents, it caused developmental shock, trauma, or stress. They will need to heal this developmental shock, trauma, and stress in their close relationships as a way of completing this essential developmental process of the codependent stage of development. The need to recreate primal trust also involves developing an "all good" view of the therapist with whom a person is healing this trauma. Clients perceive this person as kind, loving, and available to meet their needs.

  This phenomenon is similar to the blissful state of paradise experienced during the codependent stage of development when primal trust was still being established. At some point, however, the idealized therapist also betrays the person, revealing that he or she was both "good and bad" and leaving him or her feeling angry, deceived, or abandoned.

  Betrayed people feel crushed each time their innocent, childlike trust gets shattered by a beloved person who fails to play out the perfect parent they hoped this idealized person would be. The betrayal and the subsequent loss triggers a reenactment of a developmental shock, trauma, or stress related to the initial loss of primal trust during infancy.

  Betrayal can become a useful growth experience if we learn to look at what is right about it. It makes us aware of an unresolved developmental shock, trauma, or stress from the codependent stage of development. The betrayal exercise can help identify any betrayal experiences and connect the dots between betrayal experiences and unhealed developmental shock, trauma, or stress.

  We have developed several experiential tools to help people identify and heal developmental shocks, traumas, or stresses caused by betrayals early in life. One tool is a written skill practice for locating patterns of betrayal, and another is a dyad activity that involves the use of movement, music, and dialogue. For more information about betrayals and our experiential tools, see chapter 11 of *Conflict Resolution: The Partnership Way* (Weinhold & Weinhold, 2009).

Tools for Reregulating Emotions Involving Developmental Shock, Trauma, or Stress

- **TET** (described previously)
- **Breathwork Techniques** (described previously)
- **Opening the Heart Exercise** is an exercise that we have adapted from the work of Dr. Robert Gass (1991), who conducts workshops with his wife, Judith Gass, on opening the heart. We use this powerful guided meditation in our training workshops for professionals to help them experience how unhealed developmental shocks, traumas, and stresses cause their hearts to close and help them heal heart-related wounds. This exercise can also be used with clients.
- **Centering** is an important skill we adapted from our work with Tom Crum, who developed the Aiki approach to conflict resolution (Crum, 1998). Centering, a mindbody technique often used in martial arts, can be used to help people reregulate themselves after experiencing the effects of a reenactment of developmental shock, trauma, or stress. By noticing that you have become uncentered, you can be taught to quickly re-center yourself. This tool is taught in our training workshops for professionals.
- **Meditation** is a relaxation skill that helps you cope with the developmental stress that often accompanies unhealed developmental shocks, traumas, or stresses. Among the many kinds of meditation, the one form we use and teach in our trainings is a version of mindfulness or Vipassana meditation (Ray, 2002).
- **Betrayal Trauma Clearing Exercise** (described previously)
- **Empathy and Compassion Training** is a big part of our training workshops. We've found Jerry Donoghue's Compassionate Communication Course (n.d.) particularly helpful in learning how to identify people's feelings and the unmet needs that are associated with them. This skill is essential not only for clients, but for the DPW therapist and the DPC specialist in their efforts to help people integrate and reregulate their emotions.
- **EFT** (described previously)

Tools for Healing Splits within the Self and Reclaiming Dissociated Self Parts Caused by Developmental Shock, Trauma, or Stress

- **Gestalt Techniques** (Brownell, in press) are useful in helping people identify with the split-off parts of themselves. We have adapted the *empty chair* technique from gestalt therapy to help people identify their split-off parts and to begin to reunite them. We typically do not work sitting in chairs. Instead, we work on the floor and often use pillows to represent clients' split-off parts and have them move back and forth having a dialogue with each part. We have incorporated a number of gestalt therapy tools into our DPW approach that we offer in our workshops to train professionals in how to heal developmental shocks, traumas, or stresses.

- **Psychodrama Techniques** (Moreno,1985) are also very useful to help people to act out dramas where elements of their unhealed developmental shocks, traumas, or stresses will emerge. We have adapted some psychodrama tools into the DPW approach we use. Learning to use these tools is part of our training workshops for professionals.
- **Completion Process with Your Parents Exercise** (Weinhold & Weinhold, 2008) is a powerful gestalt-like process that involves dialoging with both parents about experiences of developmental shock, trauma, and stress. Because it can trigger regressive states and memories, it should be done with a therapist who can provide the appropriate support and interventions. If you are a therapist, we recommend additional training or personal work with this tool in order to use it effectively. A version of the protocol can be found in Chapter 10 of our book, *The Flight From Intimacy (2008).*
- **Reclaiming Projections Exercise.** Do you remember an incident in which you experienced a sudden rush of energy in your body and felt the blood rushing through your veins, your heart beating faster, and you froze or wanted to fight or run away? These are symptoms of an ASR that your body automatically had because you felt unsafe and are signals of an unhealed developmental shock, trauma, or stress. One of the ways that people try to avoid these feelings is by projecting them on others. Following are two simple exercises that we created for helping people reclaim any projections. You may be able to connect them with unhealed developmental shocks, traumas, or stresses.

  Projection Reclaiming Exercise 1:

  - Remember an incident where your reaction was far greater than what was called for, where you "made a mountain out of a mole hill." This indicates that your feelings may be coming from some previous incident.
  - Ask yourself, "Am I actually unsafe in the present situation?"
  - If the answer is "no," then ask yourself, "Where have I felt this way before?"
  - Realize that you have regressed back to an earlier time in your life where you felt unsafe.
  - Ask yourself, "What about that earlier situation is still unfinished that causes me to feel unsafe now?"
  - Then ask yourself, "What did I need in the past and how can I get this need met now in a way that helps me feel safe?"

Projection Reclaiming Exercise 2:

- Remember a conflict situation in which you totally focused on what the other person said or did. Overfocusing is a form of projection that helps you avoid feelings and looking at your part in causing the conflict.
- Notice what you are feeling and ask yourself: "When and where have I felt this way before?"
- Notice if you are using loaded words like "always" or "never" to describe the situation.
- This may also be your attempt to avoid intense feelings from an earlier incident.

- **Active Imagination Technique** (Johnson, 1986) is a Jungian technique in which you dialogue with a split-off part of yourself, a dream, or an inner conflict. Usually done as a writing exercise, you ask an important question that you want answered of some perceived part of yourself that you want to connect with and then use your active imagination to construct a dialogue with that part of you. This often gives valuable insights into the conflict, enabling you to see it in a different light.

Tools for Modifying Distorted Self–Other Relational Dynamics Caused by Developmental Shock, Trauma, or Stress

- **TET** (described earlier)
- **Completion Process with Parents** (described previously)
- **Weinholds' Corrective Re-parenting Techniques** (described previously)
- **Emerson's Relational Shock Clearing Therapy**· (Emerson, 2007) is an experiential therapy, offered by William Emerson's "Emerson Seminars," to professionals and nonprofessionals, which helps people learn to clear and heal shock using processes that help identify, explore, and heal wounds emanating from the prenatal and perinatal periods. Emerson's group also uses clinical tools such as Sand Tray Therapy and craniosacral work with adults and with infants and small children.
- **Levine's Somatic Experiencing** (described previously)
- **Mines' TARA Approach for the Resolution of Shock and Trauma** (Mines 2003) resolves the physiological, neurological, emotional, psychological, and spiritual impacts of shock and trauma (p. 21). A colleague of Emerson, Stephanie Mines' approach uses Jin Shin Tara, a form of acupressure, and what she calls "the language of healing" in combination with touch and intention to open new

neurological pathways. Her 10-step approach includes addressing shock immediately, identifying the lesson in an overwhelming experience, sustaining this awareness, establishing a strong relationship with one's body, developing an inner witness, bonding with nature, using laughter as the "best medicine," language and touch as healing tools, and separating past from present.

- **Castellino's Prenatal & Birth Process Therapy,** developed by Ray Castellino (2000), a former chiropractor, craniosacral therapist, and practitioner of polarity, is available for children, adults, babies, and new families. His process therapy model resolves prenatal and birth trauma using a synthesis of principles and practices drawn from energetic bodywork, craniosacral fluid tide work, psychotherapeutic approaches, trauma resolution work, and birth simulation work. Castellino's empowering approach emphasizes development that moves from the inside out, rather than from external sources. His approach facilitates personal evolution and individuation and an internal locus of control.
- **Rothschild's Somatic Trauma Therapy** (2003, pp. 25–27) is an integrated process-oriented treatment model for treating symptoms of trauma and PTSD. In development since 1992, Somatic trauma therapy is not a single method, but an integrated system of psychotherapy and body-psychotherapy tools and techniques that continues to evolve as new theory and techniques emerge in the field. Somatic trauma therapy addresses all aspects of trauma's impact—on thinking, emotions, and bodily sensations—bringing them into sync and relegating trauma to its rightful place in the past.
- **Empathy and Compassion Skill Training**. (described previously)
- **Partnership Conflict Resolution Skills** (Weinhold & Weinhold, 2009) are essential for resolving the intractable conflicts at the core of chronic relationship problems, illnesses, and degenerative diseases. These skills are some of the most unique and progressive components of DPW, as they focus on renegotiating conflict aspects of developmental shock, trauma, and stress. These very useful tools help people develop better social engagement skills and heal the effects of developmental stress. We write extensively about resolving conflicts of wants and needs, values and beliefs, and intractable conflicts in our book, *Conflict Resolution: The Partnership Way* (2009).
- **Reclaiming Projections Exercises** (described previously)
- **Weinholds' Model for Creating Conscious, Committed Partnership Relationships** (Weinhold & Weinhold, 2009) is described at length in Chapter 12**.** This is at the heart of recovery from the effects of developmental stress. Conscious committed relationships may take many forms—friends, business partners, parents and children, or romantic couple relationship. Commitment can be defined in many ways. For our purposes, the most common aspects of

commitment include the willingness of both people to stay engaged in the relationship and not run away when the unhealed developmental shocks, traumas, or stresses emerge; the willingness of both people to change; and the willingness of both people to be emotionally honest.

Consciousness refers to the degree to which people are aware of their behavior and are able to understand what motivates them to do what they do. *Cooperative* means willingness to help each other in the healing process. Many codependent relationships are competitive rather than cooperative in nature. In a cooperative relationship, people freely teach and learn from each other instead of withholding information or using it to manipulate and control their partner.

We have found that conscious, committed relationships provide an ideal crucible for healing developmental shock, trauma, or stress. This, we believe, is love and intimacy at its highest and best. While most people define intimacy as only those warm, close, maybe sexual times that are all blissful and serene, we discovered that expanding the definition of intimacy leads to a different kind of intimacy. If you include the times that involve a cooperative effort to help each other heal the effects of developmental shock, trauma, or stress that show up in your relationship, you may find a deeper kind of intimacy. This helps to heal wounds and make the spirit whole, and it can be an exciting adventure that opens you to the depths of LOVEvolution.

WORDS OF COMFORT, SKILLFULLY ADMINISTERED, ARE THE OLDEST THERAPY KNOWN TO MAN.

LOUIS NIZER

CHAPTER ELEVEN

An Annotated Analysis of the Transcription of an Individual DPW Session

This session was transcribed from a DPW demonstration videotaped during a conflict resolution class. We obtained permission from this client to videotape and transcribe it for inclusion in this book. The name of the client has been changed. This session contains many of the components of DPW and illustrates how it functions as a therapeutic modality. Serena is an ideal client, as she has already done a great deal of work on herself and also understands our developmental model very well. Serena is able to follow her own process and to quite effectively witness and describe her internal world. Clients with less self-awareness and developmental information would not be able to shift as quickly as Serena does in this session.

In this typical DPW session, Janae is sitting on the floor with Serena on cushions. This position not only offers more opportunities for body and movement signals to appear in the client's process, it also makes it easier for experiential work with intrapsychic splits and relational dynamics.

This session with Serena is a good representative example of our corrective parenting techniques and contains many of the elements that characterize them. It also emphasizes the impact of the therapist's ability to emotionally and relationally attune with the client in ways that are energetically supportive. This allows Serena to process from the place of a witness and to stay in control of her parasympathetic nervous system.

Typically, the presenting problem is a conflict, either internal or with others; a body symptom; or a dream or a dilemma that has the client confused or interested in working on. It is important to first build rapport with the client before jumping into the presenting problem. Often that rapport can be built verbally while the client is describing the issue or problem by showing understanding and compassion for what the client is presenting. In addition, nonverbal signals will also help attune. Facing the client at a safe distance, making eye contact, and mirroring his or her posture can help with the attunement process.

In the example that follows, Serena's presenting problem is an internal conflict about work. Janae skillfully helps her go deeper into the unconscious elements of the conflict that reveal the hidden effects of an unhealed developmental shock, trauma, or stress contained in the conflict. She is looking for evidence of any incomplete developmental processes and the unmet developmental needs associated with them. Once she finds them, she begins to help Serena connect at a feeling level with these missing pieces in her developmental history so that she can recover the split-off parts of herself that contained these missing pieces.

Janae: Serena, could you give me some background on the issue that you'd like to work on today? Then we can make a contract about it.

Serena: The issue that I want to work on comes out of my behaviors of workaholism that I got into trying to meet everybody's needs except my own. It got to a point where I hit a wall. I spent 3 months on a medical leave of absence and knew then at the end of that time, I was not well enough to work full time and keep all the lids down. I made a decision to give up my full-time work.

The option that was available to me was to work full time or work as a temporary employee, which meant that I did not have a regular income or regular hours. I am a person who needs structure in her life, and I do best when I have ordinary stuff to do. The unpredictability of working as a temp was difficult for me, but I chose that, believing that my need was greater for more margin in my life than to try to work full time while meeting the needs of my family.

Both my elderly mother and my husband's elderly father live locally, and I have extended family needs that I have to take care of. In the beginning, in fact, while I was working full time, I tried negotiating with my employer about the possibility of working as a permanent part-time employee. I got nonanswers about why that was not possible. I don't expect them to meet all my needs at their expense. I wanted to negotiate something that is workable for both of us. But that moved to the front burner when I made the decision not to work full time anymore. This process is excruciating slow. *(Serena moves her arms in a flailing motion.)*

The feedback I get at work is that "we are working on it. Be patient; we will come to you. Don't be bugging us—that's counterproductive." Recently, I came across a job listing that was for a permanent part-time position, but in another department of the company. I have applied for that position. If it is offered to me, it will mean that I will take a two-dollar an hour pay cut in order to have regular hours and regular income.

I am struggling to see if I really want to do that or survive with the challenge of irregular hours and pay. Part of the conflict I have is that, for whatever reason, when I try to be clear about what my wants and needs are and try to be open to negotiation, I just keep getting cut off. I am told, "We know better"—a real authoritative parental stance.

Does this give you enough to work with?

Janae: Yes, that is a lot to work with. If I am hearing you correctly, what you'd like to work on is learning why you feel stuck in this conflict at work. Is this true?

Serena: Yes, I'd not only like to know why I am stuck, I would also like to get unstuck.

(Contract articulated and agreed upon.)

Janae: I noticed as you were talking, the more that you went into it, the more it seemed to touch a deep feeling place inside. Could you go inside for a moment and notice what are you feeling and where you feel these feelings in your body?

(Janae asks Serena to switch from her cognitive and auditory channels to emotions and the proprioceptive channel and from her conscious awareness to her unconscious awareness.)

Serena: There is tension in my face. One of my reactions to this kind of conflict is that I cry. Crying was not acceptable in my family of origin unless you went off by yourself. I feel very self-conscious about my tendency to cry when talking about difficult things, even with just one other person but especially in a group.

Janae: This is taking a lot of courage to bring this out, Serena. Think about the kind of obstruction that you are experiencing in your job and close your eyes for a moment. Now let that whole experience that you just described settle into your body. Notice where you feel it the most. I know you feel it in your face, but can you feel it any other place? *(There is a period of silence.)*

What are you aware of, Serena? Is there anything else going on in your body?

(Janae experiments to see if Serena can go deeper into her emotions and her proprioceptive memories.)

Serena: A generalized tension in all my limbs. I would describe it as a freeze response. I don't feel I have an urge to run or a need to fight, but I feel immobilized.

(Serena indicates that she is falling into a shock state.)

Janae: Just for a moment focus on that inner experience of immobilization and see if you can intensify it and make it more intense. Just a little bit, not like you have to go into it full blown. Then what I would like, Serena, is for you to tell me about the earliest memory you have of this feeling of being immobilized. *(Serena's body becomes stiff, and she closes her eyes.)*

(Janae asks Serena to consciously amplify the signal of immobilization, while simultaneously controlling any urges she might have to withdraw into a dissociative state.)

Serena: Well, there is a memory that came to me, and I suppose it must be associated with this feeling. I don't have a cognitive connection there.

(Serena begins to witness dissociated memories stored from a developmental shock. Energetically, she is surrounded by Janae's therapeutic embrace and deeply attuned presence. Had Serena withdrawn into a dissociated state, Janae would have switched into comforting interventions to support Serena. Following her process and reading her subtle cues, Janae would intuitively determine the appropriate interventions.)

The memory that came has to do with when I was quite young, and I don't know how young. A cousin was caring me for. During my afternoon nap I soiled my pants, and that became a real issue. I am not sure if that was with her or with my mom, but those are the two people who seemed to be there.

Janae: Can you tell me more about that experience? What pieces of it do you recall? You soiled your pants. Do you remember being in the room where this happened? Were you in bed?

(Serena begins to recall visual memories related to her shock.)

Serena: The bathroom is more the room that is part of this awareness.

Janae: Do you recall anything about what your mother or this relative said to you?

(Janae is checking for auditory memory related to the shock memory.)

Serena: It is more of a feeling that I don't want to be a baby. That is what babies do. There is a real sense of shame about what happened to me. But it is stronger than that—it is that I did that.

(Serena recalls memories of shame but no auditory memories. Shame experiences almost always trigger shock states.)

Janae: What is so terrible about being a baby?

Serena: When I behave in ways that are probably normal to small children, my dad gets angry with me, and he tells me to stop it or there is just this general expectation that I am not acceptable.

(Now Serena begins recalling unspoken or telepathic messages she received from her father.)

Janae: What part of you is not acceptable, Serena? What part of you doesn't your daddy like?

Serena: He doesn't like childlike behavior. He likes predictability. When I behave in ways that are free, he doesn't like it.

Janae: He doesn't like you being spontaneous. Does this mean that he doesn't like you being spontaneous when you play? Spontaneous when you cry? Or spontaneous when you are whatever?

(Janae asks Serena to be more explicit about her father's implied message.)

Serena: Pretty much whenever I am whatever.

Janae: You had this spontaneous soiling in your pants. This reminded you that you were not supposed to be spontaneous. You are not supposed to let anything out—not even in your pants, especially in your pants. You are supposed to keep everything contained and not be an inconvenience to people. Does this feel true?

(Janae checks to see if her interpretation of Serena's father's message fits.)

Serena: *(Nods her head, indicating yes.)*

Janae: Close your eyes and just let yourself sit with this whole idea, Serena. Let yourself feel the impact of this message. There is a little girl whose mom and dad don't want her to be free, and they don't want her to be spontaneous. They want her to give up anything spontaneous. What do you feel inside when you hear me say these words?

Serena: I am afraid.

(This is Serena's conscious process.)

Janae: What are you afraid of?

Serena: I won't get the approval of the people that I want it from—my mom and my dad.

Janae: What will happen if you don't meet their approval?

Serena: What came to mind was isolation, yet I don't remember that that tool was used as a punishment for me as a child.

Janae: There are many types of isolation. Sometimes we can be isolated and be right in the middle of a whole group of people. It is more about how we experience it than how it looks like physically. When you were spontaneous, was there some kind of punishment? Did they exclude you, shun you, and shame you?

Serena: I certainly felt shamed in that incident.

Janae: Do you feel like they loved you?

Serena: Yes, I think that.

Janae: What is your fear—if they didn't love you, what would happen?

(Janae seeks to deepen Serena's unconscious process.)

Serena: They wouldn't take care of me.

Janae: What would happen if they didn't take care of you?

Serena: I couldn't take care of myself

Janae: What would happen to you because you couldn't take care of yourself?

Serena: I would die.

(Serena's unconscious process and core belief is, "If I don't do what my parents want me to do, they will not take care of me and I will die.")

Janae: You became afraid. If you did this terrible thing and were spontaneous, you ultimately might die. This is where it took you step by step. When you think about that whole memory, what do you feel?

(Janae checks to see if there is more emotional content related to this memory.)

Serena: I feel the tension in my body.

(Serena's body becomes stiff and tears begin to trickle slowly down her cheeks.)

Janae: *(Janae moves her cushion closer to Serena to deepen the empathic attunement between them and to offer emotional support.)*

Perhaps this is the tension you had in your body to keep you from dying. This is what you probably did as a little girl. You made yourself get tense and stay alert so you wouldn't do some terrible thing and bring on this awful consequence.

(Janae identifies the impact of Serena's memories of hypervigilance on her sympathetic nervous system.)

Serena: I became very vigilant about where other people were at and the nuances of my response.

(Serena states this in her own words.)

Janae: This one time maybe you were taking a nap or something, but you lost your vigilance and you soiled your pants, and there was this terrible consequence. People didn't like what you did, and they didn't like you. Is that true?

(Janae check to see if her summary of Serena's experience is accurate.)

Serena: I certainly felt that way.

(Serena validates Janae's summary.)

Janae: That is your reality. Somehow the littlest thing you did wrong could have some horrible consequence for you. It must have been terrifying to live like that, Serena. *(Tears trickle down Serena's cheeks.)* How awful for this little tiny girl to be walking around on eggshells for fear she would do some unknown thing that would just destroy her and could be the end of her world.

(Janae validates the shocking aspect of Serena's experience and puts her hand on Serena's knee to help her stay in her body while she is processing the memory.)

It is okay. Just let yourself feel this terror. Nobody saw how wounded you were, how tense, how frightened you were. You lived in this little, quiet, and terrified world. How terrible, Serena, that nobody could see this happening to you. This must have been really, really painful for you. You started shutting down all the joy, playfulness, and all the liveliness because you were so afraid. Sounds like you lived in constant fear. It must have happened a lot. One slip and that could be the end. The end of everything.

(Janae describes the long-term implications of this early shock experience on her subsequent development.)

Serena: I am thinking that this played out a lot. This thread is throughout all of my significant childhood memories. It has played out in my marriage as well.

(Serena begins to see how this early experience has created cycles of traumatic reenactment in her life.)

Janae: One small slip, and it is the end of the world.

(Janae validates the life-and-death nature of this trauma.)

I just want to acknowledge that this pain that you have gone through your whole life has come from some belief that you formed as a very tiny child, that one small slip and it is the end of the world.

(Janae helps Serena identify the distorted belief that she formed as the result of her traumatic experience.)

How much pain and tension has it caused you? It is really traumatic about how many times you had to shut yourself down—over and over again for fear if you let yourself out it would be the end.

(Janae's comforting and affirming words help Serena recognize how this trauma has kept her in protection rather than growth modes during her life.)

It is okay to feel it. You don't have to hold it in any longer. I will be right here with you. Just keep feeling it until you get to the bottom of it. Really deep. It hit your soul and wounded you right in the core of your very being.

(Janae provides a safe container to help Serena go into the core emotions related to this trauma.)

What made it even worse is that the people who could do this to you were the people that you depended on.

(Janae helps Serena identify the betrayal component in her trauma.)

Keep letting yourself feel it. A mother whose love you cherished and desired could somehow abandon you is a terrible wound. Let yourself go into it as many times as you need to in order to go to the bottom of it.

(Janae helps Serena plumb the emotional depths of this shock memory so that she can clear it from the black hole.)

Serena: Do you want me to share?

(Serena is emerging from the memory and the black hole.)

Janae: Whatever you want to share. Sometimes it helps to tie the story together to speak it out loud, to make sense out of it.

Serena: I am getting in touch with my anger and having to deal with the current conflict and my sense of dilemma that I feel in all these times when there is no way for me to win.

The conflict between what I know my needs are and what I felt I needed to do in order to meet my own needs. When I made the decision to quit working full time, my husband was opposed to that decision and accused me of doing further damage to our marital relationship because of the loss of income to our family. I felt like I had to choose between meeting my own needs and trying to please everybody else. I feel that my employer has the ability to lessen the impact about this and refuses to do it for reasons that I cannot understand. That is the core of my current dilemma, and it is where I always get hung up.

(Serena begins to connect her past trauma to present-time events and see the common pattern in them. This indicates an internal shift into the neocortex part of her brain and the autonomic nervous system's social engagement system.)

Janae: It is happening with your husband and your boss just like it did when you were a young child. All these things are the same, happening over and over.

(Janae restates Serena's words and emphasizes the pattern aspect of the shock memory.)

Serena: The people that I look to who can meet my needs refuse to do so for reasons that I can't understand, and I keep trying to figure that out. Is it something in me that is causing this to happen?

(Serena reveals her "they are okay/I'm not okay" intrapsychic split.)

Janae: You were taught to believe that it is your fault that this is happening. You keep looking at this as if it is your fault. Is that right? *(Janae shifts her position and places her hand on Serena's other knee)*

(Janae states the split more directly.)

Serena: That is the belief system that I grew up with.

(Serena confirms this clarified split.)

Janae: Let's go back to the earliest time in this memory and see if we can figure out what needs to be repaired there and see if healing it affects these other pieces.

(Janae searches for the incomplete developmental process and unmet needs that are associated with it.)

Let's go back to the memory that you had when you were a little girl and you soiled your pants. At that time, what would have helped you create a different belief? What could have been different? What could your mother or your cousin have said or done that would be different?

(Janae asks Serena to identify the missing relational pieces needed to heal the trauma.)

Serena: They could have said that it happens sometimes, you are still a big girl, and it doesn't mean you are bad. We will just clean it up, and you can go out and play. *(Serena gestures with her hands.)*

(Serena speaks the healing words and message implied in them.)

Janae: What you needed was an affirmation that it was okay that this happened. This didn't mean that there was some major flaw in who you were. It needed to be done in a kind, loving, understanding way that validated who you were.

(Janae states Serena's words more emphatically.)

Serena: What I am remembering, and who knows if it is accurate or not, but I kind of have a sense that my mom didn't make a big deal out of it except that she made me clean it up myself.

Janae: What was the message in that?

(Janae helps Serena connect her mother's behavior with its meaning and using shame as a tool for rejecting her.)

Serena: If you have to suffer the consequences of it, then you won't do it again.

Janae: What was the message in that?

Serena: I should have done better than I did.

Janae: I think there was another message in it, Serena. I think in a very subtle way your mother was saying, "You are too big for me to take care of you like that. You are not a baby, and you have now lost a certain set of privileges. The real message I am hearing in this is that you need to be self-sufficient. Yes, you had an accident like you were a baby. You are not allowed to regress. You are not allowed to show the places where you still need your mother. You are not allowed to show the parts of you that still have some baby needs in them. You are done with being 'baby.' That's done and that is all you are going to get." Do you hear any of that?

(Janae interprets a message in Serena's mother's behavior and unspoken words that Serena does not hear and checks to see if Serena hears what she hears.)

Serena: Yes, I do, and I am connecting it to a time frame when my younger brother was born. I think it was when my cousin came to help my mom with the new baby. She had four children.

(Serena not only hears this expanded explanation, she is able to apply it to other situations that also reaffirm it.)

Janae: I would like to do a direct intervention. Would you be willing to let me play the kind of mother that I think you would have needed?

(Janae sees the possibility of healing this trauma in the relationship channel where it originally happened.)

Serena: Yes.

Janae: Okay, Serena, if you'd like, I'm willing to be your functional mother for a few moments and say the words that you indicated would help you heal this memory.

Serena: Yes, that would be great.

Janae: *(Making a developmental intervention, Janae places an empty cushion across from Serena and moves over to sit on it.)*

I'm speaking now as your mother. "I see how really sad you are about soiling your pants. I know you must feel very embarrassed. I know how hard you try to control everything and not be spontaneous. For you to have soiled your pants means there must be something really difficult going on inside you. We have a new baby here, and you are not the baby anymore. Some part of you realizes that you are not the baby anymore and that you will never get to be the baby again.

"You are done being 'baby' and you must feel really sad about that. When you soil your pants, I see that there is a part of you that is grieving the fact that you are not the baby anymore. I really understand. It is really hard to lose that place in the family.

"We want you to know we love you. Even if you soil your pants and might be a little angry, and this is the only way you can show it, because you are so afraid to show how you really feel in our family. I see how hard you are struggling to keep our love so we won't desert or abandon you, so you won't die.

"We understand you are having a really deep and painful experience right now. We see it, and we want to hold you and support you and reassure you of our love. We won't go away, and we won't let you die. It doesn't matter how many times you are spontaneous and forget to hold yourself in and how many times you soil your pants, we will always love you."

(Janae speaks the words of unconditional love that a nurturing and aware mother would have spoken to her child in such a situation.)

Serena: *(Serena's body and face look frozen.)*

Janae: Serena, I'm shifting back to being Janae now. What is going on in your body now? What are you feeling?

(Janae moves back to her original cushion as she releases the mother role.)

Serena: Push pull. There is a part of me that wants to really accept this and a part that says this is not real.

(Serena is working at the edge between her conscious and unconscious awareness, and she is caught between past, present, and future realities.)

Janae: What would be the value of it not being real? What would be important or valuable about receiving what you just heard?

(Janae's work at the edge looks for the opposing beliefs that prevent Serena from taking in the words and changing her behavior and beliefs.)

Serena: If it's not real, it would allow me to hold on to old patterns that are very familiar and have worked reasonably well for me.

Janae: It seems to me that the words put you at a choice point. If you receive them, experience being loved unconditionally, and change your old belief, then what you are confronted with is a new belief and a new way of being. This means that you can go into any company you work for and negotiate to get your needs met. You can expect to be heard, expect to be honored, valued. In this new way of being there is no place to be a victim. It is a huge turn in the road. It can be a very difficult one to make, Serena.

(Janae supports Serena working at the edge between maintaining her past behavior and moving to a new behavior pattern.)

This path started so early and is so woven into the fabric of who you are. Changing it means you have to be willing to let go of a major way of living. It is scary. You'd have to learn "if I am not a victim, who am I?" This is what we all have to learn—how to get our needs met and let people love us, honor, respect, and cherish us in the way we want to be. You don't have to make any big choices right now. You just need to know that you are at a choice point. This is a powerful place to be and to know that a new way is opening to you. It is sort of like letting go of an addiction.

You don't let go of an addiction or the pattern of being a victim until you can imagine a new way of being. When you can build this picture, then it will happen. You don't have any experience of living as not being a victim.

(Janae affirms that Serena has the power to choose. She continues working at the edge by giving Serena a choice about her future.)

Serena: Actually, I do feel that I am moving out of it.

(Serena's body begins to shift as she changes her position, indicating a shift into the kinesthetic channel and a shift in consciousness.)

Janae: Well, that is good news. Tell me about it. What would it look like to not be a victim?

(Serena has psychologically moved out of her shock state and is beginning to engage socially with Janae, as she begins helping Serena create a vision of a different future. Now Serena, emotionally attuned with Janae in the relational channel, also begins working internally in the visual channel.

(Janae backs her cushion away from Serena and removes her hand from Serena's knee.)

Serena: Part of it is in being in a class like this. I am much freer, much less worried about what I say and how that will be received by other people, much less vigilant about projecting about how people are responding on how I behave. I feel much more comfortable about myself and how I contribute. More importantly, I am able to make a mistake and not be afraid of dying if I say something foolish. Even taking a risk like this.

(Serena affirms that she is already moving into a new reality where she is not a victim.)

Janae: You did not die—you are very much alive. You did one of the scariest things. You went right into the shock, experienced the feelings, and then found its meaning. You also let others witness this, and you are sitting right here looking very alive. Congratulations! This is a big change in your patterns.

(Janae confirms the new reality again.)

The question is, "How can you empower yourself to really walk into this new way of being?" You are learning to recognize the automatic response that signals the approach of the victim place. That place you cut yourself off, where the fear captures you.

(Janae affirms that Serena is powerful and able to consciously stop her pattern of being a victim and shifting from the trauma to the LOVEvolution track of development.)

Serena: Part of it is awareness. This has been a piece of it. I am really learning to trust my process. I don't have to fix it in one dialogue with you. It has been part of the process to get in touch with one more memory and to see more of the connection throughout my developmental process. As I get more connected with it, the length of time that I feel overwhelmed by the fear gets shorter. I can cognitively take risks like I did in volunteering for this demonstration and knowing that, if I was selected, it would be part of my process. If I was not selected, God was providing for me to work on my process through another person. So I was equally all right with whether I was chosen or not.

(Serena confirms her healing experience and personal power.)

Janae: This is tremendous growth that you are describing. Leaving a very deep life pattern of traumatic experiences. This is pretty awesome.

(Janae helps Serena anchor her new beliefs about herself.)

Serena: This has been most of a decade's journey. I do know that it is a process. It also allows me to be more compassionate and gentle with other people in their processes. I have to honor their processes.

Janae: With this kind of resource base, let's look at how you can apply some of this information to the conflict that you have in the workplace. Based on this new orientation, how might you react differently to these people who seem to be playing out your unsupportive mother?

(Janae asks Serena to return to the visual in which she began her work and to integrate it into the relational channel to anchor her learning into her life.)

Serena: I am learning to be clearer about verbally expressing my needs with no expectations for a certain outcome. When my employers are not willing or able to meet my needs, I am more okay with allowing a process rather than becoming reactively angry or deciding to go off from them, isolating, and attempting to meet my needs in my own way.

(Serena says this with great clarity.)

Janae: What we are seeing is how this 3-year-old trauma has been circulating in your life in different ways. When you get in these different places, you still have this 3-year-old child reaction. You feel deeply wounded. You feel unseen, unvalued. They don't meet your needs, you feel shame, and then you want to pull away and go nurse your wounds in private. You haven't been able to have a reaction in either of these places in your life that is not tainted by this very early experience. A piece of the hurt gets cycled through both of these places. *(Serena nods her head in agreement with Janae's remarks.)*

(Janae articulates the dynamics of traumatic reenactment in Serena's life.)

Serena: What I am trying to learn to do differently is to be more open to a process, rather than making an event out of it. It is not black or white.

(Serena's comment indicates that she is moving beyond the splitting stage in the counterdependent stage of development.)

I am able to say that, "For now, you are not able to meet my needs. I will meet my needs in the best way I can, and then I will come back to you and ask again, 'Isn't there some way that we can work together on this?'"

(Serena's comment indicates that she is developing "both/and" thinking.)

Janae: This is something you could not do with your mother. Your mother said, "You soil your pants, and you clean it up." There was no negotiation with her. Every time you use your skills in conflict resolution, and you talk about wants and needs or values and beliefs that you have, about companies that need to value their employees, and the investment that they have made in you and family-friendly work environments, you break the pattern. You don't necessarily have to have this wounded child piece in you. You can go in as an advocate for yourself.

(Janae helps Serena connect the inner child part of her psyche with her adult part and affirms this important move toward the independent and interdependent stages of development.)

Serena: More and more I am able to do that. It is just when there is a situation that catches me off guard and throws me back there. Then I am back in the 3-year-old child, the tears are there, and I feel a real sense of shame.

(Serena realizes that there might still be some unhealed pieces of this developmental shock that could trigger her in the future.)

Janae: Another missing piece to this shock is that there was no advocate there for you as a child. Your cousin could have advocated for you. She could have said, "It's okay. She is just having a reaction because there is a new baby. Most kids regress and will wet their pants. It is really normal.

Come here, sweetie, and I will clean you up and hold you. Your mom is just a little overwhelmed right now with the new baby."

(Janae finds another place where she can include a relational intervention that Serena needed, this time with her cousin.)

So when you go in and advocate for yourself, you internalize the piece that is missing for you. You can be the adult advocating for the little girl who needs to have her needs met.

(Janae helps Serena integrate her adult and child parts in her psyche.)

Serena: What I am getting in touch with is that maybe I am still looking for the advocate outside of myself.

(Serena identifies the external locus of control component of her victim pattern.)

Janae: The advocate in a traumatic situation is called the rescuer.

(Janae brings in dynamics from the drama triangle.)

Serena: Even though I am being an advocate for myself, I think my little girl self inside was wanting someone to rescue me. *(Serena puts her hands on her chest as she speaks.)*

Janae: You did need a rescuer as a child. The problem is that when we still carry this internal victim around with us, we can also act out the persecutor role. We can go into the company we work for and say, "You are a terrible company to work for. Haven't you heard of family-friendly practices? Where have you folks been? Get with it. This is the 21st century."

(Janae helps Serena understand what is right about wanting a rescuer and how this unmet developmental need for protection helps create drama triangle dynamics in her life.

If you get into this kind of anger and shame others the same way that your mother shamed you, you lose the ability to be assertive. *(Janae moves her hands forward in an assertive motion.)* In this situation, you are still acting out your own trauma of victimization, perpetration, or needing rescue. Now that you've gotten in touch with this old wound, you will be able to get your needs met more effectively, and you will be able to go into these kinds of situations with a lot more clarity.

(Janae emphasizes how this piece of her healing work can change Serena's life.)

Janae: Let's go back now to see if there is anything that is not finished about this issue, so you can see how this trauma and this pattern is playing out in your life.

(Janae returns to the original contract.)

It appears that the conflicts that you are having in the present with work and your husband and in the past with your mother are a reflection of an internal conflict about "Can I really get my needs met? If I can't get my needs met, does it mean that I will die? I must get my needs met. If I say what my needs are, then I could die." This internal dialogue creates an internal reenactment cycle that you can't escape from. "I need, but my need means I might die." No wonder you feel frozen and immobilized. There is no resolution to this internal conflict.

(Janae helps Serena integrate her contract with the work that she just completed and affirms her reason for making it.)

Serena: That is really how it has felt.

Janae: You have this part of you that is needy and another part that wants to be spontaneous. They are both in conflict with the part of you that says you will die if you speak up, so you better sit down and be quiet. Imagine these parts coming together inside of you. There is a way to get your needs met and not die. It is very clear that you are on the mastery road to doing that. *(Janae touches Serena's knee in an affirming way.)*

(Janae helps Serena see the developmental source of an early relational conflict and how to integrate her conflicted intrapsychic parts.)

Serena: Thanks, Janae.

Janae: Your face looks quite different right now. How are you feeling right now? How is your back feeling right now?

(Janae checks to make sure that Serena is anchored in her body after processing dissociated memories.)

Serena: Tired. It is mostly that my feet are asleep. *(Serena moves her feet, stretches out her legs, and lifts her knees as she moves off her cushion.)*

Janae: If we were to stop our work right now, would there be anything missing?

(Janae checks again to make sure that the therapy contract is complete.)

Serena: I just have a sense that my wish to take care of my own needs is just very early and probably goes back even further than the 3-year old incident. I just now had a sense that I really knew at that moment that there was earlier history already in play.

(Serena is identifying the next step in her healing process.)

Janae That seemed to be a really life-altering experience when your mother drew the line and said, "That is it. No more being baby."

Serena: Yes.

Janae: "You soil your pants, you clean it up."

Janae: If there are earlier events that are important for you to remember, they will emerge.

(Janae briefly touches Serena's knees as a way of affirming their relational connection.)

Janae: Thanks for being so brave and sharing in front of so many people.

Serena: Thanks for the opportunity.

It is very clear that Serena recognizes the "process" aspect of DPW. Few clients are able to identify the next step in their work as quickly as she does. Because DPW can open clients to very early dissociative and regressive memories, it is important to begin therapy by building a strong, resonant relationship with them. This allows them to feel safe as they begin looking at the presence of developmental shock, trauma, and stress in their lives.

Because Serena had already done a lot of work on herself and had some personal history with Janae as an instructor prior to this demonstration, she was able to open herself up without a great deal of preparation. The danger in moving too fast with DPW is that it can overwhelm clients' autonomic nervous system and re-shock or re-traumatize them. Rushing clients can not only switch clients into the protection mode and lower the trust level, it also slows down the healing process and creates ethical issues.

When men and women are able to respect and accept their differences, then love has a chance to blossom.

John Gray

CHAPTER TWELVE

A Systems Approach to Healing Developmental Shock, Trauma, and Stress in Couples

Developmental systems theory (DST) and developmental process work (DPW) use a systems approach for healing the effects of unhealed developmental shock, trauma, and stress in couples. A central DPW goal in working with couples is teaching them how to regulate their emotions effectively during relationship conflicts. A conscious, committed partnership relationship provides a safe place where both members can help each other heal their developmental shocks, traumas, and stresses and learn how to quickly reregulate their emotions when triggered by memories anchored in early developmental shock, trauma, and stress. This supports the completion of the essential developmental processes of the couple, which allows the couple system to evolve.

Our theory holds that couple relationships go through the same developmental stages as an individual. Using this premise, the DPW counselor or social worker looks for the signs of unhealed developmental shocks, traumas, and stresses and incomplete developmental processes in their conflicts that might be causing stuckness in the couple system. By helping them resolve their conflicts, the couple not only discovers these processes and works to complete them, but the couple can also be taught how to work cooperatively to heal the developmental shocks, traumas, and stresses that are related to them.

DPW as a Systems Approach to Healing Developmental Shock, Trauma, and Stress in Couples

DPW couples therapy principles apply to relationships between any two committed people, whether they are friends, family, coworkers, or a committed couple. Generally, the closer a couple relationship becomes, the more likely that the partners will trigger conflicts containing reenactments of unresolved developmental shocks, traumas, and stresses. The commitment aspect is that both parties agree to stay engaged during conflicts and to work cooperatively in finding a resolution. This kind of commitment provides the kind of safety needed to heal developmental issues that are inherent in intractable relationship conflicts. The cooperative healing of unhealed developmental issues can not only restore the emotional resonance between the partners but also deepen the intimacy in their relationship.

The evolution of couple relationships follows a developmental sequence paralleling that of individuals. As the relationship and the individuals involved grow and mature, the relationship moves through a series of predictable stages. When you enter an intimate relationship, you bring with you your developmental issues involving the effects of unhealed shocks, traumas, and stresses. As intimacy levels deepen, any incomplete developmental processes connected to these issues will eventually surface during relationship conflicts. These conflicts begin with competing needs and wants, and then progress to differing values and beliefs. Eventually, they emerge as intractable conflicts that recycle in the relationship without getting resolved. While unhealed developmental shock, trauma, or stress can be an underlying cause of any conflict, our experience is that all intractable conflicts are caused by unhealed developmental shock, trauma, or stress.

Our own developmental issues surfaced once we felt emotionally safe and secure in our relationship. We gradually experienced an increase in the number of conflicts that began triggering issues involving unhealed developmental shocks, traumas, and stresses. For a period of time, we, like many couples, tried to avoid the issues that triggered conflicts by trying to keep the peace and maintaining an artificial sense of harmony. Once we decided we wanted more intimacy and risked going deeper, our unhealed developmental issues surfaced even more quickly, and we found ourselves triggering each other in unexpected and surprising ways.

Because of our own couple experiences and our clinical work with many other couples, we believe that conscious, committed, partnership relationships are an ideal crucible for helping couples evolve in their individual and couple consciousness. Couple relationships provide many rich opportunities for healing the effects of developmental shocks, traumas, and stresses and completing the incomplete developmental processes from each individual's own development. The trick is learning how each person can help the other reregulate his or her emotions whenever they get triggered, so that they can complete any incomplete developmental processes they brought with them into the relationship.

The four stages of couple relationship development are codependent, counterdependent, independent, and interdependent. Table 12.1 lists both the essential

TABLE 12.1

The Essential Developmental Processes of Couples

Stage of Development	The Essential Developmental Processes in Couple Evolution	Experiences for Completing the Essential Developmental Processes in Couples
Codependent (Harmony)	• Create secure and consistent bonding experiences with each other • Establish deep primal trust in each other • Develop ways to quickly repair any disruptions to couple resonance • Establish good communication and social engagement skills with each other • Establish an identity as a couple • Create secure bonding experiences in the family between parents and children • Establish primal trust among family members • Establish healthy emotional communication and social engagement skills among family members • Establish an identity as a family	• Establishing a friendship as a valued quality of the relationship • Attuning to each other and learning how to sustain that attunement • Recognizing and acknowledging each other's spiritual essence • Exchanging nurturing touch and talk • Respecting and validating each other's needs and feelings • Giving and receiving unconditional love • Exploring common interests, values, beliefs, and goals
Counterdependent (Conflict)	• Become functionally separate individuals in the relationship • Identify and accept individual differences in thoughts, feelings, and behaviors • Resolve internal conflicts between needs of self and other • Develop effective partnership ways to resolve conflicts of wants and needs and of values and beliefs	• Supporting each other to explore interests outside of the relationship • Separating nurturing touch from sexual touch • Establishing individual goals, values, and beliefs within the couple relationship • Establishing and receiving respect for each other's boundaries • Identifying self-needs vs. other-needs • Negotiating directly to get needs met

(continued)

TABLE 12.1 *(continued)*

Stage of Development	The Essential Developmental Processes in Couple Evolution	Experiences for Completing the Essential Developmental Processes in Couples
Independent (Resolution)	• Listen empathically and nondefensively to each other • Communicate feelings directly and responsibly • Take responsibility for the influence of past shocks, traumas, and stresses on your behavior • Master financial, psychological, and professional self-sufficiency within the relationship • Move beyond an idealized, romanticized approach to love and intimacy • Develop core values and beliefs as a couple • Achieve object constancy as a couple • Bond with nature as a couple	• Achieving a balance between individual and couple needs and interests • Identifying individual goals, values, and beliefs within the couple relationship and operating from them as both individuals and as a couple • Experiencing object constancy with each other in spite of conflicting needs and wants or values and beliefs
Interdependent (Partnership)	• Create a well-differentiated and clearly defined sense of self within the relationship • Support each partner's development • Learn to cooperate with each other in getting important needs met in the relationship • Experience the deepest human connection possible with each other • Develop equality in the relationship • Cooperate to help each other heal developmental shocks, traumas, and stresses • Cooperate to develop each person's fullest human potential	• Using transformative methods of resolving conflict • Building and sustaining a spiritual dimension in the primary relationship • Utilizing the relationship as a tool for individuation and mutual spiritual evolution • Mutually affirming each other's spiritual values and goals and acting from them • Identifying situations where couple devotion can be extended to others outside the relationship • Committing to resolving intractable conflicts at their source

Source: From *The Flight from Intimacy,* by J. Weinhold & B. Weinhold, 2008, Novato, CA: New World Library. Reprinted with permission of the author.

developmental processes for each stage in couple relationships and ways that couples can complete them.

When couples seek therapy, they usually are in an intractable conflict and emotionally escalated. While they may relate similar stories, and each partner's story has various perspectives, the common theme is often, "We had a wonderful relationship in the beginning. We got along so well. Then we started to get on each other's nerves and began having fights." Sometimes the two people have been in conflict long enough to create a reservoir of ill will between them from holding grudges and hanging onto resentments. If this is the case, our first task is to help them use some of our tools to drain the reservoir.

Dramatic conflicts in a relationship actually indicate that the relationship is maturing. The most visible shift is the shift from the codependent stage to the counterdependent stage of relationship. During the codependent stage, or "honeymoon stage," couples ignore issues and topics that might trigger conflicts to preserve the good feelings and sense of attunement. Some relationships remain in this stage for a long time, particularly if the individuals involved are skilled at maintaining a shallow level of intimacy that keeps them from getting too close and if they are living very busy separate lives. The more contact, the more there will be opportunities for couples to trigger each other.

When the relationship does move into the counterdependent stage, differences once ignored or avoided come to the forefront. Usually, one member of the relationship gets uncomfortable with "walking on eggs" and brings up a conflict he or she is having. This may initially be upsetting, as it can activate fears that the relationship will end. As in individual development, the shift from the codependent to the counterdependent stage of development often is sparked by the desire for more autonomy.

The desire for more separateness in a relationship typically does not happen simultaneously. One person usually wants to seek out individual activities before the other person is ready for this to happen. This creates an imbalance between one partner's need for separateness and the other's need to maintain oneness. The shift into the counterdependent stage of relationship development may begin quite innocently and end up in a conflict that feels catastrophic. For example, he wants to take a trip with his buddies, or she wants to get an advanced degree that involves taking night classes. These kinds of relational changes may trigger reactions connected to issues containing unhealed developmental shocks, traumas, or stresses. These issues could contain fears of abandonment in the person wanting to maintain the oneness, or fears about suffocation or being controlled in the person wanting more separateness.

The biggest problem during the counterdependent stage of couple relationships is that the partners are unaware of their underlying developmental issues and often think the other person is the cause of the conflict. Partners may nag, cajole, threaten, or use other manipulative ploys to change the other person's mind. This strategy, of course, is seldom successful. So the partner wanting more freedom feels trapped. Caught in a dilemma, that person often feels like his or her only choices are either to leave the relationship to look for a more compatible partner or stay in the relationship, suffer, and feel resentful. This is the point where partners often decide to seek either individual or couples counseling.

What couples need at this point is systemic information about how relationships grow and mature as the individual partners are growing and maturing. With this kind of support, couples counseling can really make a difference. Counselors and social workers using DPW's systemic approach can help couples understand the developmental stages of couple relationships, why they trigger each other, and what they can do about it.

Training DPW Therapists to Utilize a Systems Approach in Counseling Couples

Counselors and social workers using DPW's systems approach with couples need a solid grounding in the core individual counseling skills. In addition, DPW counselors and social workers need a variety of other counseling skills to use as they follow their couple clients' process. In order to know which tool to use and when to use it, DPW-trained counselors and social workers need to be able to build a resonant field with each individual member of the couple and with the couple as a unit. This skill is obviously more difficult than building and sustaining a resonant field with an individual, particularly if the couple is not able to do this between themselves. In this case, we recommend using a cotherapy model—two therapists for two clients. The cotherapists can then create and hold their own attuned field, which helps stabilize the couple both individually and as a pair.

To understand and practice DPW's system approach, it is important to understand family systems theory. This involves understanding how an individual as a system is different when part of a couple system. This more complex dynamic requires a paradigm shift, as it shifts from linear to circular causality.

Linear causality refers to the concept of cause and effect. One person's action causes another person's predictable reaction. An example of linear causality is:

cause   effect
man drinks——————————>woman nags

In this linear model, the man's drinking causes the woman to nag. This explanation is perfectly acceptable, but it may not be a complete explanation. If we were to ask the man to explain his drinking, he might report:

cause   effect
woman nags——————————>man drinks

Again we have an acceptable linear, cause-and-effect explanation for the behavior. The man drinks because he cannot tolerate the woman's nagging, and the drinking dulls his anger toward her.

Circular causality considers both explanations and incorporates them in a more complete systemic conceptualization of the problem. The wife nags to stop her husband from drinking, and the husband continues to drink because it helps him tolerate his wife's nagging. This circular understanding of the problem is:

circular causality
drinking————————————nagging

A DPW counselor or social worker working with this couple would understand the problem more completely by conceptualizing it through the circular causality model. According to this view, the behavior of both persons maintains the problem behavior. The couple's problem may not necessarily be either the drinking or the nagging but, rather, their inability to resolve the power struggle concerning whose needs will dominate in the relationship. At a deeper level, both are likely trying to control emotions they fear might erupt if they are triggered. The DPW counselor or social worker looks for interventions that move couples to deeper levels of interaction.

In addition to being able to work with circular causality, DPW counselors and social workers must have cleared their own developmental issues involving relational shock, trauma, and stress in order to effectively support the couple system. Otherwise their therapy may be distorted, and the content of the couple's issues will trigger them. This situation is very difficult and very serious. We recommend that DPW counselors and social workers get constant monitoring, ongoing supervision, and continued personal counseling in order to prevent countertransference issues.

DPW training programs require potential counselors and social workers to examine their own personal histories and to identify any developmental issues involving unresolved shock, trauma, and stress. While typical counselor and social work training programs are not equipped to provide personal therapy for their trainees to heal developmentally related issues, we insist our trainees get individual or couples counseling while they are in the training program to clear them.

A vital component in our training of DPW counselors and social workers for couples work is providing ample time for them to process their own unhealed developmental shocks, traumas, and stresses. These unhealed developmental issues often show up as projections on their fellow trainees or their trainers. During these spontaneous teachable moments in our classes, we allow time for trainees to process their projections. These authentic moments may be even more important than the scheduled content.

As trainees become more aware and skilled, and as the training group becomes more cohesive, we have found that training groups naturally shift into the developmental–constructivistic model, which we discussed in Chapter 9, where we often recognize that our approach may be incomplete. Because we value trainees' experience and promote active learning, we encourage and expect trainees to become cocreators of our process-oriented approach.

We recognize that each trainee brings his or her unhealed developmental issues involving unresolved shock, trauma, and stress into our trainings, and we see this as part of both their experiential learning and the cocreative context of our trainings. Rather than seeing these unresolved issues as a stigma, we provide a supportive and compassionate environment that frames their traumas as opportunities for personalizing our DPW model. This approach also helps them recognize when they get triggered by their clients' behaviors or issues and what to do when it happens.

The Core Skills DPW Therapists Need to Utilize a Systems Approach in Counseling Couples

Next we describe 12 essential skills for counseling couples. They build on the same skills that were described in Chapter 9. In this chapter, we will describe how these core skills serve as a foundation for those training in DPW to use a systems approach in counseling with couples (Fenell & Weinhold, 2003).

Core Skill 1: Attuning with Couples

In couples' counseling, attuning with a couple is often called *joining* (Minuchin, 1974). This is similar to Schore's concepts of emotional synchrony and resonance. The effective DPW therapist must attune with each member of the couple system, as each person in a couple relationship needs support in describing his or her part of the conflict and needs to feel heard, understood, and respected by the counselor. The first session or two is also the time to assess the current level of functioning of each of the members of the couple. It is important to observe the behavior of each partner to determine whether he or she might be experiencing symptoms of shock, trauma, or stress and to use the appropriate interventions identified in Chapter 10 to support them.

DPW couple counselors and social workers need excellent listening skills and effective verbal and nonverbal communication skills so that each partner feels understood and supported. For example, if one partner regresses into a developmental shock state and is not communicating, the counselor or social worker must address this individual issue before going any further. If joining and attuning are successful, the counselor or social worker will serve as a significant source of self-esteem for each person (Minuchin & Fishman, 1981). When a partner in a couple expects the counselor or social worker to meet some of his or her self-esteem needs, the counselor or social worker has increased power and ability to intervene effectively with him or her.

In couples therapy, the story that each member of a couple describes in the conflict is typically about the partner. The effective therapist will hear and understand each version of the story without favoring either of the versions. This skill takes practice, as counselors and social workers can be triggered by elements of one member of the couple's story and lose their objectivity. Once a counselor's or social worker's unhealed developmental issues become obvious to clients, their ability to intervene in creative and powerful ways is limited. Again, our recipe for guarding against even the perception of countertransference is conjoint couples counseling. Then each counselor or social worker can join with the one member of the couple with whom he or she seems to relate to better without alienating the other.

Generally, the male counselor or social worker joins better with the male client, and the female counselor or social worker can then join with the female client. If it is not possible to find a counselor or social worker of the opposite gender as a cotherapist, we recommend two same-gender therapists collaborate to prevent the appearance of drama triangle dynamics. In counseling with gay couples, it is better to have same-gender therapists, if possible. In our own practice of conjoint counseling, we are able to flow back and forth in the way that we support each person. This shows couples that the two of us are united as a therapeutic team and that we support them individually and as a couple. This is the most important aspect of working conjointly in couples therapy.

Core Skill 2: Information Gathering with Couples

In individual counseling, open-ended questions help the counselor or social worker gather more information than closed questions. The same is true in couples counseling. Open-ended questions allow clients to respond in multiple ways; a closed question lends itself to yes–no responses. An example of an open-ended question would be: "Tell me about your relationship with Mike." A closed question would be: "Do you get along with Mike?" Minimal encouragers also aid in information gathering. A minimal encourager prompts the client to provide additional information, as, for example, in "Tell me more" or "Give me an example of that."

Core Skill 3: Structuring with Couples

In couples counseling, structuring is of critical importance. At the onset of couples counseling, clients are frequently stuck in conflicts involving interlocking patterns of developmental shock, trauma, and stress. Despite their ongoing experiences of pain, they often continue to repeat the same behaviors and dialogues because they are components of unconscious individual and intergenerational reenactment patterns involving developmental shock, trauma, and stress. In couples counseling, structuring begins with the first telephone contact. Often, the person contacting the therapist has decided who really needs the counseling. The spokesperson for the couple is already active and apparent (1) in setting up the counseling session, and (2) in determining who should be present in the counseling session.

The therapist must recognize that this person, no matter how well intentioned, may attempt to control the counseling and may even be the one who has the most investment in maintaining the dysfunction. Therapists are most effective in helping couples engage in new behavior sequences by being more collaborative than authoritarian. For example: The wife may call to set up a counseling appointment and tell the counselor that the session has to be scheduled around her husband's work schedule. The counselor or social worker must respond in a way that acknowledges the wife's concern for her husband's schedule but does not let this concern set a precedent in attempting to direct other aspects of the counseling session.

Core Skill 4: Information Giving with Couples

At times in DPW couples counseling, the therapist must give information to the couple. Again, the readiness of the couple to hear this information is paramount. These teachable moments have to be timed in such a way as not to overwhelm them, while also offering information regarding their issues that may expand their therapy experience. The reasons for offering information are to identify choices, to evaluate their choices, and to correct erroneous information. In giving information, it is important to be brief and accurate and to present the information gradually, only when the couple is ready to hear it.

In couples counseling, information giving takes on increased importance for two reasons. As couples' counseling often tends to be brief, clients need information to begin making changes relatively quickly in the therapy. To alter dysfunctional relational patterns, couples need to understand and recognize dysfunctional patterns, such as the drama triangle. Even if the counselor or social worker identifies the developmental issues involving shock, trauma, and stress and provides information about them, the couple still must recognize them when they appear and learn how to change this dynamic. The information provided by the counselor should meet the following criteria:

1. The information is understood and accepted by the couple.
2. The information does not overwhelm the couple.
3. The information is accurate.
4. The information is provided at the appropriate time.

Core Skill 5: Reflecting Content with Couples

Reflecting content is an important skill for the couples therapist. It helps couples crystallize their thoughts and feelings by having them restated in a more concise manner. It also helps counselors check their perceptions to make sure they are congruent with what the couple is communicating. Although the focus is often more on content, the counselor also acknowledges and validates each person's feelings.

For example, if the female member of a couple says, "I don't know about him—one moment he is as nice as can be, and the next he is a real jerk," the therapist might say, "So he seems like a pretty inconsistent guy who is hard for you to be with, and his erratic behavior keeps you pretty confused?" In this reflective statement, the counselor is careful not to agree with her perception but to show acceptance of it while also checking it for accuracy.

For counselors and social workers to provide information to couples about their current patterns of behavior, they must be able to recognize their interlocking developmental patterns involving shock, trauma, or stress. When therapists notice a certain repetitive behavior, they can reflect their observation of that behavior to the couple. For example, "Mary, I notice that whenever Bill seems to have trouble gathering his thoughts, you jump in and speak for him. Are you aware of this?" After listening to Mary's response, the therapist should check out this same observation with the other member of the couple. "Bill, are you aware of this dynamic?" If either partner resists the therapist's effort to identify behavior patterns, the timing was likely not right for this intervention, and the counselor should back off rather than pushing it.

Core Skill 6: Reflecting Feelings with Couples

This skill helps couples increase self-awareness and self-understanding. In reflecting feelings, counselors and social workers express clients' most visible emotion. As in individual therapy, this skill has three aspects: listening for feeling, timing, and reflecting the feeling. In listening for emotions, also listen for emotions that are not being expressed. The information in Chapter 10 describing the differences between clients' presenting behaviors indicates when a client might be experiencing shock, trauma, or stress.

It is also possible to observe nonverbal behaviors, such as breathing patterns, lack of eye contact, a sigh, a blush, a stammer, a glazed-over look, or swallowing to determine whether they connect to memories of developmental shock, trauma, or stress. Verbal clues include the use or lack of use of feeling words and tone of voice. Good timing requires that the counselor or social worker wait for an appropriate moment before reflecting and is careful not to cut off an internal flow or disturb the focus of thought. It is also important not to lag behind the couple. Reflecting feelings requires the use of a feeling word when the client may not have said one. For example, if a client says, "I wish I could get Jim to listen to my feelings like this," the therapist might say, "You seem to be feeling frustrated that Jim doesn't seem to hear your feelings when you express them."

Core Skill 7: Summarizing Content and Feelings with Couples

There are times in couples counseling when the counselor or social worker needs to recapitulate, condense, or crystallize the essence of the couple's thoughts and feelings. Although this skill resembles reflection of content and feeling, it is more comprehensive and includes deeper aspects that the clients are struggling with. Summarization can be used at the beginning of a session to review aspects of the previous session or at the end of a session as a review. This technique is also helpful when clients ramble, are unclear, are at the end of a discussion on a particular topic, or are in conflict.

Summarization during couples therapy can pull together the critical aspects of a session. Counselors and social workers will want to be certain that their summarizations include the thoughts of each partner as much as possible. Summarization should be expressed tentatively then checked with the couple to confirm that it is accurate. Generally, couples therapists use summarization of content more frequently than summarization of feeling.

Core Skill 8: Self-Disclosure with Couples

In counseling couples, therapists may want to share personal thoughts, feelings, and experiences that are relevant to a couple's situation. Self-disclosure primarily involves listening to clients, reflecting content and feelings, and telling the partners what the therapist hears and feels related to what the couple is sharing. For example, "I hear how much the two of you have suffered because of this issue. I feel sad about your loss of connection to each other and your fear that the relationship might end."

Couples therapists must be careful not to use self-disclosure inappropriately. Frequently, counselors and social workers think self-disclosure means to share or describe a situation in their own lives that was similar to what the couple is experiencing. While this might be useful, often it is not. Because the problems that couples bring to counseling are common to all couples, it is also possible that the couple's behaviors or interactions will remind the counselor of a similar situation in his or her own life. Therapists should be careful when discussing their own similar situations because it could shift the focus away from the couple's experiences and to the therapist's and stir countertransference issues.

Core Skill 9: Confrontation with Couples

Confrontation during couples counseling serves the same function as in individual counseling. It helps couple clients recognize incongruencies between what they say and how they behave. Confrontation helps couples clarify what they want and encourages movement toward that goal. Again, timing is important. Therapists should use this skill only after building a solid relationship with both members of the couple. It is also important not to seem as if you are more confrontive with one member of the couple in your confrontations. It is best to focus on their circular dynamic with caring and compassion. By framing your confrontation in systems language, it can have a positive effect. For example, you might say, "I have noticed that when Sally talks about you, you look down. What are you feeling when she talks to me about you?"

Core Skill 10: Interpretation with Couples

Effective interpretation helps couples understand the interlocking dynamics in their conflicts. When we work with couples and recognize how things have shifted from harmony to conflict in their relationship, we typically respond by saying,

"Congratulations, your relationship has now gotten close and safe enough for the developmental issues that you brought with you to the relationship to surface so they can be healed. Now what you need are some skills to help you recognize and clear them." This kind of interpretation also helps couples reframe their conflicts.

When couples come for counseling, they are generally stuck in behavior patterns that they do not understand and are unable to change. One of the therapist's first interpretations is to acknowledge and affirm the couple's genuine attempts to resolve their conflicts and to acknowledge that the current methods they are using are not working in spite of their best efforts.

Couples usually appreciate this interpretation because it shows that the counselor or social worker recognizes their struggle to change. It also affirms the therapist's proficiency in recognizing that they have been trying to solve their problems. It further offers couples a ray of hope that therapy might help them out of their stalemate.

Another critical skill for helping couples resolve their conflicts is the therapist's ability to offer new ways of perceiving their problems. Redefining the problem through *reframing* presents the couple with a new problem to solve. Because it is a new problem, the couple quickly sees the counselor or social worker as the expert who can help resolve the problem.

If one partner reacts to a reframing intervention by saying, "No, that's not it at all," the therapist's timing or wording of the interpretation may not be useful to the couple. The counselor needs to drop the effort to interpret and wait for a better time or use different words.

Reframing the problem can be a very effective form of interpretation. The couple is often in so much turmoil that they cannot get beyond their anger and hurt. For example, once the counselor determines that a couple is serious about wanting to improve the relationship, the wife's "pressuring her husband to express his feelings" can be redefined as "her need to hear that she is loved and valued." In the same manner, the husband's "withdrawal" may be redefined as "his sadness that he is unable to meet your need for closeness." This type of interpretation must be done carefully and with appropriate timing. When the partners are venting their anger toward each other, for example, they are not ready for a redefinition and this particular intervention is almost certain to be ineffective.

Core Skill 11: Behavior Change with Couples

Bringing about behavior change in therapy sessions with couples requires an advanced skill that includes all of the preceding skills. The four stages in the process each require different skills:

1. Identifying and clarifying couples issues require the use of emotional attunement, information gathering, structuring, reflection of content, and reflecting feelings.

2. Establishing workable goals requires the use of information gathering, information giving, summarization, and self-disclosure.
3. Establishing criteria for effectiveness of the action plan requires the use of confrontation and interpretation as well as reflection skills. This helps both client and therapist know when they have achieved the therapy objectives.
4. Implementation requires all of the skills—summary skills, reflection skills, confrontation skills, interpretation, and closure skills.

For a couples systems approach to be effective, counselors and social workers must help couple clients identify and clarify their interlocking patterns involving shock, trauma, or stress as a circular dynamic. This makes both partners be involved in both the problem and its solution.

Couples therapists must also establish criteria for evaluating the effectiveness of their counseling. The most common way is tracking changes in the behavior of a couple. A systems approach offers therapists multiple criteria for evaluating clinical effectiveness. A major strength of a systems approach is that couple clients are able to see the possibility of several therapeutic outcomes that would be acceptable as effective change. Therapists should be aware that system changes may occur in ways that are quite different than they anticipate. Such unexpected behavioral changes, typical of process-oriented therapy, are just as effective as changes produced by well-designed, therapist-directed treatment plans that specify outcomes.

Furthermore, therapist-directed treatment plans may also yield such unexpected outcomes. For example, a couple struggling with individuation might say that they want to stay together, so the counselor plans his or her therapy interventions to support this desired outcome. However, the partner wanting more freedom might feel so confined by the other partner's efforts to increase contact that he or she might suddenly choose to move out of their shared home. So the first treatment plan actually helped the person who moved out get clearer about needing more space. Once the couple separates instead of staying together to complete their individuation process, it is time for a new treatment plan.

Behavior changes during couples therapy occur more often when the counselor or social worker has:

1. successfully attuned with each partner;
2. followed the unfolding developmental processes of both individual partners and the couple relationship;
3. helped them identify the individual and couple issues involving unresolved developmental shocks, traumas, or stresses that each brought into the relationship and are contributing to their conflicts;
4. helped them recognize the incomplete individual developmental processes seeking completion in their relationship and understand why they are incomplete;

5. helped them develop strategies to resolve conflicts involving developmental shocks, traumas, or stresses and to complete the incomplete developmental processes they each brought to the relationship;
6. supported both partners in working cooperatively to heal their developmental shocks, traumas, or stresses by designing interventions for them to use to complete the incomplete developmental processes they each brought to the relationship; and
7. used a systems approach to provide timely developmental interventions.

Core Skill 12: Closure with Couples

One of the most common problems in counseling couples is closure. Inexperienced counselors and social workers report that this is a difficult part of the therapy process. Closure skills enable the therapist and the couple to accomplish the following:

1. Bring a particular issue or problem to some resolution
2. Bring a session to an end
3. Terminate a client's contract

In the first instance, it is sometimes necessary for the therapist to ask, "Have we gone as far as we can on this problem? Is resolution complete?" or, "If we stopped now, would we be missing anything?" It is easier to reach a mutual decision about whether resolution is complete in terms of meeting the goals of the contract when there is a specific couple contract. Without a contract, the therapist can do closure by summarizing what they have covered, asking probing questions about their satisfaction with the sessions, and reflecting content and feelings. Summarizing skills are useful in closing a session. It is usually helpful to ask each partner to summarize what he or she got out of the therapy and to evaluate the success of the counseling in light of the contract with the couple.

Some counselors and social workers are timid and would rather avoid closure, while others may be too aggressive and close prematurely. Either of these behaviors may be indicators that the therapist is caught in countertransference and unable to sort out his or her personal and client issues.

Final closure may require several sessions to complete and usually involves both some self-disclosure and an interpretation of the couple's current status, as well as a thorough review and summary of the counseling contract. Some counselors and social workers write a formal evaluation of the couples counseling. If the clients return to therapy or go to another therapist, it is easier to make a comparison between the clients' present and past levels of functioning.

Closure in couples therapy often follows one of two patterns. In brief couples counseling contracts, closure occurs as quickly as possible after the couple has begun more functional behavior patterns. To insist that a couple stay in therapy after they have made basic couple system changes might imply that the changes are not real or that they will not last. Couples should be free to end treatment as soon as they feel ready and should be invited to return if further problems develop. In order for a couple to maintain their behavioral changes, they must believe that they, not the therapist, are responsible for what happens as a result of couples counseling.

A second form of closure occurs after a couple has made systemic changes. Here counselors and social workers offer a couple the opportunity to either terminate or to remain and make the next and more complex changes in the process. This psychoeducational approach (Johnson, Johnson, & Holubec, 1993) supports the idea of teaching couples what it takes to bring about changes in their relationship. After this stage of the therapy is complete, it is time for closure.

How DPW Therapists Can Prevent Burnout in Counseling Couples

The primary cause of burnout in working with couples is the presence of countertransference issues. It is impossible to effectively join with a couple's relational system and work effectively as a DPW therapist without experiencing some symptoms of countertransference. It is easy to get triggered by clients' issues that relate to therapists' own developmental issues, particularly in activating dynamics of the drama triangle, as we mentioned in Chapter 7.

The most important strategy for preventing therapist burnout from couple counseling countertransference is regular supervision. In addition, it may be necessary for therapists to get couples or individual counseling for their own couple issues. It also helps counselors to monitor their reactions to the content during couples counseling sessions. If countertransference interferes with your effectiveness with a particular couple, you have an ethical obligation to heal the developmental issues involving shock, trauma, or stress that you are re-experiencing either through supervision or counseling of your own. If you are unable to heal the effects of your developmental shock, trauma, or stress and they interfere with your effectiveness as a DPW counselor or social worker, then you need to refer the couple to another therapist.

Therapeutic Interventions for Healing Developmental Shock, Trauma, or Stress in Couples

The following is a synopsis of therapeutic interventions that counselors and social workers can use in resolving developmental issues involving shocks, traumas, or stresses in couple relationships.

Regulating Emotions During Couple Conflicts

A central DPW goal in working with couples is teaching them how to regulate their emotions effectively during relationship conflicts. Ideally, people learn this skill in their first year of life through experiences of attunement with their parents and other bonded caregivers. If people experienced developmental shock, trauma, or stress during this critical period, they will have difficulties in regulating their emotions during relationship conflicts, particularly intractable conflicts that are triggered by lingering effects of unhealed developmental shock, traumas, or stresses in this early period of development.

We find that the experiential couple sculpting exercise we describe later in this chapter is a highly effective way to convey the effects of unhealed developmental shock, trauma, or stress in couples. For this reason, we usually do it very early in a couple's therapy contract. Sometimes we schedule the first appointment as an extended two- or three-hour session, which gives us time to gather their histories and to also do the sculpting exercise. We find this mini-intensive model very effective for couples who are in crisis and need a rapid intervention.

Emotional dysregulation in couples is typically caused by one or both partners being triggered by an unprocessed memory involving the effects of developmental shock, trauma, or stress. The triggering response immediately changes this person's time orientation from present to past or to dissociation, collapses the triggered partner's personal sense of reality, and releases stored emotions from the unhealed effects of the shock, trauma, or stress. This shift from present to past and the discharge of strong emotions can happen so quickly that both people feel stunned. Disrupting this rapid-fire process can be challenging, but it is possible. Here is how we work with this very emotionally intense situation.

We find it is easier when both partners have some understanding of shock, trauma, and stress states, for it provides a language and a context for processing the conflict both internally and relationally. The person who is triggered communicates this information to his or her partner by using the "T" hand signal used to request a time-out in sports. At this point, both partners stop all talking, yelling, and other escalated behaviors and begin working internally. Taking a physical time-out from each other for 10 or 15 minutes is often helpful at this stage.

During the time-out period, each person practices calming techniques such as centered breathing, listening to soothing music, sitting in nature, and drinking water to ground themselves. As their nervous systems quiet and the flow of adrenaline slows, the person who was first triggered reviews the period prior to the conflict in search of the cue that triggered his or her reaction. The partner of the triggered person reviews the conflict itself in search of the thing that triggered him or her. This inner work helps to separate out each person's reality and the unprocessed developmental shock, trauma, or stress that is seeking to be healed. Once each partner has determined the cue that triggered the conflict, what event in the past the cues connect with, what emotions are related to this event, and what unmet developmental needs are seeking to be met, the partners come back together.

Less experienced couple clients may need support from a therapist to do this kind of inner work and also support in helping both couple partners to share with each other the information about the sources of their conflict. They certainly will need support in finding ways inside and outside the relationship to fulfill the unmet developmental needs that appear in the conflict. More experienced couple clients can do much of this inner work and couple sharing with minimal therapeutic support. As couples grow more comfortable in negotiating to fulfill their unmet developmental needs, they may be able to do almost all of the healing work inside the couple relationship without therapeutic assistance.

Reframing Relationship Conflicts

When couples seek therapy, they often need help in reframing the problems in their relationship. As mentioned earlier, it is appropriate to say, "Congratulations! Your relationship is maturing. It is now strong enough and safe enough for these kinds of conflicts to emerge." This response may seem strange and confusing at first, and the couple might think, "This is the dumbest thing we've ever heard." Of course, therapists should explain the reasons why they are making this statement.

If a relationship reaches the counterdependent stage of development before one of the partners is personally ready for this change, this partner may feel scared, angry, depressed, or ashamed. When couples understand that relationships go through developmental stages, it helps them reframe their perceptions and view their conflicts as a sign of growth, challenging though it may be. Working from a developmental perspective can also help partners understand that the underlying causes of the conflicts were present at the beginning of the relationship, but that they needed time together and feelings of safety in order for them to surface.

Most relationships, too, contain invisible shock-, trauma-, or stress-related issues that can cause conflict. Perhaps there are subtle differences between partners regarding energy levels or the need for novelty, change, and freedom. Or there may be extreme differences between the partners in levels of sensory perceptiveness, emotional sensitivity, and social introversion and extroversion. These kinds of differences can cause imbalances in the attunement between them, and they can affect the sense of timing of their individual growth and different styles of social and relational expression that can complicate couple communication patterns.

A sensitive person, for example, may be able to perceive a potential conflict while it is just a spark, whereas the partner may not be able to perceive it until it has ignited into flames. A person who needs more freedom or wants to change the relationship may feel controlled by a partner who wants predictability, routine, and status quo. Control issues could be interpreted as unspoken messages that say, "I'm scared that you will leave me." If this partner feels afraid of being left and has unresolved abandonment traumas or conflicts, his or her partner's desire for more freedom eventually will activate these issues.

These kinds of subtleties in a relationship often create more disruption and dissension than more obvious differences such as age, religion, parenting styles, or values and beliefs. It is important to recognize these subtle differences and to look for them as possible sources of relational friction, because these kinds of differences are very difficult to change.

Moving consciously through the counterdependent stage of development is an important milestone for couples. This passage truly is an affirmation of the strength of the relationship and can be a source of empowerment for the partners to see the positive aspects of this shift. What couples need most to help them through this stage is a cooperative context for understanding the nature of their conflicts and tools for resolving with them.

Helping Couples Create a Partnership Relationship

A cooperative framework helps shift the context of a relationship from being competitive into one that is *transformative* (Weinhold & Weinhold, 2009). It provides opportunities for reframing negative perceptions into more positive perceptions that support both partners' mutual growth and shift from the trauma track of development to the LOVEvolution track. If a couple agrees that they want to develop a cooperative relationship, therapists can use the following guidelines to help them achieve this goal. Each guideline may require several sessions to ensure it becomes firmly established.

Recognize and acknowledge each other's issues involving unresolved developmental shocks, traumas, or stresses. At the beginning of a romantic relationship, couples are usually on his or her best behavior, each trying to show the other person their lovable and capable qualities. It takes spiritual courage to reveal weaknesses and liabilities to a partner, after working so diligently to impress the other with one's assets. Acknowledging that both bring unhealed developmental issues into the relationship adds an element of truthfulness to the relationship that can prevent posturing, denial, projections, and other defense mechanisms.

Giving empathic and compassionate responses to confessed weaknesses and developmental issues helps when they eventually do surface in the relationship. Couples may need empathy and compassion training in order to respond to each other in this manner. Modeling these kinds of responses during a therapy session is very important, as it makes the concept of LOVEvolution real rather than abstract.

Without a framework for helping each other heal the wounds from the past, it can feel risky for partners to expose their vulnerabilities and deficits. Including mutual healing as a higher purpose in a relationship enables the partners to shift into a conscious, committed, and cooperative relationship. The sooner partners risk acknowledging the fact that they bring unresolved developmental issues to the relationship, the better chance they have of getting them healed.

Help each other heal developmental shocks, traumas, or stresses. This step, which calls for skills in understanding and compassion, can create a larger context for the relationship. It can shift the relationship from a competitive model to a cooperative model, where real healing can happen. Then partners can each remove their projections from the other and see the wounded child hiding inside. This shift may require some extended work with some couples who trigger each other frequently.

Be willing to ask for what you want and need 100% of the time. Rather than being indirect or complaining, partners must be willing to ask directly for what they want from the other. This agreement is essential if they are going to break through the their developmental issues and related unresolved conflicts. This agreement also breaks through any residual codependent behaviors and fears of taking charge of getting their needs met without feeling guilty.

In some couples therapy, we have asked couples to contract with each other not to do anything for each other unless their partner asks directly for it or they ask permission before doing it. We call this tool *cold turkey,* and it really breaks though codependent behavior patterns and defenses preventing the healing of developmental issues.

Tell the truth about your behavior, feelings, and needs 100% of the time. Telling the truth frees a person mentally, emotionally, physiologically, and spiritually and removes barriers to intimacy. However, this often requires taking big risks. The best policy, although not the easiest, is telling the truth even if it creates a conflict. When couples do this, they develop the kind of trust in each other that allows the relationship to evolve.

Close all the exits. When the partners get triggered or encounter a lot of conflict, they must agree to stay engaged. A *no-exit agreement* can help any hidden fears surface and eliminates flight responses such as running away, either physically or emotionally, or fight responses, such as blaming the problem on their partner. Neither person can threaten to end the relationship in the middle of a conflict or to avoid facing the issues by fleeing into addictions or another relationship.

If one partner refuses to implement a no-exit agreement, it really is not safe for the other to attempt to express his or her deepest emotions and bring unhealed developmental issues into the relationship for healing. In such situations, the partner ready to face his or her developmental issues can only work alone or with a trusted friend or therapist. A no-exit agreement and cooperative work with a committed partner, however, is the fastest way for a couple to evolve.

Practice equality of power, opportunity, and responsibility. A couple can mutually evolve only if they can create a firm foundation of sharing at all levels in the relationship. Equal relationships create a spirit of cooperation, as well as mutual trust and respect. In a world with economic, social, political, and psychological inequalities, relationship equality is difficult to achieve without a conscious, concerted commitment. The partners also must commit to using cooperative conflict resolution methods.

Redefine intimacy. A couple can choose to define everything they do where they are being truthful and open-hearted as intimacy: the intimacy of cocreation; the intimacy of regressing and having your partner trigger a memory in you involving unhealed developmental shock, trauma, or stress; the intimacy of being separate; the intimacy of yelling; the intimacy of holding and comforting; the intimacy of being sexual; and the intimacy of mutual healing. This reframe may take some couples a while to master and integrate.

Respect each other's boundaries. Partners can create a great deal of freedom and inspire a great amount of respect for each other's space when they are able to identify their boundaries and negotiate clear agreements about sharing their physical and psychological space. This is where an agreement to tell the truth 100% of the time is essential. Many of the triggering experiences in a relationship involve past experiences of boundary violations, so this guideline becomes a very important part of the healing process.

Develop common spiritual practices. Spiritual practices can take many forms, from formal activities such as prayer, meditation, or attending church to informal practices involving walks in the park or exercising together. Moments of quiet, deep connection can provide important islands for attunement and intimacy.

While the outer world stops, partners touch into that place of timeless connection and eternal love. Moments such as these nourish their souls and offer support for coping with the stresses of daily living. We have found that couples who have a deep spiritual connection can better weather the storms in their relationship, particularly when they are working together to heal their developmental shocks, traumas, or stresses.

Keep all relationship agreements and negotiate any changes directly. Whenever circumstances around an agreement change, the partners must renegotiate a new agreement. Broken agreements quickly undermine relational trust and good will, especially if they are broken unilaterally and without negotiation. Breaking agreements is often related to unhealed developmental issues involving past agreements that were not kept while growing up. In addition, couples often have different standards about agreements, and it is important to negotiate some middle ground.

Work cooperatively to resolve intractable conflicts at their source. One of the most powerful and affirming parts of a cooperative relationship is helping each other heal the developmental issues at the source of conflicts. We can testify that this kind of cooperative work opens tremendous intimacy in a relationship. It is what people say they want but are afraid to ask for. The therapist's job is teaching them how to do this healing work with each other.

Helping Couples Learn the Differences between a Dominator and Partnership Relationship

One of the factors that fosters drama triangle dynamics in couple relationships is the dominator paradigm containing inequities in power. The drama triangle involves three revolving roles: the persecutor, the rescuer, and the victim. The most dominant or most powerful person in the relationship often acts out the persecutor role, the second most dominant person acts out the rescuer role, and the weakest person acts out the victim role.

Dominator relationships involve splitting and polarization, such as positions of dominator/dominated, passive/aggressive, and win/lose, to create hierarchical structures. These dualities do not support couples in revealing and healing the issues involving developmental shock, trauma, or stress that they brought into the relationship. Conscious, committed cooperative relationships involve interdependent interactions based on unity, mutuality, sharing, and the creation of nonhierarchical structures. We compare these two relationship paradigms in Table 12.2.

You can see in the comparison the critical differences in the philosophy and practice of dominator and cooperative relationships. Most contemporary relationships exhibit some characteristics of both paradigms, but the dominator form of relationship is still by far the most prevalent form in this country.

DPW Processes for Healing Developmental Shock, Trauma, and Stress in Couple Relationships

In Table 12.3 we show common presenting issues that clients might bring to a couples therapy session. The table can be used as a guide to help identify potential therapeutic interventions for each specific presenting problem. You can also use this list to assess the degree that this problem or issue is present in your client's history.

If the issue is present in one of the partners, the other person can serve as a *high witness* and remain silent but present for the work of the healing process

TABLE 12.2
Differences between Dominator and Partnership Relationships

Dominator Relationships	Partnership Relationships
Use force or threat to enforce domination	Use the vision of higher consciousness to encourage linking for the common good
Create inequalities in power and decision making	Create equal opportunities for money and share power in decision making
Value violence and exploitation	Value nurturing qualities such as compassion and nonviolence
Enforce rigid sex roles	Fluid gender roles
Are competitive	Are cooperative
Use fear to create separation	Generate hope and high ideals to create unity
Are materially oriented	Are spiritually oriented
See women and children as property	See women and children as equal, unique individuals
Support codependent and counterdependent behaviors	Support interdependent behaviors and intimacy
Follow a path of fear and protection	Follow a path of learning and discovery
Use control, manipulation, and deception in communicating	Use truth, empathy, and directness in communicating
Value either the needs of the relationship or the needs of the individual	Value both the needs of the individuals and the needs of the relationship

Source: From *Conflict Resolution: The Partnership Way* (2nd ed., p. 155), by B.Weinhold and J. Weinhold, 2009, Denver, CO: Love. Reprinted with permission.

during the therapy session or can participate if appropriate. The role of high witness is important for those who are healing developmental issues because most early shock, trauma, and stress happened in isolation and without interventions from a caring person. This lack of external validation and support often makes people question within themselves about whether or not these early relational events actually happened and wonder whether it was just their imagination or whether they are crazy.

Witnessing a partner's healing process during therapy can be very useful in teaching the second partner how to be supportive if the issue emerges outside of therapy. In therapy, it is important, however, not to work with only one person in the relationship on their issues. Make sure each takes a turn to keep a balance

TABLE 12.3

Inventory for Identifying Therapeutic Interventions for Healing Developmental Shock, Trauma, or Stress in Couples

Directions: Place a number in the column marked "Degree Issue Is Present."
Use a scale of 1 to 4 to rate the degree to which an issue is present in your life:
1 = Almost Never, 2 = Occasionally, 3 = Usually, 4 = Almost Always

Presenting Problem or Issue	Degree Issue Is Present	Possible Incomplete Developmental Process from Childhood	Suggested Therapeutic Interventions for Healing Developmental Shock, Trauma, or Stress
Fear of intimacy		Emotional, sexual, physical abuse or invasion of boundaries by caregivers	Use empty chair technique to help release feelings with the counselor serving as a protector.
Anxiety or compulsive behaviors		Possible abuse or neglect of basic needs, shame-based discipline	Teach clients relaxation and meditation techniques.
Passivity, letting others lead		Little support for independent thoughts and/or actions	Role-play parents and give supporting messages for independent thoughts and actions.
Fear of trying new things		Received more "no" messages than "yes" messages	Role-play a parent and give client "yes" messages.
Fear of touch combined with compulsive eating		Experienced sexual and/or physical abuse	Identify possible perpetrators. Have client express previously unexpressed feelings (use pillow to express them on). Ask partner to provide compassion and comfort.
Bored easily, externally motivated		Experienced lack of support for exploratory behavior, may have been a "play pen baby"	Support client in exploring new ideas and activities.
Rejects help from others		Shame-based discipline possibly used to set limits	Help client express feelings about being shamed.
Strives for perfection		Shame and/or other abusive methods of discipline used to control and set limits	Provide unconditional messages to client.
Unable to admit mistakes		Severely punished for mistakes with either shame or hitting	Role-play a parent, giving the client understanding of what happened to them when they made a mistake. Provide positive messages about mistakes being the way to learn.

(continued)

TABLE 12.3 *(continued)*

Presenting Problem or Issue	Degree Issue Is Present	Possible Incomplete Developmental Process from Childhood	Suggested Therapeutic Interventions for Healing Developmental Shock, Trauma, or Stress
Inability to follow through with agreements		Self-management skills were not taught effectively, personal boundaries not respected	Create written agreements with client. Have client decide on a consequence for breaking an agreement and implement it, if necessary.
Inability to handle time and money effectively		Lack of support for self-care	Explore the relationship between "mother" and the material world with your client. Provide client with a time-management tool where all time is structured. Have clients hire a financial counselor to teach them how to manage their finances.
Intimidation or manipulation used to resolve conflict		Not allowed to make own age-appropriate decisions, had "helicopter" parents	Create and enforce a "no-power-plays" contract with your clients. Teach them to express feelings of shame directly.
Difficulty in giving compliments		Lack of support and positive feedback for efforts to be independent	Give client a specific kind and amount of positive feedback every session. Ask them to write positive affirmations.
Overpersonalization of conflicts and other issues, moody behavior		Shame and guilt used to prevent development of independent ideas or actions	Have client use journaling to recover early memories of traumas. Role-play with client to get them to express the feelings and any unfinished conversations.
Low tolerance for frustration and/or ambiguity		Efforts to become separate either overtly or covertly sabotaged, failures were punished	Have client sign up for a wilderness experience or ropes course to develop risk-taking skills.
Unwillingness to be responsible for actions		Lacked effective limit setting, raised with permissive discipline	Teach client to use goal- /limit-setting structures in their life (time, money, energy) to structure realistic goals/limits.
Follows direction of others vs. trusting own wisdom and intuition		Received messages that it was not safe to be a separate person, attempts to separate were punished or ignored	Have client take a public speaking or leadership development class. Have client explore some new activity outside his or her comfort zone that pushes client to take more risks.

(continued)

TABLE 12.3 *(continued)*

Presenting Problem or Issue	Degree Issue Is Present	Possible Incomplete Developmental Process from Childhood	Suggested Therapeutic Interventions for Healing Developmental Shock, Trauma, or Stress
Fear of the future, fears of being left behind, feelings of inadequacy, low self-esteem		Possible unprocessed birth trauma or early abandonment experiences where bonding needs were not met	Use breathwork with client. Affirm client by offering unconditional love.
Difficulty relaxing, chronic body tension		Early tactile deprivation and a lack of constant care as an infant	Have client get massages to experience nurturing, nonsexual touch.
Compulsive eating, smoking, drinking, or sex		Deprivation of nourishment and/or love, basic needs may have been neglected	Give client nurturing messages and support.
Feeling unconnected to others or isolated in the relationship		Early abandonment by those charged with care	Role-play a parent or caregiver providing client with nurturing messages.
Trouble trusting others, suspicious of the motives of other people		Birth trauma and lack of attention to needs at birth	Put clients under a blanket in a quiet room filled with soft lights and soothing music. Have them ask their partner to lead them on a trust walk.
Feeling unloved by the partner		Insufficient loving messages from parents and/or other caretakers, socialization taught through criticism rather than praise	Provide clients with reassurance in time of doubt or fear. Ask clients to identify all the things they wish their parents had said and done during childhood, and then have them ask you to say those things to them.
Unable to define wants and needs, expects others to know how to meet these needs		Parent(s) may have hovered so that needs for feeding, affection, diapering were anticipated and met without the child having to give appropriate cues	Role-play clients' parents and give clients permission to identify their needs and affirm their right to get them met. Ask clients to contract to ask directly for things they want and need.
Unwillingness to negotiate to get needs met		Subjected to win–lose methods of conflict resolution, negotiation interpreted as losing	Ask clients to enroll in a class in conflict resolution and learn win–win methods for conflict resolution. Teach them how to express past feelings about situations where loss was experienced and affirm their feelings and/or have their partner do this.

(continued)

TABLE 12.3 *(continued)*

Presenting Problem or Issue	Degree Issue Is Present	Possible Incomplete Developmental Process from Childhood	Suggested Therapeutic Interventions for Healing Developmental Shock, Trauma, or Stress
Inability to shift from oneness to separateness without great difficulty		Rigid black-or-white atmosphere, some traumatic experiences between the ages of 1 and 2	Assist clients in identifying instances of trauma or repression and encourage clients' expressions of feelings about these experiences. Teach them to learn to identify the gray area in situations
Avoidance of intimacy through workaholism or other compulsive activities		Abusive, invasive, or neglectful relationship with an adult during childhood that made intimacy unsafe	Help clients identify instances of abuse or invasion and witness their expression of feelings about these experiences. Provide the comforting messages they needed to hear from their abusers.
Resistance to developing spiritual practices		Spiritual traumas between the ages of 4 and 12, religious abuse	Help clients identify instances of spiritual trauma and witness their expression of feelings about these experiences.
Fear of abandonment		Removal from mother too soon at birth and taken to nursery, abrupt or extended separation from mother during the first year of life, reinforced by later experiences of traumatic separation	Contract with clients to give them appropriate messages, such as, "I'm leaving now, and I'll be back at ____ " at times of separation. Help them do inner child work to validate and release the feelings of loss and trauma during early childhood.
Breaking and/or forgetting relationship agreements		Unpredictability of parents, broken agreements, sadness and anger about broken agreements	Create a commitment contract with clients about keeping agreements with consequences for breaking them. Process feelings.
Unwilling to accept past conflicts as the source of current conflicts		Unprocessed rage from abusive and/or shame-based discipline and limit setting	Help clients identify instances of abusive and/or shame-based discipline and provide a safe place for the expression of their feelings about these experiences.

Total Score _______________

Scoring*:* Add up the numbers in the ***Degree Issue Is Present*** column for each question to get your score. Check below for the interpretation.

Interpretation:

If your score was between:

30–62 = Little evidence of unhealed developmental shock, trauma, or stress

61–80 = Moderate evidence of unhealed developmental shock, trauma, or stress

62–100 = Significant evidence of unhealed developmental shock, trauma, or stress

100–124 = Strong evidence of unhealed developmental shock, trauma, or stress

between them. It is important to tell the couple that each will be taking turns, and ask which one wants to go first. This prevents one member of the couple from becoming the "sick" or identified patient and the other appearing as "well."

A good place to begin healing shock, trauma, or stress is using clients' current symptoms or conflicts and tracing them back to early childhood events containing unhealed developmental shock, trauma, or stress and incomplete developmental processes. Table 12.3 serves as a self-inventory with lists of common symptoms and their possible causes and suggests interventions to use in treating them.

Table 12.3 contains criteria for identifying developmental shock, trauma, or stress during couples counseling and any related incomplete developmental processes. We designed many of the interventions we suggest in this table to heal the relational aspects of developmental shock, trauma, or stress. Particularly, we have utilized those interventions to heal the effects of developmental shock, trauma, and stress that occurred in clients' relationships with their mothers or other primary caregivers during infancy and early childhood.

It is also likely that these same relational components are present in a couple's current relationship. Any unhealed developmental shock, trauma, or stress will continue to recycle in clients' lives until they complete the essential developmental processes that were interrupted or not supported in the codependent and counterdependent stages of their development. The inventory shows how to connect the current issues involving unresolved developmental shocks, traumas, or stresses that might be recycling in a couple's current relationships, along with information about their possible source.

Working with the Narcissistic–Borderline Dynamic in Couples Counseling

We recognize Joan Lachkar (1992) for her groundbreaking psychodynamic research in this particular aspect of couples counseling. She was one of the first to identify the symbiotic union between two people with complementary patterns of relational wounds. Those with shock, trauma, or stress during the codependent stage of development enter relationships as people who have a great need for structure, are emotionally dependent, have a fragile sense of themselves as valuable individuals, and carry feelings of worthlessness. In our developmental model, codependent behaviors are a milder manifestation of these issues, and borderline behaviors are more extreme manifestations.

In their need to be dependent on someone, those with a borderline personality disorder often fuse psychologically with others to the degree that they are emotionally unable to distinguish between their own identity and that of their partner or their children. On the outside, they often appear soft, compliant, and accommodating. Inside, however, they are like very young children begging for attention and love. They have poor impulse control and live anxiously, fearing that they will be abandoned. During the splitting phase of the counterdependent stage of their development, they likely created the belief that "You're okay, I'm not okay."

Those who primarily suffered shock, trauma, or stress during the counterdependent stage of development enter relationships with unhealed narcissistic issues of entitlement, grandiosity, euphoria, and omnipotence. These characteristics are very visible in those with a narcissistic personality disorder. These individuals often appear as very arrogant, charismatic, extroverted, and attention seeking. They are typically demanding, perfectionistic, self-entitled, and have a great need for approval and ego stroking.

Narcissistic adults were almost always abused either physically or emotionally by their parents during childhood. They were forced to deny their own needs and their sense of self and forced to create a false self that pleased their parents. Often they were expected to perform and excel in ways that make the parents look successful in the eyes of the world. The loss of their true self left them with a deep sense of personal inadequacy. The false self hides this inner inadequacy and helps create a set of behaviors that makes them extremely emotionally vulnerable to rejection. In the splitting phase of the counterdependent stage of their development, they created the belief that "I'm okay, you're not okay."

So the narcissist has a need for attention and an "I'm okay, you're not okay" belief, while the borderline has a need for love and a "You're okay, I'm not okay" belief. The complementary nature of each person's beliefs about who is okay and who is not fit like a hand in a glove, so it is not surprising that these two personality types are often attracted to each other in an unconscious attempt to get their reciprocal needs met.

In choosing a marital partner, the narcissist (more commonly the male) makes sure his partner will adoringly follow his lead in every aspect of their lives. He expects to be mirrored perfectly, to receive absolute loyalty, adulation, compliance, and selfless service. This particular kind of couple has an unspoken understanding that the narcissist will never have to admit mistakes, nor will his faults and failings ever be pointed out, even in the slightest way. If problems arise, the borderline partner is to gladly assume responsibility for them.

The dependent borderline willingly makes this contract with the charming, charismatic, caring, and loving narcissistic hero who has come to rescue her. Now relieved of being responsible for herself, she focuses all her attention on her partner in an all-out display of her devotion. She sacrifices herself, her energy, her interests, her beliefs, her values, and her self-worth in the hope that her devotion will draw him closer to her. Finally, she fantasizes, she will find the perfect parent with whom she can unconsciously complete her unfinished bonding work.

This symbiotic bond unfortunately operates more like a "bond" that fuses them together in a "dance of intimacy" in which neither can ever get what he or she wants, in spite of their great efforts. Their complementary projections serve as a kind of psychic glue in which each needs the other to play out personal relational dramas involving unidentified and unhealed development shock, trauma, or stress.

While Lachkar typically works alone with narcissistic–borderline couples, we always work as cotherapists. This allows us to support both partners without getting caught in drama triangle dynamics that are so common with couples struggling with narcissistic–borderline dynamics. The therapeutic goals we focus on are simple in principle, but complicated in practice, as these particular couple dynamics are complex.

The first principle is to support the partner with codependent, one-down borderline characteristics in becoming stronger and emotionally more self-sufficient. The second principle is to support the person with counterdependent, one-up narcissist characteristics in releasing the false self beliefs and behaviors in order to discover the hidden or dormant true self. Both of these processes take time. In order for them to be effective, however, both people must really want to change. Otherwise, therapy just becomes a circus of drama, projection, blame, splitting, denial, and magical thinking, particularly with the more codependent borderline partner.

Working with clients who have narcissistic behaviors is a specialty that requires that the counselor or social worker possess a very strong and highly developed sense of self and the ability to stay centered under duress of criticism, to tolerate one-up power plays, and circumvent strategies designed to "win the game." James Masterson (1993) wrote what we consider to be the definitive clinical book, *The Real Self: A Developmental and Object Relations Approach to the Treatment of the Closet Narcissistic Disorder of the Self.*

Clinical work with borderline clients is a very different kind of specialty that also requires a strong sense of self, the capacity for coping with lots of drama, tolerance for manipulation and threats, and the ability to cope with a lot of ambivalent behavior. While we have found many good books on this topic, our favorite is *I Hate You, Don't Leave Me* by Jerold Kreisman and Hal Straus (1989). We prefer this book because it is written in layperson's language that more sophisticated clients can read.

The therapist's goal is to stay centered throughout these cycles of extreme behavior and to serve as a stabilizing force. This constancy and consistency provides an emotional container that helps borderline clients gradually feel safe and protected and helps them to trust that they can find the middle ground in their needs, wants, and behaviors. Both therapists and clients can use Table 12.3 to help identify symptoms of developmental trauma that appear in both codependent/borderline and counterdependent/narcissistic therapy issues.

DPW Therapeutic Intervention: Sculpting Diagnostic Exercise for Couples

We have used this diagnostic exercise many times and always found it extremely useful in quickly identifying core developmental issues that are keeping the relationship stuck. It helps us quickly identify the interventions needed to move the couple forward in the healing process. Plan to take at least 1½ to 2 hours to complete the process with a couple.

Preparations and instructions for the couple

- Preface sculpting with an overview of how couples' traumatic histories interlock and have a kind of "cosmic perfection" to them. The sculpting exercise shows couples how "right" they are for each other from the perspective of triggering and healing each other's developmental issues. The rightness in choosing to be with each other often has a feeling of being guided from some higher level of knowing that often feels and appears "cosmic" in nature to couples.
- If possible, videotape the sculpting to use in working with the couple. Let them take it home with them after you have seen it. You may even use a session to go over it with the couple to point out things they may have missed in the process. When they get stuck in unraveling their individual pieces of their dynamic, you can refer back to the dynamics displayed in the sculpting.
- Work with one person at a time. Have them decide who will be the sculptor and who will be the sculptee. The sculptor looks at his or her part of their relationship dynamic first.

Step 1: Identifying the link between the past and the present

a. Remember the very worst conflict you have had, one where you hit the wall and were left feeling hopeless about finding a resolution to it—perhaps you thought about leaving the relationship.
b. Using no or very few words, make a freeze-frame kind of photo of this conflict.
c. Show what this conflict looked like by moving your partner so that his or her body, body language, and facial expression illustrates how he or she looks to you during the conflict.
d. Now sculpt yourself without words. Show how you react when your partner goes into this body posture through positioning your body, gestures, body language, and facial expression.
e. Ask the sculptor to close his or her eyes and report what he or she is feeling at the moment of the impasse. Then ask some of the following questions:
    - When you go into this interaction with your partner, what feeling do you feel?

- What is the earliest memory of feeling this feeling?
- How old do you feel? What was happening in the memory?
- Where do you feel this feeling in your body? Focus on this body feeling and breathe into it so that you can feel it more deeply.
- Who from the past event does your partner represent in present time?
- What did you need from this person in the past conflict to have resolved it?

f. Take a few minutes to process the results of this step with the sculptor. Ask:

- Were you aware that you were regressed to an earlier age when you reached the impasse?
- What didn't you get to say or do in the original conflict or encounter?
- What needs didn't you get met then that are still trying to get met in this relationship?
- What did you do to protect yourself in the original conflict that you still use today when you get in a conflict like this one?

g. Ask the person who was sculpted the following questions:

- Were you aware that when you are in this kind of conflict, your partner is regressed to a young age (state the age if it was shared)?
- How does learning this about your partner help you see him or her in a different light?
- Were you aware that you appeared the way your partner sculpted you?
- Does knowing his or her perception of you help understand his or her behavior in the conflict?

Step 2: Clarifying the vision of the couple's future

a. Context: "If you could work through this conflict in present time, what would your future together look like?" This question helps determine whether the couple is working more on individuation issues or if one of the two is more invested in getting divorced. This is important in determining the course of counseling.
b. Assuming that you are able to get through this impasse, make a sculpted snapshot of your vision of your future together. Shape your partner and then shape yourself in relationship to him or her.
c. Ask each person how this vision feels, beginning with the sculptor.

Step 3: Using the future vision of the relationship to resolve the present-time conflict (assuming that it indicates staying together)

a. Have couple resume sculpting postures created in Step 1.
b. The goal is to help the couple develop a pathway from the present impasse to the vision of a future without this impasse.

c. Tell the sculptor that he or she is 100% responsible for changing his or her part of the conflict by changing his or her behavior during the conflict in order to move toward the vision he or she has.
d. The internal part of this shift involves:
   - recognizing that he or she is in a regression and that the partner in present time is not at the source of the conflict and
   - initiating proactive shift in behavior to return him- or herself to an adult state of consciousness.

e. Reconnect step by step nonverbally with the partner using micro-movements and no words to move toward the vision that contains the resolution of this conflict.
   - Make it a reciprocal process where the sculptor takes a step and then asks the sculptee to take a step as well, if he or she feels able.
   - Identify what he or she needed from the other person in the past conflict.
   - Share this information with the partner.

f. Discuss how it felt to take full responsibility for resolving the conflict.
   - Repeat the process in slow motion so that the steps are clear.
   - Talk about the reciprocal nature of the process so that each positive step by one person evokes a positive step by the other.
   - Ask the person being sculpted how it felt to see the other person taking the lead to get the conflict resolved and what shift occurred in them as a result.

Step 4: The therapist uses content from the first sculptee's part of the exercise to summarize his or her history of developmental shock, trauma, or stress.

Step 5: Reverse sculptor/sculptee roles

- Repeat Steps #1–4 above

Step 6: Sit down with the couple and review the exercise with them.

a. Couples often get very emotional during this exercise, particularly when they process through the regressive pieces in both the sculptor/sculptee roles. Help them process their feelings and identify and summarize how they see their patterns of trauma interlocking.
b. Focus on the ongoing resolution of the trauma for each person using Step 3, focusing on the future vision of the relationship to resolve the present-time conflict (assuming that it indicates they want to stay together).
c. In some cases, it becomes clear that their visions of the future are not very compatible. If that is the case, you will need to explore with them their options for the future. You can suggest continuing counseling to help them re-

form their relationship in a new way to create a more compatible vision or to help them end their relationship in a healthy way. We make sure to tell couples that we are not invested in them staying together unless that is what they decide.

Case Example: Using DPW in Counseling with a Couple

Craig and Lindsey came to us for therapy in the midst of an intense relationship crisis. On the verge of a physical separation, they were concerned their marriage was in permanent breakdown. Both had been married and divorced before, Craig twice and Lindsey once. Having been through the cycles of grief and feelings of failure in their earlier breakups, they were not optimistic that they could make it through another round of this kind of suffering. Their goal was learning why their relationship was not working in spite of the effort that they had put into it and to learn new skills that would help them become closer.

We began by administering and reviewing their completed inventories on codependency, counterdependency, developmental trauma, and addiction to adrenaline. Then we conducted an extensive intake with them about their early childhood experiences, their relationships in their families of origin, and also their previous marriages and significant relationships. Lindsey had no children but was an avid pet lover, while Craig had two teenaged children with his first wife.

We noticed as we were discussing their early childhood experiences and relationships in their families of origin that they each described them as fairly normal, without traumatic, shocking, or stressful events and with the past as having very little influence on either their histories of broken relationships or their current marital issues.

When we listened to Lindsey's version of their problems, she spoke at length about her efforts to make Craig happy. She tried to come home from work early to do all the housework, get outside chores done, and make dinner before he got home from work. She made a special effort to eat with Craig and listen to him talk about his day. Her biggest issue was Craig's complaints that she was not able to meet his needs despite her best efforts. Lindsey said Craig complains about how she does things and tends to pick at her about little issues. The food may not be prepared exactly to his liking or she may have failed to complete a chore that he wanted done. His constant criticism, she said, was driving her away. More and more she had been spending time with her parents and friends.

Craig's version of their problems was quite different. His biggest complaint was that Lindsey was always distracted with other interests and did not seem present even when she was with him. He had become suspicious that she was having an affair and had begun watching her outings away from home more carefully. He also described his discomfort about how she behaved around men in her family and in the community, seeing her as overly affectionate and somewhat flirtatious with them. He also did not like how she cuddled with her dog rather than with him.

Then we asked Craig about his two previous marriages and why he thought they failed. His response to this question was quite revealing. For several minutes he talked negatively about his former wives, their faults, their problems, and their inability to meet his emotional needs. When we asked what specifically he had contributed to the failed marriages, he could not think of anything other than he had just married the wrong women.

In a similar exchange with Lindsey about her failed relationships, she talked mostly about herself, how early she had married the first time, how few relationship skills she had as a new bride, and about how her parents' marriage had been a poor role model for her. After her divorce, she lost confidence in herself as a marriage partner and had avoided marrying again until she met Craig.

The two of us could see some of the underlying problems Craig and Lindsey brought into their marriage. Rather than analyzing them and giving a lot of information about our perceptions of the problems, we decided to do the sculpting exercise to identify their underlying issues.

Lindsey took the first turn as sculptor, with Janae coaching her through the sculpting process to seek the source of her part of their intractable conflict. Lindsey began by sculpting Craig so that he had his hands on his hips and a stern and disapproving scowl, as he looked down on her. Then she positioned herself below him, on her knees, looking up at him. When we asked her what she was feeling, she said "sad, scared, overwhelmed, and judged." The earliest memories she had of these feelings were when she was about 5 years old, when she watched her mother being yelled at and criticized by her father.

For a few moments, she went inside and then sank deeper into this memory and the feelings that began flooding her. Then she slowly looked up at Craig and said, "When you yell at me and criticize me, I feel just like Mama. And you sound just like my dad. Mama couldn't stop him from yelling at her—she just stood there frozen. And that's how I feel with you—frozen." Craig looked shocked when she said all this, and then he looked confused.

During the time Lindsey had been turned inward, Janae stood close to her and focused on creating and surrounding her with an attuned field of energy to support her as she moved close to the edge of a shock state. After Lindsey began to talk, Janae asked what she needed when her parents were caught up in their fight. Lindsey said, "I needed them to know how scared I was and that I was feeling everything they were feeling—Daddy's anger at Mama, Mama's terror, and their fear that they were on the edge of a divorce. I was totally overwhelmed with it all, and they didn't even know it. Then Daddy drove off in the car, and Mama went into the bedroom and laid down. I just sat there all alone in the living room not knowing what to do."

Then Janae asked Lindsey, "What did you need when you were sitting alone in the living room?" and she said, "I needed my Mama to come and hold me. Or my grandma, anybody! I was just so scared." "So," Janae said, "when you and Craig get into a fight and he yells at you, you regress back into this memory and feel like you are 5 years old again. Is that right?" Lindsey nodded. Janae looked over at Craig and saw the stricken look on his face. "Were you aware this is what was happening inside Lindsey when the two of you get into a fight?" "No," he said. "I had no idea. I thought she was just playing victim and trying to make me feel bad for hurting her feelings."

At this point in the sculpting process, Lindsey had shown us how this particular childhood event left a shock imprint on her nervous system, one that contained unmet needs for safety, protection, and comforting, and a sensitivity to criticism, yelling, blaming, and being abandoned both emotionally and physically. Because she had not been able to resolve her internal conflict about wanting emotional and physical support from the very people who were hurting her, she became immobilized and triggered into a shock state during her conflicts with Craig.

After connecting the dots between unresolved developmental shock during Lindsey's childhood with her present-time conflicts with Craig, we wanted to determine whether the relationship was so irretrievably broken that it could not continue, or whether the relationship dream was still alive for Lindsey and hope remained for continuing it. So Janae asked her to sculpt her vision of the future between her and Craig, assuming they were able to heal the old traumas that were keeping them in conflict.

Lindsey thought for a while, then went to stand beside Craig and joined her left hand with his right. Then she began walking with him side by side, alternately looking forward and then at him. She looked very happy to be with him and to be moving toward some unseen but anticipated future together. This told us that our focus with her would be supporting her in making the relationship with Craig work.

Then Barry coached Craig while he sculpted his perception of their conflict. Craig placed Lindsey standing with her arms crossed and with an angry, disgusted look on her face. He positioned himself several feet from her, with a yearning look on his face. Then he reached out his arms toward her, holding them for a moment before dropping them. His face looked sad, lonely, hopeless, and powerless. Lindsey stayed unresponsive to him and ignored his outreached hands. Barry asked Craig to close his eyes and then notice what he was feeling in this freeze-frame of their conflict. Craig was quiet for a moment and then said, "I feel like a failure. I can't accomplish what I want to."

Then Barry asked Craig to feel these feelings as deeply as possible and then to search back in time to the earliest memory he had of feeling this way. He was quiet for a long moment and then said, "I felt like this when I discovered my first wife was having an affair and I couldn't do anything about it." After a minute or so, he said, "I also felt this way after my grandma's death when I was 6. She loved me so much and no one told me directly that she had died. I overheard the news in a phone conversation my dad was having with my aunt. Everyone was so upset because her death was unexpected, and they all went into this panic. But they ignored me. No one even knew how much I loved her, more than my mother even. No one ever talked with me about her death, about what happened. No one could see how much it affected me, and no one helped me through it. I had to do it all alone."

Barry asked Craig what he needed at the time of his grandmother's death. He thought about it for a moment and then said, "I wished they had just spent time with me, talked with me about what happened, and helped me understand it all. People just turned it into a big secret!" Then Barry asked him what he needed in that moment. He said, "for someone to understand what I was feeling, how lost I was after that, how much I missed Grandma. I probably needed to cry about losing her."

Then Barry asked Craig if he saw any similarities between what happened after his grandmother's death, his first wife's infidelity, and his conflicts with Lindsey. He thought about this for a while and then said, "Well, it helps me understand how early I began feeling alone, about how I have this expectation that those I love will either ignore me or leave me, and that I sometimes push people away to protect myself from the possibility of losing someone I love again. Maybe I really haven't let Lindsey in my heart and keep her at a distance by criticizing her."

Barry stopped for a moment at this point to check in with Lindsey. When he asked her how she felt watching Craig regress into his 6-year-old memories and relive his experience of losing his grandmother, she teared up a bit and said, "I had no idea that's what was really happening. I just thought he was a man with a hard heart."

After helping Craig connect the dots between the unresolved developmental trauma during his childhood with his present-time conflicts with Lindsey, we wanted to determine whether the relationship was so irretrievably broken that it could not continue, or if his relationship dream was still alive and hope remained for continuing it. So Barry asked him to sculpt his vision of the future between him and Lindsey if they were able to heal the old traumas that had them trapped in conflict.

Craig looked uncomfortable and stood silent for a minute or so. Then he moved to within about 3 feet of Lindsey and held his arms out toward her. He looked at her with a loving expression on his face and waited. Lindsey responded to the look on his face and outstretched arms by reaching out her own arms and smiling back at Craig. Then Craig moved closer to her, and they embraced, holding each other ever so gently.

The last step in this session with them was helping them understand the steps they each needed to take to break through their patterned behaviors of rejection and disengagement. In slow motion, each walked step by step from the original freeze-frame sculpting of his or her present-time conflict and moved toward their images of a happy future together, alternately embracing and walking hand in hand. This helped them understand in a very concrete way that change is a slow process, that it moves step by step, that each has to be aware when they are projecting their internal conflict and feelings on the other, and that their commitment to be together provides the power and strength needed to help them get through the tough places.

Then we sat and debriefed the sculpting exercise for about 20 minutes. It was interesting to observe how their once very different perceptions of their conflict had shifted, and they began recognizing the similarities between them. Both, they recognized, were imagining that the other was judging and then rejecting. Both saw how they retreated when they got triggered, and Craig could see how he yelled at Lindsey the way his father yelled at his mother. Perhaps most interesting was Craig recognizing that he had been playing out his father's relational patterns of having several broken marriages and relationships. We could see the relief on Lindsey's face when Craig talked about this, as she seemed to understand only too well how much he is like his father.

Craig and Lindsey's homework assignment was to work on re-patterning their responses to each other when they got triggered. We suggested that they take a time-out if they got into a conflict to keep it from escalating. During this time-out, each person was instructed to look at him- or herself and his or her part of the conflict, using a list of questions for resolving intractable conflicts (Weinhold & Weinhold, 2009, p. 135). Each agreed to be 100% responsible for breaking his or her part of the relationship dynamic and to removing the projections each was putting on the other.

About 3 weeks later, Lindsey made an appointment to see Janae. She explained when she first arrived that she and Craig had attempted to use the tools that we had suggested but without much success. Initially, she said, they got closer, and she started opening up more to Craig, but then he refused to look at his part of conflicts during their time-outs. Instead, he returned with a laundry list of complaints about what she was doing wrong and filibustered during conflicts to make sure that he was absolved of any responsibilities.

We were not terribly surprised, as we had seen the strong narcissistic–borderline dynamics between them from the very beginning. Lindsey's efforts to accommodate to Craig's needs appeared to have pushed him beyond his intimacy comfort zone and stirred up repressed emotions and awarenesses that he was not ready to address.

Of particular interest was Lindsey's description of Craig's satisfaction with our joint therapy session, mostly because he really felt heard and emotionally supported. His biggest problem continued to be Lindsey's lack of willingness to take all the responsibility for their problems and to devote herself more to him and his needs. He was, it appeared, looking for a woman who would dote on him and indulge his need for perfect narcissistic mirroring in the way that his beloved grandmother had. About 2 months later, Lindsey moved into her own place and continued to work on herself. She decided not to hurry through the process of legal separation and perhaps divorce until Craig no longer did things that triggered her. She had come to understand that he served as a great mirror for her and began to feel grateful for learning so much about herself in this relationship.

To put the world right in order,
we must first put the nation in order;
to put the nation in order,
we must first put the family in order;
to put the family in order,
we must first cultivate our personal life;
we must first set our hearts right.

Confucius

CHAPTER THIRTEEN

A Systems Approach to Healing Developmental Shock, Trauma, and Stress in Families

The evolution of family relationships follows a developmental model that parallels that of individuals and couple relationships. Adult members of a family bring with them into their family system all the unresolved conflicts and issues involving developmental shocks, traumas, and stresses from both the individual and the couple stages of development. This relational baggage eventually surfaces as drama triangle conflicts within the family system.

We define a family system as intimate relationships involving three or more individuals, whether they are parents and a child, three friends, or three coworkers. Most people do not understand that a dramatic shift occurs in relational dynamics when a relational system shifts from two to three people. You may notice that the word "dramatic" contains the word "drama." This is no coincidence. As soon as three people enter a relationship, it contains sufficient players to physically fill all the roles in the drama triangle. These dynamics often do not appear until after a period of time that allows for the development of sufficient trust and intimacy. Once this foundation of security is in place, the effects of the unhealed developmental shocks, traumas, and stresses of all three people are likely to surface. For this reason, conflicts involving relationships of three or more tend to be some of the most intractable and most related to issues containing unhealed developmental shocks, traumas, and stresses.

Staying conscious and clear in a family can be quite difficult, as members' unhealed developmental issues almost effortlessly trigger conflict. The success of family or three-way relationships depends on the degree to which each person has healed his or her developmental issues. In addition, individuals must know how to stay clear of drama triangle dynamics and have completed the splitting phase of the counterdependent stage of development. DPW-trained professionals may have difficulty in navigating relationships with two or more people for the same reasons.

The four stages of family development, like those of individuals and couples, are codependent, counterdependent, independent, and interdependent. The essential developmental processes for each stage are illustrated in Table 13.1. When each individual member of the system, including the parents in their couple relationship, are able to complete their essential developmental processes, the family system can proceed to the next stage of development.

DPW as a Systems Approach for Healing Developmental Shock, Trauma, and Stress in Families

To be effective in working with families, DPW therapists need to understand the uniqueness of family counseling and be able to conceptualize family problems systemically (Fenell & Weinhold, 2003). This means that they must be able to recognize the family as a functioning human system connected by relationships, history, and shared emotional experiences. Further, the effective family therapist or social worker must be able to conceptualize the family system as the client and as the focus of treatment. In addition, the counselor or social worker must develop the skills necessary to attune with each family member and develop interventions that impact the entire family system.

Developing a Family Systems Perspective

To understand family systems and to practice therapy from a systemic approach, therapists must understand that systems exist at many levels. One of the easiest ways to understand the concept of living systems is to examine the human being. The human is a living system composed of subsystems, which in turn are composed of other subsystems.

Just as humans are living systems composed of subsystems, each individual lives in a subsystem of a larger living system. This point is essential in learning to provide therapy for families: The individual human is a subsystem of a larger living system called the family. The family is part of a living system called the extended

TABLE 13.1

The Essential Developmental Processes in Families

Developmental Stages and Processes	Essential Developmental Processes of Family Evolution
Codependent (Bonding)	• Create secure bonding experiences in the family between parents and children • Establish primal trust of family members with each other • Establish healthy emotional communication and social engagement skills among family members • Establish an identity as a family
Counterdependent (Separation)	• Parents and children learn to assert their individual needs and have them supported by other family members • Use of fair, equitable, and nonshaming methods of limit setting and discipline • Resolve conflicts effectively between needs of parents and needs of children
Independent (Mastery)	• Develop individual and couple autonomy within the family structure • Develop core values and beliefs as a family • Achieve object constancy as a family • Bond with nature as a family
Interdependent (Cooperation)	• Build consensus in decision-making skills among family members • Family members learn to cooperate with each other so all get important needs met • Create rituals that sustain a spiritual dimension in the family • Create divisions of labor based on individual interests and abilities • Family members cooperate to help each other to heal their developmental shocks, traumas, or stresses • Family members cooperate to develop each member's fullest potential as a human being

family, which is part of a larger system called the community. The community is part of a larger system, perhaps known as the state, which is also part of a larger system, and so on.

Developmental systems theory (DST) states that when the essential developmental processes are not complete in one stage of a subsystem of a social organization, there may be problems in all of the organization's subsystems. This concept is especially important when a counselor or social worker treats a family in which the problem seems to reside primarily in one of the members. Family systems therapists recognize that, although an individual exhibits the presenting problem, it may be maintained by behaviors of other family members. Furthermore, the systems counselor or social worker recognizes that the problem behavior affects the behavior of other members of the family system.

Most of the family theorists and researchers mentioned in Chapter 2 were initially schooled in models of psychotherapy that emphasized treatment of the individual. These models focused on problems of an intrapsychic nature—problems that resided within the mind of an individual. Each of these theorists sought to understand the nature of problem formation in a more inclusive theoretical orientation. Rather than viewing the client's problem as being intrapsychic in nature, they came to view the psychological problem as a symptom of dysfunctional patterns (Minuchin, 1974) in the identified patient's family system. Thus, they presented a new way of conceptualizing problem formation. With this new conceptualization of problem formation came new models and strategies for problem resolution. This shift in problem formation formed part of the foundation for DST.

The movement from an individual perspective to a systems perspective of problem formation and resolution is recognized as a paradigm shift (Haley, 1971), a term frequently used in the family therapy literature. To most effectively employ systems-based counseling interventions, counselors must experience this paradigm shift and learn to understand how an individual's symptoms are one aspect of a family's interactive sequences of behavior and may serve to stabilize and maintain the current family system.

A classic example of this concept is the case of a child whose symptoms divert the focus of the parents from their marital problems and thoughts about divorce to the problems of the child. By manifesting psychological symptoms, the child has preserved, at least temporarily, the unity of the family system through the symptomatic behavior. The parents rarely dwell on their marital problems when they are needed to help their child. The result of the child's symptomatic behavior is the preservation of the larger system, the family. Thus, the symptoms of the child can mask a larger problem with the family system.

Sources of Developmental Shocks, Traumas, and Stresses in Families

The birth of the first child usually precipitates the shift from couple to family dynamics. The change in dynamics becomes more visible when the child begins separating from the mother or primary caregiver during the counterdependent stage of development. This stage, characterized by a lot of conflict, is the time when adults often use "reverse psychology" on the child to cope with the frustration of psychological splitting exhibited by the child's oppositional and defiant behaviors. When a parent is directive and authoritative, the child may become oppositional and set off a power struggle between them. The child's independent behaviors can trigger the parents' unhealed developmental shock, trauma, or stress.

Family conflicts are complicated because two parallel levels of dynamics are happening simultaneously. The first level is occurring between the child and parents in present time. The second is occurring inside of each of the parents in past time. Psychodynamic psychology recognizes that adults often unconsciously regress to the chronological age of their child and reenact unprocessed feelings and traumas (deMause, 1982, p. 135). This psychological phenomenon, known as regression–progression, stimulates an unconscious restaging or reenactment of the parents' own developmental issues involving shock, trauma, and stress. This restaging provides the parents with a venue where they unconsciously reprocess the shock, trauma, or stress related to same-age experiences from their own childhood. In essence, these parent–child conflicts function as an unconscious "therapeutic" process for the parents.

Parents can be expected to replay their own unhealed developmental shock, trauma, and stress through each stage of their child's development, particularly during the counterdependent stage of development. Each parent becomes psychologically vulnerable to regression–progression experiences during family conflicts, especially when the other parent or caregiver is in conflict with the child. The parents' symbiotic bond and strong identification with the child trigger their own unhealed developmental issues, activating latent feelings and behaviors related to their own struggle for separation.

In short, the boundaries between the parents' experiences of the past and their experiences with their children in the present become blurred. Similar to a posttraumatic stress flashback experience, the past feels as though it is still happening in the present. Parents experience exaggerated feeling states that relate more to their past than the present. For example, when the mother is in conflict with the child, the father may identify with the child as the victim and perceive the other parent as the persecutor. This symbiotic identification with the child triggers rescuer behavior in the father and activates the dynamics of the drama triangle between the two parents and the child.

In another common parent–child drama, a parent sees the child as an enemy. For example, the father perceives that the mother is more attentive to the child than to him. This triggers the father's memories of unresolved developmental issues involving sibling rivalry, stimulating him to criticize the mother for "spoiling" the child. Unable to identify his own unmet needs for nurturing, the father attempts to diminish the strong bond between the mother and the child. Parenting provides a stage upon which both parents can unconsciously or consciously seek resolution to the impact of their own unresolved developmental issues. The recycling of trauma through family dramas is a major cause of intractable family conflicts.

One of the most fascinating aspects of family conflict is the regression–progression phenomenon. While it sits on a foundation of love-based symbiosis between parent and child, it can suddenly shift into a hate-filled situation in which the parent perceives the child as an enemy. The realization that a young child could appear threatening to an adult indicates the presence of psychological projections. Projections involving splitting between past/present, self/other, and us/them are prevalent in family conflicts. Parents' inability to separate past from present and self from other can suddenly trigger a small present-time conflict to erupt into a life-threatening episode of family violence that triggers parents' deepest emotions. The parents' loss of reality and accompanying emotional dysregulation indicates symptoms of either unresolved shock or trauma, critical causes of intractable family conflicts.

The problem with the regression–progression restaging is that it allows adults to unconsciously use children as projective or "therapy" objects to purge themselves of their feelings anchored in their own unresolved developmental shock, trauma, and stress. Rather than working consciously on these issues through counseling or parenting classes, parents simply reenact their trauma with their children. This reenactment is the primary cause of intergenerational patterns of child use and abuse. The solution to regression–progression is conscious parenting in which adult family members use external resources such as therapy or support groups to clear themselves of their unresolved developmental issues. This recommendation applies not only to parents rearing children but also to all adults who provide custodial care for children, such as childcare personnel, schoolteachers and officials, athletic coaches, and church supervisors and teachers.

Parents who are intentionally curtailing their practice of regression–progression typically have done extensive personal work in therapy and support groups to resolve their developmental issues. Most significantly, however, these parents learned to redefine the nature of their wounds. Rather than seeing themselves as "broken," we help them reframe their problems as "developmental delays." This helps them depathologize their dysfunctional behaviors and to accept their projections and episodes of emotional overreactions as cues for looking at their own developmental histories. This reframing helps create a vision for complete healing of developmental shocks, traumas, and stresses and the full realization of their potential.

Acting out through regression–progression, some parents lay traps, lie, threaten violence, manipulate, withdraw their love, humiliate, distrust, scorn, ridicule, coerce, terrorize, and commit violence against their children. Doing these things to their children is a way of proving to themselves that their parents really did love them. This denial and repression of abusive and traumatic experiences is a major force in the replay of conflictual family patterns.

Intergenerational Family Patterns

One of the best ways to identify developmental shocks, traumas, and stresses is by looking for the fractal patterns a family uses to transmit them intergenerationally.

This shows how the same developmental shocks, traumas, and stresses flow from one generation to another when there is no external intervention in the family's behavior patterns. Most people experience a moment of frightening awareness when they see a family pattern or developmental issue begin showing up in their children and grandchildren.

In his book, *Breaking Family Patterns* (Weinhold, 2006b), Barry listed 12 common behavior and relational patterns that are transmitted intergenerationally that contain unhealed developmental shock, trauma, and stress. We list and describe them briefly here, but for full descriptions and ways to heal them see his book. At the end of this chapter are two self-inventories taken from that book that show how to begin the process of identifying these intergenerational family patterns and their connections to developmental shocks, traumas, and stresses.

General Pattern 1: The Reappearance of Unresolved Parental Conflicts

What you know about how to form relationships you learned as a child in your relationships with your parents and siblings or from other adults such as teachers, relatives, and friends. All the attitudes, values, beliefs, feelings, perceptions, and unresolved conflicts you have that impact your current relationships are anchored in what you learned in these earlier relationships by the age of 10. In addition, they left you with many questions that didn't get answered that have carried into your current adult relationships. As a result of these gaps in your understanding, you likely unconsciously recreate in your current relationships the behaviors, attitudes, needs, and feelings that you are still trying to understand. Then you will need to heal the effects of developmental shocks, traumas, and stresses that may have caused these misperceptions and mistaken beliefs.

It is common to selectively perceive and even provoke the reappearance of aspects of your unresolved conflicts in your current partners, coworkers, and bosses. For example, if you had a father who had a bad temper and you never learned how to cope with his temper as a child, you will attract a spouse, boss, coworkers, or friends who have a bad temper "just like my dad." There is an unconscious compulsion to attract people to you who can help you heal your developmental shock, trauma, or stress.

General Pattern 2: The Instant Replay of Codependent and Counterdependent Family Patterns

If your relationship with one of your parents was full of conflict or confusion and contained little emotional acceptance, you may recreate in your current relationships the same kind of relationship dynamics that you had with your parents. For example, if you were a parentized child who was expected to take care of your parents' feelings or needs by being obedient, thoughtful, and subservient to their wishes instead of taking care of your own wants and needs, you may find yourself doing the same kinds of codependent caretaking in your adult relationships.

Most children do not receive the tools they need to help them become emotionally and psychologically separate from their parents, so their most familiar relationship pattern is one involving codependency. When children leave their parents, it is often from a position of counterdependency ("I'll show you I don't need you anymore. I can make it on my own."). They are likely still in this position when they form adult relationships. They may also fall back on the more familiar codependent patterns and alternate them with counterdependent ones. This "co-counter" dance of relationships is one of the primary barriers to intimacy in adult relationships.

General Pattern 3: Living Out Your Parents' Relationship

If your parents' relationship was conflictual and confusing to you, you may try to understand your parent's relationship by recreating it in your adult relationships. You may find yourself fighting the same way they did and may even fight over the same issues, such as money, child-rearing methods, or religion. Also, you may still attempt to "fix" your parents' relationship as a way of finally winning their love and approval.

Specific Family Patterns

Under each of the three general family patterns there are three specific family patterns that relate to the general one. We briefly describe each below.

Specific Pattern 1a: The Parental Disapproval Syndrome

In the first general pattern, you attract relationships in which the personality traits of your parents that you did not learn how to cope with as a child may show up in your current relationships You may find that the things that your parents disapproved of in you when you were a child are some of the same things that you are "sensitive" about and can be easily hurt by with others. Your old wounds may cause you to be triggered into a body memory of the times you were hurt as a child by something someone said or did to you. These represent shocks, traumas, or stresses that have not been healed, and it may seem to you that you are actually drawing this kind of person to you. In truth, that is exactly what is happening. It is your attempt to finally heal the wounds connected to these early developmental shocks, traumas, and stresses.

Labels like "selfish" or "unappreciative" may cut deeper if these were ways you were hurt as a child. You may even use them to disapprove of yourself. Also, you may disapprove of the same things in others that your parents disapproved of in you. In short, you may hold prejudices, beliefs, and values similar to your parents although you may not even be aware of this fact. Again, most of these prejudices, beliefs, and values are formed before the age of 10.

Specific Pattern 1b: Getting Even

You may find yourself using these same disapproval methods with those you perceive as weaker than you. Revenge is a very common way that people cope with feelings of betrayal. It is called the *talionic response* and is characterized by the "eye for an eye" form of retribution that is still legally used in some countries to punish people. This can become a collective method of trying to heal wounds by taking out hurt and angry feelings on others. However, the only way these wounds can heal is by feeling the feelings and expressing them in more appropriate ways. Acting them out on others tends to keep you from feeling your true feelings. You may blow up at someone in order to avoid feeling the emotional pain that you are experiencing.

Specific Pattern 1c: Self-Condemnation

The other way you act out this first general pattern is by "beating yourself up" by using the same disapproval methods and expressions your parents used on you as a child. Sometimes you may hear your inner critic judging your mistakes, saying almost verbatum what your parents said to you as a child. This kind of self-hatred is very destructive to your self-esteem. Have you ever done something embarrassing and then heard yourself calling yourself names such as "stupid" or "you jerk" or some other degrading term that you remember your parents using on you as a child?

Specific Pattern 2a: Acting Weak and Helpless

Under the second general pattern, you tend to recreate in the present the same conflictual relationships you had with your parents when you were a child. You may find yourself acting weak and helpless toward your spouse or boss the same way you did toward your mother when you were a child. You may let others take responsibility for your life either because you do not feel able to do it for yourself or because it is easier to blame them if something goes wrong. Many people get stuck in these dependent behavior patterns and spend the rest of their lives trying to get other people to take care of them. Most alcoholics have this pattern.

Specific Pattern 2b: Life Is a Struggle

Because of the struggles you had with your parents while growing up, you may find comfort and familiarity in your adult lifestyle and relationship struggles. So when there is an absence of struggle or conflict, you may get anxious and uncomfortable and unconsciously attempt to create some chaos or a conflict. It is possible to become addicted to the steady flow of stress hormones that come from the drama of struggle and conflict, making it difficult to tolerate peace and harmony in your life. This can be related to the addiction to adrenaline that we discussed in Chapter 8.

Specific Pattern 2c: Sexual Repression

This specific issue concerns repressed sexual feelings, which can also affect your adult sexuality. Because you are a sexual being and because in most families sex is never openly discussed, normal sexual feelings between parents and children are never verbally acknowledged. Instead, many parents and other adults either overtly or covertly act out their repressed sexual feelings on their children or push them away both physically and emotionally when the child begins to develop sexually. If this happened to you, you may have learned to repress your sexual feelings. You may have been victimized by your parents' sexual acting out or their rejection. In these cases, your adult sexual relationships can be profoundly affected.

Repressed sexual feelings are the most common causes of impotence and frigidity in both men and women and can severely limit your freedom to express your sexual feelings freely and appropriately in your adult relationships. Promiscuous sexual behavior and teenage pregnancies often are the result of perceived parental rejection.

Specific Pattern 3a: The Parentized Child

The third general family pattern involves growing up too fast and taking on adult responsibilities while still a child. This is very common if one of the parents is absent from daily household activities or if a parent is incapacitated by mental and/or physical illness or from drug or alcohol abuse.

Another cause of this pattern is underlying incompatibility problems between the parents that leave both partners with unmet emotional needs. In this case, fathers may parentize their daughters and mothers may parentize their sons by discussing issues and problems that should be the responsibility of adults, such as finances, job problems, relational problems, and extended family conflicts. Most damaging, however, is parents' discussing their marital and sexual problems with their children. These kinds of behaviors, which are considered emotional incest, can be very damaging to children's emotional development.

Unresolved loyalty and legacy issues with your family of origin can confuse matters even more. You may feel you owe your parents great debts that you can only repay by being loyal to them and conforming to their wishes. Becoming an extension of your parents' unresolved lives is another form or parentizing. Here you serve as an object that your parents can manipulate to satisfy their unmet needs. You must break this particular pattern before you can build sustainable adult relationships.

Specific Pattern 3b: The Fear of Success

If you were taught to take care of your parents' wants and needs first and deny your own wants and needs, you may find yourself feeling afraid of being more financially, socially, educationally, and psychologically successful than your parents.

You may limit yourself and your adult relationships in these ways so as not to make your parents feel bad or appear unsuccessful.

Specific Pattern 3c: The Fear of the Unfamiliar

Under the influence of this pattern, you may limit your adult relationships just because you are afraid of the unknown. Breaking your family patterns means venturing out onto unfamiliar waters well beyond those traveled by your parents or other members of your family. Your success in dealing with the unknown will depend partially upon how your parents supported your attempts to explore new and unknown territory. Most parents encourage and support their children's ventures into new and better relationships. They recognize the limitations that they had to overcome and will want their children to have an easier and happier life.

In your innocence, you may have expected this kind of love and support from your parents. Instead, you may have been greatly disappointed and confused when they held on, criticized, controlled, and discouraged your efforts to live a freer and happier life, often asking you to live out their fear of the unknown.

Breaking Intergenerational Patterns

As you become aware of these transgenerational patterns, you can see how your parents are (or were) also scared children with unhealed developmental shocks, traumas, and stresses. You can have compassion for their struggle as people and as parents rather than holding on to resentment and anger over their lack of support. When you are able to see your parents as they really are and not in the idealized way you would like them to be, then you are able to see yourself and others the way you and they really are. This more realistic perspective will set you free to grow up and take charge of healing your wounds, finally establishing the loving, effective adult relationships that you have always wanted.

The best way to break these family patterns is to:

1. Consciously decide to shift from the developmental trauma track to the LOVEvolution track of life.
2. Reexamine your childhood experiences from an "optimal parenting" or LOVEvolution perspective to determine the essential developmental processes in your childhood that are still incomplete.
3. Look for symptoms of unhealed developmental shocks, traumas, and stresses from your early childhood.
4. Identify and plan ways to complete these essential developmental processes in your current couple and family relationships.
5. Express any and all feelings you were not permitted to express as a child.
6. Repattern your relationship dynamics to eliminate the effects of all shock-, trauma-, or stress-related distortions.

TABLE 13.2

DPW Interventions for Completing the Essential Developmental Processes of Families

Stage of Development	Essential Developmental Processes of Families	DPW Interventions for Completing These Processes
Codependent	• Creating secure bonding experiences in the family between parents and children • Establishing primal trust of family members with one another • Establishing healthy emotional communication and social engagement skills among family members • Initiating a healthy family vision and inducting family members into it • Establishing a healthy identity as a family	• Help reestablish consistent parenting practices for the children. • Teach family members how to give and receive unconditional love. • Create a process for parents to exchange nurturing touch and talk between parents and children and between siblings. • Help the family establish effective rules and roles (family sculpting can be used). • Initiate activities to help create common interests, values, beliefs, and goals among family members.
Counterdependent	• Parents and children learning to assert their individual needs and have them supported by other family members • Using fair, equitable, and nonshaming methods of limit setting and discipline • Parents being able to set effective limits for themselves and their children • Resolving conflicts between needs of parents and needs of children effectively	• Encourage parents and children to individually explore interests outside the family. • Help parents learn to recognize the unique characteristics and life path of each child. • Help parents identify their needs and the needs of the children. • Help parents build appropriate boundaries between children and parents.
Independent	• Supporting development of individual initiative in family members • Developing individual and couple autonomy within the family structure • Setting limits on children, selves, and extra-family involvement to preserve couple relationship/couple autonomy within the family structure	• Have parents provide children with independence training in managing time, money, school, and extracurricular activities. • Help parents develop a consequence-based method of discipline for children. • Teach parents to establish and maintain boundaries between adult activities and interests and parenting activities.

(continued)

TABLE 13.2 *(continued)*

Stage of Development	Essential Developmental Processes of Families	DPW Interventions for Completing These Processes
Independent (continued)	• Developing core values and beliefs as a family • Achieving object constancy as a family • Bonding with nature as a family	• Help the family learn to achieve a balance between adults' and children's needs. • Help parents to support children's development within and away from the family. • Help the family experience constancy of family relationships and structure during times of stress and/or conflict.
Interdependent	• Building consensus in decision-making skills among family members • Teaching family members to cooperate with each other so all get important needs met • Creating rituals that sustain the spiritual dimension of the family • Creating divisions of labor based on individual interests and abilities • Cooperating to help each other heal developmental shocks, traumas, and stresses • Cooperating to develop each member's fullest potential as a human being	• Teach parents how to manage family affairs through regular family meetings. • Help family members to value and keep agreements between family members. • Help parents to set limits on children, selves, and those outside the family. • Help family members to use power equitably between adults and adults, adults and children, and between children and children. • Help the family to create a high level of physical, mental, emotional, and spiritual resources for all members.

Training DPW Therapists in a Systems Approach to Counseling Families

To be effective in working with couples and families, therapists need to understand the unique concepts of family therapy and to conceptualize family problems systemically. This means that the counselor or social worker must be able to recognize the family as a functioning organism connected by relationships, history, and shared experiences. They must also be able to make effective interventions in the powerful intergenerational fractal patterns that lock families into dysfunctional behaviors and relational structures.

Core Skills for DPW Therapists to Utilize a Systems Approach in Counseling Families

Changing the Regression–Progression Dynamic

The first step therapists can use to stop the regression–progression family dynamic is psychoeducation. Once therapists get family members to understand the nature of developmental shock, trauma, and stress and the regression–progression phenomenon, they can help them consciously decide not to participate in this dynamic. They need to get family members to commit to redefining themselves as transformers of it and to reframing their own life experiences to break free of the developmental trauma track of evolution. Breaking free from the regression–progression dynamic specifically requires that adults become totally responsible for their residue of unhealed developmental shock, trauma, and stress. Making this shift might mean having to shift their whole reality base.

Once therapists have done their own work, they are in a better position to help family members develop an internal sense of object constancy and "I'm okay, you're okay" thinking. This allows members to retain their sense of self-worth even when they have moments of feeling rejected or unworthy during family conflicts. Therapists can teach family members how to create a family environment that supports its members in their effort to develop object constancy. However, when a family member is not able to do this, it indicates the presence of unresolved issues from the splitting subphase of the counterdependent stage of individual development and may require individual therapy.

Resolving Conflicts of Wants and Needs in Families

Family members can be taught how to resolve the most common source of family conflicts—wants and needs. Here we present an eight-step method for resolving conflicts of wants and needs that can be taught to all family members in therapy or in a class that is an adjunct to family therapy.

1. Describe objectively your perception of the problem or behavior. Begin with *I statements*. Avoid using harsh or judgmental language, *you statements,* threatening body language, and a strident voice. For example, you might begin, "I noticed that you didn't clean up your dishes after you ate last night."
2. Share the way you feel about the person or problem. Keep your focus internal, specifically on your inner experience of the conflict to help you stay centered so you do not escalate or lose your objectivity. Continuing with the previous example, you might say, "I felt angry with you when I saw the dishes sitting there."
3. Describe the tangible effects or results of the problem or issue on you and/or your relationship. Speak authentically in a way that helps the other person realize that his or her behavior has created a consequence that affects the bond or connection between you. Tell the other person how what he or she

did affected you by saying, "When I had to clean up your dishes to use the sink, I didn't feel close to you and I didn't look forward to being with you tonight."

4. State directly what you want from the other person. Formulate this request ahead of time in your mind so you can speak precisely. Be prepared to enter into a negotiation process, if necessary, to get your need met by having a series of options or solutions that might be acceptable. Emphasize how much you value and care for the other person. In the example, you might say, "What I want is to be able to feel close to you, and to do that, I want you to keep your agreement to clean up your dishes after you eat."
5. Ask the person directly for what you want. Asking directly gives the other person a choice. When people have choices, they are more likely to act cooperatively and to be willing to negotiate if the initial suggestion is not acceptable to them. You need to ask directly, "Are you willing to do that?"—then be prepared to respond to a refusal of cooperation with the question, "Well, what are you willing to do?"
6. Use reflective listening. At this point, the other person may likely give an explanation for his or her behavior. Repeat what you hear, so the partner feels heard and understood, before going on to the next step. Avoid getting bogged down here by defending yourself, blaming the other, complaining about him or her, or escalating by bringing in other issues. Focus on your feelings of compassion and caring for your partner as you reflect what you think he or she is feeling. You can say, "When I get angry about these things, you look like you're feeling hurt and angry. Is this true?" Once you have reflected the statement, you may want to return to your original question: "Would you be willing to do that?"
7. Negotiate if there are differences between what you want and what the other person is willing to give or do. If the other person refuses to cooperate with your initial request, ask, "What would you be willing to do?"
8. If you are unable to negotiate the differences, look for other sources of the conflict. In this case, you may have to agree to disagree and invite the other person to join you in exploring the conflict further. You might say, "I see that we just don't agree on this issue, and I accept our disagreement. Would you also agree that we can't find a partnership solution at this time?" Or you might say to the other person, "Would you be willing to explore our differences further, looking for possible conflicts of values or beliefs or look for other possible sources of this conflict?"

Resolving Conflicts of Values and Beliefs in Families

Conflicts of values and beliefs are usually more complex and more difficult to resolve than conflicts of wants and needs. They require a different set of skills and have to be directed more on developing mutual understanding and respect for differences than trying to change the other person's values and beliefs. A seven-step process for resolving conflicts of values and beliefs follows.

1. Take turns listening to each other's views of the conflict using reflective listening. Identify the feelings as well as the content. Agree not to state your own opinion or position until you agree that you have reflected what the other person has said. For example you might say, "You seem to be saying that you think I'm trying to control you, and you also seem a little angry and scared to me. Do I understand accurately what you're saying and feeling?" When the other person indicates feeling heard, move to Step 2.
2. Take turns finding the sources of the value or belief conflict. Each person talks about personal experiences that may have led to the formation of this value or belief. You might ask your partner, "What other experiences have you had in your life where you've felt that people were trying to control you?" Again, listen and reflect back the feelings and content for each other before moving forward to the next step.
3. Take turns finding the sources of the feelings. Focus on the feelings and reflect what you hear from the other. Ask, "What other times in your life have you felt this way?"
4. Determine any shifts in awareness. Take turns restating any new perceptions. You might say, "Based on your exploration of the sources of your values or beliefs and your feelings, do you have any new perceptions of your value or belief? Are you feeling any different about my views?" Again use reflective listening.
5. Explore areas of agreement and disagreement. One way to do this is to say, "I think we can now agree that what we originally identified as control was really a desire for more directness in our relationship. Because of our history, where other people tried to control us, we're indirect in our communication with each other. Do you agree that this could be a problem for us?"
6. Make plans to handle any areas of disagreement. This might take the form of saying, "If either of us feels controlled by the other in any way, can we agree to bring it directly to the other so we can talk about it again?"
7. Make plans to handle any strong feelings or reactions. If this conflict brings up strong feelings and reactions in either of you, you may have to look deeper to locate the source of these strong feelings and reactions. You may have hidden developmental shocks, traumas, and stresses that prevent you or the other person from completely listening and communicating respect and understanding. If both parties are willing, a therapist or mediator may utilize the process outlined in the next section for resolving intractable conflicts at their source.

Resolving Intractable Conflicts at Their Source in Families

Intractable conflict is obviously the most difficult kind of conflict to resolve and usually involves unhealed developmental shock, trauma, and stress. To do this conflict resolution in a couple or family, you first need a mutual commitment to work cooperatively on these kinds of conflicts. Then you can utilize the following step-by-step process for resolving intractable conflicts at their source.

1. Ask your partner to role-play the person with whom you had the original unresolved conflict. Ask your partner to participate by saying something like, "Would you be willing to play my father and listen while I express the anger I felt toward him when he divorced my mother and left our family?"
2. Identify the element in the conflict that is unfinished or unresolved. To inform your partner about what you may be needing, you can set the stage by saying something like, "I never got to express my anger at my father and to hear him acknowledge and accept my feelings."
3. Make a contract with your partner. The request must be specific: "Would you role-play my 'functional father' and accept my feelings of anger and really hear my feelings? After I've expressed my anger, I want you to tell me that I have a right to be angry and that you still love me and won't abandon me. Would you do that?"
4. Complete the contract. Sit across from your partner and express your anger at your "father." Your partner, who is role-playing your father, replies, "You have a perfect right to be angry at me. What I did changed your life and made life difficult for you. I'm glad you have the courage to tell me how you feel. I still love you and won't abandon you."
5. Allow yourself to feel the full impact of the role-play. The impact of the role-play may be dramatic or subtle, so allow enough time to fully feel the changes in awareness that might result. You might report, "I'm feeling much lighter and freer. My jaw seems looser, and I notice I'm feeling a little sad. I must be grieving the loss of my dad's presence in our family for the first time since he left. My anger must have blocked me from feeling the sadness."
6. Ask for any additional support. If you need support or feedback from your partner after completing this risky contract, ask for it: "Would you hold me or comfort me while I experience my sadness and grief?" If you do want to be held, clarify whether it is your father or your partner who is doing the holding. If you need to be held by your father, you must renegotiate with your partner to role-play the father. The roles and relationships always must be clear and separate.
7. Allow your partner to leave the role. Use a direct statement to acknowledge that your partner has completed the role play, so you can reenter the present. Say to your partner, "I feel complete now in our role play. We can return to present time." Thank your partner for helping you complete this unfinished business with your father.
8. Return to the current conflict. After completing the unresolved elements from your past conflict, return to the current conflict to see if it now can be resolved. It is usually easy to resolve the current issues once the issues from the past have been resolved.

Holding Family Meetings

Family meetings are an important way to implement partnership couple relationships into a family structure. Here children learn to participate in group decision making, to negotiate to get their needs met, to solve problems, and to resolve conflicts effectively. Children who learn skills by participating in family meetings can apply them outside the family setting. Emphasizing this learning can make implementing family meetings easier, as some members may not see the significance of family meetings. They should be normalized and made a regular part of family life, perhaps structured around family meals.

Couples who are transforming their family structures into a partnership system often notice that their children resist the parents' attempts at reform. These children, who have learned how to function in a dominator family with secrets, triangulation, power plays, and other forms of dirty fighting, may fear losing their position of power in the family hierarchy. Once a new partnership structure is operationalized, the children usually find that family meetings support them in getting their needs met more directly.

Therapeutic Interventions for Healing Developmental Shock, Trauma, and Stress in Families

Read over the list of common issues related to developmental shocks, traumas, and stresses and the related incomplete developmental processes shown in Table 13.3. In the blank before each item in the Common Issue column, place a number from 1 through 10 (1 = not at all, 10 = all the time) that best represents how much that issue was present in your family of origin. Score and interpret your answers after taking the inventory. Then look at the suggested ways to intervene if you are a family counselor.

Pay particular attention to those items that had scores of 7 or more. Your response to these items indicates a strong presence of developmental shocks, traumas or stresses. These situations need to be addressed to heal the developmental shocks, traumas, or stresses that are causing them.

How DPW Therapists Can Prevent Burnout in Counseling Families

Again, the key for the DPW therapist is doing his or her own personal work and getting effective clinical supervision. In addition to these practices, it is imperative

TABLE 13.3

Self-Inventory: DPW Interventions for Healing Developmental Shocks, Traumas, and Stresses in Families

Common Issue	Incomplete Developmental Processes from Childhood	Suggested DPW Interventions for Healing Developmental Shock, Trauma, and Stress
___ 1. Fear of being consumed	Child subjected to "helicopter parenting," parent hovers over the child	Role-play or have a family member role-play a parent who is doing this behavior and ask family members to express any unexpressed feelings.
___ 2. Addiction to activity	Love and acceptance as conditional	Teach family members relaxation and meditation techniques. Have family do them with each other.
___ 3. Victimization	Emotional, physical, and sexual abuse or shame-based discipline	Identify possible developmental shocks, traumas, and stresses and teach family members to use TET process to heal them.
___ 4. Fear of influence from outside the family	Family secrets, an us vs. them attitude	Help family members to uncover any family secrets and look at the impact they have had on the family system.
___ 5. Secrets between family members	Shame-based parenting	Help the family identify possible use of shame to discipline children and the effects it has had on the family system. Teach family members to ask for nurturing support from others in the family.
___ 6. Unequal rights between adults and children	Authoritarian parenting style	Ask family members to examine the source of their beliefs and values. Explore new parenting strategies to help preserve diversity of values and beliefs.
___ 7. Rejecting help from others even when needed	Neglect of needs, shame-based messages about expressing needs	Teach family members to respect and take seriously all expressions of needs by family members. Ask them to examine the source of any resistance to doing this.
___ 8. Control and manipulation used to get needs met	Love and acceptance conditional	Teach family members how to ask for unconditional support and acceptance from others in the family.
___ 9. Lack of respect for personal boundaries	No rights to privacy, children seen as extensions of parents	Teach parents how to say "no" as many ways as they can.
___10. Unwillingness to assume responsibility for actions	Self-management skills not taught effectively, personal boundaries not respected	Teach parents how to structure regular family meetings where all agreements are written down. Each family member decides on his or her consequence for breaking an agreement, if necessary.

(continued)

TABLE 13.3 *(continued)*

Common Issue	Incomplete Developmental Processes from Childhood	Suggested DPW Interventions for Healing Developmental Shock, Trauma, and Stress
___11. Inability to handle time and money effectively	Little support for self-care	Ask the family to invest in time- and money-management tools to improve these skills. If necessary, ask the parents to hire a financial advisor to teach them how to manage their finances.
___12. Intimidation or manipulation used to resolve conflicts	Not allowed to make own age-appropriate decisions	Help parents create and enforce a no-power-plays contract. Encourage and support direct expression of feelings of shame.
___13. Suppression of feelings	Shame used to prevent independent ideas and actions	Teach family members how to use j ournaling to recover early memories of traumatic experiences. Contract with family members to support each other while they express their feelings about this.
___14. Belief in scarcity	Lack of support and positive feedback for independent efforts, no modeling of healthy expression of feelings	Ask family members to give each other specific kinds and amounts of positive feedback every day. Teach family members how to write positive affirmations.
___15. Lack of personal accountability	Efforts to become separate either overtly or covertly sabotaged, failures punished	Ask family members to sign up for a risk-taking, skill-building workshop to develop teamwork and confidence.
___16. Rebellious and acting-out behavior, testing limits	Lacked effective limit setting, raised with permissive discipline practices	Teach parents to set realistic limits for themselves and other family members on a daily basis.
___17. Indirect communication	Received messages that it was not safe to be a separate person, attempts to be separate punished	Ask parents or other family members to take a public speaking or leadership development class. Teach family members how to learn to communicate their feelings and needs directly.
___18. Angry and/or violent behaviors	Possible unprocessed birth trauma or early abandonment experiences in which bonding needs were not met	Teach family members to use breathwork techniques with each other present. Ask family members to hold and affirm each other by offering unconditional love.
___19. Addictive behaviors such as drinking, smoking, eating disorders, and drug use	No support for expressing feelings	Have family members give each other foot massages and other nurturing touch.
___20. Compulsive eating, smoking, drinking, or sex	Deprivation of nourishment and/or love, basic needs possibly neglected	Teach each family member how to identify and ask directly for help in meeting his or her needs.

(continued)

TABLE 13.3 *(continued)*

Common Issue	Incomplete Developmental Processes from Childhood	Suggested DPW Interventions for Healing Developmental Shock, Trauma, and Stress
___21. Feeling unconnected to others or isolated in the relationship	Early emotional or physical abandonment by those charged with caretaking	Help each family member to identify unmet needs and ask each other directly for help in getting them met.
___22. Trouble trusting, suspicious of the motives of others	Birth trauma and lack of attention to needs at birth	Ask parents to arrange for family members to bathe in a quiet room filled with soft lights and soothing music. Have family members lead each other on a trust walk.
___23. Parents using children to make themselves look good to others	Not enough mirroring of children's essence and positive responses from parents	Encourage family members to ask for reassurance from each other in times of doubt or fear. Have them identify all the things they wish their parents had said and done during their childhood, and then ask family members to say or do what was missed.
___24. Inability to define wants and needs, expecting others to just know how these needs should be met	Needs were anticipated and met prior to expression of children's needs for feeding, affection, changing diapers; parents possibly hovered and did not wait for signals for needs to emerge	Teach family members how to identify their own needs and affirm their right to get them met. Teach them to ask directly for things they want and need.
___25. Inability to shift from oneness to separateness without difficulty	Rigid atmosphere with everything either black or white, some traumatic experiences between ages of 1 and 2	Help family members to identify instances of trauma or repression in the family and to ask other family members for support to express their feelings about these experiences.
___26. Unwillingness to negotiate to get needs met	Subjected to win–lose methods of conflict resolution; negotiation interpreted as losing	Ask family members to enroll in a class in conflict resolution and learn win–win methods for conflict resolution. Show family members how to express past feelings about situations where loss was experienced.
___27. Avoidance of intimacy through workaholism or other compulsive activity	Abusive or invasive relationship with an adult during childhood that made intimacy unsafe	Help family members uncover instances of abuse or invasion and ask for support in expressing their feelings about these experiences.
___28. Resistance to participating in spiritual practices	Spiritual trauma between ages of 4 and 12, religious abuse	Help family members to identify instances of spiritual trauma and ask for support in expressing their feelings about these experiences.

(continued)

TABLE 13.3 *(continued)*

Common Issue	Incomplete Developmental Processes from Childhood	Suggested DPW Interventions for Healing Developmental Shock, Trauma, and Stress
___29. Fear of abandonment	Removed from mother at birth and taken to nursery, abrupt or extended physical separation from mother during the first year of life reinforced by later experiences of traumatic separation	Teach parents how to effectively communicate with young children about leaving for any reason, "I'm leaving now, and I'll be back at ___." Teach family members to do inner-child work to validate and release the feelings of loss and trauma during early childhood.
___30. Breaking relationship agreements	Unpredictability used as a way to avoid abuse, invasion, or punishment from caregivers	Have family members develop written agreements with each other, with agreed-upon consequences for breaking them.
___31. Unwilling to accept past conflicts as the source of current conflicts	Unprocessed rage from abusive and/or shame-based discipline and limit setting	Help family members identify instances of abusive and/or shame-based discipline and for support to express feelings about these experiences.

Total Score ______________

Scoring and Interpretation

If your score was between:

310–250 = Presence of many symptoms of developmental shocks, traumas, or stresses in your family
249–100 = Presence of some symptoms of developmental shocks, traumas, or stresses in your family
99–31 = Very few symptoms of developmental shocks, traumas, or stresses in your family

that therapists monitor their level of involvement with their clients and make sure they are not working harder than the clients in resolving a problem.

The other important way to prevent burnout is to monitor carefully any countertransference issues or cues that trigger you in your counseling with families. Working with families is bound to bring up memories of any unhealed developmental shocks, traumas, or stresses for you to heal. Working with families therefore provides the counselor with a unique opportunity to identify his or her own developmental shocks, traumas, and stresses and use the tools that he or she has to heal them.

Case Example: Using DPW in Counseling with a Family

The following example shows how we used DPW with a family. As you read through the description, see if you can identify the key DPW principles.

Leonard, a single professional father with five children, came to us with his fiancée, Melanie, for couples counseling. The two of them had been dating for about a year and were beginning to experience recurrent conflicts. Some of the conflicts were related to their couple relationship, but the most difficult ones involved family issues.

Leonard had been divorced for 4 years and recently had gained custody of his children through a lengthy legal battle. Their mother was unhappy about her loss of custody and was filing a countersuit. Melanie, a single woman with no children, had been spending a lot of time with Leonard and his family and saw problems within the family system. The children, whose ages ranged from 3 to 14, were exhibiting signs of posttraumatic stress, including bedwetting, fighting, dependency, and poor academic performance at school. Leonard had hired a housekeeper to provide childcare, cleaning, and laundry services for the family. The housekeeper sometimes brought her own two children with her to work.

Melanie actually made the therapy appointment for the couple and identified several concerns that she felt needed to be addressed in their counseling. First was a conflict between her and Leonard regarding the children's need for therapy to help them adjust to their new home and school environments. The second was the number of recurring intractable conflicts between the two of them. These conflicts had been present prior to the children coming to live with Leonard but had increased after they arrived. The third concern involved problems with the housekeeper bringing her children with her to her job at Leonard's home and the regular conflict between her children and Leonard's. The fourth issue related to the stress created by Leonard's former wife's attempt to regain custody of the children.

This complex case involved several levels of work. After the initial session with Leonard and Melanie as a couple, we counseled them separately to look at the individual issues they were bringing into their relationship. We did an intake of their personal history and administered a series of diagnostic inventories to assess their individual development. After discussing the results of these assessments with them, we helped each of them understand the role of unhealed developmental shocks, traumas, and stresses in their intractable conflicts with each other, their children, and the housekeeper. This was a rather difficult task, as both Leonard and Melanie preferred to see Leonard's former wife and her parenting as the source of all of their family problems. It took a lot of patience and empathy to mirror and validate the impact of their own very significant childhood shocks, traumas, and stresses on their current conflicts and problems.

Initially, we rotated between individual counseling with Leonard and Melanie and conjoined couples counseling. We also administered the diagnostic inventories for couples and helped them see how the conflicts in their relationship mirrored unhealed individual issues from their childhoods. We also spent a considerable amount of time helping them recognize the traumatized parts of each other and develop compassion for each other's wounds. This helped them identify their childlike behavior that emerged when they regressed during conflicts. They began to work cooperatively to help each other heal the effects of their developmental shocks, traumas, and stresses and get some of their unmet developmental needs met. This skill increased the level of intimacy between them and strengthened their relationship sufficiently to progress to the next level of intervention.

We gave Leonard a number of books on parenting to read and then began a series of family counseling sessions. Because of the size of Leonard's family, we conducted these sessions in his home. We have found home visits to be extremely effective. The children tend to behave more spontaneously, without the kind of constraints that office visits create. This allows us to see family dynamics very quickly. We helped Leonard design and implement a format for family meetings that would help build a more democratic family structure. This was the first experience for Leonard in parenting these children, as his former wife had been the children's primary caregiver. In one of the first family meetings, we suggested that Leonard ask all the children to present their perspectives on the problems in the family, while he took notes.

During these meetings, we were able to observe more closely the children's behavior and the relationships between them and with Leonard and Melanie. From these interactions, we were able to see their unmet developmental needs, incomplete developmental processes, and determine their levels of development. The children participated in problem-solving family issues that involved them, such as conflicts between siblings, laundry, homework, and kitchen cleanup.

One of the most poignant moments of our family intervention came during a family meeting and involved the children giving Leonard feedback about how they appreciated his efforts to be a father and make a loving home for them. Leonard had just shared his feelings of discouragement about their fighting and lack of cooperation. While we saw how much the children loved their father, we also saw how he was seldom able to see beyond the struggles he was having. We encouraged the children to speak their love and appreciation directly to him one at a time. As they did, Leonard's eyes welled. By the time the last one finished, he was sobbing uncontrollably. This authentic encounter with his children bolstered his sagging confidence as a father.

Once the family meeting structure was firmly established in the system to address their day-to-day problems, Leonard invited the housekeeper and her children to attend a family meeting. As we observed the dynamics between her and Leonard's children, it was clear that her job in Leonard's home was very stressful for her. While she was able to perform the physical aspects of housekeeping, the childcare component was complicated by the presence of her own two children. We recommended that she find separate childcare for them, which she did for a period of time. She eventually decided to terminate her position with the family, and Leonard hired a new housekeeper without children to take her place.

The behavioral problems with Leonard's children continued, however, in spite of our efforts. We eventually recommended individual therapy for those exhibiting the most problems, including attachment therapy for one of the younger children. We consulted periodically with the therapists of these children regarding the family situation and gave them feedback after our family meeting sessions. On several occasions, we also went to their schools and consulted with the counselors regarding the developmental issues of the children who were not in therapy and made recommendations to their teachers regarding possible interventions. We also went to court and testified as expert witnesses during a custody hearing.

The complexity of the problems in Leonard's household overwhelmed Melanie. Though she struggled to ride the regular waves of family chaos and conflict, she found her experiences there kept her flooded with posttraumatic stress symptoms. She undertook an earnest program of personal counseling to help her cope. While she did free herself from many of these symptoms, she eventually decided that she was not physically or emotionally able to be a full-time stepmother to Leonard's children. She continued to be friends with Leonard and his children for a period of time and then entered a new relationship. Leonard continued in individual therapy for a while to help him adjust to this loss. He also continued to provide for some individual therapy for his children.

Our experience with this family has served as a laboratory for expanding our clinical skills in DPW and for refining our partnership model of conflict resolution. This example illustrates the complexity of working with large systems and the amount of perseverance required to address the complexity. It also presents a realistic picture of the interface between individual development and couple, family, and social systems, as well as the limitations in changing larger systems when the individuals who comprise them are restricted in the internal resources that are needed for transformation.

This case also helped us develop patience and realistic expectations about working with large systems. Change does not happen overnight, and the effects of interventions are often not visible in the short term.

Self-Inventory: What Are Your Family Patterns?

In the blank before each item, place a number from 1 through 4 that indicates how true it is for you.

1 = Almost Never 2 = Occasionally 3 = Usually 4 = Almost Always

____ 1. My current relationship conflicts remind me of conflicts I had as a child.

____ 2. My partner says or does some things that irritate me and remind me of the way my parents treated me.

____ 3. My partner disapproves of some things I say or do just the way my parents did.

____ 4. I criticize others and myself the way I was criticized as a child.
____ 5. Even though I don't want to, I find myself saying and doing things that hurt my children or partners the same way people hurt me while I was growing up.
____ 6. When I get upset at myself, I say some of the same critical things to myself that my parents or others said to me when I was a child.
____ 7. The way my partner relates to me reminds me of the way my parents related to me when I was a child.
____ 8. I find myself acting weak and helpless so others may feel sorry for me or help me out.
____ 9. I can see similarities between the kinds of intimate relationships I now have and the relationship my parents had or still have with each other.
____10. I tend to feel uneasy when everything seems to be going well in my relationships.
____11. When I have conflicts with others, I tend to focus on what they did to cause the conflict.
____12. I tend to give more than I receive in my relationships.
____13. I have trouble enjoying sex the way I would like.
____14. I am afraid to be "too successful."
____15. I don't like to take risks and prefer to stay with what is familiar.
____16. I feel like my intimate partner treats me unfairly.
____17. When asked, I have trouble thinking about or listing positive traits about myself.
____18. I cannot express my feelings the way I would like.
____19. I encounter people who tend to treat me like my parents treated me.
____20. I feel controlled by the expectations of others.
______ Total Score

Scoring and Interpretation

Add the numbers in the column to the left of the statements to get your total score. Use the following guidelines to help you interpret the possible meaning of your score.

If your score was between:

20–40 = A few family patterns are likely sources of your present conflicts.
41–60 = Many family patterns are the likely sources of your present conflicts.
61–80 = Almost all of your present conflicts have their source in unprocessed family patterns.

Self-Inventory: What Is the Level of Dysfunction in Your Family of Origin?

Using the following 25 characteristics of dysfunctional families, rate your own family of origin. In the blank before each item, place a number from 1 through 5.

1 = Not present at all, 2 = Present to a small degree, 3 = Present sometimes, 4 = Present most of the time, 5 = Present all of the time

____ 1. The family promotes competition rather than cooperation. This means that children are compared with each other and sibling rivalry is actually promoted.

____ 2. There is a misuse of parental power. Parents may use their power to threaten, intimidate, control, and subjugate their children to obey their orders. This usually involves a deliberate, but often unconscious, attempt to break the will of the child, often while the child is still an infant. It is often justified as necessary "for their own good."

____ 3. There is no respect for the basic human rights of children or women. Women and children are treated like chattel or property, without basic human rights. Children are expected to be seen and not heard and have no needs or wants of their own.

____ 4. There are rigid, compulsive rules. There is an attempt to overcontrol or overregulate the behavior of family members through the use of rigidly enforced rules. Reasons for rules are usually not provided and obedience is mandatory.

____ 5. There are rigid gender roles. The boys or men are supposed to follow their traditional roles and the girls or women theirs. No exceptions are allowed. People tend to interact with each other through their roles rather than through their individual interests and needs.

____ 6. There is no sharing of housework or household chores. Women and girls are expected to handle the household chores; the boys and men are exempt from these duties. Boys growing up in this type of family often expect to be waited on by their spouses when they get married.

____ 7. There are no joint family activities planned. This type of family is very fragmented, and there are no structures or planned activities, such as family outings, that promote unity and family bonding.

____ 8. The economic condition of the family is kept secret from family members. In these families, children are not told about the family's income and little or no financial responsibility is shared appropriately with other family members.

____ 9. There is no respect for personal privacy. Children do not have their own personal space or property. Toys, clothing, bedrooms, furniture, and personal items are considered belonging to the family not individuals. Parents do not respect their children's needs for privacy or boundaries.

____10. There is no shared decision making in the family. The head of the household makes all the major decisions, and other family members have very little say in these decisions.

____11. There is no shared parenting. Almost all parenting is done by one parent, usually the mother. The father is absent or not involved in the day-to-day parenting and perhaps is only involved occasionally in disciplining the children.

____12. There is no support for the expression of feelings. Family members are taught to hide their feelings or are punished for their attempts to express normal feelings such as anger, sadness, fear, or even joy.

____13. The main forms of discipline utilized are spanking, threats, or sham- ing. The level of physical or emotional violence is high in these families. Usually there is abuse of alcohol or drugs by one or both parents.

____14. Win–lose conflict resolution methods are utilized. Whenever there is a conflict, someone wins and someone loses, instead of finding a solution where both parties can win. Partnership resolutions require a set of problem-solving skills that most parents don't have.

____15. No one admits making a mistake or apologizes for their actions. Parents are always right in these families, and they present themselves as infallible. If they make a mistake, they try to hide it or explain it away instead of owning it and apologizing to those who were affected by the mistake.

____16. Problems are blamed on others. There is a defensiveness in the family; when something bad happens, there is a quick attempt to blame it on someone else. There is no personal accountability or responsibility for one's own actions.

____17. There is resistance to outsiders. There is a "we versus them" attitude toward anyone outside the family. The family is not opened to guests coming in or to sharing with others outside the family.

____18. Loyalty to the family is seen as a duty. Children are expected to defend the family against any outside criticism, even when the family is in the wrong. Protecting the family name is overemphasized.

____19. There is resistance to change. Even though the family has obvious dysfunctional elements, there is strong resistance to changing them. There seems to be a fear that any change may bring about something worse. Sometimes people have lived for generations with these dysfunctional patterns and have become comfortable with their "familiarity." To change them means going into unfamiliar territory.

____20. There is no family unity. In this type of family "two against one" triangles develop to create some unity or safety. There is often a lot of indirect communication in which one person may communicate to another through a third person.

____21. There is no protection from abusive acts. Children may be emotionally, physically, or sexually abused by one or both parents, and the other parent does nothing to protect the child from this abuse. This can also be true in sibling abuse, where an older sibling abuses a younger one and neither parent does anything to stop the abuse or protect the younger child.

____22. Conflicts in the family are often ignored. In this type of family, every conflict is swept under the rug rather than resolved effectively. This often causes a heavy, oppressive family atmosphere in which there is conflict in the air and no one is talking about it.

____23. There are a large number of family secrets. Almost every family has some secret they don't want people outside the family to know. The children are admonished not to reveal these secrets. However, in many instances the children are not told these secrets, and the presence of these secrets colors relationships among family members. Often some members know the secret and others don't, creating "unholy alliances" within the family.

____24. There is little joy or laughter in the family. In these families, parents often feel overburdened or overwhelmed by the job of parenting, so they can't have fun or allow laughter in the family. In some families, the only laughter that is permitted is when someone is teased or made the butt of a joke. This is a dysfunctional form of humor.

____25. The children are unplanned or unwanted. More than 50% of all children born in this country are either unplanned or unwanted. Children often know they are unplanned or unwanted, even though no one ever tells them. An illegitimate birth is often kept as a family secret.

______ Total Score

Scoring and Interpretation

Add the numbers in the left-hand column to record the total score of how you perceive the level of dysfunction present in your family of origin and compare it to the suggested interpretation.

If your score was between:

0–25 = There was almost no evidence of dysfunctional elements present in your family of origin. Caution: Too rosy a picture of your family of origin could indicate some denial of these dysfunctional elements and their possible effects on you.

26–75 = There is some evidence of dysfunctional elements present in your family of origin.

76–125 = There is considerable evidence of dysfunctional elements present in your family of origin.

From *Breaking Family Patterns* (pp. 21–23), by B. Weinhold, 2006, Swannanoa, NC: CICRCL Press. Used with permission.

PART FIVE

Developmental Process Consultation

I DON'T KNOW WHAT YOUR DESTINY WILL BE,
BUT ONE THING I DO KNOW;
THE ONLY ONES AMONG YOU
WHO WILL BE REALLY HAPPY ARE THOSE WHO
HAVE SOUGHT AND FOUND HOW TO SERVE.

ALBERT SCHWEITZER

CHAPTER FOURTEEN

Developmental Process Consultation

Process consultation uses structured activities to help members of an organization work together more cooperatively. Process consultants or trainers observe the interactions among members of the organization in the normal flow of work and in the way they conduct their meetings. They then provide feedback to members of the organization or group to help them identify the attitudes and behaviors that are helping or hindering the organization's success. From this information, the members of the organization are able to function more effectively.

Developmental Process Consultation: A Systems Approach to Healing Developmental Shock, Trauma, and Stress in Organizations

Those who use developmental systems theory as a foundation for their process consultation with organizations are known as *developmental process consultants* (DPC). This is an expansion of the process-consultation model long recognized in organizational development circles as an effective tool for changing organizations. The DPC helps members of an organization specifically identify any incomplete developmental processes in the organization that might be causing social disengagement practices and interfering with interpersonal communication.

Organizational issues are complex because people unconsciously bring their unhealed developmental shocks, traumas, or stresses and social disengagement defenses to work with them. These unidentified issues contain a residue of unprocessed emotions and relational dynamics that will eventually surface in the workplace as drama triangle dynamics. When people overreact during their relational interactions, it is helpful for them to recognize when they get triggered and are experiencing the reenactment of a previous event containing developmental memories of unhealed shock, trauma, or stress.

DPCs train managers, supervisors, and employees to spot incomplete developmental processes and the effects of developmental shocks, traumas, or stresses that may be causing them. They also train others in the organization or group to understand the developmental principles that are inherent in their intrapersonal, interpersonal, and intergroup relationships and help them increase their members' social and relational effectiveness. This is the most productive way to advance the evolution of their school, company, church, nonprofit agency, or other large organization or nation–state.

This chapter discusses how to apply the principles of developmental process consultation to companies, schools, churches, nonprofit agencies, and other large organizations. The goal of DPC is providing planned interventions to maintain a sense of object constancy or psychological objectivity, both individually and collectively in the system. These interventions include training in empathy, conflict resolution, and communication skills that discourage splitting behaviors and support decision-making strategies that identify at least three options or choices when making a decision. These skills help people maintain their self-worth even when they experience moments of feeling rejected or unworthy during a conflict or period of reorganization.

Rather than judging or criticizing, it is more effective to react from a compassionate and empathetic perspective—both toward others and toward yourself. DPCs teach organizational members empathy skills that enable them to respond with compassion so that people can learn how to work internally on themselves whenever they get triggered.

The systemic nature of the reenactment of events involving unhealed developmental shock, trauma, or stress often makes it difficult to identify and resolve them. Corporations, businesses, and other organizations are typically organized around a formal network of horizontal and vertical structures designed to accomplish the goals of the organization. A lack of awareness of the havoc that unhealed developmental issues wreak on an organizational structure inadvertently encourages dysfunctional relational dynamics such as the drama triangle and the need/obligate system, which will be explained.

Quantum theory and chaos theory suggest that besides the formal organizational structure, another, more informal and invisible self-organizing structure actually determines how the organization functions. Chaos theory says strange attractors, or organizing forces within any system, create fractals of predictable behavior patterns that direct the system's behavior. One of the most common strange attractors in organizations is the unhealed developmental issues of its members involving shock, trauma, or stress.

In one company where we served as DPCs, we attended several executive committee meetings. During one of these meetings, we noticed that the group tended to discount the comments of the manufacturing vice president. Other members of this executive committee also seemed to ignore him at breaks, cut him off when he spoke, or attempted to rescue him by trying to explain to others what he meant to say. The members perceived him as weak and passive and then supported their perceptions by preventing him from speaking out in their meetings. They seemed to have put him into a category. They kept him socially disengaged as a way of avoiding fears and anxieties about the potential for their own marginalization that he triggered.

We shared our observations regarding this man's marginalization in one of the committee meetings and then waited to see if it would reappear. After it did, we met with this vice president and asked him if he was aware of being ignored. When he said he was, we asked him how he felt about the situation. With our coaching, he was able to tell his colleagues how he felt ignored and hurt about the way they were treating him.

Once he expressed these feelings directly, told others about the effect their behavior was having on him, and asked them to stop treating him that way, the other group members began treating him differently. They encouraged him to speak more in their meetings. Once this happened, they learned that he had a lot of good ideas and that he was not weak and passive as they had previously believed. His colleagues began using some of his suggestions and found them to be helpful. People began to gravitate more to him at breaks, and he slowly became perceived as a valuable resource in meeting discussions.

The group had targeted this man because they projected some of their own unhealed developmental issues on him related to feeling weak and being rejected. He likely reminded many of his colleagues of a weak or passive father who let them down or was emotionally unavailable to them. When the VP became more emotionally available, they stopped projecting weakness and passivity on him. Projections involving unhealed developmental issues can affect the morale, productivity, and wellness of the workplace. Unfortunately, our consulting contract did not include helping people in that organization heal their developmental shocks, traumas, or stresses, so it is likely that they emerged in other ways in this organization.

When people work closely together over a period of time, it is only natural for unhealed developmental issues from their families of origin to surface. When people feel safe enough, they let down their guard a bit and their wounds emerge. Organizations need structures in place that help people both identify and heal the effects of these wounds when they do emerge. One of the best ways to address this need is conceptualizing a workplace structure as a functional family.

In her excellent book, *Family Ties, Corporate Bonds* (1985), Paula Bernstein described such a vision:

> Tomorrow's corporate family will be headed by a man or a woman—not necessarily in the old-fashioned father or mother role, but more an adult friend, a protector, and advisor to his or her adult children, cousins, siblings, and stepchildren. We will be

> grown-ups working with grown-ups, but still fulfilling our own individual, special emotional needs. (p. 176)

According to the tenets of DST, the evolution of organizations follows a developmental process similar to that for individuals, couples, and families. The four stages of organizational evolution are the codependent, counterdependent, independent, and interdependent stages. The essential developmental processes that must be completed at each stage of evolution of the organization were presented in Chapter 1 and are repeated in Table 14.1.

Organizations that create a supportive environment where individual members are encouraged to contribute as partners will evolve to a higher, more effective stage. Some organizations create an organizational identity that helps its employees bond socially with each other rather well but then they fail to support them in getting their individual needs met. The company may be struggling with a split between management and labor that is visible in low wages or meager benefits for the employees but provides for managers' needs in ways that create distrust and competition between the two.

This split and the inability to do "both/and" thinking then becomes a barrier to the organization's evolution. Employee turnover in this kind of company is usually high and affects the company's esprit de corps. Rapid turnover and the loss of friendships have a big impact on employees' emotional stability. Most corporate environments, unfortunately, do not help people deal with these social and emotional losses. Unprocessed emotional losses in a workplace can trigger employees' memories of previous losses in their lives, causing them to regress and lose the present-time focus they need for high productivity.

In order to facilitate incremental evolution into higher stages of organizational development, management must make a conscious effort to address employees' work-related experiences in functional ways and create opportunities for the development of healthy social engagement. This includes the ability to recognize and process unhealed developmental issues when they emerge. Otherwise, drama triangle dynamics will get activated, employee morale will fall, productivity will decline, and the organization will stagnate.

The human interactions where developmental shocks, traumas, or stresses typically appear in an organization are in the following areas:

1. Communication and social interactions
2. Roles and functions of members in group meetings
3. Group problem-solving and decision-making meetings
4. Group norms and group process in meetings
5. Leadership and authority in meetings
6. Intergroup cooperation and competition

TABLE 14.1

The Essential Developmental Processes of Organizations

Stage of Development / Primary Task	Essential Developmental Processes of an Organization
Codependent (Bonding)	• Create bonding experiences for employees • Build trust between employers and employees • Create an organizational identity • Provide for the basic needs of employees and managers • Foster healthy emotional communication and social engagement skills with employees and employers • Build an organizational esprit de corps
Counter-dependent (Separation)	• Support employees in asserting their needs and have them taken seriously by employers • Identify and promote the unique contributions of each employee to the organization • Use fair, equitable, and nonshaming methods of limit setting with employees • Establish rules and policies in equitable ways • Resolve internal conflicts between the needs of employees and the needs of employers • Understand the influence of incomplete developmental processes on work performance and provide ways to heal developmental traumas at work
Independent (Mastery)	• Employers create an organizational culture with mutually determined values and beliefs • Individual autonomy is supported by employers and employees within the organizational structure • Employees are given responsibility for self-regulation of emotion and self-care • Employees achieve true pride in their work • Employers provide specialized training and development for each employee to enhance individual contributions to the organization
Interdependent (Cooperation)	• Create organizations run cooperatively by employees and employers • Utilize team-building activities • Promote cooperation building between teams • Create rituals that build and sustain employee morale • Create divisions of labor based on individual interests and abilities • Foster cooperation that helps each employee develop his or her fullest potential as a human being

Woven through all of these processes, however, are the effects of unhealed developmental issues involving shocks, traumas, or stresses and the inherent need for ways to identify and heal them.

How Developmental Process Consultants Work with an Organization

The steps that a DPC uses when consulting with an organization are as follows (Schein, 1969):

Step 1: Establish contact with the organization. A member of the organization, usually an executive, seeks your help in addressing a specific problem. The most difficult part of this step is encountering a hierarchical doctor–patient orientation that gives you expert status as an outsider. This approach ignores the inherent wisdom of the people who work within the organization regarding the causes of the problem and workable solutions for it.

During a face-to-face meeting between you and a committee of organizational members, offer them a different approach. At this meeting, outline your alternative consultation approach and seek their interest in participating with you in it. In some instances, you may find a lack of compatibility regarding your approach and their goals. In these cases, you can decline their offer to retain your consulting services.

If you find the organization receptive to your ideas, it is important to define your relationship via a formal contract stating when and how much you will be paid, the exact nature of services you will provide, the time frame when you will be providing services, and the outcome goals you hope to achieve. It is very important to make the outcome goals as explicit and concrete as possible.

Step 2: Observe the organization's essential developmental processes during key meetings. Look at how people communicate with each other, particularly how much of their communication is via emails or phone calls rather than face-to-face. If most of their communication is indirect, too many social disengagement practices are in place. Attend key meetings to learn more about how their face-to-face communication affects the organization and its processes. Here you can observe how the organization functions and what developmental components might be targeted for further study.

Observe top-level meetings first, as these meetings reveal most about how members of the organization communicate with each other. Provide a context for your presence in these meetings to help people get to know you and explain your purpose for being in the meeting. Before attending these meetings, you may also choose to interview some key people, not to gather data, but to build relationships.

Once they know and trust you, they are more likely to cooperate when you recommend changes.

By attending key meetings, you can identify specific incomplete developmental processes for later follow-up. For example, we participated in a strategic planning process at a small company that was part of a large corporation. One activity asked employees to list their personal goals for the next year. These personal goals would be compared with the branch company's goals and with the goals of the overall corporation. One employee after another presented their personal goals written on a large piece of newsprint. It was interesting to discover that each employee actually presented not personal but organizational goals (e.g., "I am going to increase my attendance at supervisory meetings," or "I am going to work late to keep the paperwork from piling up"). Their goals did not focus on an outcome for themselves (e.g., "I am going to work for a promotion by the end of this year," or "I am going to join the company bowling team and spend at least one evening a week having fun"). We saw this as a sign pointing to the incomplete developmental processes around bonding that employees were bringing to work and that were creating social disengagement practices.

We also saw this as a reversal process present in this company where employees believed that their primary task was supporting the company's needs rather than having the company support their needs. Through interviews and questionnaires, we confirmed that many employees came from families with reversal patterns: Many of these employees had taken care of their parents more than their parents had taken care of them. They were unaware that they brought this dysfunctional family pattern to work with them. When we disclosed this in our reports from the data-gathering phase of our consultation, the management decided to implement policies that encouraged more of a balance between the welfare of the company and the needs of the employees.

Step 3: Conduct collaborative data-gathering activities. Unlike other consultation models, those used by a DPC do not rely just on the intuition and personal expertise of the consultant to diagnose the organization's problems. Instead, the DPC provides activities designed to actively involve everyone in the organization in discovering the nature of its problems. The five kinds of data-gathering strategies utilized by the DPC are observations, interviews, questionnaires, focus groups, and executive coaching sessions. It is good to use a combination of all of these. Having everyone fill out questionnaires helps highlight any incomplete developmental processes that could block the fulfillment of organizational objectives. The two self-inventories at the end of this chapter can be used as part of these data-gathering activities.

In addition, the DPC conducts structured interviews with key people who represent a cross-section of the organizational structure. Even in situations where the organizational objectives and goals have been jointly determined, it is best to have everyone identify the developmental processes that they see are necessary to achieve corporate goals and objectives. These interviews should also help identify what they see is preventing the organization from reaching its goals and objectives.

Step 4: Analyze the results of the data gathering and report back to the organization. Once you have analyzed the results of your data-gathering activities, report your findings back to the organization. This prepares it for any interventions you might advise. All organizational members should have access to a written report of your findings. This step sets the stage for future developmental interventions. Your report should provide information about what you found in the six main areas of the organization identified earlier in this chapter.

Step 5: Interventions. Here are some ways to intervene as a developmental process consultant:

a. Observe key meetings and provide process feedback that can help people change dysfunctional behaviors and processes.
b. Conduct coaching sessions with key executives who have the maximum impact on the organization and serve as role models.
c. Train all employees in key skills that can address the presence of the effects of unhealed developmental shocks, traumas, or stresses in the organization (i.e., conflict resolution training, counseling, or coaching for individuals or groups). Make these interventions be a part of the contract you have with the organization.
d. Give process feedback to the groups you observe by allowing time for process analysis at the end of each meeting. You can focus this analysis through key questions based on what you observed. For example, if you observe some nonverbal reactions to a decision made during a meeting, you might ask: "How did all of you feel about how the decision was made about topic X? Did you feel that you had enough input into the decision in order to personally support it?"
e. Giving process feedback to individuals or groups often leads to coaching or counseling sessions with the people involved. When given feedback about how their behavior affects others, people ask, "What can I do to change this behavior?" As a DPC, you can help key people identify how they might be reenacting the effects of their unhealed developmental shocks, traumas, or stresses and then help them find resources for healing them.

Trainings should be built around the results of your data-gathering activities. Structure them around specific topics, such as drama triangle dynamics, the need/obligate system, social engagement skills, and identifying the effects of unhealed developmental shocks, traumas, or stresses. Perhaps you can offer basic training courses for everyone and more advanced training to the key executives.

Step 6: Evaluate the results. The primary goal of the developmental process consultant is to improve the overall effectiveness and functionality of the organization. Some of the best indicators of this outcome are that the company begins allocating more time for social engagement activities, as well as creating structures for reviewing and analyzing its important decision-making processes.

The most important DPC outcome is enhancing the social engagement skills of all members of the organization by helping them to identify and encouraging them to address the effects of any unhealed developmental issues through therapy or executive coaching. It may be helpful to train one or two members of the organization in more advanced DPC skills so that they can function as internal consultants. These people would be able to identify and heal their own developmental issues when they arise and then assist those at any level within the system: individual, couple, family, and group.

People spend more than one-third of their life in the workplace, which presents many opportunities to reenact unhealed developmental issues. This is also true because workplaces unconsciously remind people of their families of origin and therefore trigger memories of any early unhealed shock, trauma, or stress. Currently, in most companies the only formal structure in place to resolve these issues are grievance procedures, which do not address the real issues involved. Most employees avoid using these resources because of their adversarial and confrontational nature. Without corporate-endorsed structures such as employee assistance programs that offer real support to employees who might be reenacting their unhealed developmental issues in grievance processes, most people will develop avoidant or indirect means such as the drama triangle or the need/obligate system to deal with their unhealed developmental issues.

If all employees are taught how to help each other identify and heal the developmental shocks, traumas, or stresses that interfere with workplace productivity, a company can save enormous amounts of time and money and greatly increase its employee productivity. Why don't companies invest more in training employees to do this? Some enlightened ones do, but most of them do not seem to understand the benefits.

For example, a middle manager of a large high-tech company where we proposed employee training on this topic said with great seriousness, "Our employees don't have personal issues at work. They leave them all at the door." We wondered if the company's reputation for high levels of executive alcoholism might be related to this denial. We also wondered if these employees carried home their work-related frustrations and dumped them on their families. Unfortunately, this attitude is still quite common among corporate leaders and school principals, ministers, and agency heads, who simply do not understand the impact of unidentified and unhealed developmental shocks, traumas, or stressors on the operation and evolution of their organization.

Teaching employees how to effectively recognize and heal these issues is just good management practice. Bernstein (1985) wrote that when she interviewed employees, the conversation always returned to one theme: the lack of good management, the need for it, and how much the employees hungered for it. The employees she interviewed longed for fairness, leadership, and justice, and for simpler, less convoluted, and more straightforward conflict-free relationships.

The structure of an organization or company determines how many personal issues will be present in that organization. Litwak (1961) found that the potential for personal issues to show up at work is greater in centralized, more highly bureaucratic organizations than in organizations with fewer centralized structures. Likert and Likert (1976) developed a method for rating organizations on a continuum between rigidity and flexibility.

According to the Likerts, the most effective organizations are adaptable to changing conditions and needs. The following criteria developed by the Likerts (1976), which we include in our organizational systems theory, help determine the flexibility and adaptability of an organization.

1. *A minimum of rules and regulations.* The openness of a system can be determined by identifying the number of rules and regulations and how long these have existed. Most open systems have very few rules and use a set of operating principles for each subsystem of the organization. These principles are determined by the group or team most directly involved.
2. *Decision-making at the level of implementation.* Another quick way to assess a system's openness is checking the number of levels a decision must pass through before it can be implemented. In an open system, all important decisions are made at the level of implementation.
3. *A minimum number of hierarchical levels.* An open system is relatively flat in organizational structure. The more levels that information and decisions must pass through, the more chances of error or misperceptions and the more opportunities for conflict.
4. *Maximum data flow with external systems.* To determine this, notice how the system exchanges information, resources, and data with the systems that are contiguous to it. In open systems, established communication methods insure a reciprocal flow of information, resources, and data.
5. *Collectively determined goals and purposes.* Identify how goals and purposes are determined. In an open system, they are determined collectively by those directly involved in the process. Input is also sought from members of the larger contiguous system to accommodate changing needs and purposes.
6. *Direct, wide-band, face-to-face communication.* In closed organizations, communication tends to become indirect (memos, voice mail, email, etc.). Open systems use more direct, face-to-face, wide-band (information and feelings) communication. This offers some potential for group decision making. By

checking how information is transmitted, it is possible to assess the openness of a system. Structures must also encourage the direct expression of both positive and negative feelings.

7. *Neutralized power.* Power plays are common in organizations. In open systems, power is distributed through all levels. There are no one-up/one-down power moves and no win–lose decision making or conflict resolution strategies. A good way to check the openness of an organization is to look for evidence of misuse of power.
8. *Flexible developmental processes.* The developmental processes (daily schedule, flexibility of hours, curriculum, etc.) in open systems are very flexible and dynamic. They can easily be changed in response to the changing needs of those involved. In less open systems, curriculum guides or job tasks are rigidly enforced and time schedules are inflexible.
9. *Open, permeable system boundaries.* Rather than operating as an enclave, an open system extends its boundaries into the next larger system. The goals, purposes, and processes of the organization are completely visible. Open systems seek to blend their information, resources, and data flow with the next larger system. Open schools, agencies, churches, and corporations operate as integrated, rather than separate, systems that enfold the daily lives of the people involved.
10. *Flexible role definitions.* Job descriptions and rigid role definitions can affect the degree of openness in a company, school, church, or agency. In an open system, the roles that people are assigned or choose to play are flexible and able to change. The Openness to Change Inventory at the end of this chapter is also drawn from this research and may be used to assess the relative openness of your organization.

Likert and Likert (1976) found that more rigid organizations tended to manage personal issues poorly. They found that the personality and methods of the managers and supervisors also made a big difference. Less defensive managers who could receive feedback and were naturally supportive of others tended to prevent personal issues from interfering with performance. The leadership style of the managers and supervisors generally set the tone for personal conflict management. Those managers and supervisors with good communication skills, supportive attitudes toward those they supervised, the willingness to be emotionally honest, and the ability to facilitate the resolution of conflicts generally had fewer personal issues to handle among those they supervised.

The culture of the organization can also play a part in the resolution of personal issues. Organizations with competitive, everyone-for-themselves cultures have more personal issues than those with a spirit of cooperation for achieving the organization's goals. Some organizations unwittingly create a competitive climate because of the presence of punitive, petty, and divisive organizational policies and procedures. These kinds of policies traumatize people and ultimately gnaw at morale, erode productivity, affect the health of employees, and eventually impair the organization and its productivity.

The stability of an organization is an important factor in managing personal conflicts. Organizations experiencing high levels of change are more vulnerable to internal personal conflict. The way in which an organization manages change can destabilize employee morale and increase personal conflict. Organizations experiencing rapid change can handle conflicts effectively when the institutional climate supports the use of effective conflict resolution strategies. When conflict is denied or avoided, any change that reverberates through the company will increase conflict.

The Adverse Impact of Unhealed Developmental Shock, Trauma, and Stress in Organizations

Any interaction involving three or more people increases the probability of the unconscious acting out of unresolved developmental issues from people's families of origin. Why does this happen? The unhealed shocks, traumas, or stresses initially occurred in the family of origin. When people leave there, they carry with them the incomplete developmental processes connected to these unhealed shocks, traumas, or stresses. It is natural for humans to replay their unhealed developmental shocks, traumas, or stresses. This is why a boss may remind you of your father or mother and trigger memories related to the shocks, traumas, or stresses you experienced with them and why the things certain coworkers say or do may activate posttraumatic triggers involving a parent or sibling.

Organizations also have invisible structures built around fractal family patterns. It is quite common, for example, for founders or presidents of a company to reenact their unhealed developmental issues in the way they manage the company. The workplace becomes a stage for reenacting any unhealed family-of-origin dramas. They then hire managers who support their concept of how an organization should be run. Employees are perceived as family members and become players in the founder's traveling family-of-origin drama.

An employee of one such large company perceived its corporate dysfunction as the replay of the founder's alcoholic family dynamics. The founder was acting out the dysfunctional ways that he was treated in his family in the way he organized and operated his company, which triggered employees' unhealed developmental issues. This employee saw how company policies were designed to avoid conflict, play favorites, keep secrets, rigidly define the roles of subordinates, and use unpredictable decision-making strategies. The manager in question used temper-tantrums to get his way and threw lots of company parties where the alcohol flowed freely. This behavior perfectly describes the profile of an alcoholic family.

Family-of-origin patterns are an even more important factor in the success or failure of small businesses. Family dynamics can become so complex and entangled that they provide an ideal setting where almost everyone can reenact their unhealed developmental shocks, traumas, or stresses. This adversely affects corporate productivity and decision making. The dysfunctional family patterns woven into a company structure can even dictate the story line of the company's progress. The typical story line of many small companies is a period of initial rapid growth, followed by a stabilizing and leveling-off period, and then a decline in productivity that may lead to the company's demise.

Jongeward (1973) stated that a company story line "may depict a comedy, a saga, a tragedy, a farce, or a dull plodding drama going nowhere" (p. 6). We see that the family-patterned story line is like a fractal that determines the company's cast of characters, their dialogue, the script they carry out, the dramatic actions they take, and the ultimate fate of the company.

Company policies are one of the most visible places to see family patterns and drama triangle dynamics in action, as the rules often resemble the structure of the founder's family of origin. For example, if the founder's family avoided conflict, it is likely that the company will also have policies that support avoiding conflict. In some companies, the founder runs the company like an authoritarian parent whose word is law and decisions are unquestionable. In a company with a noncollaborative leader, the boss is isolated from the problems inside the organization because employees are afraid to provide the boss with information they think he or she does not want to hear. For example, they will not share information about changing markets and what the company's position is in those markets. Without this information, he or she is likely to make poor decisions.

Drama Triangle Dynamics in the Workplace

Bolton (1976) wrote about how the behavior of dysfunctional employees can impact the more functional employees. He described how some people carry an "emotional plague" that undermines the effectiveness of those who are working constructively in the organization. Employees who have little self-awareness about their developmental histories often use the drama triangle to process their unhealed developmental shocks, traumas, or stresses, particularly through the victim role. It is important to recognize when an employee is reenacting his or her unhealed developmental shock, trauma, or stress in the workplace and to refuse to play with them in the drama triangle. In most organizations, it is not easy to recognize drama triangle dynamics until you are deep in the middle of them. The following sections detail some of the common ways this gets played out in organizations.

The Good Old Boy/Old Girl Drama Triangle

One of the most common ways the drama triangle gets played out in organizations is through the "good old boy/good old girl" networks. These are codependency-based agreements that enable people to maintain their dependencies. This is one of the most common ways that developmental shocks, traumas, or stresses circulate through the organization without detection.

This dynamic also involves the unconscious *need/obligate system* between two employees that we discussed in Chapter 7. Employee A, for example, identifies something that Employee B needs and provides him with it. This obligates Employee B to pay back the favor, even though it was performed without his request. Because Employee B does not like to be obligated, he does a favor for employee A to get him obligated in return. This need/obligate system keeps both persons stuck in a codependent relationship. Both participants keep score to make sure that the tally comes out even. The problem with this system is that both parties end up feeling used by the other, which triggers memories of unhealed developmental shock, trauma, or stress from the past.

For example, Sally is usually the first one at work because her husband drops her off on his way to work. She makes the coffee for everyone, even though it is Milly's job to do so. When Milly gets to work and finds that Sally has already made the coffee, she feels conflicted. She likes to make the coffee her own way, which is a little stronger than the way Sally makes it. She also feels as though she now owes Sally a favor, which is a source of some discomfort because it reminds her of times growing up when she felt obligated to do things her parents wanted her to do that she really did not want to do. When Sally asks Milly to cover for her so she can leave work a little early to do some shopping, Milly feels obligated to do so, even though she does not want to, because Sally made the coffee for her. This inability to be emotionally honest and look at the source of their discomfort causes strained relations between the two coworkers. This kind of system triggers memories of unhealed developmental shock, trauma, or stress that can be related to a sibling in their families of origin who they felt was the favorite or had certain privileges that they didn't have.

The conflict between Milly and Sally finally erupts when both get to the copy machine at the same time. The conflict is not really about the copy machine—it is about making the coffee and leaving work early, although it is not even about that. Unless they can sort out the unhealed developmental shock, trauma, or stress involved and get to the core issues and end the need/obligate system, it is difficult to resolve the conflict effectively. A framework has to be put in place within the organization that makes it possible for Sally and Milly to help each other look for the core issue related to unhealed developmental shock, trauma, or stress and then help each other to heal it.

Another common way that employees start the drama triangle is from the victim role. For example, an employee, John, is tardy or absent, but no one says anything, so his tardiness continues. A female employee complains to his or her mutual supervisor (triangulation): "I don't see why John is always late and nobody says anything. Maybe I'll just start coming in late, too."

The supervisor (persecutor) decides to get tough with the tardy employee and issues an ultimatum to John: "If you are late one more time, you will be fired." John (victim) feels angry with his boss and asks one of his colleagues (rescuer) to intervene with his boss. The colleague defends John's behavior with his boss, discovers the name of the woman who complained about John's tardiness, and then tells John, who confronts her (persecutes). The woman feels guilty when she finds out that John was given an ultimatum about his job. She then goes to their supervisor and pleads John's case (rescues): "But he was only late three times and then by just a few minutes." The supervisor (now feeling like the victim), who is tired of hearing about this problem, finally says: "Since you are the one who caused this problem in the first place, maybe I should fire you instead" (persecutes).

This game can go on forever until people refuse to get their needs met by being victims and begin asking directly for what they want or need without involving others. The best way to break the power of the drama triangle and the need/obligate system is by making agreements that everyone will ask directly for what they need and negotiate directly with those involved when conflicts arise.

The Gossip Mill: A Breeding Ground for Traumatic Reenactment

One of the most destructive forms of communication in organizations is the gossip mill, which typically involves triangulation; drama triangle dynamics; and developmental shocks, traumas, or stresses. It also involves splitting that creates divisiveness and a lack of trust among members of organizations.

It is tempting to engage in splitting during workplace conflicts. Here is how it usually begins. People often fear going directly to those with whom they have a conflict because they anticipate repercussions. Splitting transactions, which involve someone being "good" and someone else "bad," sound something like this: "Do you know what she did to me? Well, let me tell you." This indirect expression of anger during a conflict can escalate into a major drama where someone becomes the organizational scapegoat and suddenly departs from the organization or drags as many people as possible into the conflict.

The best way to avoid these drama triangle dynamics is to refuse to get between two other people and to insist that they resolve their conflicts directly with each other. When people come to you with information about another person, you can do the following:

- Refuse to get in the middle of their relational issue. Ask them to deal directly with the other person involved.
- Refuse to even listen to their issues with other people, as this contaminates your relationship with the other person.
- If they persist in sharing the conflict with you, warn them that you will share everything you hear with the other person involved unless they agree to go directly to this person with the conflict.

- You may also offer to help mediate the conflict if you want to and both people agree to letting you serve in that role.
- Agree to serve as a mediator only if the two people involved directly ask you for help.

How Employees Can Identify Unhealed Developmental Shock, Trauma, and Stress

Employees often hope their bosses will be the "good parents" they always wanted, dreaming that the corporation or organization will give them what they did not get in their family of origin. The family patterns of employees and those of the company are often remarkably congruent, creating a stage where everyone triggers each other's unmet needs and unhealed developmental shocks, traumas, or stresses. People seem to be unconsciously drawn to workplaces with compatible family issues. Career choices and corporate positions are often made because of unresolved family patterns. I (Barry) am very aware of how they have influenced my career:

> I came from a post-depression family that had little financial stability during my early childhood. I felt a lot of tension in the house over money issues. I eventually saw how my decision to become a university professor was influenced by the need for financial predictability and security. As my awareness grew about the ongoing influence of developmental shock, trauma, or stress, I saw how my supervisors and deans exhibited elements of my mother and father. Many of my conflicts with these people were actually reenactments of unhealed developmental shocks, traumas, or stresses with my parents.

You may choose a role at work that is different from the one you played in your family of origin. However, it is likely to be a role that was played out by someone else in your family. If you were persecuted by an abusive mother or father, for example, you may assume the persecutor role at work when you are promoted to a supervisory position. The reasons for doing this are typically unconscious, but it is usually an attempt to heal any wounds you still carry about being victimized. You may use your position at work to discharge feelings of anger and resentment left over from your family-of-origin shocks, traumas, or stresses. Some people find it safer to act out their repressed feelings in the workplace than at home. If you do find yourself reenacting your family-of-origin conflicts in your workplace, be compassionate toward yourself. Just focus on identifying what triggered you so that you can identify the unhealed developmental shock, trauma, or stress and heal it.

If you do have unhealed developmental shock, trauma, or stress from your family of origin, it will surely appear at your workplace. Begin by identifying the events or people at work that trigger you and cause greater than normal reactions. Then use the tools you have learned to heal the effects of the shock, trauma, or stress. If you are able to do this, the workplace can become an exciting forum for healing your family-of-origin dramas.

If you are not able to do this, you run the risk of reenacting these shocks, traumas, or stresses at work. This vulnerability can affect your job effectiveness. Without an awareness of what triggers your responses, you are unable to prevent the replay of these developmental shocks, traumas, or stresses at work. This can have a significant impact on your career, and it may be at the root of an unstable employment history.

Perhaps the corporation of the future will develop "functional family" policies that facilitate LOVEvolution. The traditional corporate model not only undervalues family life but often forces employees to sacrifice their family life for the good of the company. Some corporations understand that this policy is both exploitive and destructive in the long run but do little to change it. However, more employees are now demanding changes in corporate structures that make the workplace more humane and family friendly.

In order to keep their employees, more progressive corporations provide benefits for employees that demonstrate an appreciation for creating a family-friendly workplace. They also provide more worksite policies and programs, such as flexible work hours, recreation programs, and on-site childcare facilities. These innovations foster a family-like atmosphere at work and provide for the creation of a functional family structure. In this time of unsettled social and economic conditions, rising divorce rates, and single-parent families, the workplace can be a stabilizing force in the lives of people.

In addition to these innovative policies, progressive organizations of the future will train their employees to identify and then support them in healing the developmental shocks, traumas, or stresses that show up at work every day. While this may seem like a radical and expensive policy, it is actually a cost-saving policy in the long term. When an organization makes that kind of commitment in its employees, the loyalty and discretionary effort that it creates will have a positive impact on the overall success of the organization.

At the end of this chapter are several exercises to help you identify developmental issues that could show up at work. One instrument helps identify family-of-origin patterns and the developmental shocks, traumas, or stresses connected with them. Another diagnoses the developmental components of your workplace dramas and shows how to use the principles and tools of DPC to heal any lingering impact of these dramas.

The vision of the corporation of the future as a functional family can become a reality when you learn how to use your corporate or work–family shocks, traumas, and stresses as a valuable source of evolutionary information. When you do, you will be able to help create a healthy corporate family to help members of the workforce shift to the LOVEvolution track of development.

Healing the Effects of Developmental Shock, Trauma, and Stress at Work

The following are the most effective ways to handle developmental traumas when they show up at your school, church, company, or agency:

- Teach about the dynamics of the drama triangle, the need/obligate system, and how to recognize unhealed developmental shock, trauma, or stress.
- Get a consensual agreement from all members to ask directly to get their needs met.
- Educate colleagues about the destructive power of triangulation and splitting.
- Train people to help each other to heal these developmental shocks, traumas, or stresses. This training should be experiential and provide ample opportunity for skill practice.

DPC can provide all employees with skills in identifying developmental shocks, traumas, or stresses and teach them to support each other through the healing process. Unless training in these skills is offered to all members, however, the organization has no framework for addressing these issues, and they will continue to slow down or stall the evolution of your organization.

Using Developmental Process Consultation to Facilitate Organizational Change

At the core of DPC is the principle that following the process of an organization will help you identify how and where it is developmentally stalled and show you which interventions are needed. The inventories at the end of this chapter can be used to assess your company's stage of development and evolution.

Another important principle of DPC is that every system is always in the process of evolving or devolving. It is possible to move this process forward when people understand how organizations and the people in them evolve and know how to accelerate or redirect this evolution.

With help, people and progressive organizations can identify the behaviors and beliefs that obstruct their development and change. Healthy organizations periodically review the effectiveness of their structures to determine how well they support their objectives. Individuals who are trained as DPCs are able to facilitate this change process.

Training Developmental Process Consultants to Use a Systems Approach in Organizational Consulting

A DPC needs the same core skills as a DPW, plus advanced skills for working effectively with large organizations, including nation–states. The advanced skills include training in the application of chaos theory; cross-cultural psychology; conflict resolution; dialogue; process consultation; organizational development; appreciative inquiry; large-group dynamics; cross-disciplinary team building; and data-collection, evaluation, and analysis skills.

The most effective skill development training is offered in experiential intensive workshops that begin with participants identifying and healing their own developmental shocks, traumas, or stresses. Self-development is the first priority for those who want to work as DPCs.

To become a certified DPCs, it is necessary to attend an introductory training, three week-long trainings in Healing Developmental Trauma, and an advanced training intensive in DPC. Completion of the core skills training is a prerequisite for the advanced training in DPC.

The Essential Skills of Developmental Process Consultants for Using a Systems Approach in Organizational Consulting

Mental health professionals who are helping their clients heal developmental shocks, traumas, or stresses in both small and large systems need a set of basic skills to help them achieve the goals of DPC. These basic skills are:

1. *Contracting skills.* You must establish a clear contract with your clients, whether they are individuals, couples, families, groups, or organizations. Both you and your client need clear outcome goals for both the duration of the consulting contract and for each aspect of the contract. After getting a clear consulting contract, with each consulting contact you need to ask your client: "What would you like from our work together today? Let's see how that fits with your consulting contract. What specifically would you like from me today related to your goals?" The contracting component of DPC solicits client participation in the intervention, which prevents you from acting out the rescuer role in the drama triangle. Contracting also creates safety for the client, as it establishes clear boundaries and teaches the client important negotiation skills.

2. *Visioning skills.* Visioning is a critical component of DPC. A clear consulting contract requires that you help the client create a vision of the desired outcomes. Without behaviorally based goals or a clear vision of a positive outcome, consulting rarely produces positive change. Individuals and members of larger social

systems need a positive vision to focus their energies and create lasting change. Without a vision, the energy of the individual or system eventually stagnates or dissipates, preventing the successful completion of goals and objectives.

A DPC must also ensure that the client does not create a negative consulting vision that focuses mostly on eliminating negative behaviors. Negative visioning ends up reinforcing the behavior or situation that is causing the problem. An example of this is "cutting down on turnover" or "eliminating employee conflicts." Both of these goals focus on the undesirable behaviors and lack a positive vision related to the health or wellness of the organization.

An example of the power of a positive national vision is President Kennedy's dream of landing an American on the moon by 1970. At the time he articulated this vision, the technology did not exist to accomplish this dream. His vision helped focus the nation's collective energies toward completion of this seemingly impossible task. An example of a negative vision goal is the attempt to reduce the size of the national debt. A more positive transformation of this negative national vision might involve using our nation's resources to create a more humane and responsible society.

3. *Empathy skills.* DPCs must first identify and heal their own developmental shocks, traumas, or stresses, which opens their hearts and makes them more emotionally available and supportive in their work with others. This is the best way to develop empathy and compassion for the wounds of others.

Through their own healing work, consultants learn the right brain–to–right brain synchronization process that is necessary for processing and regulating emotions. Through these personal experiences, consultants are then able to help their clients learn the emotional self-regulation skills they missed in their childhood.

4. *Process skills.* The most important skill needed to use DPC effectively is following the client's process as it unfolds. This includes:

- creating a trusting, protective relationship with organizational clients;
- giving positive support and validation for the organizational client's presenting problems;
- helping the organizational clients reframe their presenting problems to help them better understand their source;
- reflecting back aspects of the organizational client's reality that appear to be unseen by them;
- experiencing emotional synchrony and relational resonance with the client organization;
- making appropriate interventions in the organization to heal the effects of developmental shocks, traumas, or stresses;
- reprocessing distorted cognitions or beliefs among the members of the organization;

- healing organizational splits within the client organization; and
- repairing any damaged relationship dynamics in the client organization.

5. *Assessment skills.* Clinicians need system-specific inventories to assess an organization's current functioning level. These inventories correlate with Table 14.1. Intake data from these assessment tools need to be combined with oral intake information from the members of the organization to create a profile of the organization's current stage of development.

6. *Intervention skills.* The diagnostic profile created in the previous step is utilized to implement behaviorally based interventions that interrupt the fractal patterns of reenactment of unhealed developmental shock, trauma, and stress. These interventions also help clients get their developmental needs met and complete their essential developmental processes so that they can move forward in their evolution.

7. *Evaluation skills.* Both qualitative and quantitative tools must be used to evaluate the effectiveness of interventions. These include pre- and post-test quantitative measures. These include the Openness to Change and the Stages of Consciousness inventories at the end of this chapter, structured interviews, focus groups, and follow-up interviews with clients to provide additional post-intervention qualitative data that can be fed back into the design portion of the intervention process to ensure more effective organizational work.

8. *Cross-disciplinary team-building skills.* The systemic nature of DPC requires the skills for working in cross-disciplinary teams. Most traditional education, unfortunately, trains people as specialists with limited information and experience in other disciplines. DPCs who work with organizations, for example, learn very quickly that they must have skills in family counseling as well.

These services may require them to create a larger system of collaboration involving school officials, social service agencies, and the legal system. DPCs often observe the processes of teams that review the entire structure of the organization, requiring knowledge of the language and duties of a number of disciplines employed in that organization.

9. *Large-group process skills.* DPCs who do organizational consulting or work with national or international groups organizations also need large-group skills. In addition to public speaking and dialogue facilitation skills, they must be able to understand and facilitate group dynamics and to synthesize and summarize complex group issues. These skills are best learned through working with groups of increasingly larger size with the assistance of mentors or of a cotrainer.

10. *Cross-cultural skills.* DPCs need skills in working with a variety of cultures to gain specialized cross-cultural skills. The term cross-cultural can apply to corporate cultures involving top managers, middle managers, and employees; to

ethnic, racial, religious, social, economic, and political groups within a community, state, or nation; and between nation–states.

These skills include communication skills in values/beliefs clarification and specialized language and customs. These are best learned through immersion experiences in various cultures and training offered by groups or organizations that specialize in these areas.

Self-Inventory: Identifying Family Patterns in the Workplace

Complete this self-inventory by placing a number in the blank preceding each statement to indicate how true it is for you:

1 = Almost Never, 2 = Occasionally, 3 = Usually, 4 = Almost Always

____ 1. My feelings about my boss remind me of those I had with a parent when I was growing up.
____ 2. My boss says or does things that irritate me and remind me of ways that my parents treated me.
____ 3. My boss disapproves of things I say or do just the way my parents did.
____ 4. I criticize others and myself the way I was criticized as a child.
____ 5. Even though I don't want to, I find myself saying and doing things that hurt my coworkers the same way people hurt me while I was growing up.
____ 6. When I get upset at myself at work, I say some of the same critical things to myself that my parents or others said to me when I was a child.
____ 7. The way my boss relates to me reminds me of the way my parents related to me when I was a child.
____ 8. I find myself acting weak and helpless so others at work will feel sorry for me or help me out.
____ 9. I can see similarities between the way I relate to my colleagues and the way I related to my siblings.
____10. I tend to feel uneasy when everything seems to be going well at work.
____11. When I have conflicts with others at work, I tend to focus on what they did to cause the conflict.
____12. I feel underpaid and unappreciated at work.
____13. I feel so stressed by my job that I have no energy for play or exercise.
____14. I am afraid to appear too successful at work.
____15. I avoid taking risks at work and prefer to do what others expect of me.
____16. I sacrifice myself and/or my family life for the sake of the company.
____17. When asked, I have trouble thinking about or listing positive traits about my work responsibilities.

____18. I cannot express my feelings the way I would like while at work.
____19. I encounter people at work who tend to treat me like my parents treated me.
____20. I feel controlled by the expectations of people at work.
_______Total Score

Scoring and Interpretation:

Add the numbers in the column to get your total score.

Use the following guidelines to help you interpret the possible meaning of your score.

20–40 = A few family patterns are likely sources of your present work conflicts.
41–60 = Many family patterns are the likely sources of your present work conflicts.
61–80 = Almost all of your present work conflicts have their source in unprocessed family patterns.

Review each item where you answered 3 = Usually or 4 = Almost Always. These items can offer clues to family patterns present in any of your current work conflicts. For example, if you answered almost always to "I feel that I give more to my work than I receive back," explore the possibility that you were parentized in your family of origin and required to take care of others more than yourself. This might create work situations where you feel angry, unappreciated, and resentful. If this is true, it would be important to begin redirecting your anger toward family-of-origin members who expected you to deny your needs. Then learn effective ways to get your needs met in your current work relationships.

Self-Inventory: The Openness to Change Inventory

Directions: Place a number in the column that best represents your experiences of living within your organizational culture. Never = 1, Sometimes = 2, Usually = 3, and Almost Always = 4.

____ 1. The salary/wages I receive are fair for the work I provide.
____ 2. The benefits I receive meet my health care and other important needs.
____ 3. I trust that those who supervise me have my best interests at heart.
____ 4. My superiors listen to me and respect me as a person.
____ 5. When I have a problem or need, I know my superiors will respond seriously and effectively to my request for assistance.
____ 6. I have sufficient time to develop relationships with my coworkers.
____ 7. My superiors encourage me to contribute any new ideas I might have.

____ 8. There are few rules to restrict my freedom in this organization.
____ 9. I am consulted on decisions that directly affect me.
____10. Information and important decisions are shared in face-to-face meetings where I feel free to express my opinions and feelings.
____11. Important information and decisions are communicated in memos, policy letters, telephone calls, faxes, or email.
____12. When I want an answer to something, I have to check with numerous people.
____13. I am encouraged to wear as many "hats" as the situation calls for.
____14. I am free to change what I am doing in response to my needs or the needs of my customers, clients, and coworkers.
____15. If I perform above my expected level, my superiors will praise me.
____16. Managers, supervisors, and employees work together toward common goals and objectives.
____17. I have the power to make the decisions that affect me most directly.
____18. My superiors support and/or reward my efforts toward personal growth and mastery.
____19. The approved procedures and schedules are loosely followed in this organization.
____20. The goals and purposes of this organization are determined through input from all those involved in the organization.
____21. When I have a conflict with a supervisor or administrator, I anticipate an equitable resolution.
____22. The opportunity exists in this organization for people to take cooperative and collective action to reach their goals and objectives.
____23. The basic attitude of everyone is to look out for themselves; looking out for each other is actively discouraged.
____24. A top priority of this organization is the personal growth and development of each employee.

Scoring and Interpretation:

This inventory yields four subscores and a total organizational score. Total your ratings for each subscore, then apply the interpretation of scores to each subscore. Finally, consult the interpretation of the total organizational score.

______ Incomplete Developmental Processes in the Codependent Stage (Add your scores for items 1–6)
______ Incomplete Developmental Processes in the Counterdependent Stage (Add your scores for items 7–12)
______ Incomplete Developmental Processes in the Independent Stage (Add your scores for items 13–18)

______ Incomplete Developmental Processes in the Interdependent Stage (Add your scores for items 19–24)
______ Total Organizational Score (Total of all the subscores)

Interpretation of Your Subscores:

21–24 = Most major developmental processes appear to be complete in this organization.
15–20 = A few incomplete developmental processes may be present in the structure of the organization.
11–14 = Clear evidence of the presence of major incomplete developmental processes in the structure of the organization
6–10 = Major reorganization of some of the basic structures of the organization may be necessary.

Interpretation of Total Organizational Score:

79–96 = Most essential developmental processes are being supported in this organization.
60–78 = A few incomplete developmental processes are present in this organization. (Check the lowest of the four subscores to locate the gaps.)
42–59 = Clear evidence of incomplete developmental processes in this organization. (Check the lowest of the four subscores to locate the gaps.)
24–41 = Major reorganization of the basic structures and processes of this organization may be necessary.

The SOC Inventory

Complete the self-inventory by placing a number in the blank preceding each statement to indicate how true it is for you:

1 = Almost Never, 2 = Sometimes, 3 = Often, 4 = Almost Always

____ 1. Conflicts just seem to happen to me, and I have no idea why.
____ 2. In a conflict situation, someone has to win and someone has to lose.
____ 3. In a conflict situation, I feel victimized by the actions of others.
____ 4. I can see the underlying patterns in my recurring conflicts.
____ 5. I have the skills to help others successfully resolve their conflicts.
____ 6. If I have a conflict, I turn it over to God or my higher power.
____ 7. In a conflict situation, I tend to see myself as right and the other person as wrong.
____ 8. In a conflict situation, I try to shoot down the arguments of the other person.

____ 9. As the result of resolving my conflicts, I am better able to understand myself and why I got into a conflict with this person.
____10. I have altered some of my values and beliefs as the result of my conflicts.
____11. I wish that the people who bug me would just go away.
____12. In a conflict situation, I end up not getting what I want and the other person does.
____13. I lack confidence in my ability to resolve my conflicts successfully.
____14. I can see the causes of my current conflicts stemming from similar unresolved conflicts I had as a child.
____15. I have the ability to locate and resolve any unresolved conflicts from my past.
____16. In a conflict situation, I am afraid that I will lose myself if I consider the other person's position or needs.
____17. I believe that the past is the past; you have to put it behind you and go on.
____18. I depend on the instruction of my teachers, because they have more knowledge and experience than I do.
____19. I am able to see how the patterns of unresolved conflicts from my past are controlling my life.
____20. I am able to change the major underlying dysfunctional patterns of behavior that have controlled my life.

Scoring and Interpretation:

To get a score for each of the five stages of consciousness, add the numbers for the four items keyed to each stage:

Stage One (Add items 1, 6, 11, and 16) = _______
Stage Two (Add items 2, 7, 12, and 17) = _______
Stage Three (Add items 3, 8, 13, and 18) = _______
Stage Four (Add items 4, 9, 14, and 19) = _______
Stage Five (Add items 5, 10, 15, and 20) = _______

After receiving information about what each stage represents, you can use the following interpretation of your scores. The stages of consciousness where you had your highest scores are the ones that you are most likely to use in a conflict situation. The higher the stage of consciousness where you have your high scores, the better chance you have of being successful in using the Partnership Way to resolve your conflicts.

In each of the five stages of consciousness, a score of 10–16 = a high score, 5–9 = a medium score, and 1–4 = a low score.

References

American Institute on Domestic Violence. (2001). *The Human Factor.* Retrieved from http://www.aidv-usa.com/statistics.htm

Anonymous. (n.d.). Please don't circumcise. *Complete Mother Magazine.* Retrieved from http://www.compleatmother.com/circ.htm

American Psychiatric Association. (1994). *Diagnostic and statistical manual of mental disorders* (4th ed.).Washington, DC: Author.

Babcock, D., & Keepers, T. (1976). *Raising kids OK.* New York: Grove Press.

Bandler, R., & Grinder, J. (1979). *Frogs into princes: Neuro linguistic programming.* Moab, UT: Real People Press.

Bandura, A. (1986). *Social cognitive theory.* Englewood Cliffs, NJ: Prentice-Hall.

Bateson, G., Jackson, D. D., Haley, J., & Weakland, J. (1956). "Towards a theory of schizophrenia." *Behavioral Sciences, 1,* 251–264.

Becker, R. O. (1998). *The body electric: Electromagnetism and the foundation of life.* Quill.

Bernstein, P. (1985). *Family ties, corporate bonds.* New York: Henry Holt.

Bodack, P. (1998, Fall). The latest rage … incidents of road rage are on the rise. *American Automobile Association,* p. 8. Retrieved from http://www.paturnpike.com/tools/newsletters/fall98/page08.htm

Bolton, T. (1976). *People skills.* New York: Simon & Schuster.

Bowen, M. (1978). *Family therapy in clinical practice.* New York: Jason Aronson.

Bowlby, J. (1969). Attachment and loss. In J. Bowlby, *Separation: Anxiety and anger.* (Vol. 1). New York: Basic Books.

Boyle, P., & Brawley, O. (2009, July/August). Prostate cancer: Current evidence weighs against population screening, *CA: A Cancer Journal for Clinicians, 59,* 220–224.

Braden, G. (2000). *The Isaiah effect: Decoding the lost science of prayer and prophecy.* New York: Random House.

Braden, G. (2004). *The God code.* Carlsbad, CA: Hay House.

Bradshaw, J. (1988). *Healing the shame that binds you.* Deerfield Beach, FL: Health Communications.

Bradshaw, J. (1990). *Homecoming: Reclaiming and championing your inner child.* New York: Bantam.

Brawley, O., Ankerst, D., & Thompson, I. (2009, July/August). Screening for prostate cancer. *CA: Cancer Journal for Clinicians, 59*(4) 264–273. Retrieved from http://www3.interscience.wiley.com/cgi-bin/fulltext/122477069/HTMLSTART

Briggs, J., & Peat, F. (1989). *The turbulent mirror.* New York: Harper & Row.

Brodie, W. (2001). *The cancer personality: Its importance in healing.* Retrieved from http://www.healingcancernaturally.com/emotions-and-cancer-healing.html#cancerpersonality

Brodie, D. (1997). *Cancer and common sense, combining science and nature to control cancer.* Reno, NV: Winning.

Brown, L. (2008). *Plan B 3.0: Rescuing a planet under stress and a civilization in trouble.* New York: W. W. Norton.

Brownell, P. (in press). *Gestalt therapy: A guidebook for mental health professionals*, New York: Springer.

Buckley, W. (1968). *Sociology and modern systems theory.* Englewood Cliffs, NJ: Prentice-Hall.

Bureau of Labor Statistics. (2005). *National census of fatal occupational injuries.* Washington, DC: Author.

Bureau of Labor Statistics. (2008). *Employment characteristics of families summary.* Washington DC: Author. Retrieved from www.bls.gov/news.release/famee.nr0.htm.

Burgan, M. (2009). *Nikola Tesla: Physicist, inventor, electrical engineer.* Mankato, MN: Capstone Press.

Callahan, R. (2001). *Tapping the healer within: Using thought-field therapy to instantly conquer your fears, anxieties, and emotional distress.* Chicago: Contemporary Books.

Cashdan, S. (1988). *Object relations therapy: Using the relationship.* New York: W. W. Norton.

Castellino, R. (2000). The stress matrix: Implications for prenatal and birth therapy. *Journal of Prenatal and Perinatal Psychology & Health, 15*(1), 3–22.

Centers for Disease Control and Prevention (CDC). (2003, April). *Costs of intimate partner violence against women in the United States.* Atlanta, GA: Author.

Chamberlin, D. (1998). *The mind of your newborn baby.* Berkeley, CA: North Atlantic Books.

Chamberlain, D. (1999). Selected works by David B. Chamberlain. *Journal of Prenatal & Perinatal Psychology and Health, 14*(1–2), 1–194.

Chamberlain, D. (2003). *Early and very early parenting: Very early parenting starts before conception.* Retrieved from http://birthpsychology.com/lifebefore/early9.html

Chappell, P. (2003). *Emotional healing with homeopathy: Treating the effects of trauma.* Berkley, CA: North Atlantic Books.

Chrousos, G., & Gold, P. (2002). Stress system malfunction could lead to serious, life threatening disease, *NIH Backgrounder.* Bethesda, MD: National Institute of Child Health and Development.

Circumcision resources link. (n.d.). *The compleat mother: The magazine of pregnancy, birth and breastfeeding.* Retrieved from http://www.compleatmother.com/circ.htm

Clarke, J. (1978). *Self-esteem: A family affair.* New York: Harper & Row.

Clarke, J., & Dawson, C. (1989). *Growing up again: Parenting ourselves, parenting our children.* Minneapolis, MN: Hazelton.

Clow, B. (1991). *The liquid light of sex: Understanding your life transitions.* Santa Fe, NM: Bear & Co.

Clow, B. H. (2007). *The Mayan code: Time acceleration and awakening the world mind.* Santa Fe, NM: Bear & Co.

Cook, A., Blaustein, M., Spinazzola, J., & van der Kolk, B. (2003). *Complex trauma in children and adolescents.* White paper from the National Child Traumatic Stress Network Complex Trauma Task Force, Durham, NC.

Coolidge, F. (1999). *Coolidge assessment battery.* SIGMA Assessment Systems, P.O. Box 610984, Port Huron, MI 48061-0984.

Cooper, K. (1982). *Aerobics program for total well-being: Exercise, diet, and emotional balance.* New York: Bantam Books.

Courtois, C. A. (1993). Vicarious traumatization of the therapist. *NCP Clinical Newsletter, 3*(2) 1–4.

Craig, G. (n.d.). *Emotional freedom technique.* Retrieved from http://www.emofree.com

Crenshaw, T. (1997). *The alchemy of love and lust.* New York: Pocket Books.

Crum, T. (1998). *The magic of conflict: Turning a life of work into a work of life.* New York: Simon & Schuster.

DeAngelis, T. (2007). A new diagnosis for childhood trauma? *Monitor on Psychology, 38*(3), 32.

deMause, L. (1982). *Foundations of psychohistory.* New York: Creative Roots.

deMause, L. (1991). The universality of incest. *The Journal of Psychohistory, 19*, 123–164.

Dewey, J. (1963). *Experience and education.* New York: Collier. (Original work published in 1938.)

Diamond, J. (1989). *The addiction to adrenaline inventory*. Self-published paper.

Diamond, A., & Doar, B. (1989). The performance of human infants on a measure of frontal cortex function, the delayed response task. *Developmental Psychobiology, 22*(3), 271–274.

Dilts, R., & Green, J. (1982). Applications of neurolinguistic programming in family therapy. In A. M. Horne & M. M. Ohlson (Eds.), *Family counseling and therapy*. Itasca, IL: Peacock.

Donoghue, J. (n.d.). *Inner empathy: Gently revealing our disowned core needs and holding them in compassionate presence*. Unpublished manuscript.

Dykema, R. (2006). How your nervous system sabotages your ability to relate: An interview with Stephen Porges about his polyvagal theory. *Nexus Magazine*. Retrieved from http://www.nexuspub.com/articles/2006/interview_ma.htm

Eisler, R. (1987). *The chalice and the blade*. Pacific Grove, CA: Harper-Collins.

Eisler, R. (2003). *The power of partnership*. Novato CA: New World Library.

Ellis, A. (1995). Rational emotive behavior therapy. In R. J. Corsini & D. Wedding (Eds.), *Current psychotherapies* (5th ed.). Itasca: IL: Peacock.

Emerson, W. (1993). *Treatment outcomes*. Petaluma, CA: Emerson Training Seminars.

Emerson, W. (1996). Points of view. *Pre- and Perinatal Psychology Journal, 10*(3), 125–142.

Emerson, W. (2007). *Emerson seminars, workshops and trainings*. Retrieved from http://docs.google.com/gview?a=v&q=cache:0tU_bEtiQM8J:www.emersonbirthrx.com/ESschdl07_email.pdf+relational+shock+clearing+process+2007&hl= en&gl=us

Erikson, E. (1959). *Psychological issues*. New York: International Universities Press.

Farrant, G. (1988, Summer). Cellular consciousness and conception, *Pre- & Perinatal Psychology News, 2*(2).

Farrant, G., & Larimore, T. (1997). Egg and sperm memory: Universal body movements in cellular consciousness and what they mean. *Primal Spirit, 2*(1), 1.

Federal Bureau of Investigation, Uniform Crime Reporting Program. (2005). Hate crime statistics. Washington, D.C. Retrieved from http://www.fbi.gov/ucr/hc2005/index.html

Feinstein, D., Eden, D., Craig, G., & Bowen, M. (2005). *The promise of energy psychology: Revolutionary tools or dramatic personal change*. New York: Tarcher/Penguin.

Fennel, D., & Weinhold, B. (2003). *Counseling families: An introduction to marriage and family therapy* (3rd ed.). Denver, CO: Love.

Feuerstein, G. (1996). *The shambhala guide to yoga* (1st ed.). Boston & London: Shambhala.

Figley, C. R. (Ed.). (1978). *Stress disorders among Vietnam veterans: Theory, research, and treatment*. In the Psychosocial Stress Book Series. New York: Brunner/Mazel.

Figley, C. R. (Ed.). (1985). *Trauma and its wake: The study and treatment of post-traumatic stress disorders*. In the Psychosocial Stress Book Series. New York: Brunner/Mazel.

Figley, C. R. (Ed.). (1986). *Trauma and its wake: Traumatic stress disorders: theory, research, and treatment* (Vol. II). In the Psychosocial Stress Book Series. New York: Brunner/Mazel.

Figley, C. R. (Ed.). (2006). *Mapping the wake of trauma: Autobiographical essays by the pioneers of trauma research*. In the Psychosocial Stress Book Series. New York: Routledge.

Figley, C. R., & Leventman, S. (Eds.). (1980). *Strangers at home: Vietnam veterans since the war*. New York: Praeger.

Figley, C. R., & McCubbin, H. I. (Eds.). (1983). *Stress and the family: Coping with catastrophe* (Vol. II). In the Psychosocial Stress Book Series. New York: Brunner/Mazel.

Figley, C. R., & Nash, W. P. (Eds.). (2007). *Combat stress injury theory, research, and management*. New York: Routledge.

Fleming, T. (n.d.). *TAT professional's manual*. Retrieved from http://store.tatlife.com/index.php?main_page=product_info&cPath=22&products_id=86

Ford, D., & Lerner, R. (1992). *Developmental systems theory: An integrative approach*. Newbury Park, CA: Sage.

Forward, S., & Buck, C. (1978). *Betrayal of innocence*. New York: Penguin Books.

Fosar, G., & Bludorf, F. (2001). *Vernetzte Intelligenz*. Düsseldorf: Auf Lager.

Framo, J. (1982). *Explorations in marital and family therapy.* New York: Springer.

Freire, P. (1994). *Pedagogy of the oppressed.* New York: Continuum.

Freud, S. (1921). *Jenseits des Lustprinzips [Beyond the pleasure principle].* Zurich, Switzerland: International Psychoanalytical Publishing House.

Frye, V. (2001). Examining homicide's contribution to pregnancy-associated deaths. *Journal of the American Medical Association, 285*(11), 1510–1511.

Gariaev, P. (Ed.). (1997). *Wave genetic code* (in Russian). Moscow: Izdatcentr.

Gass, R. (1991). *Opening the heart: Guided imagery and music (*audiocassette recording). Boulder, CO: Spring Hill Music.

Gazmararian, J. A., Petersen, R., Spitz, A. M., Goodwin, M. M., Saltzman, L. E., & Marks, J. S. (2000). Violence and reproductive health: Current knowledge and future research directions. *Maternal and Child Health Journal, 4*(2), 79–84.

Gimbutas, M. (1982). *The goddesses and the gods of old Europe: 6500–3500 B.C.* Berkeley & Los Angeles: University of California.

Glazov, J. (2001). Male circumcision (Part 2)—Much more than the mutilation of sexual pleasure. Retrieved from http://97.74.65.51/readArticle.aspx?ARTID=25206

Gleick, J. (1987). *Chaos: Making a new science.* New York: Penguin.

Goerner, S. (1995). Chaos, evolution, and deep ecology. In R. Robertson & A. Combs (Eds.), *Chaos theory in psychology and the life sciences.* (pp. 17–38). Mahwah, NJ: Erlbaum.

Gold, M. S., & Tabrah, H. (2000). Update on the ecstasy epidemic. *Journal of Addictions Nursing, 12*(3/4), 133–142.

Goleman, D. (1996). *Emotional intelligence.* New York: Bantam.

Goleman, D. (2006). *Social intelligence: The new science of human relationships.* New York: Bantam.

Goleman, D. (2009). *Ecological intelligence: How knowing the hidden impacts of what we buy can change everything.* New York: St. Martin's Press.

Goulding, M., & Goulding, R. (1978). *The power is in the patient: A gestalt approach to psychotherapy.* San Francisco: TA Press.

Green, J. D., & Dilts, R. (1982). Neuro-linguistic programming in family therapy. In A. M. Horne, & M. M. Olsen (Eds.), *Family Counseling and Therapy*. Itaska, IL: Peacock.

Grof, S., & Grof, C. (n.d.). Retrieved from http://www.breathwork.com

Gutmann, G. (1990, July/August). Blocked atlantal nerve syndrome in infants and small children [English translation from *Manuelle Medizine* published by Springer-Verlag in 1987]. *International Review of Chiropractic.*

Gyatso, T. (1989). *Dalai Lama's peace prize acceptance speech.* Retrieved from https://ssl4.westserver.net/spiritual/peace/dalilama.htm

Haley, J. (1971). *Changing families: A family reader.* New York: Grune & Stratton.

Hamer, R. (2000). *Summary of the New Medicine.* Switzerland: Knautsch.

Hamer, R. (n.d.) GNM paradigm. *Learning German New Medicine.* Retrieved from http://learninggnm.com/

Hardwick, C. (2008). Geeks take their cue from Thomas Edison's napping technique, *Wired Magazine.* Retrieved from http://www.wired.com/gadgets/miscellaneous/magazine/16-06/st_napping

Havighurst, R. (1972*). Developmental tasks and education*. New York: David McKay.

Hay, L. (1984). *You can heal your life.* Carlsbad, CA: Hay House.

Henderson, B. (2005). *Cancer-free: Your guide to gentle, non-toxic healing.* San Antonio, TX: Get And Stay Well.

Hepper, P. G. (1996). Fetal memory: Does it exist? What does it do? *Acta Paediatr* (Stockholm). Suppl 416:16–20.

Herman, J. (1992). *Trauma and recovery.* New York: Basic Books.

Hess, E. H. (1975). The role of pupil size in communication. *Scientific American, 233,* 110–119.

Hoeller, S. (1989). *The gnostic Jung and the seven sermons to the dead.* Wheaton, IL: Quest Books.

Hofer, M. A. (1990). Early symbiotic processes: Hard evidence from a soft place. In A. Glick & S. Bone (Eds.), *Pleasure beyond the pleasure principle*. New Haven: Yale University Press.

Hooks, B. (1994). *Teaching to transgress*. New York: Routledge.

Horner, A. (1979). Object relations and the developing ego in therapy. New York: Jason Aronson.

Horon, I., & Cheng, D. (2001). Enhanced surveillance of pregnancy-associated mortality—Maryland 1993–1998. *Journal of the American Medical Association, 285*(11), 1455–1459.

Horsfield, K., Dart, G., Olson, D. E., Filley, G. F., & Cumming, G. (1971). Models of the human bronchial tree. *Journal of Applied Physiology,* 207–217.

Houlihan, J., Kropp, T., Wiles, R., Gray, S., Campbell, C., & Greene, A. (2005). *Body burden: The pollution in newborns*. Washington, DC: Environmental Working Group.

Hughes, F. (2007, March 9). Cancer and heart disease cured by new discovery. *Columbia Star* (Columbia, SC), 1.

Hurley, D. (2006). *Natural causes*. New York: Broadway Books.

Huttenlocher, P. (1984, March). Synapse elimination and plasticity in developing human cerebral cortex. *American Journal of Mental Deficiency, 88*(5), 488–496.

International Transport Workers Federation. (2000). *Air rage: The prevention and management of disruptive passenger behaviour. A guide to good practice and practical action for aviation trade unionists, the transport industry and safety regulators*. London: ITF Publications.

Izzo, J., Sica, D., & Black, H. (Eds.). (2007). *Hypertension primer: The essentials of high blood pressure: Basic science, population science, and clinical management* (4th ed.). New York: Lippincott-Williams & Wilkins.

Jackson, D. (1965). Family rules: The mantel quid pro quo. *Archives of General Psychiatry, 12,* 589–594.

James, B. (1994). *Handbook for treatment of attachment-trauma problems in children*. New York: The Free Press.

James, L., & Nahl, D. (2006). *Flight attendants worldwide rally against "air rage."* Retrieved from http://www.drdriving.org/rages/air2.htm

Johnson, D. W., Johnson, R. T., & Holubec, E. J. (1993). *Circles of learning: Cooperation in the classroom.* (6th ed.). Edina, MN: Interaction Book Co.

Johnson, R. (1986). *Inner work: Using dreams and active imagination for personal growth.* San Francisco: Harper & Row.

Johnson, S. (1987). *Humanizing the narcissistic style*. New York: W. W. Norton.

Jongeward, D. (1973). *Everybody wins: Transactional analysis applied to organizations.* Menlo Park, CA: Addison-Wesley.

Jung, C. (1968). *Archetypes and the collective unconscious* (Collected works, Vol. 9, Part 1). Princeton, NJ: Princeton University Press.

Kammerman, S. B. (2000). From maternity to parental leave policies: Women's health, employment, and child and family well-being. *The Journal of the American Women's Medical Association, 55,* 96–99.

Kaplan, L. (1978). *Oneness and separateness.* New York: Simon & Schuster.

Kaplan, L. (1984). *Adolescence: The farewell to childhood.* New York: Simon & Schuster.

Karpman, S. (1968). Fairytales and script drama analysis. *Transactional Analysis Bulletin, 7,* 39–43.

Kaufman, J., & Zigler, E. (1990). The intergenerational transmission of abuse. In D. Cicchetti & V. Carlson (Eds.), *Child maltreatment: Theory and research on the causes and consequences of child abuse and neglect.* New York: Cambridge University Press.

Kegan, R. (1994). *In over our heads.* Cambridge, MA: Harvard University Press.

Kelder, P. (1985). *An ancient secret of the fountain of youth.* New York: Doubleday.

Kellogg, C. (1991). Postnatal effects of prenatal exposure to psychoactive drugs. *Journal of Prenatal and Perinatal Psychology and Health, 5*(3), 233–252.

Kernberg, O. (1976). *Object relation's theory and clinical psychoanalysis.* New York: Jason Aronson.

Kiely, L. (n.d.). *Top-down yoga: The evolutionary" 'body" of our humanity.* Retrieved from http://tdynyc.50megs.com

King, S. (2005). Miasms in homeopathy. *Classical Homeopathy.* Retrieved from http://homepage.ntlworld.com/homeopathy_advice/Theory/Intermediate/miasm.html

Klaus, M. (1995, September 30). *Importance of post-natal relationships.* Speech given at the 7th International Congress Association for Prenatal and Perinatal Psychology and Health, San Francisco, CA.

Klaus, M., & Klaus, P. (2000). *Your amazing newborn.* New York: Perseus/ HarperCollins.

Kolb, D. (1984). *Experiential learning.* Englewood Cliffs, NJ: Prentice Hall.

Krause, A., & Haverkamp, B. (1996). Attachment in adult child–older parent relationships: Research, theory and practice. *Journal of Counseling and Development, 75,* 85–86.

Kreisman, J., & Straus, H. (1989). *I hate you, don't leave me: Understanding the borderline personality.* Los Angeles: Avon Books.

Krishnamurti, J. (1986). *The future of humanity: Two dialogues between J. Krishnamurti and David Bohm.* Largo, FL: Miranda Press.

Lachkar, J. (1992). *The narcissistic-borderline couple: A psychoanalytic perspective on marital treatment.* New York: Bruner/Mazel.

LaGoy, L. (1993, August). *An imprint for life.* Presented at Pre- and Perinatal Psychology Congress in Washington, DC. Retrieved from http://primal-page.com/lagoy.htm

LaGoy, L. (2007). *An exploration into the vanishing twin syndrome and its possible psychological influence on the surviving twin.* Unpublished doctoral dissertation. Retrieved from http://www.beba.org/programs/research/PhD_Nancy.pdf

Lander, J., Brady-Fryer, B., Metcalfe, J. B., Nazarali, S., & Muttitt, S. (1997). Comparison of ring block, dorsal penile nerve block, and topical anesthesia for neonatal circumcision. *Journal of the American Medical Association, 278,* 2157–2162.

Landreth, G. (2002). *Play therapy: The art of the relationship.* (2nd ed.). New York: Brunner-Routledge.

Last, W. (2007). Sexual energy in health and spirituality. *Nexus magazine, 14*(3), 25–26.

Last, W. (n.d.). *The new medicine of Dr. Hamer.* Retrieved from http://www.whale.to/cancer/last.html

LeBoyer, F. (1975). *Birth without violence.* New York: Knopf.

LeBoyer, F. (1980). *Frederick LeBoyer's 4 June 1989 letter to Rosemary Romberg-Weiner.* Retrieved from http://intact.wikia.com/wiki/Fred%C3%A9rick_Leboyer%27s_4_june_1980_letter_to_Rosemary_Romberg-Weiner

LeBoyer, F. (2002). *Birth without violence.* Rochester, NY: Healing Arts Press.

LeDoux, J. (1994, June). Emotion, memory and the brain, *Scientific American,* 50–57.

LeDoux, J. (2002). *Synaptic self: How our brains become who we are.* New York: Viking.

Lehrer, P., Woolfolk, R., & Sime, W. (Eds.). (2007). *Principles and practice of stress management* (3rd ed.). NY: Guilford.

Levin, P. (1988a). *Becoming the way we are.* Deerfield Beach, FL: Health Communications.

Levin, P. (1988b). *Cycles of power.* Deerfield Beach, FL: Health Communications.

Levine, P. (1997). *Waking the tiger: Healing trauma.* Berkeley, CA: North Atlantic Books.

Levine, P. (2005). *Healing trauma: A pioneering program for restoring the wisdom of your body.* Boulder, CO: Sounds True.

Levine, V. (1999). *Mind and body therapies.* Chicago: Lowell House.

Lewis, T., Amini, F., & Lannon, R. (2000). *A general theory of love.* New York: Vantage Books.

Lewis, H. B. (1980). Narcissistic personality or shame prone superego mode. *Comprehensive Psychotherapy, 1,* 59–80.

Likert, R., & Likert, J. (1976). *New ways of managing conflict.* New York: McGraw-Hill.

Lipari, J. (2000, July/August). Raising baby: What you need to know. *Psychology Today.* Retrieved from http://www.psychologytoday.com/articles/200007/raising-baby-what-you-need-know

Lipton, B. (1986). Cellular consciousness. *Planetary Association for Clean Energy Newsletter, 5,* 4.

Lipton, B. (2001). *Nature, Nurture and Human Development*. Retrieved from http://www.brucelipton.com/conscious-parenting/nature-nurture-and-human-development

Lipton, B. (2005). *The biology of belief.* Santa Rosa, CA: Mountain of Love/Elite Books.

Lipton, B. (2006). *As is above … so is below: An introduction to fractal evolution*. Talk given at the International Conference on Science and Consciousness, April 27, 2006, Santa Fe, NM.

Litwak, E. (1961). Models of bureaucracy which permit conflict. *American Journal of Sociology, 67,* 177–184.

Lowen, A. (1994). *Love, sex and your heart.* NY: Penguin/Arkana.

MacLean, P. (1974). *Triune conception of the brain and behaviour.* Toronto: University of Toronto Press.

Magid, K., & McKelvey, C. (1989). *High risk: Children without a conscience.* New York: Bantam.

Magill, F., & Tilghman, T. (1965). *Magill's Quotations in Context.* Harper & Row.

Mahler, M. (1980). Rapprochement subphase of the separation-individuation process. In R. Lax, S. Bach, & J. A. Burland (Eds.), *Rapprochement: The critical subphase of separation-individuation* (pp. 3–19). New York: Jason Aronson.

Mahler, M., & Furer, M. (1968). *On human symbiosis and the vicissitudes of individuation.* New York: International University Press.

Mahler, M., Pine, F. & Bergman, F. (1975). *Psychological birth of the human infant: Symbiosis and individuation.* New York: Basic Books.

Malaspina, D. (2006). In session with Dolores Malaspina, MD, MSPH: The impact of childhood trauma on psychiatric illness. *Primary Psychiatry, 13*(7), 33–36.

Malaspina, D., Harlap, S., Fennig, S., Corcoran, C., & Susser, E. (2003). Maternal stress and offspring schizophrenia risk. *Biological Psychiatry, 53*(suppl), 168S.

Mandelbrot, B. (1980). Fractal aspects of the iteration of z for complex , (1–z). *Annals of the New York Academy of Sciences, 357,* 249–259.

Markolin, C. (2009). *Introduction to German new medicine.* Retrieved from http://learninggnm.com/

Markolin, C. (2010). *The five biological laws.* Retrieved from http://learninggnm.com

Masterson, J. (1993). *The real self: A developmental and object relations approach to the treatment of the closet narcissistic disorder of the self.* Philadelphia: Bruner/Mazel.

McAuliffe, G., & Eriksen, K. (2000). *Preparing counselors and therapists: Creating constructivist and developmental programs.* Virginia Beach, VA: Donning.

McCraty, R., Atkinson, M., & Tomasino, D. (2003). *Modulation of DNA Conformation by Heart-Focused Intention.* Boulder Creek, CA: HeartMath Research Center, Institute of HeartMath, www.heartmath.org.

Mead, V. (2006). *Facilitating mindbody dialogue in chronic illness: The parasympathetic nervous system.* Retrieved from http://www.veroniquemead.com/pns.php

Meichenbaum, D. (1994). *A clinical handbook/practical therapist manual: For assessing and treating adults with post-traumatic stress disorder (PTSD).* Waterloo, Ontario: Institute Press.

Miller, A. (1981). *Prisoners of childhood.* New York: Basic Books.

Miller, A. (1984). *For your own good.* New York: Farrar, Straus & Giroux.

Miller, A. (1986). *Thou shalt not be aware.* New York: New American Library.

Miller, A. (1988). *Banished knowledge.* New York: Doubleday.

Miller, A. (1991). *Breaking down the walls of silence.* New York: Dutton.

Miller, A. (2005). *The body never lies: The lingering effects of hurtful parenting.* New York: W. W. Norton.

Miller, J. G. (1978). *Living systems.* New York: McGraw-Hill.

Mindell, A. (1983). *Dreambody.* Santa Monica, CA: SIGO Press.

Mindell, A. (1985a). *Rivers way.* Boston: Routledge and Kegan Paul.

Mindell, A. (1985b). *Working with the dreambody.* Boston: Routledge and Kegan Paul.

Mindell, A. (1987). *The dreambody in relationship processes.* Boston: Routledge and Kegan Paul.

Mines, S. (2003). *We're all in shock: How overwhelming experiences can shatter you and what you can do about it*. Franklin Lakes, NJ: New Page Books.

Minuchin, S. (1974). *Families and family therapy*. Cambridge, MA: Harvard University Press.

Minuchin, S., & Fishman, C. (1981). *Family therapy techniques*. Cambridge, MA: Harvard University Press.

Moreno, J. (1985). *The autobiography of J. L. Moreno, M.D.* (Abridged). Cambridge, MA: Harvard University, Moreno Archives.

Nannini, A., Weiss, J., Goldstein, R., & Fogerty, S. (2002). Pregnancy-associated mortality at the end of the twentieth century: Massachusetts, 1990–1999. *The Journal of the American Medical Women's Association, 57*(3), 23.

National Center for the State Courts. (1996). *Examining the work of state courts, 1995: A national perspective from the court statistics project*. Williamsburg, VA: Author.

Nelson, B. (2007). *The emotion code.* Mesquite, NV: Wellness Unmasked.

Nelson, C., & Luciana, M. (Eds.). (2008). *Handbook of developmental cognitive neuroscience* (2nd ed.). Cambridge, MA: MIT Press.

Ney, P. (1988). Transgenerational child abuse. *Child Psychiatry and Human Development, 18,* 151–168.

Nicholls, D., & Ferguson, S. (2002). *Bioenergetics* (3rd ed). New York: Academic Press.

Niehoff, D. (2002). *The biology of violence: How understanding the brain, behavior and environment can break the vicious circle of aggression*. New York: The Free Press.

NIH Press Release. (2002, September 9). *Stress system malfunction could lead to serious, life threatening disease*. NIH Backgrounder. Rockville, MD: Author. Retrieved from http://www.nih.gov/news/pr/sep2002/nichd-09.htm

NIH State-of-the-Science Conference Statement. (2004). *Preventing violence and related health-risking social behaviors in adolescents.* Rockville, MD: U.S. Department of Health & Human Services.

Noble, E. (2003). *Having twins and more: A parent's guide to multiple pregnancy, birth and early childhood.* New York: Houghton Mifflin.

NOVA Video Series.(2000). *Life's First Feelings.* Boston: WGBH.

Odent, M. (1994). *Birth reborn.* New York: Pantheon.

Odent, M. (n.d.). How effective is the accordion method? Evaluating our preconceptional programme. *Primal Health.* Retrieved from http://birthpsychology.com/primalhealth/primal8.html.

Oneida Indian Nation. (2007, February 18). Retrieved from http://www.oneidaindiannation.com/about/government/27273129.html

Orr, L. (n.d.). *Rebirthing breathwork.* Retrieved from http://www.rebirthingbreathwork.com

Orr, L., & Ray, S. (1977). *Rebirthing in the new age*. Milbrae, CA: Celestial Arts.

Palmer, L. (2002). The chemistry of attachment. *API News, 5*(2). Retrieved from http://www.attachmentparenting.org/support/articles/art chemistry.php

Pearce, J. C. (1998). Waking up to the holographic heart: Starting over with education. *The Corporatization of Education Edition of Wild Duck Review, 4*, 2.

Perry, B. (1996). Incubated in terror: Neurodevelopmental factors in the cycle of violence. In J. Osofdsy (Ed.), *Children, youth and violence: Searching for solutions* (pp. 59–87). New York: Guilford Press.

Pert, C. (1997). *Molecules of emotion: The science behind mind-body medicine.* New York: Touchstone Books.

Piaget, J. (1951). *The child's conception of the world.* New York: Humanities Press.

Piaget, J. (1971). *Psychology and epistemology.* Harmondsworth, England: Penguin.

Prescott, J. (1997). *Perspectives on violence: Excerpts from the origins of human love and violence.* Retrieved from http://www.birthpsychology.com/violence/prescott.html http://www.birthpsychology.com/violence/prescott.html

Prescott, J. (2002). Paper presented at the Society for the Scientific Study of Sex and The Brain Conference, Midcontinent & Eastern Regions, June 13–16, 2002, Big Rapids, MI.

Porges, S. (1995). Orienting in a defensive world: Mammalian modifications of our evolutionary heritage. A polyvagal theory. *Psychophysiology, 32,* 301–318.

Porges, S. (2001). The polyvagal theory: Phylogenetic substrates of a social nervous system. *International Journal of Psychophysiology, 42,* 123–146.

Porges, S. (2003). Social engagement and attachment: A phylogenetic perspective. In J. A. King, C. F. Ferris, & I. I. Lederhendler (Eds.), *The roots of mental illness in children* (1008: 31 doi: 10.1196/annals.1301.004). New York: New York Academy of Sciences.

Pyterek, A. (n.d.). Circumcision: The root of misogyny. *The Compleat Mother.* Retrieved from http://www.birthpsychology.com/birthscene/circ.html - pyterek

Quilligan, J. (2007, March/April). Mobilizing for a global Marshall Plan: toward a transformational foreign policy. *Tikkun Magazine.* Retrieved from http://www.tikkun.org/article.php/Quilligan-mobilizingaglobalmarshallplan

Rand, M. (1996). The importance of bonding. As it was in the beginning: The significance of infant bonding in the development of self and relationships. *Journal of Child and Youth Care, 10,* 4.

Ray, R. (2002). *Indestructible truth: The living spirituality of Tibetan Buddhism.* Boston: Shambhala.

Reich, W. (1948). *Listen, little man!* New York: Orgone Institute Press.

Reik, W., & Walter, J. (2001). "Genomic imprinting: Parental influence on the genome." *Nature Reviews Genetics, 2,* 21+.

Reno Integrative Medical Center. (2008). *What is cancer?* Retrieved from http://www.renointegrative.com/nature.html

Rhinehart, J. (1999). Neonatal circumcision revisited. *Transactional Analysis Journal, 29,* 215–222.

Rife, R. (1931). *Resonant frequency therapy: Building the Rife bare device.* Self-published by author.

Robertson, T. (2005). *Fertility and the mind-body connection.* Retrieved from http://www.birthpsychology.com/lifebefore/concept11.html

Robinson, M., & Wilson, G. (2006). *Sex and addiction.* Retrieved from http://www.reuniting.info/science/sex_and_addiction

Rogers, C. (1986). The Reist workshop: A personal overview. *Journal of Humanistic Psychology, 26,* 23–45.

Rogers, C., & Ryback, D. (1984). One alternative to planetary suicide. In R. F. Levant & J. M. Shlien (Eds.), *Client-centered therapy and the person-centered approach: New directions in theory, research and practice.* New York: Praeger.

Rothbart, M. K., Taylor, S. B., & Tucker, D. M. (1989). Right-sided facial asymmetry in infant emotional expression. *Neuropsychologia, 27,* 675–687.

Rothschild, B. (2000). *The body remembers: The psychophysiology of trauma and trauma treatment.* New York: W. W. Norton.

Rothschild, B. (2003). Applying the brakes. *Body Mind Spirit Magazine, 21.* Retrieved from http://www.saskworld.com/bodymindspirit/edition21/17_article_rothschild.htm

The Rush. (n.d.). Retrieved from http://www.therush247.com/abouttherushs18.php

Sager, C. J., & Kaplan, H. S. (1971). The marriage contract. *Family Process, 10,* 311–326.

Sandel, S., Chaiklin, S., & Lohn, A. (Eds.). (1993). *Foundations of dance/movement therapy: The life and work of Marian Chace.* Washington, DC: American Dance Therapy Association.

Satir, V. (1988). *The new peoplemaking.* Palo Alto, CA: Science and Behavior Books.

Schaaf, R. C., & Miller, L. J. (2005). Occupational therapy using a sensory integrative approach for children with developmental disabilities. *Mental Retardation and Developmental Disabilities Research Reviews, 11*(2), 143–148.

Schein, E. (1969). *Process consultation: Its role in organizational development.* Reading CA: Addison-Wesley.

Schiff, J. (1970). *All my children.* New York: Pyramid.

Schiff, J. (1976). *The cathexis reader.* New York: Harper & Row.

Schore, A. N. (1991). Early superego development: The emergence of shame and narcissistic affect regulation in the practicing period. *Psychoanalysis and Contemporary Thought, 14,* 187–250.

Schore, A. N. (1994). *Affect regulation and the origin of the self: The neurobiology of emotional development*. Nahwah, NJ: Erlbaum.

Schore, A. (1996). The experience-dependent maturation of a regulatory system in the orbital prefrontal cortex and the origin of developmental psychopathology. *Development and Psychopathology, 8*(1), 58–87.

Schore, A. (1999). *Affect regulation and the origin of the self: The neurobiology of emotional development.* Hillsdale, NJ: Erlbaum.

Schore A. (2001). The effects of early relational trauma on right brain development, affect regulation, and infant mental health. *Infant Mental Health Journal, 22,* 201–269.

Schore, A. (2003a). *Affect regulation and disorders of the self.* New York: W. W. Norton.

Schore, A. (2003b). *Affect regulation and the repair of the self.* New York: W. W. Norton.

Schore, A. (2004, August 30). Raising baby: What you need to know. *Psychology Today.* Retrieved from www.psychologytoday.com

Seligman, M. (1998). *Learned optimism: How to change your mind and your life*. NewYork: Free Press.

Senge, P. (1990). *The fifth discipline.* New York: Doubleday.

Shapiro, R. (2009, July 9). *Personal blog*. Retrieved from http://traumatherapy.typepad.com/trauma_attachment_therapy/

Shapiro, F., & Forrest, M. (1997). *EMDR: The breakthrough "eye movement" therapy for overcoming anxiety, stress, and trauma*. New York: Basic Books. Retrieved October 22, 2009, from http://www.emdr.com/

Sjoo, M., & Mor, B. (1987). *The great cosmic mother: Rediscovering the religion of the earth.* San Francisco: Harper & Row.

Society for Human Resource Management. (2002). *Workplace violence study.* Alexandria, VA: Author.

Southern Poverty Law Center. (2009, Fall). For the record. *Intelligence Report, 135,* 62–64.

Stamm, B. (Ed.). (1995). *Secondary traumatic stress: Self-care issues for clinicians, researchers, and educators*. Lutherville, MD: Sidran Press.

Straus, M. (1980). *Behind closed doors: Violence in the American family*. New York: Anchor Press.

Thayer, S., & Nathanson, S. (1997). *Interview with an angel.* New York: Dell/Random House.

Tronick, E. Z. (1989). Emotions and emotional communication in infants. *American Psychologist, 44,* 112–119.

van der Kolk, B. (1988). The trauma spectrum: The interaction of biological and social events in the genesis of the trauma response. *Journal of Traumatic Stress, 1*(3), 273–290.

van der Kolk, B. (2005). Developmental trauma disorder: A new, rational diagnosis for children with complex trauma histories. *Psychiatric Annals, 35,* 401–408.

van der Kolk, B., McFarlane, A., & Weisaeth, L. (Eds.). (1996). *Traumatic stress: The overwhelming experience on mind, body and society.* New York: Guilford Press.

Van Lancker, D. (1991). Personal relevance and the human right hemisphere. *Brain and Cognition, 17,* 64–92.

Verny, T. (Ed.). (1984). *Pre-and perinatal psychology, An introduction.* New York: Human Sciences Press.

Verny, T. (1988). *The secret life of the unborn child.* New York: Delta Books.

Violata, C., & Russell, C. (1994, July 1). *Effect of non-maternal care on child development: A meta-analysis of published research.* Poster session presented at 55th Annual Convention of the Canadian Psychological Association, Penticton, BC, Canada.

Von Bertalanffy, L. (1968). *General systems theory: Foundation, development, and applications.* New York: Brazillier.

Waldfogel, J. (2001). *What children need: (The family and public policy).* Cambridge, MA: President and Fellows of Harvard College.

Walker, M. (2002). Profile of the holistic cancer therapist W. Douglas Brodie, MD, HMD. *Medical Journalist Report of Innovative Biologics*. Retrieved from http://findarticles.com/p/articles/mi_m0ISW/is_2002_Feb-March/ai_82881801/?tag=untagged

Wallerstein, E. (1985). Circumcision: The uniquely American medical enigma. *Symposium on Advances in Pediatric Urology: Urology Clinics of North America, 12,* 123–132.

Weiner, N. (1954). *Cybernetics, or control and communication in the animal and the machine* (2nd ed.). Cambridge, MA: MIT Press.

Weinhold, B. (2000). Unpublished research paper on methods of shifting consciousness. University of Colorado at Colorado Springs.

Weinhold, B. (2006a). *Spreading kindness; Volume I: Implementing the kind and safe schools initiative.* Swannanoa, NC: CICRCL Press.

Weinhold, B. (2006b). *Breaking family patterns.* Swannanoa, NC: CICRCL Press.

Weinhold, B., & Weinhold, J. (1989). *Breaking free of the co-dependency trap.* Walpole, NH: Stillpoint.

Weinhold, B., & Weinhold, J. (1992). *Counter-dependency: The flight from intimacy.* Colorado Springs, CO: CICRCL Press.

Weinhold, B., & Weinhold, J. (1994, September/October). Developmental process work in marriage and family therapy. *Family Counseling and Therapy Journal, 2*(6).

Weinhold, B., & Weinhold, J. (2000). *Conflict resolution: The partnership way.* Denver, CO: Love Publishing.

Weinhold, B., & Weinhold, J. (2008a). *Breaking free of the co-dependency trap.* Novato, CA: New World Library.

Weinhold, J., & Weinhold, B. (2008b). *The flight from intimacy.* Novato, CA: New World Library.

Weinhold, B., & Weinhold, J. (2009). *Conflict resolution: The partnership way* (2nd ed.). Denver, CO: Love.

Weiss L., & Weiss, J. (1989). *Recovery from co-dependency.* Deerfield Beach, FL: Health Communications.

Wheatley, M. (1992). *Leadership and the new science: Discovering order in a chaotic world.* San Francisco: Bennett-Koehler.

Wilber, K. (1980). *The Atman project: A transpersonal view of human development.* Wheaton, IL: Theosophical.

Wilber, K. (1996). *A brief history of everything.* Boston: Shambhala.

Wikipedia. (n.d.). *Ryke Geerd Hamer.* Retrieved from http://en.wikipedia.org/wiki/Ryke_Geerd_HamerR

Wilcock, D. (2007). *Kozyrev: Aether, time and torsion.* Retrieved from http://www.divinecosmos.com/index.php?option=com_content&task=view&id=334&Itemid=30

Wilson, J. P., & Lendy, J. D. (1994). *Countertransference in the treatment of PTSD.* New York: Guilford.

Winnicott, D. W. (1965). *The maturation process and the facilitating environment.* New York: International University Press.

Winstone, C. (2003). Pre- and peri-natal shock: Considerations for psychotherapy. *Insights Magazine—B.C. Association of Clinical Counsellors, 8,* 1–24.

Wittling, W. (1997). The right hemisphere and the human stress response. *Acta Physiologica Scandanavica, 640* (Supplement), 55.

Wright, M. S. (n.d.). *Perelandra.* Retrieved from http://www.perelandra-ltd.com/

Yamada, H., Sadato, N., Konishi, Y., Muramoto, S., Kimura, K., Tanaka, M., et al. (2000). A milestone for normal development of the infantile brain detected by functional MRI. *Neurology, 55,* 218–223.

Zhang, Y. (2007). *Transforming emotions with Chinese medicine: An ethnographic account from contemporary China.* Albany, NY: SUNY Press.

Zinn, H. (2001). *A people's history of the United States: 1492 to present.* New York: Perennial Classics.

Name Index

Subject Index